A GERMAN WOMEN'S MOVEMENT

A German Women's Movement

NANCY R. REAGIN

Class and

Gender in

Hanover,

1880–1933

The

University

of North

Carolina

Press

Chapel Hill

& London

1995

The paper in this book meets the guidelines for permanence and
durability of the Committee on Production Guidelines for Book
Longevity of the Council on Library Resources.

Library of Congress Cataloging-in-Publication Data
Reagin, Nancy Ruth, 1960–
A German women's movement : class and gender in Hanover, 1880–
1933 / Nancy R. Reagin.
p. cm.
Includes bibliographical references and index.
ISBN 0-8078-2210-8. — ISBN 0-8078-4525-6 (pbk. : alk. paper)
1. Feminism—Germany—Hannover—History—19th century.
2. Feminism—Germany—Hannover—History—20th century.
3. Women—Germany—Hannover—History—19th century.
4. Women—Germany—Hannover—History—20th century.
I. Title.
HQ1623.R43   1995   94-39348
305.42′0943—dc20   CIP

99   98   97   96   95   5   4   3   2   1

FOR BILL

Contents

Tables

Acknowledgments

One of the most gratifying aspects of completing this study—beyond the golden knowledge that this project is finished—is that it gives me the chance to acknowledge all of the colleagues, friends, and relatives whose criticisms, encouragement, and help made this book possible. My work benefited from the assistance of many individuals and institutions. I was fortunate to have Vernon Lidtke as my doctoral advisor while I was doing the initial research on this topic. His encouragement and criticisms, especially the latter, pushed me to make my arguments more comprehensive and complex than they otherwise would have been. I am also grateful to his colleagues in the Johns Hopkins Department of History, Mack Walker and Toby Ditz, who read this study in various stages of preparation, and whose comments and suggestions helped improve it.

My research and writing were supported by grants from the Deutscher Akademischer Austauschdienst, the Johns Hopkins University, the National Endowment for the Humanities, and Pace University. The source material for this study came from a variety of institutions and individuals, some of whom generously shared private documents and correspondence. My thanks go to the following: the Niedersächsisches Hauptstaatsarchiv; the Hanover Stadtarchiv, and especially to the members of its staff, who shared their knowledge of Hanover's history with me; the Landeskirchliches Archiv der Evangelisch-lutherischen Landeskirche Hannovers; the Katholischer Deutscher Frauenbund; the pastor and staff of the Reformed Protestant Church in Hanover; the Deutscher Evangelischer Frauenbund, which permitted me to work in its private archive, a valuable and extensive collection of sources for studies in German women's history; the Hanover Stadtbibliothek; and the women who agreed to be interviewed for this study, especially Annamarie Feesche, Frida Glindemann, and Jutta Rexhausen.

My German colleagues and friends helped to make my research more fruitful and my life in Germany more pleasant. In particular, I would like to thank Adelheid von Saldern, Angelika Döring, Siegfried Müller, Anna Rieke-Müller, Buka and Dietz Denecke, and Klaus and Katja Fülberg-Stolberg. Monika Sonneck and Christiane Schröder located and photocopied primary sources for me, for which I am very grateful. Doris Marquardt deserves a special mention. She has generously shared her time, her knowledge of local sources, and the fruits of her own research. She also helped proofread the manuscript, a truly tedious task. I am grateful for her friendship and encouragement.

I owe an enormous debt to the New York–based German Women's History Study Group: Bonnie Anderson, Dolores Augustine, Maria Baader, Rebecca Boehling, Renate Bridenthal, Jane Caplan, Belinda Davis, Katharina Feil, Atina Grossmann, Amy Hackett, Young Sun Hong, Marion Kaplan, Jan Lambertz, Molly Nolan, and Heidrun Suhr. Collectively, its members' work helped to create the field I work in. The women who belong to this group read and critiqued a large part of my study, and came up with a title for it. Their comments and suggestions were enormously helpful; overall, our meetings were both stimulating and supportive. I am particularly grateful to Renate Bridenthal; she read most of this study, and shared her own research with me. Her insights and support have been invaluable. Claudia Koonz also provided me with valuable assistance, when it was most needed. Marilyn Shevin Coetzee gave my manuscript a careful reading, and made a host of helpful suggestions.

My family and friends contributed to my work in ways that were different, but no less essential, than the help I received from colleagues. I have been fortunate in having the steadfast friendship of my colleagues Marilyn Thornton Williams and Mary Pickering. My parents were sure that I would complete this project long before I ever was, which also gave me confidence. Mary Masters gave me expert and thoughtful assistance in compiling my index. Anne Alworth provided affectionate child care for my daughter while I worked on this study. My deepest debt, however, is to my husband, Bill; he gave me the assistance, companionship, and affection and provided the bulk of the child care necessary to finish this work. This book is for him.

A GERMAN WOMEN'S MOVEMENT

Introduction

The entire strength of the women's movement derives
from the conviction that the woman, different from the
man anatomically down to her teeth, is just as different
in her psyche, and that she can therefore bring other char-
acteristics . . . to the task of developing human culture.
—Helene Lange

The conviction that the two sexes were divided by innate and far-reaching differences was widespread among all the women's movements of the late nineteenth and early twentieth centuries. Even some supporters of equal rights feminism, who sought to obtain the same rights and roles that men had, embraced and celebrated the concept of gender difference. The movements that emerged in almost all Western societies during this period were divided not over the question of gender difference, but over the problems raised by this conviction: whether or how difference should be reflected in feminists' goals and strategies.[1]

A so-called radical minority within the Wilhelmine women's movement pursued a strategy of equal rights feminism, but the "moderate" majority within the leadership of the movement's umbrella organization, the Bund Deutscher Frauenvereine, or BDF, grounded its analysis and proposals in essentialism, the belief in innate gender differences.[2] In Germany, gender difference was articulated within the framework of a philosophy that became known as the doctrine of spiritual motherhood. This school of thought was originally developed by the women who were associated with the social reformer Friedrich Froebel, and popularized within the broader women's movement by Henriette Goldschmidt. Its proponents held that all women possessed certain innate maternal qualities, including the capacity to nurture and educate the young, ill, poor, or otherwise dependent persons. Married women, they argued, exercised these talents in their capacities as wives and mothers, but unmarried women could and ought to function in maternal roles, too, especially as teachers, nurses, and social workers. Furthermore, all women could exercise a maternal influence in society as a whole through volunteer work, especially social work.[3]

Indeed, increasing women's "maternal" influence in the public sphere was the *Kulturmission* of the moderate majority. These women argued that contemporary German society was distorted by the one-sided predominance of male values and leadership, which caused many of Germany's undeniable social problems. Thus, women deserved more rights and roles because they were different, and therefore complemented men, and women's influence would improve the entire community.

Some of the movement's historians have been critical of its rejection of equal rights feminism, arguing that this rejection led to a turn to the right, politically, before 1914.[4] Other writers have concluded that the embrace of gender difference was linked to a broader political conservatism, which undermined the resistance that the women's movement might have offered to the rise of National Socialism, and which predisposed many bourgeois women to accept some Nazi doctrines.[5]

These arguments have been sharply rejected by the most recent historians of the movement, who claim that the movement's espousal of essentialism led to a form of feminism that had no affinities with National Socialism, but rather fostered a wide-ranging, radical critique of the male dominated social and political structures of imperial Germany. A recent study of the kindergarten movement, and of German feminists' work in the area of family policy and children's welfare, argues that the movement's acceptance of gender difference did not lead to political conservatism, but rather was a springboard for a socially transformative ideology.[6]

Another study of the bourgeois women's movement goes even further, to claim that "male" political labels and categories (such as "liberal" or "conservative") cannot be applied at all to the supporters of spiritual motherhood. This study, of the women's movement in Bremen, concludes that women of this period inhabited an entirely different culture from men, with their own values, and cannot be analyzed using concepts that derived from male culture. Using these values, Bremen women developed a critique of male society that was articulated largely through a vigorous temperance movement and a "morality" movement to end the regulation of prostitution in the city.[7] A study of the Bremen movement cannot help us understand the politics of the German women's movement as a whole, however, because it was among the "most radical" local movements in all of Germany; furthermore, this monograph fails to examine the Bremen movement from the standpoint of class or *Stand*.[8]

An examination of class interests and class divisions within women's movements is crucial, however, as the body of work done in American women's history on women's organizations and movements makes clear. Historians have documented the presence of a shared "women's culture" and "women's values" among nineteenth-century middle-class American women, analogous to the distinct values shared by bourgeois German women; but this women's culture rarely transcended class, and did not preclude class conflict. A leading American women's historian notes that middle-class female activists who came out of this "women's culture" developed solutions to social problems that "lessened working-class women's control over their own lives and instead increased the powers of the dominant class in shaping the most intimate aspects of working-class women's lives."[9]

Recent work on the Wilhelmine women's movement has thus demonstrated admirably that, in the hands of some members of the German movement, essentialism and the concept of spiritual motherhood became the basis for a potentially radical feminist critique of male hegemony. These historians fail, however, to acknowledge the fact that terms like "morality" and "spiritual motherhood" were politically ambiguous, capable of being incorporated into a variety of political agendas; they tend to overlook the ways in which much of the German movement reflected class interests, which were linked to its heavy emphasis on gender differentiation. Lacking this focus on class and political context, these studies cannot explain the German movement's steady drift to the right, which began at the latest by 1908, and which accelerated during the Weimar period.[10]

The BDF's shift to the right has sometimes been ascribed to the influence of the large conservative women's groups that joined it, such as the Deutsch-Evangelischer Frauenbund (German Protestant Women's League, or DEF) and the rural and urban housewives' associations. This is begging the question of why these associations became so popular and powerful to begin with, however.[11] Furthermore, like the politically progressive wing of the BDF, conservative groups also based their arguments on essentialism and the doctrine of spiritual motherhood, but they used these concepts in a way that supported a larger politically conservative agenda. Indeed, these right-wing associations differed from "radical" feminist reformers *primarily* in a party political sense, and *not* in their espousal of women's "cultural mission" and maternal nature: it was largely their partisan political differences with the "radicals" that earned the DEF and its allies the designation "conservative." Thus, "masculine" political categories are essential for understanding these groups. Any study of the German movement and its mainstream's emphasis on gender difference should include a political analysis of the entire spectrum of organizations that used this maternalist orientation, from left to right, or it is truncated, and powerless to convey fully the stalemated position that the women's movement found itself in by 1930.

Thus, another local study of the German women's movement is needed, one that can capture the entire political spectrum of the movement and which does not focus on the liberal or left-wing bastions of Berlin, Bremen, or Hamburg. Hanover is a good example of how the movement also flourished in the provinces; in many ways, the city typified the German movement at the grass-roots level. The German women's movement as a whole found its membership largely in urban, Protestant, Prussian areas; Hanover was all of these. An analysis of the Hanover movement helps explain the conservatism manifested in national congresses of the women's movement; there, representatives from grass-roots movements across the empire voted for leaders and policies that slowly shifted the movement to the right. Hanover's movement is more accessible than many other provincial movements, moreover, because of the ample sources preserved in its city and state archives.

A local study also captures aspects of the women's movement and of bourgeois women's experience that are difficult to flesh out in research that focuses exclusively on the national leadership. Local chapters of national organizations were forums for the expression of clubwomen's anxieties and aspirations, which were then directed into collective action. At the local level, one can examine the relationships between chapters of different organizations, to see how the movement functioned in a coordinated fashion. In addition, a local study can grasp the social foundations of the movement, showing how it was embedded in and influenced by the familial, political, and social networks that existed in bourgeois society. A grass-roots study thus gives insight into the movement's diversity and complexity.

Finally, a local study can convey the extent to which the women's movement transcended the BDF (which has provided the organizational parameters for almost all previous work on the movement), by including all the groups that were active on the local level, whether they belonged to the BDF or not. Many of the largest bourgeois women's organizations in Germany, such as the Catholic Women's League and the Vaterländischer Frauenverein (the women's auxiliary to the Red Cross) never joined the BDF, while the influential DEF and the two huge national housewives' associations did join the BDF, only to leave later. In addition, the right-wing women's groups that arose during the 1920s openly opposed the BDF.

Yet I would argue that all of these groups should be included in a local study of the bourgeois women's movement, because all of them (when compared, for example, with a women's choral group) actively sought to mobilize women to effect social change, and to help themselves or other women (although these groups had different definitions of what constituted "help").[12] On the local level, membership in the BDF cannot be used as an indicator of membership in a city's women's movement, since chapters of both sorts of women's groups—those that did and did not belong to the BDF—cooperated in promoting local projects and a united women's agenda. In Hanover during the Weimar period, for example, both sorts of associations joined the Women's City League, the umbrella organization for the local movement. In addition, the membership of organizations within and outside of the BDF overlapped substantially in Hanover. Thus, at the grass-roots level, using the BDF to delineate the women's movement is artificial and misleading.[13]

Using a more inclusive definition of the women's movement, my study of the Hanover movement reveals that the women's movement at the grass-roots level was in fact intensely political, although in a fashion that could not be easily pigeonholed before 1914. Each member of the movement—in Hanover and nationally—should be located somewhere on a graph composed of two variables: first, the spectrum of party politics, which ran from the left to the right; and second, the spectrum of feminist theory, which ranged from radical to conservative in terms of challenging traditional gender roles or accepting gender role polarization. Each leader, each women's group stood at a particular point where these two spectrums intersected (or collided, in some cases).

Members of the radical minority wing of the BDF, such as Minna Cauer, frequently embraced both equal rights feminism and progressive liberalism (which were philosophically compatible), but this linkage was not automatic; a few women, such as Käthe Schirmacher and Marie Lischnewska, championed both radical feminism and right-wing nationalism.[14] On the other side of the spectrum, members of the DEF frequently supported policies based on extreme gender differentiation, along with very conservative party political positions; but this linkage, too, was not always a given. Gertrud Bäumer, a national leader who developed an elaborate body of theory based on essentialism, also had strong liberal party political affiliations for most of her career. Mathilde Drechsler-Hohlt, a leader in the Hanover movement, supported equal rights feminism while belonging to the center-right Deutsche Volkspartei during the 1920s.[15]

An examination of the Hanover movement indicates that much of the bourgeois women's movement was indeed politically conservative, but this fact was not caused by its embrace of gender difference and "spiritual motherhood"; instead, its conservatism was reflected in the ways in which the movement used and redefined these malleable concepts. As this study will show, although the movement's politics were sometimes subtle or complex, they certainly can be discussed using conventional political categories, because their ideas were shaped by considerations of class and partisan politics, as well as gender.

At the national level, the BDF tried to overcome party political divisions within its ranks by embracing a doctrine of *Überparteilichkeit* (being "above" party political divisions, or "neutral" in a partisan sense). This was easier before 1908, when the laws regulating voluntary associations in most German states prohibited women from joining political associations, or even attending meetings where "public affairs" were discussed. These laws were superseded in 1908 by the new *Reichsvereinsgesetz*, which finally allowed women to join political parties. As long as women could not formally participate in politics throughout most of the empire, the BDF could paper over internal political differences, and uphold the idea that it sought only goals that were "above" politics and would benefit both women and the community or nation.

Tensions arose within the women's movement after 1908, as leaders joined different political parties. Increasingly, the BDF was constrained from taking specific positions on women's issues, since the more detailed its proposals were, the more obviously its program would resemble that of specific political parties, which would leave the BDF open to charges that it was violating its duty to be politically neutral. The disputes and divisions over what form of women's suffrage the movement ought to work for (three-class suffrage or not) were only one example of the difficulties that *Überparteilichkeit* could lead to.[16]

On the local level, however, *Überparteilichkeit* was more easily achieved. In Hanover, the movement developed a feminine analogue of the approach taken toward local politics by men's parties in many cities. As in many other German cities, Hanover's local notables strove to achieve "professional," efficient, nonpartisan local government; municipal officials (even elected ones) were expected to be impartial with respect to partisan politics. The Hanover women's movement thus came of age during a period when the local government was dominated by the motto "party politics have no place in city hall."[17]

At the same time, Hanover's municipal political environment was also profoundly antidemocratic. The "neutral" local government was elected on the basis of an extremely restricted municipal franchise. Furthermore, the Social Democratic Party (or SPD) and its supporters were excluded from the gentlemen's agreement of "neutrality"; the SPD was the object of open attacks by the local political establishment. In this environment, support from an organized mass political party was irrelevant, while personal connections and the appearance of efficiency and professionalism were all-important.[18]

The "neutrality" pursued by the local women's movement was shaped by this environment. All of the women's associations founded before World War I in Hanover (and most even thereafter) were *überparteilich* and officially eschewed partisan politics. Instead, they shared the BDF's goal of expanding women's maternal influence in the public sphere; the movement tried, especially through social work, to create for women the role that Henriette Goldschmidt called "mothers of the community," an analogue to male "city fathers."[19] Women's work here would serve the politically "neutral" goal of combating "social degeneration," such as intervening in working-class families to promote proper standards of hygiene and better approaches to child-rearing and housekeeping. The movement was able to substantially expand bourgeois women's influence in the local public sphere, and to gain generous support from city officials before World War I, because its leaders presented bourgeois women as efficient and increasingly professionalized workers for the common good, fighting social degeneration and, hence, the roots of poverty and misery.

The women's movement was thus able to build a consensus among Hanover notables that supported its supposedly unpolitical maternal social work and growing influence. In practice, however, the movement's goals and work were simultaneously charitable *and* political, although seldom in an overtly partisan political fashion before 1914. Instead, the movement pursued the politics of class, promoting bourgeois values. In a broader sense, the women's movement was promoting bourgeois cultural hegemony by seeking to inculcate working-class women and girls with bourgeois standards and styles of housekeeping and child-rearing. The movement in effect prescribed a style of family life modeled on bourgeois norms as the cure for supposed social degeneration. Since this life-style was never presented as being explicitly bourgeois—but rather as being better, more rational, and more hygienic—the movement's work could be seen as *überparteilich* and for the common good.

In a narrower sense, the Hanover women's movement pursued bourgeois interests by openly working against the SPD, seeking to limit its influence among young working women. Within the local political environment that shaped the movement, attacks on the SPD were seen as compatible with the duty to uphold partisan neutrality, since hostility toward the SPD transcended bourgeois political parties, and united bourgeois public opinion. Thus, the Hanover women's movement made no secret of its desire to combat the SPD, and so bourgeois women created organizations for young female factory workers, servants, and shopgirls that simultaneously tried to promote bourgeois family values and protect members from the SPD's influence.

The Hanover movement reached its high-water point between 1914 and 1918. The outbreak of World War I led local women's organizations to form a cartel for social welfare work called the Nationaler Frauendienst. The Nationaler Frauendienst merged with the city's government during the course of the war, and within it, women leaders were able to exercise great influence over municipal social policy, and to obtain new positions for bourgeois women within city government.

The movement declined rapidly after 1918, however. The city's political system was swept away by the German Revolution, which introduced universal adult suffrage on all levels of government. Local notables' unquestioned hegemony was broken, as Social Democrats and Communists were elected to the city council; under the new regime, the movement's leaders lost their privileged relationship with Hanover's municipal government, along with automatic approval of their requests for subsidies from the city. Instead, the city expanded its own social welfare agencies, which replaced the private social welfare services run by women's associations. In effect, much of the movement's domain was nationalized.

In many senses, then, the introduction of a new political system after 1918 pulled the rug out from underneath the Hanover women's movement; it was now somewhat outmoded. Local women leaders had received their training in an environment where personal connections with city officials were the means to power, and they were not prepared to deal with the new system of party politics at the municipal level. The city's assumption of many of the social welfare services that had been created by the local women's movement was also a mixed blessing. The women's movement had always argued that the state should ultimately assume the responsibility for social services, but women leaders had intended that the new government welfare agencies should be run by women, a feminine jurisdiction. Instead, the new Hanover municipal welfare agencies were led by men, although women staffed the lower echelons. In addition, these municipal social workers obtained their jobs on their own; previously, individual women could only gain access to social welfare work through joining a women's voluntary association. In effect, the local women's movement had worked itself out of a job. In addition, the achievement of women's suffrage and legal equality appeared to solve the "woman question," and to render the movement superfluous. In Hanover, and in Germany as a whole, the movement groped for a new raison d'être.

Set adrift in Weimar Hanover, the organizations that made up the center and liberal section of the local women's movement attracted fewer new women; the movement as a whole was aging. The introduction of local democracy had not proved a happy development for the movement. In addition, the members of the women's movement, like other bourgeois Hanoverians, suffered materially during the Weimar period. The inflation of 1923 hit many clubwomen, dependent on pensions or fixed incomes, particularly hard.

The growth within the women's movement in Hanover during the 1920s was on the right, by associations that largely rejected the BDF, but that nevertheless were part of the world of bourgeois clubwomen: some of these conservative organizations even belonged to the league of women's associations organized by local BDF leaders. These right-wing groups

carried forward the prewar movement's "unpolitical" defense of bourgeois interests, and elaborated it, so that it evolved into a set of overtly
partisan political positions. These new right-wing women's groups were
usually closely affiliated with masculine nationalist organizations, and rejected the Weimar "system" as a whole, especially the treaty of Versailles
and the foreign policies developed by different Weimar administrations.

The enormous growth of the Hanover Housewives' Association during this period is typical of this shift to the right. The Housewives'
Association was led by an anti-Semitic woman who was active in the local
Deutschnationale Volkspartei; she also articulated her organization's hostility toward women who worked outside of the home. Her association
was joined by other, even more strongly nationalist and *völkisch* women's
groups. The emergence of this wing destroyed the Hanover movement's
prewar tradition of coalition building across confessional lines, which had
included the local Jewish Women's League.

The Housewives' Association, along with other groups from the center
and right of the Hanover women's movement, kept up a constant drum-
beat within the world of Weimar clubwomen, an angry discussion on
such topics as the decline of the German family; the need to increase the
German birthrate; the necessity of protecting *Deutschtum* within and
outside of Germany's borders; and repeated denunciations of the postwar
settlement, which trumpeted Germany's oppression by the rest of the
world. Many of the leaders of these organizations were affiliated with the
"Harzburg front," an electoral alliance in the early 1930s between right-
wing political groups and the National Socialists. They shared much of
the Nazis' *Weltanschauung*, although they were divided about the Nazis'
plans to exclude women from politics. Although these women did not
join the Nazi Party until after 1933, their work and rhetoric before 1933
had helped to prepare bourgeois women for many of the National Socialists' themes.

Once the National Socialists had taken power, however, clubwomen
did not get what they had bargained for. Their affinities with Nazi
ideology could not save right-wing women's organizations. Almost all
of the Hanover women's associations, from right to left, were *gleichge-
schaltet*. The Nazi seizure of power in fact marked the end of the first
German women's movement, which passed into history in 1933.

CHAPTER I

The Urban Backdrop

The city of Hanover, which provided a fertile field of operations for a bourgeois women's movement, also presented features that influenced the course of this movement; these features would also impose some constraints on its development. Hanover was not "representative" of other cities in the German Empire, but then neither was any other city. Hanover was typical only in the sense that it shared a number of particular local characteristics with many other cities. The Hanover women's movement was thus the product of a specific urban environment. Local women's associations were shaped by the city's basic, persistent features—the confessional distribution of its population, for example—and also by the constant changes that Hanover was undergoing during this period, including rapid industrial development and an expanding population. In addition, Hanover women's organizations were influenced by the city's political environment, which set the parameters within which the local women's movement would develop. Finally, the goals that the movement would pursue were influenced by the values of bourgeois culture as a whole, and those of bourgeois women's separate sphere in particular.

The women's movement in Hanover, and across Germany, was first and foremost a response to the social problems created by industrialization and urbanization; the first women's groups were charitable associations, and social welfare organizations made up the backbone of the movement throughout the Wilhelmine era. None of these groups would have emerged except for the unparalleled changes taking place within the cities that nurtured the women's movement. Urban historian Jürgen Reulecke has written that the expanding cities of imperial Germany fell into two categories. The first category consisted of cities that "sprang out of the ground," small towns or villages hosting industries that grew explosively. These cities had skewed class and occupational distributions:

essentially, they were enormous settlements of industrial workers. The second category included cities that were regional centers for commerce, administration, and transport. They attracted industrial development, but the industrial sector was usually diversified; this type of city grew more slowly than the first category of cities, but at a steady pace.[1]

Hanover is an example of the second type of metropolis. The city was the administrative hub for the province of Hanover, with about 10 percent of all workers employed by the local or provincial governments. In addition, Hanover's position in the railroad network guaranteed that it became the regional center for transportation and commerce. Laws passed after 1866 to encourage industrialization contributed to growth in the manufacturing sector; by 1875, Hanover boasted 470 large factories, including heavy industry, chemical production, and textile plants. The city's demographic profile reflected its economic development. Hanover's population grew from about 87,000 in 1869 to almost 210,000 in 1891; it would increase to 316,000 before 1914.[2]

Most of the city's population was Protestant. The city's expansion did not affect Protestants' overwhelming domination of the local urban environment: in 1867, Protestants comprised 90.5 percent of the city's population, while Catholics made up 7.4 percent, and Jews accounted for 2 percent of Hanover's inhabitants, a distribution that hardly changed over the next forty-five years.[3] Hanover's elite groups were almost exclusively Protestant; local Catholics were disproportionately working-class immigrants from other regions who had been drawn to the city by its industrial development. As a result of this confessional distribution, Hanover's women's movement would be dominated by Protestants: Catholic and Jewish women, surrounded and outnumbered, would form their own, separate confessional women's associations.

Hanover's position as a center for administration and commerce meant that the city had a broad middle class: civil servants, white-collar employees, professionals, businessmen, and the traditional *Mittelstand* groups, including merchants, artisans, well-to-do peasants, and shopkeepers. Collectively, these groups referred to themselves as the *Bürgertum*. The *Bürgertum* has been a problematic social group in German historiography; historians differ over the extent to which *bürgerliche* social groups can be treated as a single class, or if indeed it makes sense to speak of a German "middle class."[4]

The *Bürgertum* of the nineteenth century cannot be defined simply by any single criterion. It included a wide range of occupational groups. In terms of income, bourgeois social groups ranged from impoverished academics, eking out a living as *Privatdozenten*, to prosperous factory owners. The educational background of German burghers was equally varied; those from the traditional *Mittelstand* were usually apprenticed as soon as they finished the *Volksschule* (elementary school), whereas professionals, academics, and high-level civil servants completed university degrees. The varied social groups that made up this bourgeoisie often had conflicting economic interests. The German bourgeoisie was also divided by confession. The Protestant majority tended toward disdain and suspicion of Catholics, whom Protestants suspected of being blindly loyal to Rome, and thus insufficiently patriotic. In addition, Jewish Germans were discriminated against by Protestants and Catholics alike, and still faced substantial social and professional barriers.[5]

In spite of these divisions, however, bourgeois society was also united in several important ways. Members of the *Bürgertum* shared the perception that as a group, they were caught between two other powerful forces: the working class and the aristocracy. *Bürgerliche* society was also held together by a set of values that included a drive for self-improvement and success. Personal worth was measured by achievements—intellectual goals in the case of the *Bildungsbürgertum*, and material success for other middle-strata groups. Qualities that furthered personal achievement—diligence, self-discipline, conscientiousness, and thrift—were particularly admired. Gambling, excessive drinking, profligacy, sexual irregularities, and other activities that would tend to interfere with work and success were condemned. These values unified bourgeois social groups that were otherwise disparate and bound them into what Rudy Koshar calls a "moral community."[6] *Bürgerliche* society was thus simultaneously a collection of disparate social groups in the process of consolidation and a community with a shared ideology.

Bourgeois women had their own beliefs, some of which overlapped with the values of men of their class, and some of which were uniquely their own. Generally speaking, bourgeois women tended to be more religiously observant, and more fervent in their celebration of religion than their husbands and fathers. Linked to this stronger religious orientation, *bürgerliche* women adhered more closely to the code of sexual conduct and morals prescribed by organized religion; they tended to reject the idea of a double sexual standard for men and women, and espoused the idea of a "single morality" of chastity for men and women. In this code, a woman's physical integrity and chastity were closely tied to her personal honor.[7]

These beliefs were an obvious departure from the behavioral norms observed by most men, but in some ways this was to be expected, since both bourgeois men and women embraced polarized definitions of masculinity and femininity. The two sexes were seen as being both antithetical and complementary. In this schema, men were rational, assertive, strong, and dominant, whereas women were supposed to be more pious, emotional, intuitive, nurturing, and submissive. The sexual division of labor in bourgeois society was grounded in these polarized stereotypes: women's emotional, nurturing nature assigned them to the private sphere of home and family, whereas men's rationality and aggressiveness suited them to the masculine public world of work and politics. Women's domain was separate from, and by no means equal to, the masculine realm.[8]

Bourgeois women also subscribed to many of the values that bound *bürgerliche* society together, however. Bourgeois women valued such qualities as thrift, diligence, and conscientiousness; but for women, these attributes were supposed to serve a different function than they did for men. These characteristics were admired in men because they furthered personal achievement, and material success; in women, these qualities were valued insofar as they were expressed in domestic life. Bourgeois women shared a specifically feminine subset of values, which stressed domesticity: the management of an orderly household, and the maintenance of an affectionate, strictly moral family life.

Efficient, capable housewifery was an essential component of a family's claim to bourgeois status and respectability. Respectability was achieved not just through the husband's educational level or income, but also through the cleanliness, orderliness, and manners displayed by the family in its private life. Indeed, the wives of civil servants had to maintain an orderly and respectable homelife, since this was a requirement for their husbands' employment and advancement.[9]

The most obvious norm in the constellation of bourgeois feminine values, visible as soon as a visitor crossed a family's threshold, was an extremely high standard of cleanliness. Middle-class housewives strove to keep their homes spotless, an ideal that impressed one British visitor, who claimed that German housewives of her acquaintance put their curtains through ten separate rinses when washing them. "The extreme tidiness of

German rooms is a constant source of surprise," she commented, "They are as guiltless of 'litter' as the showrooms of a furniture emporium. . . . Each chair has its place, each cushion, each ornament. Even where there are children German rooms never look disarranged. . . . [In one flat] I saw everywhere the exquisite order and spotlessness the notable German housewife knows how to maintain."[10]

The bourgeois emphasis on thrift found its domestic expression in housewives' careful consumption and detailed household accounts. Washing curtains by hand, instead of sending them to the cleaners as our English visitor did, was one of a hundred small ways to conserve money. When the feather stuffing in bolsters, which could not be cleaned at home, had to be sent to the cleaners, the good housewife went along, and watched to make sure that she got her own feathers back.[11] The obligatory Sunday dinner, a joint of meat or roasted goose, made repeated appearances later in the week, as every bit of the "leftovers" was used. Thrift, documented through detailed bookkeeping, helped bourgeois families accumulate capital for sons' tuition fees or daughters' dowries.[12]

Besides the endless cleaning, baking, washing, sewing, knitting, darning, canning, and shopping, bourgeois housewives had to make time for bearing and rearing their children, which was in fact their primary responsibility. Here, the bourgeois value of conscientiousness found expression in a particular style of child-rearing, which stressed intense involvement and supervision by the mother over her children's lives. It was during this period that the sentimentalization and glorification of motherhood were reaching new heights, and bourgeois mothers were expected to provide a secure, nurturing, and loving environment for their children.

Mothers organized their children's days, arranging the children's walks, meals, lessons, story reading, and games, which were supervised by the housewife herself, or a servant. Mothers taught their children, especially daughters, skills such as piano playing or sewing; older daughters had to be chaperoned when they went out into public. In addition, bourgeois mothers were expected to teach their children appreciation for German culture, even high culture, by exposing them to the classics. This style of child-rearing was intended to produce well-behaved, obedient, polite children, who were trained for upward social mobility, and whose public behavior enhanced the respectability of the family.[13]

Most observers agreed that German bourgeois housewives did all this work with the aid of fewer servants than their French or English counterparts. Unlike English ladies, who were not expected to enter the kitchen or dirty their hands, most German housewives continued to perform all kinds of housework, even after their families had enough wealth to make this unnecessary; this may have been related to the emphasis on extreme thrift. A British observer commented that unlike French or English bourgeois mothers, who almost all employed nurses or nannies, the typical German "mother spends her time with her children, playing with them when she has leisure, cooking and ironing and saving for them and husband. . . . The German mother leaves her children less to servants than the English mother does. . . . [She] will do cooking and ironing when an Englishwoman of the same class would delegate all such work to servants."[14] The German emphasis on the personal work, involvement, and responsibility of the housewife would be reflected in the movement later created by bourgeois women: it was a style of housewifery and child-rearing that bourgeois women believed could be adopted by every woman, regardless of income level.

Bürgerliche women thus shared the values of the broader bourgeois public sphere, but they expressed these norms in their own way, within a domestic context. Overall, bourgeois women strove to reflect the ideals of thrift, hard work, extreme cleanliness, and orderliness and to produce well-reared, polite children. Realizing these values, they believed, would enhance the family's happiness; it also bolstered the family's respectability and the individual housewife's status among her acquaintances.

These values, nurtured within the bourgeois household, would be expressed in the work undertaken by clubwomen outside the home. Cleanliness, order, and discipline were tantamount to German civilization for bourgeois men: their wives and daughters tended to see *domestic* cleanliness, order, and discipline as the essence of civilized life, a view that would find expression within women's associations. Reforming working-class households to reflect these norms would become an important part of the *mission civilazatrice* of the bourgeois women's movement.

The movement that bourgeois women would create depended on an organizational form already widespread in bourgeois society, the local voluntary association (*Verein*). Voluntary associations first began to play a significant role in German public life during the last half of the eighteenth century. Early associations were agricultural societies, reading circles, and musical clubs; philanthropic societies and sociable clubs were soon added to the growing list of voluntary organizations that were being founded across Germany. After 1815, political associations became widespread, along with groups devoted to arts and sciences, professional societies, and humanitarian reform organizations.[15] By the mid-nineteenth century, every German locality had developed a network of voluntary associations, clubs, and societies.

With the exception of professional groups, voluntary associations were not restricted to a single occupational group and were formally democratic. Although most associations were, in fact, exclusive (the degree of exclusivity varied, but bourgeois societies rarely admitted working-class members), they accepted members from differing social backgrounds. Citizens who joined bourgeois organizations left their families, guilds, and neighborhoods to associate with other members from different occupations. This mingling of members with different occupational backgrounds worked to break down barriers between *bürgerliche* social groups; voluntary associations thus built bridges within the *Bürgertum*, and contributed to the integration of different middle-strata groups into a unified community.

Within the *Bürgertum*, voluntary associations helped to fill members' leisure hours, and became one the chief forums within which bourgeois culture was articulated. The increasing specialization of associations devoted to various arts and sciences led to the creation of an educated public, an audience for new works of art or for scientific debates. Other bourgeois voluntary organizations, devoted to philanthropy or reform, acted as adjuncts to the state in supporting schools, public hygiene, and social welfare projects. The voluntary association thus became an agency for the expression of bourgeois civic and artistic values.[16]

Women could not join many voluntary associations because most German states (including Prussia) forbade women to belong to organizations that engaged in politics, or to attend meetings at which public affairs were discussed; in addition, women were denied the right to vote, except in a handful of local elections in some states. The term "public affairs" (*öffentliche Angelegenheiten*) was usually construed broadly, and police could forcibly break up meetings where public policy was debated if women were present.[17] Instead, bourgeois women formed their own associations, organizations that, as we shall see, were expressions of specifically feminine bourgeois beliefs. These associations sought to promote the values that underlay women's ideology of domesticity and moral purity in the community at large. Only after the turn of the century would women begin to challenge the laws that restricted their participation in public life, especially their exclusion from the electorate.

Women were excluded from politics, but men's voluntary associations could function as substructures for political pressure groups and local government, and did. Besides acting as auxiliaries to local governments (for example, by financing civic improvements), bourgeois men's associations were forums within which political leaders maintained contact with their constituencies and attracted support for political programs. Clubs, sociable organizations, and civic associations thus mediated between the general public, political parties, and government.

Every local political party had voluntary associations, which it used as adjuncts, but men's clubs and voluntary organizations were especially important to *bürgerliche* liberal political groups. The political strategies of liberal politicians—in Hanover and in other localities—were not based on large, bureaucratized political organizations, with national constituencies (such as the SPD or Center Party); in addition, liberals tended to reject ideologies designed to court mass constituencies. Rather than looking downward, toward a mass base for support, liberal political leaders tended to reach out to their social peers: family, friends, business associates, and fellow club members. Liberal politicians in municipal administrations made decisions based on a consensus that had been reached among local *Honoratioren* (notables), and clubs and associations played an important role in articulating this consensus.[18]

Lacking a popular base of electoral support, or extensive political organizations, liberal politicians across Wilhelmine Germany were able to dominate many municipal governments (including Hanover's) only because many localities placed tight restrictions on local franchises.[19] In some cities, restrictions on local franchises were loose enough to permit SPD candidates to win municipal elections, but not in Hanover. Hanover's National Liberal Party leaders, who dominated local government, successfully defended the city's 1858 constitution against attempts to reform suffrage restrictions and broaden popular participation. Municipal franchises were restricted according to a complicated set of requirements based on length of residency, income level, the amount of taxes paid, and whether a resident owned property. Men who met these requirements still had to apply for the right to vote in local elections, and these applications were not always approved. The net result was to severely limit the number of voters in local elections: in 1907, when Hanover had about

277,000 residents, approximately 10,000 citizens were qualified to vote in local elections.[20] In essence, this amounted to a government by local notables: factory owners, professionals, important businessmen, and high-level civil servants.

This system buttressed rule by the National Liberals. The city had two burgomasters (mayors) during the period under consideration, and both were National Liberals. The only serious opposition that the National Liberals faced within the local *Bürgertum* was from Guelph partisans (represented by the German-Hanoverian Party), who refused to accept Hanover's annexation by Prussia and yearned for the return of the Guelph dynasty. Guelph sympathizers were watched by local police, however, and were unable to wrest power from the National Liberals in local elections, although they did win some provincial level elections.[21]

Political developments after 1890 undermined the National Liberals' position on both the provincial and national levels, but did not weaken their control over Hanover's municipal government. The most serious challenge to the National Liberals, and indeed to the entire local bourgeoisie, was the steady growth of the Hanoverian branch of the SPD. The rapid expansion of the city's industrial sector had resulted in a substantial increase in the SPD's natural constituency, the urban working class. In every election after 1878, the SPD reached the runoff for the city's Reichstag seat; by 1884, the SPD's constituency had grown large enough that the party's candidate, aided by left-liberal voters, won Hanover's Reichstag mandate. After the lapse of the Socialist Law, the SPD simply could not be stopped. After 1898 the SPD won an outright majority in almost every first-round Reichstag election, and kept the Hanover seat through 1932.[22]

The SPD could win only in Reichstag elections, of course, because all other provincial and local elections were based on restricted franchises. The SPD thus could not threaten the liberals' control over Hanover's municipal government; the SPD's rapid growth and firm hold on Hanover's Reichstag seat must nevertheless have been galling to both the National Liberals and Guelphs. Local social reform groups that arose after 1890 (including women's organizations) would reflect this sense of anger and unease regarding the SPD, as well as continuing divisions between Guelph partisans and those who accepted Prussian rule.

The National Liberals were able to retain local notables's support, and thus control over local government, because they were seen as competent, professional administrators, who kept the city's government "neutral" in party politics or, at least, neutral vis-à-vis the bourgeois political parties. Although they dominated Hanover's municipal government, the National Liberals did so in a curiously nonpartisan fashion. Municipal senators and city councilmen did not meet or sit as part of party caucuses; officially, at least, city council members and senators were without formal party affiliations. Their partisan affiliations were never mentioned in municipal records. In elections, candidates for city council were not identified by party, and did not run on party lists. Overtly partisan politics were frowned on at the local level. Burgomaster Heinrich Tramm, who dominated the city's government between 1891 and 1918, personified this "neutral" approach to municipal politics. As a National Liberal politician, Tramm held seats in Hanover's provincial parliament (Landtag) and in the Prussian Diet; as burgomaster, however, his motto was "party politics have no place in City Hall."[23]

This attitude was a response to the expansion of municipal government during the Wilhelmine period. Across Germany, municipal governments were forced to assume new responsibilities and to offer new services in response to the needs of rapidly growing urban populations. This resulted in an increase in the number of municipal officials, and the bureaucratization of city governments. Increasingly, competence, education, and administrative skills were supposed to be prerequisite for appointment or election to public office: efficiency, not ideology, ought to determine the selection of municipal leaders and policies. This approach rewarded those who could demonstrate administrative and technical skills, and penalized politicians who appeared to be overly ideological or partisan.[24]

Like the system of restricted municipal franchises, the elevation of nonpartisan municipal administration promoted government by notables, thus benefiting liberals and excluding the SPD from local government. In Hanover, Burgomaster Tramm and other National Liberal municipal leaders were perceived by their peers as qualified, competent, nonpartisan administrators. SPD leaders, on the other hand, were seen as unsuitable for municipal leadership, since the SPD was the party of class struggle and, thus, "partisan." In order to assure the continued dominance of "competent" officials, liberal notables argued, municipal franchises had to be restricted; otherwise the SPD would undoubtedly win local elections and bring unsuitable, partisan leaders into city government.[25]

The SPD was simply beyond the pale for those who endorsed municipal political "neutrality." In practice, municipal officials in Hanover were expected to behave impartially only toward the representatives and policies of bourgeois political parties. The SPD was excluded from the gentlemen's agreement that "nonpartisan" municipal administration represented, and the SPD's policies were never included in the *bürgerliche* consensus according to which the city was run.

This was the political environment within which the Hanover women's movement developed. Local women's associations were founded in a rapidly growing urban economy, a society that was politically dominated by local notables. The *Bürgertum* itself was initially split by rivalries between National Liberal and Guelph sympathizers, but was united in the face of the threat posed by the SPD. Hanover's political elite defended its position through an extremely restricted local franchise, which effectively excluded the SPD from local politics.

The man who dominated this political environment after 1890, Heinrich Tramm, was an effective administrator, popular among Hanover's bourgeoisie; his influence over the city's development was so great that to this day, the Wilhelmine period is referred to in local histories as the "Tramm Era."[26] His elevation to the pinnacle of the city's government would ultimately benefit the women's movement. As we shall see, Tramm's wife was active in several women's associations after the turn of the century, and Tramm himself was on good terms with several key leaders of women's organizations. More important, Tramm would support many of the chief objectives of the local women's movement, and his assistance would secure municipal subsidies for many projects proposed by women's organizations. Women leaders' personal contacts with Tramm would help determine the course the local women's movement would take.

Hanover's women's movement would thus come to maturity in an environment of economic and political inequality, and local women leaders would absorb the lessons of this environment. They learned that personal connections and the appearance of competence were assets, while popular support or partisan affiliations were not. In fact, the appearance of professionalism and competence was linked in the minds of local notables to political "neutrality," a position that in any case was forced on bourgeois women by the laws regulating women's participation in voluntary associations. Women leaders would therefore remain *überparteilich*, or politically nonpartisan, but, like their male counterparts, they would still work to protect bourgeois hegemony and to undermine the SPD. The SPD was so far beyond the pale that denunciation of the party was not seen by bourgeois men and women as a violation of "neutrality." Besides the lessons of their political environment, bourgeois women would also bring their own values to the creation of a movement: domesticity, order, cleanliness, morality, and a particular vision of motherhood. These factors would shape the tactics and thinking of local women leaders for over thirty years.

CHAPTER 2

Running Sewing Circles

and Visiting the Poor:

Women's Associations

before 1890

After the turn of the century, one local observer wrote that the Hanover's older women's organizations, those founded before 1890, displayed a kind of uniformity in their goals and work; they shared so many characteristics that he referred to them collectively as *Frauenvereine der älteren Gestalt* ("the older type of women's associations").[1] There were indeed substantial differences between most of the women's organizations founded in Hanover before 1890 and those established thereafter, differences in membership profiles, style, and goals. Most of the women's societies founded in Hanover before 1890 were simple charitable groups, organizations that promoted service to the sick and poor as work worth doing for its own sake, innocent of any overarching social philosophy as to the causes of and remedies for poverty. A few, however, were larger associations, which went beyond the sewing circles to try to treat the causes of poverty in a more systematic way; these groups were forerunners to the more elaborate system of social welfare organizations that would be created by the women's movement after the turn of the century.

After 1890, local clubwomen would begin to try to police the domestic lives of the poor, until by the turn of the century, women's associations came to see themselves as promoting not charity, but social work: systematic intervention in working-class families, designed to reform the values and life-style of the urban working class. After 1890, the local women's movement would establish a number of self-help associations for bourgeois women, organizations in which members pursued their own self-interest, rather than providing charity for the less fortunate. In so doing, Hanover women's associations were belatedly following examples that had been set by leaders of the national women's movement as early as the 1870s. Much of the rhetoric and goals of the later Hanover women's movement had been articulated by leaders of the national movement decades before, but these early trends in the national women's movement were generally not taken up in the provinces until after 1890.

The "woman question" had first become a subject of national debate during the 1860s as a part of the larger "social question." Feminists like Luise Otto, who had fought for women's political rights during the Revolution of 1848, and who were suppressed during the ensuing conservative reaction of the 1850s, welcomed the fact that women's position in society was now the subject of discussion by social commentators, educators, and reformers. Feminists defined the woman question as including the need for expanded political rights for women, as well as the improvement of their social and economic position, so that women could develop independent, self-sufficient personalities. Most of the liberal, male commentators who wrote about the issue and shaped public opinion, however, perceived the "woman question" more narrowly; they were concerned solely with the need to provide unmarried bourgeois women with professional training and opportunity, so that they might support themselves in a manner appropriate to their class background should their parents be unable to provide for them.[2]

Bourgeois observers were concerned about the plight of bourgeois spinsters because they believed that Germany suffered from a surplus of women, women who would never marry and thus would remain economic burdens on their families.[3] Married women and widows did not fall within the purview of this debate, since liberal commentators firmly endorsed the traditional, patriarchal family structure; the 1860s discourse over the "woman question" was concerned solely with single women who could not be accommodated within the traditional family structure. The question was thus framed by male writers as an economic one, not a political issue, and even progressive liberal commentators rejected feminists' proposal that women be granted full political rights. The liberal approach to the woman question was reflected in the German reception of John Stuart Mill's treatise *The Subjection of Women*. The liberal German press praised Mill's arguments for expanded educational and professional opportunities for women, while ignoring or rejecting those sections of the work that asserted that women should be treated as equal and independent human beings and given full political rights.[4]

The concern in liberal circles about the woman question was sufficient to ensure support for the first associations created to expand educational opportunities for women. These were the Lette Society, founded in Berlin in 1866, and the General German Women's Association (Allgemeiner Deutscher Frauenverein, or ADF), founded in Leipzig in 1865. The Lette Society focused on practical measures to assist bourgeois women, and ran a job referral service for genteel spinsters, as well as a trade school for *bürgerliche* girls and a ladies' restaurant for professional women.

The ADF, which did not have the financial resources of the Berlin association, initially had to confine itself to agitation for expanded educational opportunities for women.[5] The ADF was founded by Luise Otto and other feminists, but it did not agitate for political rights for women. To do so would have invited forcible dissolution by the police, since it would have violated the Law of Association; Otto and her associates, moreover, appear to have settled for working on projects that were attainable. The ADF was still radical in some respects, however, when compared with the Lette Society. Its educational programs sought to promote the general education and cultivation (*Bildung*) of its members; the ADF's leaders hoped that through such *Bildung*, women would become more self-sufficient, independent, and thus more worthy citizens.[6]

Although the ADF was more ambitious than the Lette Society, its program still represented a retreat from the feminist agenda articulated by Luise Otto in 1848, which had demanded political as well as social emancipation for women. Real leadership in the ADF rested with Auguste Schmidt and Henriette Goldschmidt, who focused the ADF's work on professional training for women, and generally reframed the ADF's goals in a more conservative fashion than Otto had originally conceived. Goldschmidt in particular worked to introduce nationalist sentiment into the ADF's rhetoric, and argued that professional women did not pose a challenge to the traditional family structure, but rather should be integrated into the existing social order.[7]

As a result, the German women's movement distanced itself from the struggle for emancipation that had initially characterized at least one of its wings, adopted an agenda that focused on economic rather than political gains, and by the 1870s had begun to promote women's entry into the public sphere under the rubric of "spiritual motherhood" (*geistige Mütterlichkeit*). This doctrine, which was originally formulated by educational reformer Friedrich Froebel and his female associates, equated femininity with maternal qualities, broadly defined: true femininity, they asserted, consisted of nurturing, caring, guiding, and teaching. According to this line of reasoning, women ought to be admitted to such professions as nursing and teaching not merely out of economic need, but because single women could use their innate, maternal qualities in these careers for the benefit of society as a whole. The doctrine of spiritual motherhood was popularized within the women's movement, especially by Henriette Goldschmidt. It was enormously appealing not only because it was compatible with established gender stereotypes, but also because it spoke to married as well as unmarried women. Unmarried women were provided with an additional argument to support their entry into new professions, while married women were encouraged to leave the confines of their homes (temporarily) in order to undertake unpaid social work of all kinds; they would use their maternal qualities in work with the poor, alleviating class hatred and divisions. The doctrine of spiritual motherhood stressed service and duty, not rights, and in this way helped to legitimatize the women's movement in a society that, during the 1870s, was turning away from the tenets of classical liberalism, with its celebration of individual rights.[8]

These developments—professional training for bourgeois women and the emergence of the doctrine of spiritual motherhood—were initially confined to a handful of large cities, primarily Berlin, Leipzig, and Hamburg. The organized women's movement was embodied first by the ADF and later by the Bund Deutscher Frauenvereine (or BDF), the League of German Women's Associations, an umbrella group for all bourgeois women's associations created at the behest of ADF leaders in 1894. The ADF and BDF did not influence developments in most provincial cities, however, until after 1890. In Hanover, the only reaction to the debate on the woman question was the creation of the Association for the Advancement of the Job Skills of the Female Sex (Verein zur Förderung der Erwerbsfähigkeit des weiblichen Geschlechtes), established by a small group of wives of local notables, assisted by some of the members' husbands, in 1867. The association was modeled on the Lette Society, and aimed to enhance bourgeois women's professional opportunities, but it evidently did not attract enough support, and dissolved itself only a few months after its creation.[9]

During the 1870s and 1880s, Hanover clubwomen were generally not concerned with "surplus," unmarried bourgeois women, and still less with obtaining women's political rights: instead, local women's associations overwhelmingly focused on the growth of urban poverty in Hanover during these years and on poor relief. Women's associations during this period were only part of the city's system of poor relief, a system that was struggling to keep pace with Hanover's growth. Those who administered local poor relief were in the process of rationalizing assistance to the poor, and beginning to experiment with ways to police the lives of relief recipients.

Hanover grew at a rapid pace between 1871 and 1890, as the city's population almost doubled. One consequence of the city's rapid development was an increase in the number of families that relied on municipal charity for regular support, especially during the economic recession of the late 1870s. The traditional causes of poverty—the death of a breadwinner, illness, old age, or a natural catastrophe such as a bad harvest—were now supplemented by economic depressions and industrial rationalization, new sources of poverty endemic to a capitalist economy.[10]

Hanover's system of municipal charity was not equal to the demands made on it during economic downturns. The city's municipal assistance program predated the Prussian annexation and was preserved essentially unchanged throughout the Wilhelmine period. Three types of assistance were dispensed under this system: municipal assistance; proceeds from charitable endowments (*Stiftungen*); and money, food, and clothing distributed by private charitable associations.

The city government's program of poor relief was a variation of the Elberfeld system, a model of charitable assistance popular among German cities of the period. Hanover's central poor relief committee (*Armenkollegium*), consisting of city officials and clergy, appointed and supervised a corps of municipal almoners. Municipal almoners were not paid for their work, but neither were they volunteers: an almoner who refused his appointment lost his municipal franchise and was assessed municipal taxes at an increased rate. Each almoner was responsible for all poor relief recipients living on his street. He received all applications for municipal support, investigated the applicants' economic circumstances and lifestyle, and recommended whether the application ought to be approved.[11]

The role assigned to the municipal almoner under this system was Janus-faced. On the one hand, he was supposed to befriend and advise poor relief recipients, but, on the other hand, he had to monitor and—to a certain extent—police their domestic lives. Municipal relief could alleviate poverty and prevent starvation and suffering, but it was never to be as profitable as wage labor. It constituted an alternative means of support for the working poor, but the system tried to ensure that it was an unattractive alternative. Indeed, poor relief under the Elberfeld system was so unattractive that it contributed to workers' ultimate acceptance of factory discipline by making alternative means of support unpalatable.[12]

The shortcomings of municipal poor relief were alleviated in some areas, however, by assistance from private charitable associations. The amount of assistance available from these associations increased substantially between 1871 and 1890. Like Bismarck's workman's compensation and old-age pension plans, the social service programs and charitable institutions founded by private associations represented an attempt by the middle and upper classes to render the urban working class politically quiescent. By providing the working poor with a sort of social safety net and by encouraging the poor to be industrious, orderly, and thrifty, philanthropists and reformers hoped to forestall the Social Democrats and to integrate the urban working class into the rest of society.[13] The supervision over the poor that the Elberfeld system entailed was geared toward this end, but it was only a forerunner of later, more elaborate programs that sought to intervene in and remold the lives of poor families.

Most of the charitable programs directed toward Hanover's poor during this period were sponsored by the Protestant Association (Evangelischer Verein), founded in 1865 by a group of Lutheran clergy, civil servants, and businessmen. The Protestant Association had a substantial endowment fund, and it used the accrued interest to subsidize an array of institutions that assisted, educated, or disciplined the working poor. Some of the projects were affiliated with the city's Inner Mission, while others were independent of the Lutheran Church; they included a library, a reform school for boys, a home for handicapped children, and a labor camp for vagabonds.[14]

In addition to the larger programs and institutions sponsored by the Protestant Association, the poor of Hanover received food, clothing, and money from a variety of charitable endowments, parish poor relief funds, and neighborhood charitable associations. Until 1885, the assistance distributed by these smaller charitable groups was not coordinated or overseen by any central agency. As a result, city officials complained that assistance did not go "to the deserving and needy but rather to those who are skilled at seeking out every source of charity. . . . [This situation] worsens each year, especially because most of our charitable citizens simply cannot accustom themselves to giving only to those poor persons whose circumstances have been thoroughly investigated."[15]

In 1885, therefore, the city, clergy, and various charitable associations cooperated in founding the Voluntary Poor Relief Association (Verein für freiwillige Armenpflege). The association would coordinate and centralize all almsgiving in order to avoid duplication of effort and to investigate all recipients of private charity. In its flyers and press releases, the organization admonished the public that "he who gives without knowing the recipient well, causes more damage than good. . . . this undisciplined almsgiving must be guided into proper channels."[16] The Poor Relief Association was an attempt to rationalize charity in the private sector, to establish a private, auxiliary system of poor relief that would parallel the municipal poor relief network.

The "proper channel" for private charity henceforth was the Poor Relief Association's network of poor relief districts and parish almoners (*Armenhelfer*). Patterned on the municipal poor relief system of districts and municipal almoners, the association's network divided each parish into parish almoner jurisdictions which usually had the same boundaries as the corresponding municipal almoner's assigned beat. The parish almoner investigated all recipients of private charity within his or her assigned area, and was supposed to consult regularly with the neighborhood's municipal almoner. Although municipal almoners were all men, the Voluntary Poor Relief Association accepted female volunteers as parish almoners. The association was thus the first of the large, citywide charitable programs to admit women volunteers, and Hanoverian women took advantage of this opening: from the start, over 60 percent of the parish almoners were women.[17]

For many years, however, the association remained the only large voluntary organization or charitable program that admitted women as members. Most of the women who worked in voluntary organizations in Hanover before 1890 did so within small women's associations that were independent of larger associational networks such as the Inner Mission. With only a few exceptions, the women's associations of this period existed in order to promote voluntary charitable work, and most were run with relatively little financial support or advice from city officials, clergy, or other men.

All but two of the women's associations listed in Table 2.1 were ostensi-

Table 2.1. Hanover Women's Associations Founded before 1890

Name of Association	Year Founded
Childbed Association	1813
Association of the Day-Care School of the Inner City of Hanover	1834
Frederica Association	1840
Jewish Women's League	1844
Women's Association for the Care of the Indigent Ill of the *Vorstadt* Neighborhood	1845
Women's Auxiliary of the Gustav Adolf Association	1861
Invalids' Linen Association	? (after 1865)
Association for the Advancement of Job Skills in the Female Sex	1867
St. Elisabeth Society	1868
Patriotic Women's Association	1873
Magdalene Society	1877
Women's Educational Association	1877
Dorcas Society	1878
Society for the Sale of Female Needlework	1881
Maria Society	1882
Boedeker Creche Society	1883
Association of Christian Spinsters (ran a day-care center)	1889
Reformed (Calvinist) Women's Society	1889

Note: This list includes all women's associations founded in Hanover prior to 1890, with the exception of three small charitable groups which each existed for only a few months and for which no sources are available.

bly charitable organizations, but in fact most were also sociable associations. Sewing circles and women's groups that gave benefit concerts to raise money for the poor were indeed of some service to impoverished families, but the chief value of these associations for members was sociable. Small women's groups that met one afternoon a week to sew or to discuss fund-raising tactics offered the women who came the chance to escape their household duties and children for a few hours, and to socialize with like-minded women.[18]

The first sociable and charitable women's organization in Hanover was the Association for Poor Married Women in Childbed (Verein für bedürftige verehelichte Wöchnerinnen, hereafter referred to as the Childbed Association). Founded in 1813, the association's original name was simply "The Women's Association"—since there was no other women's group at the time, no more detailed name was thought necessary. The association was established by a group of aristocratic women to collect money and clothing for the German armies that opposed Napoleon. After Napoleon's defeat in 1815, the organization solicited contributions to support widows and orphans of German soldiers. In 1817, it was reconstituted as the Childbed Association, and thereafter raised money to assist poor expectant mothers. The Childbed Association paid for doctors' fees, medicine, and infants' clothing. The women who received support (who generally came from one of Hanover's downtown parishes) were required to submit a letter from their pastors, which attested to their poverty and married status. During the 1880s the Childbed Association assisted several hundred women a year. Hanover's oldest women's association was also one of the most exclusive: of the fifteen women active in the Childbed Association during the 1880s, five were aristocratic, and almost all came from long-established Hanoverian families. As far as can be determined, the association admitted neither Jewish members nor women from the "Prussian colony," a term that referred to the families of Prussian administrators transferred to Hanover after the Prussian annexation, who were not accepted by the rest of the city's bourgeois community for many years.[19]

Like the Childbed Association, most of the rest of the city's women's organizations were founded in order to work on small charitable projects or services. Most of these projects involved personal service to the poor; a popular form of service was participation in a sewing circle that produced clothing for poor families. The Reformed Women's Society (Reformierter Frauenverein) was one example of this type of charitable service: female members of Hanover's Reformed (Calvinist) congregation gathered twice a month to finish clothing to be distributed among the congregation's poorest families at Christmas.[20] The Dorcas Society (Tabea Verein), named after Dorcas, the New Testament figure who distributed clothing to the poor, was established in 1878 by women from the "Prussian colony"; they met once a week to "cut out" pieces of fabric, which were then distributed to poor female cottage workers. The society then sold the finished clothing and gave the proceeds back to the cottage workers.[21] The Society for the Sale of Female Needlework (Verein zur Verwertung weiblicher Handarbeit), founded three years later by women from families that were Guelph partisans, performed a similar service for poor seamstresses.

The women's associations of this period generally consisted of only one or two dozen members; their memberships of these associations were socially homogenous. Members might share a confessional affiliation, come from the same neighborhood, or their organization might be a women's auxiliary of a men's association to which their husbands belonged. The Reformed Women's Society was one example of a group with a shared confessional affiliation, as was the Jewish Women's League, whose members visited and assisted the indigent and ill of the Jewish community.[22] The members of the St. Elisabeth Society did similar work among Hanover's poor Catholic families, while the women who created the Invalids' Linen Association (Krankenwäscheverein) were almost all wives of men who belonged to the Protestant Association. The Linen Association was not, however, an auxiliary of the Protestant Association; it maintained a stock of linens and nightclothes to be loaned out to poor invalids. The Dorcas Society, as mentioned earlier, was established by Prussian "outsiders"; other examples of associations whose members shared common bonds included associations that ran day-care centers. The social homogeneity of these organizations makes sense, when one considers that they were also sociable groups; members probably preferred to meet, sew, and chat with women who were their social peers, and who shared their interests.

Women's associations presented themselves to the public as charitable groups, and hence surviving records stress these organizations' service to the poor, not their sociable function. Occasionally, however, sources reflect the sociable aspects of a small charitable association, as can be seen in this account of an excursion undertaken by the ladies of the Reformed Women's Society.

On Friday, May 3, just as in previous years, the Women's Society sponsored an excursion to the Kirchrode Tower [located in a city park], to mark the end of the winter's work. Thirty-six ladies came along. The table around which we assembled [at a coffeehouse by the tower] had been decorated by our host with flowers and leaves, and the ladies participating spent a pleasant hour gathered around it. As in previous years, the excursion included a visit to a local charitable institution. After a half-hour's walk through the refreshing verdery, the ladies arrived at the Home for the Blind, where they were graciously received. Director Geiger gave us the benefit of his expertise during an extensive tour of the institution.[23]

A handful of local women's associations set up programs that were more ambitious than the sewing circles' activities, and which grew into charitable institutions. The Magdalene Society established a home for "fallen women" in 1879, which took in pregnant unmarried women and former prostitutes. Regular labor and intensive religious training were thought to be the key to the fallen woman's rehabilitation; therefore, several dozen penitents were supervised by a staff of deaconesses (sisters of the Inner Mission). The home's inmates divided their days between religious instruction and employment in a laundry run by the home, which defrayed some of the institution's expenses. The society set policy and raised the balance of the home's budget. After a one- or two-year stay, the women were given jobs as domestic servants in local families.[24]

Another more ambitious association was the Frederica Association, which sponsored the Frederica Home, a small hospital and a home for older women. As in the Magdalene Home, the Frederica Association employed deaconesses to do the day-to-day work of running the institution. The Frederica Association's members committed themselves personally to visiting penurious families that had applied for assistance to the association. The association did not give financial support to these families, since "to give alms without demanding work in return in very many cases amounts to nourishing the body and killing the soul; it increases poverty and produces more applications for support."[25] Instead of cash, the association ladies offered moral support, along with occasional gifts of food and job referrals.

> [After the head of the association] established that [the applicants] not only were truly needy, but also were really willing to be helped and to submit themselves to the guidance and care of the association, then the family in question was entered into the list of those who received regular support. Thereafter they received weekly . . . visits from the association ladies; a different member visited them each time. The assignment given to the lady who came to call was twofold. First, she was to discover the causes of the family's impoverishment and the best means by which the poor family might be helped. Second, she had to win the trust of the poor family and assist them with advice and deeds, especially paying attention to the entire household, reviving [the applicants'] sense of industry, thrift, order, and cleanliness, thus improving the situation of the poor family from the inside out.[26]

The Frederica Association clearly took as its model one of the first Protestant women's charitable groups in Germany, an organization founded by Amalie Sieveking in Hamburg in the 1830s. Founded in the wake of a cholera epidemic, Sieveking's group also did not dispense financial assistance directly, but rather tried to intervene in poor families to promote bourgeois domestic values: thrift, cleanliness, and orderliness.[27] These were the qualities that underlay the respectability and prosperity of the members' own households, and both the Hanover and Hamburg associations were sure that the acquisition of these attributes would eliminate poverty.

The Frederica Association and the Magdalene Society were different from the city's sewing circles and other small charitable organizations because they were not sociable groups; the descriptions of these two organizations' work makes it clear that members did little socializing within the context of association work. In addition, the Frederica and Magdalene societies differed because they subscribed to a rationale that sought to explain the causes of poverty and immorality, and set up rehabilitation programs based on these rationales. Other women's associations promoted personal service to the poor and sick as work worth doing for its own sake; no broader social philosophy was ever put forward by these groups.

The Magdalene Society and the Frederica Association, however, were influenced by male social commentators and philanthropists, who attributed poverty to the moral deficits of the working class. These reformers sought to integrate the working class into the rest of society by promoting *bürgerliche* values among the urban poor, a philosophy that provided the ideological underpinnings for the work done by the Frederica and Magdalene groups. The women of the Frederica Association thus paved the way for clubwomen from organizations established after the turn of the century, who would advance more elaborate theories about the causes of and cures for urban poverty.

Unlike the sewing circle groups, these two women's service organizations cultivated extensive contacts with charitable programs sponsored by men. Both associations received financial support from the city and from the Protestant Association, and had members of the Protestant Association on their steering committees or as advisors.[28] Perhaps because they were influenced by and connected with male service associations, the Magdalene and Frederica organizations adopted bureaucratic modes of operation: they had statutes, published annual reports, and kept records—

a substantial set of sources, especially in comparison with the scanty records left by the sewing circle associations.[29]

Men were also involved as advisors and officers in the local branch of another service organization, the Patriotic Women's Association (Vaterländischer Frauenverein), the women's division of the German Red Cross. Before 1890, the association was not yet large or very active in Hanover. It ran a small outpatient clinic and maintained a stock of linens, clothing, and medical supplies for use in wartime or in case of a natural disaster.[30]

Finally, Hanover's clubwomen relied upon masculine advice and assistance in the creation of another set of institutions founded during this period, a group of day-care centers (*Warteschulen*). What amounted to a day-care movement developed in the city to match the expansion of the local industrial sector: between 1880 and 1890 alone the number of day-care centers more than doubled, growing from six to thirteen.[31] By 1890, approximately one out of every twelve children in Hanover between the ages of one and six attended a day-care center.[32]

Hanover's day-care centers were created by bourgeois philanthropists, male and female, who were concerned about the growing number of working-class mothers employed full-time outside of the home, and the effect that mothers' employment might have on children. Day-care centers, one association leader argued, would keep children of working mothers from running wild, unsupervised by adults; they would "protect children from the dangers of wandering about on the streets, or from being left alone in a cramped apartment."[33] At the same time, the women who founded day-care centers took steps to ensure that only mothers who were forced to seek employment sent their children to day care. The center, one day-care association's annual report insisted, "is not for parents . . . who seek to rid themselves of the care for their children for the day."[34] Like the city's poor relief system, the day-care system promoted *bürgerliche* values. Mothers who could afford to stay home were to take care of their children without any assistance, whereas women who were forced to seek outside employment were allowed to leave their children in the centers, which would provide the sort of nurturing that children ought to receive: discipline, supervision, and care.[35]

Of the thirteen Hanover day-care centers in operation in 1890, two were sponsored by men's associations, one was financed by a charitable legacy, and one was run by a local textile factory for the children of its employees. Most of the rest were sponsored by women's associations, such as the Boedeker Creche Society. Established in 1883, the society ran a parish creche and day-care center, which took in over 150 children daily. The society employed a deaconess of the Inner Mission to run the center. Like other small women's associations, the Boedeker Society attracted members from a specific social circle. Of the fourteen women active in the society during the 1880s, the majority had husbands who belonged to the National Liberal Party; five of these men were also top municipal officials. The society had several male advisors, some of whom were husbands of steering committee members.[36]

Different women's associations did indeed tend to attract different and characteristic memberships: women from a single neighborhood; women who moved in the same circles because their husbands shared a political affiliation; or women with a shared confessional affiliation. Yet taken altogether, the women who belonged to the several small sociable and service associations that were founded before 1890 had much in common with one another. One woman who combined many of the attributes widespread among clubwomen before 1890 was Friederike Feesche. Feesche was born in Hanover in 1839; she came from an old Hanover family and entered another reputable local clan when she married Heinrich Feesche, who owned a prosperous bookstore and small publishing house. Feesche's husband was a strong supporter of the Guelph party and of the exiled Guelph dynasty; he was also on the board of the Protestant Association and belonged to other local charitable groups. Friederike Feesche herself volunteered as a parish almoner, sat on the steering committee of the Magdalene Society, and belonged to a small women's association that ran a day-care center. Feesche had one daughter, Marie, whom she occasionally took along with her on her visits to poor families in her capacity as parish almoner. After Feesche's death in 1918, Marie Feesche "inherited" her mother's position in the Magdalene Society and her parish almoner district.[37]

Friederike Feesche was typical of her generation of clubwomen in several respects. First, she was not single. Of the ninety-eight women who were active in eleven selected associations during the 1880s (see Table 2.2), the majority were or had been married. Among these women, 44 percent were married and 28 percent were widowed, while only 27 percent were single: the percentage of unmarried clubwomen would rise dramatically

Table 2.2. Occupational Background of Husbands and Fathers
of 98 Women Active in Women's Associations before 1890

Occupational Category	Number	Percentage
Academic professionals	14	14.3
Businessmen	8	8.2
Higher-level civil servants	25	25.5
Lower-level civil servants	1	1.0
Officers	11	11.2
Shopkeepers	3	3.1
Nonacademic professionals	1	1.0
Pensioners	6	6.1
Unknown	29	29.6

Note: The 98 women whose husbands and fathers are analyzed here belonged to the following organizations: The Women's Educational Association, the Childbed Association, the Association for the Day-Care School of the Inner City of Hanover, the Invalids' Linen Association, the Dorcas Society, the Boedeker Creche Society, the Association of the Care of the Indigent Ill of the *Vorstadt* Neighborhood of Hanover, and the Women's Auxiliary of the Gustav Adolf Society.

For the methods used in ascertaining the occupational background of these women's husbands and fathers, see the appendix. "Academic professionals" were men in the so-called *freie Berufe*, professionals such as doctors, lawyers, and architects, who had attended institutions of higher learning. "Higher-level civil servants" were those who had also attended universities, whereas "Lower-level civil servants" were those who had not. "Nonacademic professionals" were professionals such as apothecaries or photographers, who had had some sort of professional training but had not attended a university. "Businessmen" owned factories or large businesses, while "Shopkeepers" were small businessmen. These occupational categories were adapted from those in Kater, *The Nazi Party*.

after the turn of the century. The higher percentage of married or widowed women in women's associations founded before 1890 may be explained by the fact that membership in most of these organizations involved only a limited time commitment, usually a few hours each week, which was compatible with the domestic duties that the administration of a household involved. Alternatively, the lower percentage of single members in early women's associations may have been due to the fact that these organizations, unlike many of those founded after 1890, were not working for the benefit of unmarried bourgeois women, and were perhaps less attractive to single women.

Friederike Feesche also resembled her fellow clubwomen in coming from a prosperous, respectable family. Table 2.2 presents a breakdown of the occupational background of the husbands and fathers of the ninety-eight members of eleven associations for which membership lists were available. Except for the Voluntary Poor Relief Association, which included lower-middle-class women as parish almoners, the first women's associations in Hanover were fairly selective in their membership recruitment. Some were very selective: as noted before, one-third of the Childbed Association's members were aristocratic, as were at least twenty-two of the ninety-eight women in Table 2.2.

Feesche was typical of the period in two further respects. First, she was personally active in the association to which she belonged during this period. Few of the women's organizations established before 1890 had so called "passive" members, members who paid dues but did not contribute their time to an association's work. Passive members were more typical of the larger associations that would arise after the turn of the century. Feesche also resembled her associates in the longevity of her tenure in the societies she joined. She was on the steering committee of the Magdalene Society, for example, for over twenty years. Indeed, tenures of twenty to thirty years in associations were not uncommon among the ninety-eight women.

For decades, in fact, there was little turnover among the officers of the eleven associations listed in Table 2.2. Under these circumstances, an association might owe its creation and continued existence to the efforts of one or several key personalities, around whom the organization's work would revolve. The Reformed Women's Society, for example, was established in 1889 when Maria Eichhorn took up residence in the Reformed congregation's parsonage. Eichhorn headed the society for over twenty-five years; she also sponsored the creation of a Reformed Girls' Society, and was active in several other local women's associations.

To sum up, the women's associations that Feesche, Eichhorn, and their peers organized in Hanover before 1890—groups that, after the turn of the century, would be lumped together under the label of "the older type of women's associations"—had a great deal in common. These associations included about a dozen small sociable organizations, societies whose members raised money or produced clothing for the poor, or visited the sick and indigent. Most of these women's organizations were essentially confined to a single parish or *Stadtteil*. Their concerns were local, and they were largely isolated from citywide or national charitable networks.

Hanover's clubwomen had also created several service organizations, which were larger and not primarily sociable: the day-care associations, the Magdalene and Frederica groups, and the Patriotic Women's Association all represented a departure from the unambitious sewing circles. These groups differed from the sewing circles in their close connections with male notables and masculine charitable groups; because of these connections, women's service organizations were able to obtain sufficient funding to create ongoing projects or institutions, such as the Magdalenium. They were more bureaucratically run and shared much of contemporary male philanthropists' notions regarding the causes of poverty. From large to small, however, all of these associations had the same raison d'être. All of these women's associations were philanthropic: the members were not directly benefited by the work that they did, nor were their families or social peers.

The only exception to this rule in Hanover was the Women's Educational Association (Frauenbildungsverein), which differed in several particulars from other contemporary women's associations. Like the short-lived Association for the Advancement of Job Skills in the Female Sex, the Educational Association was inspired by the women's self-help organizations created in Berlin and Leipzig during the 1860s. Unlike the Job Skills group, however, the Educational Association was a success; for many years it was the only local women's organization affiliated with the national women's movement.

Founded in 1877, the Educational Association ran a school (Gewerbliche Fortbildungsschule), which offered courses in drawing, painting, fancy needlework, and gymnastics. Pupils could attend individual courses, or enroll in a one-year program that prepared them for the state examination for public school needlework teachers.[38] The Educational Association thus stood out from other women's organizations because its members were working for the advantage of their own social peers, since the courses were clearly intended from women of the middle and upper classes. In establishing the Educational Association, then, Hanover's clubwomen had taken a first modest step toward self-help.

The Women's Educational Association was a bureaucratically organized service group, structured along lines that would become more common after 1890. It had both active and passive members. Active members donated time and resources to an association, whereas passive members contributed only their dues and the use of their names in signed public appeals and programs. A large body of passive members, each of

Table 2.3. Hanover Men's Associations, 1890

Category	Number	Percentage
Charitable	15	6.0
Confessional	17	6.7
Professional	44	17.5
Sporting	17	6.7
Stenographic	6	2.4
Educational	3	1.2
Hobbies and recreation	16	6.3
Youth groups	2	0.7
Science and arts	5	5.9
Musical (incl. choruses)	47	18.7
Neighborhood associations (*Bürgervereine*)	9	3.6
Veterans' associations	12	4.8
Political	5	2.0
Fraternal orders and clubs	35	13.9
Reform associations	9	3.6
Total	252	100

Source: *Adressbuch der königlichen Haupt- und Residenzstadt Hannover*, 1891 ed., part II, 94–116.

Note: "Charitable" does not include *Stiftungen*, savings clubs, or funeral societies. "Professional" includes associations for the so-called *freie Berufe* as well as *Fachvereine* and civil servants' associations. "Reform" associations were groups that can be generally described as dedicated to the elimination of a particular vice or social evil; examples included the Vegetarian Society and a group that opposed cruelty to animals.

whom contributed several Marks a year in dues (such as the Educational Association possessed) guaranteed the organization a minimum budget. Furthermore, the Educational Association was given an annual subsidy by the city. The association differed organizationally from other local women's associations in another respect: it was affiliated with the national women's movement, through its membership in the ADF and later the BDF.

The membership of the Women's Educational Association was also different from those of contemporary women's societies. Of the twenty-three women active in the organization during the 1880s, eight were single, a high percentage for this period; this circumstance was probably due to the fact that the association was working on issues of interest to single women. The twenty-three association activists also included several Jewish members, which was unique: as far as can be determined, none of the other women's associations founded before 1890 had Jewish members (except, of course, the Jewish Women's League). The Educational Association thus breached the code of confessional segregation that apparently prevailed among other women's associations.[39]

Their husbands, fathers, and brothers had long since preceded Hanover's clubwomen in the development of self-help organizations, and indeed in every sort of voluntary association. The seventeen women's associations founded in Hanover prior to 1890 were scanty in number when compared with the tropical undergrowth of men's organizations that flourished during the same period. Table 2.3 presents a breakdown of the 252 men's associations functioning in 1890: they included professional, confessional, educational, recreational, musical, charitable, and political organizations. The diversity of these men's organizations serves to highlight the essential uniformity of the city's women's associations.

Unlike the city's clubwomen, Hanoverian men joined voluntary societies for a variety of reasons: recreation, education, professional advancement, self-enrichment, or to pursue political agendas. The number of recreational groups is especially striking. Apparently, men felt free to create organizations that, unlike the sewing circles, were openly and formally sociable. Men, moreover, did not operate under the same constraints as women in the pursuit of amusement, a fact reflected in a passage that reports on an excursion made by the members of the Reformed Men's Society (a sociable group led by Frau Eichhorn's husband, Pastor Edmond Eichhorn).

Many members gathered on June 15 for the annual summer excursion. . . . At 6 A.M. sharp the members met at the train station, provided with stores of food, and after a merry journey we arrived at Wildemann at 9:30 A.M. The weather was splendid and we climbed the Iberg.

As one might expect, after such exertion we had become quite hungry . . . and [on reaching the summit] we ate our packed breakfasts and were soon in high spirits. . . . [After hiking for several hours more] we took a short lunch at the Wildemann Ratskeller. We then continued through the beautiful Spiegel Valley to Lautenthal. There, in the Ratskeller garden, we took another break. Several of us began to sing, which was so well received by the other customers that we were obliged to give several encores. Unfortunately, though, the hour of departure drew near. With regret we were forced to part from our new friends, and we sang on our way down to the train station [to catch the train home].[40]

Members of the Reformed Men's Society hiked, drank, sang, and in general pleased themselves. Their hike through the countryside was certainly more entertaining than the Reformed Women's Society's visit to the Home for the Blind. The men who participated invested more money and time in their excursion than did the women discussed in the first account. The men took about twelve hours for their trip and each had to pay for train tickets, meals, and (probably) several rounds of beer. Their wives, who were responsible for their households' meals and child care, no doubt would have found it more difficult to leave home for such a long excursion. In addition, the members of the Men's Society were not afraid to draw attention to themselves in public; they were *auffällig*.

The activities and public demeanor of clubwomen thus contrasted sharply with those of contemporary men's organizations. This contrast, however, would fade somewhat after 1890. The older women's societies would continue to work quietly and were present throughout the period covered by this study, but newer women's organizations that were less self-effacing would emerge.

To a certain extent, the associations founded after 1890 represented a transition between generations of local clubwomen, since most of the leaders of these new groups were only children during the 1870s and 1880s, but the new organizations also differed qualitatively from the old. These new groups were bureaucratically organized societies, readier to appear self-serving, and were bent on effecting social change. Those new organizations concerned with helping the poor did not define their work as charity, but rather as social work, projects that were based on a detailed social philosophy. In addition, almost all of the new associations, whether social welfare or self-help groups, would embrace the doctrine of spiritual motherhood, justifying their work with reference to women's supposedly innate maternal qualities. Like the Educational Association, the newer groups would rely less on connections with individual male notables or men's charitable groups for funding, and more on direct subsidies from the city or state. After 1890, the unobtrusive sewing circle was eclipsed by newer, larger women's associations, which, through importing maternal values into the public realm, created new roles for clubwomen.

CHAPTER 3   An Ounce of Prevention:

The Tutelage of Girls'

Associations

During the years between 1890 and 1905, a new set of
women's associations was established in Hanover, organizations that differed from the older women's so-
cieties discussed in the preceding chapter. Many of these associations were
directly affiliated with the new BDF, the umbrella group for the bourgeois
women's movement. They were not only allied with national organizations, but also established coalitions among themselves; in these consor-
tiums, Hanover clubwomen would create much more ambitious programs than those established before 1890. The new women's organizations
would establish an array of social welfare services and educational institutions. In so doing, the new associations drew together to create a united
local women's movement.

Their first project was organizing girls' associations, which are the
subject of this chapter. In a sense, the local women's movement would cut
its teeth on this issue. Girls' associations were the first jurisdiction over
which the local women's movement claimed authority, and they proved a
fertile and durable fiefdom. Founding and running girls' associations
gave local clubwomen experience in administering large programs, and
in lobbying the municipal authorities for financial support. It was during
this period that clubwomen in fact began to rely on the authorities for
funding. As we have seen, before 1890, most local women's associations
were so small that they had insignificant budgets. Those that were larger,
such as the Magdalene Society, tended to rely on support from men's
associations (particularly the Protestant Association) or did private fund
raising. The new network of programs established after 1890, however,
required financing that went beyond the level that private donations and
fund-raising bazaars could provide, and so women's organizations began

to turn to municipal and provincial officials for support. By the eve of World War I, the movement would be largely dependent on public institutions for funding, a trend that began with the girls' clubs.

In addition, the arguments that clubwomen developed to justify the creation of girls' groups were the "rough draft" of a social critique they would later refine, expand, and use to make a case for other projects. For this reason, girls' associations merit special examination and analysis; this chapter also compares them with contemporary boys' organizations at various points in order to highlight differences between the reform programs that targeted young men and women.

A few boys' groups had existed in Hanover since the mid-nineteenth century, but girls' associations were a novelty during the 1890s. In establishing girls' associations, leaders of women's societies were breaking new ground, reaching out to a new clientele which was neither poor nor ill. The fact that clubwomen did so was largely due to the leadership of the Deutsch-Evangelischer Frauenbund (the German Protestant Women's League, or DEF), which sponsored the creation of a network of girls' associations. In this area, and in others, the DEF would emerge as the single most important organization in the local women's movement.

The DEF would not lead the movement alone, however. It would share leadership with the Women's Educational Association and several female teachers' organizations. The leadership and membership between the DEF and these other groups would overlap heavily, creating a core group of women who, between them, filled many of the leadership roles in the local women's movement. The DEF would often serve as the "spokesperson" for the local movement, however, because it could function as a kind of umbrella group. The Educational Association and teachers' groups by definition attracted memberships that were largely single and professional, whereas the DEF could include married women, and indeed all bourgeois clubwomen except for the movement's tiny Catholic and Jewish minorities.

The DEF was founded in 1899 in Cassel by a number of Protestant women who were supported and encouraged by Pastor Ludwig Weber, a leader in the (male) morality movement.[1] In an announcement written to advertise the association's first meeting, Weber argued that Protestant women ought to unite "in order to contribute to the solution of the woman question . . . we must not leave the debate over this question [the woman question] solely to the purely humanist, radical, or even anti-

Christian elements [within the women's movement]."[2] The DEF was thus created to act as a counterweight to liberals within the national women's movement. It was a forum for women who were essentially conservative in their outlook, yet who were interested in the "woman question," and who wished to work on issues such as improving women's education and opening new careers to women. DEF members initially espoused the narrower definition of the "woman question" put forth by liberal commentators during the 1870s, which restricted the issue to ways and means to provide for unmarried bourgeois women.

DEF members thus combined attitudes on women's issues that were progressive within the context of conservative Protestantism with more right-wing positions on other social questions; if women had had suffrage rights, there is no doubt that many DEF members would have voted for parties at the right end of the partisan spectrum. Marie Feesche (1871– 1950, the daughter of Friederike Feesche, introduced in Chapter 2), who joined the Hanover branch of the DEF, exemplified this attitude. According to her niece, whom Feesche sometimes took along on associational work, Marie Feesche was a very devout woman, who "completely despised *Emanzen* [women's libbers], because she was a woman with very traditional values. On the other hand, she thought that a girl ought to learn some sort of trade, or perhaps even attend a university; in that respect, she was very open-minded, unless of course the girl chose to enter a quite masculine career."[3]

Margarete Pagenstecher would have agreed with Feesche. In 1899, she was living in Cassel; there she belonged to a ladies' charitable association that met once a week to hear "good lectures" and to sew clothes for poor families. One week, Pastor Weber spoke at her association's meeting and announced that a meeting would be held in Cassel to found the DEF. Attracted by his announcement, which promised a discussion of careers for women, women's education, and protective laws for women workers, Pagenstecher and her sister attended. "This meeting proved to be one of the most interesting and important hours of my life," she later wrote. "My sister and I, along with many of the other ladies present, had our eyes opened to the importance of a great cause [the woman question], with which we had previously had little contact."[4]

Pagenstecher moved to Hanover that winter, and soon began to recruit women to found a local DEF branch. Leading members of the city's established, older women's organizations (discussed in Chapter 2) did not respond to Pagenstecher's invitations, but fifty local women who had read some of the DEF's literature were interested enough to attend the Hanover branch's first meeting in December 1899. Most of the women elected as officers of the new organization were wives of civil servants or clergymen. Pagenstecher had no desire to lead the Hanover DEF, and she convinced Paula Mueller to chair the first meeting, during which Mueller was elected to head the new DEF branch.[5]

Paula Mueller (1865–1946) was thirty-four years old in 1899. She was the daughter of a successful high-level civil servant. Her father, Hugo Mueller, had headed the executive bureaucracy attached to the Hanover *Landtag* before his retirement. Mueller had received the education usual for a girl of the educated classes, ten years at Hanover's secondary girls' school followed by a stay at a Swiss *Pensionat*. Her mother was a parish almoner and had introduced Mueller to voluntary charitable work. Her family's finances were such that Mueller was a woman of independent means, and she never married.[6]

Mueller was energetic and popular as the head of the Hanover DEF, and within a year she was elected as president of the national DEF; the organization's headquarters were transferred from Cassel to Hanover. For over thirty years, Mueller would dominate the leadership of the DEF, setting much of the organization's policy single-handedly. The voluminous correspondence that she left in the DEF archive shows that Mueller possessed a strong, indeed commanding personality, an enormous appetite for work, and a clear sense of what she wanted to achieve in any given situation.[7] Mueller's political orientation generally led her to sympathize with the Conservative Party, but, as we shall see, she combined conservative political beliefs with an agenda of creating new social and economic roles for women.

Under Mueller's stewardship, the DEF grew rapidly, from 18 branches with 1,300 members in 1900 to 83 branches with 9,300 members in 1907, and to 134 branches with 15,563 members in 1914.[8] The Hanover branch kept pace with this growth, attracting 300 members in its first year, and expanding to 587 members by 1913.[9] Hanover was thus the home of both a flourishing DEF branch and the association's national office. Mueller was not an officer of the local DEF after 1901, but she was very much involved in the local branch's work. The steering committee of the local branch was in fact a training ground for women who eventually rose to positions within the national leadership: by 1905, many of the women in the DEF's inner circle of leaders were former Hanover branch officers.[10]

Almost half of these DEF officers came from the nobility, and the rest were drawn from the upper middle class. Eighteen women who were officers in either the national DEF hierarchy or in the local DEF branch resided in Hanover in 1906. It was possible to ascertain the occupations of the husbands or fathers of eleven of these women (three of the remaining seven women came from noble families and were perhaps independently wealthy, while two of the other four were teachers): two were higher-level civil servants, three were military officers, two were businessmen, one was a landowner, two were physicians, and one was a lower-level civil servant.[11] The DEF, in other words, was dominated by the wives and daughters of local notables, some of whom were prominent in local government.

This social profile of the DEF's leadership supports generalizations about the DEF in current historical literature, in which the DEF is characterized as a phenomenon of "the upper middle class and the no-bility."[12] The organization's general membership, however, was more heterogenous than the leadership, and was by no means confined to the upper middle class. Table 3.1 presents a breakdown of the social profile of the Hanover branch of the DEF. Although the largest single category consisted of wives and daughters of higher-level civil servants (24.6 percent of the total), almost one-quarter of the members came from the families of lower-level civil servants, shopkeepers, artisans, and nonacademic professionals. For some women, membership in the DEF may have had snob appeal: they could not hope to be elected to leading positions within the association, but DEF meetings were a forum within which shop-keepers' wives mingled with the wives of generals and professors.

The political affiliations of DEF members were also diverse; the association was successful in attracting the wives and daughters of Guelph supporters, National Liberal politicians, and Conservatives.[13] Adelheid von Bennigsen (1861–1938), who ranked third in the DEF after Mueller and Countess Selma von der Groeben, was the daughter of Rudolf von Bennigsen, one of the leading National Liberal politicians of his generation and the former high governor of the province of Hanover. Countess von der Groeben (1856–1938), on the other hand, came from an aristocratic family with an East Elbian estate and a history of military service to

Table 3.1. Occupations of Husbands or Fathers of 289 DEF Members

Occupational Category	Number	Percentage of Total
Higher-level civil servants	71	24.6
Academic professionals	54	18.7
Military officers	43	14.9
Lower-level civil servants	29	10.0
Shopkeepers	27	9.3
Pensioners	21	7.3
Managers	12	4.2
Nonacademic professionals	9	3.1
Businessmen	7	2.4
Landowners	7	2.4
Artisans	6	2.1
White-collar employees	3	1.0

Note: For the methodology used in ascertaining the occupational background of these women's husbands and fathers, and for a definition of each category, see the appendix.

the Prussian crown; her father was a cavalry general.[14] Elisabeth von der Beck, the secretary of the national DEF, came from an old Hanover family with strong Guelph sympathies. Like the organization's officers, the DEF's general membership came from families affiliated with the pro-Guelph German-Hanoverian Party, the National Liberals, and the Conservatives; the fact that the wives of Guelph supporters worked beside members from National Liberal families reflected the declining antagonism between Guelph partisans and the rest of the city's bourgeoisie after the turn of the century.

With so many members who had strong political affiliations, the DEF became quite skilled at exploiting the ties of blood, marriage, and family friendships that connected DEF members and officers to leading politicians. Adelheid von Bennigsen, for example, was well acquainted with the city's leading National Liberal politicians, especially with deputy burgomaster Hans Eyl and *Stadtschulräte* Leon Wespy and Albert Wehrhahn (who both sat on the city's Committee on Schools). Both of these men would both help the DEF to obtain municipal support for the association's attempts to advance girls' education and vocational training (see Chapter 5).[15] Countess von der Groeben and her sister Erna von der Groeben were on good terms with the wife of provincial High Governor

Richard von Wentzel, who advised Erna von der Groeben how she might obtain funding from the high governor's office for a shopgirls' association that the DEF sponsored.[16] The DEF's files of correspondence with municipal and provincial officials document many examples of this kind of lobbying; in addition, DEF officers doubtless solicited government assistance for DEF projects when they met key politicians in social settings, but such private exchanges rarely find their way into the archives.

The DEF first used its connections to establish girls' groups. DEF leaders, and other Hanover women leaders, were able to enlist municipal support for organizing young girls because clubwomen were supposed to have inherent maternal skills that qualified them for this work. Along with the sick and needy, the young, especially young girls, were a "natural" clientele for older women, who, it was argued, could best understand and guide young girls. Hanover's notables and municipal administrators accepted this definition of women's natural sphere, and therefore supported the organization of adolescent girls by older women; this was the first of many projects in which clubwomen's maternal qualities were used to justify their involvement, and the first application by local women leaders of the doctrine of spiritual motherhood.

The consensus among municipal authorities and civic leaders that clubwomen possessed certain maternal attributes made it possible for women leaders to embark on the project of creating girls' associations, but this was not the only reason that they chose to do so. Hanover's clubwomen were one local example of a national trend among the German bourgeoisie toward creating youth groups. The rationale offered by Hanover's women leaders for organizing girls, as well as that given by local civic leaders for establishing boys' groups, mirrored arguments put forth by social commentators across Germany: youth was perceived as a distinct, problematical phase in life, one that required guidance and intervention, and youth groups would provide a forum for such intervention.

The perception of adolescence and young adulthood as a special phase in life first became widespread during the last decades of the nineteenth century. The German word for this age group, *Jugend* (which generally connotes persons between the ages of fourteen and twenty-one), first came into common usage during the 1890s.[17] Youths had a higher social profile than earlier in the nineteenth century and were more visible to social commentators because of several developments. First, there were more youths in German cities around the turn of the century than ever before, both in absolute terms and as a percentage of the population. The rapid growth in Germany's population during the nineteenth century, combined with a decline in infant mortality rates after 1870, meant the percentage of all Germans under age thirty increased substantially between 1870 and 1900; overall, Germany's population was more youthful than either England's or France's. Urban populations were especially skewed toward younger age groups, since migrants attracted to cities from surrounding rural areas tended to be young.[18]

These urban youths were noticeable not only because there were more of them, but because many had obtained jobs that made them relatively independent. Traditionally, youths had worked as apprentices, farm laborers, servants, or as cottage workers: all of these positions entailed subordination to patriarchal authority within the framework of household production. The new jobs in cities, especially factory work, often involved less supervision from adults, and paid wages that afforded young workers some economic independence. These new, "independent" youths attracted attention from social commentators and bourgeois reformers.[19]

Bourgeois reformers were increasingly aware of urban youths because these young adults fell into what one historian has dubbed a "gap in social control" (*Kontrollücke*).[20] From the time that urban adolescents left school at age fourteen until they started their required term of military service (if male) or married (if female), they experienced a degree of freedom that discomfited bourgeois observers. Social commentators feared that adolescent boys, free of teachers' control and unsupervised by their parents, would commit petty crimes, or be attracted to socialist youth organizations. Once under the influence of socialists, these young men might prove to be subversive military recruits, and ultimately undermine the ideological soundness of the army. Later in life, socialist youths would swell the ranks of Social Democratic voters. Bourgeois reformers argued that "patriotic" youth groups could help to counter the attraction of socialist youth organizations, "inoculate" young German men against socialism, and thus foster nationalist and militarist sentiments among these youths.[21]

The boys' groups organized by bourgeois reformers in Hanover after 1900 were examples of these "patriotic" youth organizations. One of the city's largest boys' associations, the Christian Youths, hosted lectures not only on "Why Do We Stay in Our Church," but also on "Germans on the Mediterranean" (about the Navy) and "Converting the Heathen in the

Goldmines of South Africa." In 1904, the Christian Youths began holding "war games" on Sundays, which eventually led to the formation of a drummer and piper corps. A surviving photograph of this corps shows a group of fifteen boys between the ages of eight and twelve, each in a uniform, carrying a drum or pipe.[22] Drummer and piper corps and war games were also sponsored by local secular schoolboys' clubs and Catholic boys' associations. Military drill and training were the raison d'être of the city's two popular *Jugendwehr* organizations. One of the *Jugendwehr* groups held courses that taught boys to use rifles, and had special naval and paramedic divisions.[23] Almost all of Hanover's boys' associations celebrated the kaiser's birthday with banquets or other special festivities.

The "gap in social control" that adolescent girls fell into was quite another matter, and the youth groups formed for girls sponsored very different activities. The fin-de-siècle bourgeois discourse about "unsupervised" young women focused not primarily on their political sympathies, but rather on their chastity, or lack thereof. In Hanover, and in other cities, bourgeois observers argued that working girls were constantly tempted and often seduced. One Hanover physician wrote that girls who, seeking work, had left their families to come to the city, "need not complain that they are lonely; often a single evening's stroll in a large city will suffice to acquaint a girl with a lover. If he becomes boring, then perhaps he has good friends, who in turn become acquainted [with her]. In short, it is not difficult for a girl, who has not sufficient occupation [in her free time] . . . to stray from the narrow path of virtue."[24] DEF leaders agreed; Paula Mueller maintained that "girls of the lower classes grow up in circumstances which are anything but sheltered. How much it must take for them to remain virtuous. . . . when heavy responsibilities and the struggle to earn their daily bread are added [to the other temptations life offers], then it often requires true heroism for them to resist [vice] and stand firm."[25]

For DEF leaders, the sexual transgressions of young women were only one aspect of widespread immorality in the society around them. The decline of public and private morals was a recurring theme in the DEF's literature, which assumed that contemporary society was seriously compromised by the spread of vice. The debate over the "morality question," as bourgeois observers called it, focused above all on the growth of prostitution; it also included broader concerns, however, about what DEF officers, and their allies, perceived as a pervasive laxity in contemporaries' private morals and behavior. Mueller gave voice to these concerns in a speech she delivered to many DEF branches in 1906, in which she warned that "under the proud achievements of the human spirit lurks a chasm of corruption, depravity, and moral decay. Boundless pursuit of pleasure has become the watchword of the day . . . [and] only too often it has replaced the promptings of chastity and morality."[26]

As far as the Hanover women's movement was concerned, however, moral laxity was only the tip of the iceberg; it was one aspect of the larger problem of "social degeneration." In championing social services, local clubwomen first made use of and ultimately entered the long-running, conflicting, and sometimes overlapping debates between (and among) a variety of interest groups: educators, philanthropists, physicians, employers, labor union officials, liberals, Catholics, socialists, social scientists, and administrators. This discursive domain, which could trace its roots back to the beginning of the nineteenth century, was concerned with the causes of and remedies for the physical misery of the lower classes and the threat which these classes posed to the Wilhelmine social order.[27] The poor, it was argued, were suffering from progressive physical and moral degeneration or decay (*Verwahrlosung*); by the end of the nineteenth century, "degeneration" had become a code word for a host of social problems. Hanover's women leaders could wield the term easily and frequently, secure that their audience understood the complex of ideas the word subsumed.[28]

Generally speaking, social commentators used *Verwahrlosung* to refer not only to the physical distress of the poor (especially their woeful housing and health) but also to the perceived loss of respect that the traditional sources of authority—the family, church, state, or employer—commanded from the lower classes. This loss of authority, in turn, was associated with increasingly widespread disregard of traditional social and religious norms. *Verwahrlosung*, or social degeneration, had thus rendered the poor susceptible to the blandishments of agitators who sought to undermine existing moral and social structures: the socialists. The moral laxity displayed by young women (and men) was thus only one part of a more sweeping and serious set of problems, which threatened to lead to social dissolution.

This was an almost apocalyptic vision of Wilhelmine society, but it was an assessment with which most Hanover women leaders tended to agree. Three tangible manifestations of immorality led them to this conclusion in dealing with young women: white slavery, the growth in prostitution, and a rise in the number of illegitimate births. Prostitution (as we shall see in Chapter 7) was endemic in Wilhelmine German cities, since many young women worked casually as prostitutes to supplement low wages or to make ends meet during periods of unemployment.[29] Illegitimacy rates were stable throughout the Wilhelmine period in Hanover, but the absolute number of illegitimate births grew along with the population; the number of pregnant single women seeking assistance from charitable institutions also grew accordingly.[30] Local women leaders drew pessimistic conclusions about their contemporaries' morals from these developments; eventually, their programs would address all three issues.

Hanover clubwomen shared their contemporaries' consensus that women had a more finely developed sense of morality than men; therefore, Mueller and her associates argued, bourgeois women's organizations had a special duty to lead the fight against depravity. Girls' associations were the first forum within which this campaign would be conducted, a means by which clubwomen could inculcate girls with "moral willpower." DEF vice-president Selma von der Groeben wrote that "to work in this area [with girls] seems to me to be one of the most urgent of our assignments . . . to help our youth to struggle and triumph [over immorality] through word and deed and with redeeming love, even after they may have fallen, but also beforehand, since to preserve is better than to salvage."[31] Mueller concurred, averring that "the conscientious care given to girls in parish girls' groups, girls' clubs, and [girls'] Bible study meetings can save many an innocent girl."[32]

Clubwomen expected girls' clubs to do more that promote chastity, however; they also were intended to inculcate political quietism as well, although in a more subtle way than "patriotic" boys' groups. The movement's analysis on the causes of "social degeneration" linked immorality with socialism and other "social poisons," and thus clubwomen hoped that by promoting religious values and chastity, they would prevent young working women from being seduced by Social Democracy. Groeben, for example, wrote that young "factory workers, shopgirls, and servants . . . are carried along with the stream, take all their opinions from their husbands or boyfriends, and are easily seduced; and if their men are Social Democrats, then they must become Social Democrats, too, even without understanding what this means. . . . we must assemble [these girls] in Christian associations and train them . . . as future housewives."[33] Helene von Fabeck, a DEF member involved in organizing domestic servants, agreed, warning clubwomen that if the women's movement did not act to organize servants, the SPD would, and would create servants' unions antagonistic to bourgeois housewives.[34]

Local clubwomen began to establish girls' groups during the 1890s; these associations were first organized on a confessional basis. Catholic women in the St. Elisabeth Society had created the Maria Society (Marienverein) in 1882, a group for female domestic servants; a group for Calvinist servants was also created by Maria Eichhorn, the wife of the local Calvinist pastor.[35] Girls who had just arrived in town and who had not yet found employment were also targeted by local women's associations, which assumed that these girls were especially vulnerable. Hanover clubwomen were afraid that while looking for work, girls from out of town might fall prey to white slavers. In 1892, local women who were concerned about white slavery founded a branch of the Society of (Female) Friends of Young Girls (Verein Freundinnen junger Mädchen, hereafter referred to as the Friends of Young Girls), a national anti–white slavery organization.

The Friends of Young Girls was primarily interested in safeguarding girls who were traveling alone. In a flyer, the leaders of the Hanover branch asserted that

> the dangers of these journeys [undertaken by young girls seeking work] are much greater than is commonly assumed. All who have worked in this area can tell of tragic cases in which [white slavers] laid in wait for these girls and pressed their attentions upon them with sophisticated cunning and malice. Many a helpless young girl who merely waited [to change trains] in a large station . . . has been lured to her ruin in a house of evil repute, or at the very least lost her luggage.[36]

The society's work reflected its motto: *bewahren ist besser als retten*. The Hanover branch established a home that sheltered girls while they looked for work, and it maintained a list of job referrals. After 1896, Hanover Friends descended on the city's train station on the first days of January, April, July, and October (the traditional dates when domestic servants entered service or changed employers and hence days when girls from out of town arrived seeking positions). Posters had been put up in rural train stations and in fourth-class train compartments, warning girls not to talk to strangers and to approach the Friends (who could be identified by the white armbands they wore) when they reached Hanover. The Friends waited by the fourth-class tracksides for young girls who arrived alone and sent those who were not met by relatives to "safe" hostels and job referral agencies. After a girl had found a position, a Friend visited her to see if she was settled in, and gave her the address of an appropriate servants' association.[37]

By 1900, then, several servants' associations had been established by local clubwomen, along with servants' hostels. In 1900, the DEF took the next step, and began to hold regular meetings for *Konfirmanden*, adolescent girls who were receiving religious instruction in preparation for their confirmation as Lutherans. These parish girls' groups were the first to organize girls who still lived at home, girls who could by no means be seen as needy. *Konfirmanden* groups represented the first steps toward an elaborate, extensive network of girls' associations that the DEF (with the assistance of women teachers) would create and dominate.

The first DEF parish girls' group was founded in 1900; about fifty girls from a single parish assembled once a week to sew shirts for poor families, while Christian literature was read aloud.[38] The meetings always closed with hymn singing. These gatherings resembled the meetings of smaller, older women's charitable associations, and perhaps the girls who attended felt "grown up." The novelty of the *Konfirmanden* group was another attraction, since these meetings were the first in Hanover to take girls and gather them together outside of the school and family for recreation; they offered a way for girls to escape from parental supervision into a peer group.

The DEF founded girls' groups in other parishes during the next three years, and all were well attended. By 1904, eleven *Konfirmanden* groups met in five parishes, attracting 600 girls a week, total; a year later, the program had expanded to sixteen weekly meetings in eight parishes.[39] The girls' parish groups were more than a source of companionship for members, since the gatherings now offered members a variety of recreational activities such as gymnastics, games, and rambles in parks or across the local countryside during the summer. Several times each year, girls' groups hosted an evening for the members' families and special assemblies for the girls' mothers, which often included slide shows. The city assisted the DEF by providing some financial support for the meetings, and also made gymnasiums and other facilities available for the girls' games and gymnastics. In 1911, the DEF persuaded the provincial

Lutheran synod to contribute 25,000 Marks a year to pay salaries to the women who led the parish girls' groups; these women were given the job title of *Gemeindehelferinnen* (parish helpers).[40]

By 1911, the *Konfirmanden* meetings were no longer the only recreational groups for Hanover girls. Starting in 1906, the DEF sponsored the creation of a chain of girls' clubs at many of the city's elementary schools. The girls' clubs sponsored many of the same activities offered by the parish girls' associations, and were usually led by a teacher who belonged to both the DEF and a female teachers' association. The DEF also established a number of special associations for shopgirls, domestic servants, and young female factory workers. Together, Hanover's girls' clubs— parish girls' and working girls' associations—numbered over forty in 1912, and had a combined membership of almost 2,000 girls, or about 10 percent of the young women between the ages of fourteen and twenty-one in Hanover. All of these girls' associations were overseen by the Committee for Girls in Hanover (which consisted primarily of DEF members, and officers from the Educational Association and women teachers' organizations). The committee held courses to train women to lead girls' associations and lobbied the provincial Lutheran Church, the provincial government, and the municipal government for financial support for girls' organizations.[41]

Local clubwomen had organized a significant fraction of the city's girls in a relatively short time, but girls' organizations were still outnumbered by their male counterparts. The combined membership of local "patriotic" (that is, nonsocialist) boys' groups was almost 5,000 in 1912, or about one-quarter of all Hanover boys between the ages of fourteen and twenty-one.[42] Apparently, it was easier to organize boys outside of the school or family than to enlist their sisters.

The DEF gave special attention to recruiting working-class girls for its associations, since these young women were presumably "unsupervised," and hence morally at risk, as well as being exposed to the blandishments of the socialists. In a pamphlet which the DEF produced for distribution among recent graduates from girls' *Volksschulen*, graduates were urged to join girls' associations and were warned

> Do not read bad books . . . preserve the purity of your hearts. . . . beware
> of men who flatter you, who make enticing promises to you, who seek
> to arouse your senses. Beware of those who offer you wine or spicy

foods. Above all beware of the "fine gentlemen," who are not of your class, and who do not respect you as a person but rather only seek girls who will yield to them.[43]

The DEF targeted working-class girls in its recruitment drives for parish girls' groups and girls' clubs, but it appears to have met with limited success. The *Konfirmanden* groups were indeed popular, but the girls who came were drawn primarily from lower-middle-class families. Frida Glindemann, a parish helper who led a *Konfirmanden* group during World War I and the 1920s, recalls that "most of the girls who came were the daughters of artisans, shopkeepers, and [minor] officials, respectable people . . . if they were alive today, I think that their fathers would be solid Christian Democratic voters. That's the kind of people they were."[44] The men who organized local schoolboys' clubs and boys' associations were equally unsuccessful at attracting working-class boys. The 5,000 members of "patriotic" boys' groups mentioned earlier were almost all students, pupils, apprentice artisans, or business employees. Very few worked in factories or as unskilled laborers.[45]

The Hanover women's movement was ultimately able to organize some working-class girls, however, within the framework of occupational girls' associations, which focused on specific "endangered" social groups: shopgirls, female factory workers, and female domestic servants. The DEF's success here contrasted sharply with the failure of "patriotic" boys' associations to attract working-class boys, who evidently preferred to join socialist boys' groups. Possibly working-class girls were less attracted to socialist youth associations than their brothers were. It seems more likely, however, that the local SPD was more interested in creating socialist youth groups for boys than for girls; there is in fact no evidence that any socialist girls' groups were established in Hanover before 1914.[46]

In addition, working-class girls may have been willing to join DEF-sponsored groups because the political orientation of these associations was much less overt than that of "patriotic" boys' organizations. "Patriotic" boys' groups openly sought to indoctrinate their members with nationalist sentiments, which some working-class youths (and parents) doubtless found objectionable. The DEF groups, on the other hand, stressed "only" chastity and domesticity, values that SPD leaders themselves espoused; the socialist movement had rejected Wilhelmine Germany's political structure, but not its sexual mores.[47] Certainly, the girls' groups were much more subtle in their political goals that other anti-SPD efforts being undertaken by contemporary male bourgeois reformers.

Compared with explicitly antisocialist groups being organized for boys under government sponsorship, the leaders of the women's movement were "only" upholding polarized gender roles and traditional sexual norms, training young women for domestic roles and housework; these were "unpolitical" values to which large parts of German society, including parts of the working class, subscribed. As Madeleine Hurd has noted, both the socialist and broader labor movement milieus stressed "enlightenment, education, and morality. . . . Education, self-control, and behavioral reform were part of the workers' political and organizational traditions."[48] These traditions nurtured a *Drang nach Kultur* evident throughout the organized working class, resulting in a steady stream of lectures, adult education courses, theater, and other offerings of science, art, and nature within the labor movement.[49] Groups for girls that stressed domestic science were of course a far cry from the "higher" cultural offerings popular among adult workers, but domestic science may have been exactly the sort of education and behavioral reform that working-class parents wanted for their daughters. This contributed to clubwomen's relative success at organizing working-class girls. Furthermore, their emphasis on domestic skills and domestic science training, which was first articulated in the girls' clubs, would surface again and again in future social welfare programs.

The activities sponsored by the DEF's servants', shopgirls', and factory workers' groups reflected bourgeois assumptions about the dangers inherent in each kind of job and the lack of domestic skills in working-class women. Factory workers, one DEF officer wrote, "have work that kills the spirit," which left them little time for learning housewifery. The association therefore

must give the female worker everything which the factory lacks: an opportunity to learn household skills in evening courses . . . and intellectual development through [attending] lectures, German lessons, art lessons, etc. These things strengthen them in morality, religious devotion, and love for the Fatherland, and thus serve as a counterweight to the rough and degrading influences and the irreligious and unpatriotic forces [within the factory—that is, Social Democracy].[50]

In 1907, The Hanover DEF branch sponsored the establishment of an association for young Protestant female factory workers, which was led by Emmi Wallmann, a DEF member (Wallmann was not a worker; her father was a forestry official). The association met once a week to sing, play games, and hear "improving" lectures, or to attend religious services on holidays. It also held courses for members in infant care, sewing, and tailoring.

The DEF was able to obtain considerable financial support from local authorities for its factory workers' group. The DEF persuaded the city not merely to pay the rent on the meeting rooms for the association, but also to pay Wallmann a salary of 500 Marks a year for her work. In addition, the DEF collected subsidies for the association from the provincial *Landesversicherungsanstalt*, which administered workers' old-age and disability insurance funds. By 1912, the association had grown so large (over 100 members) that the DEF felt it necessary to split it into two separate branches.[51]

Within these larger associations, small groups of four to eight younger girls were assigned to an older "group mother" (usually a DEF member), who visited the young members at home between meetings, encouraged them, and monitored their attendance at association activities. The maternal role that bourgeois women thus took vis-à-vis young working women, the concern they exhibited for these girls, was an expression of the doctrine of spiritual motherhood: clubwomen tried to translate mothering behavior into public roles, to help solve the "social question." At the same time, however, these girls' groups were also intended to serve a political function, to preserve young working women from the twin evils of immorality and socialism, from the temptations of Social Democracy. In addition, clubwomen hoped that these clubs would promote bourgeois values of domesticity and gender roles. A maternal role therefore also served as a vehicle for bourgeois women's own class interests and values, a linkage that would surface repeatedly in the local movement's programs.

Factory workers were not the only objects of clubwomen's concern. DEF officers concluded that shopgirls were another "endangered group." Since they were obliged to dress well "and seldom have any real work to do," they often came to think of themselves as ladies, and ran the risk of becoming idle and vain.[52] In 1904, Countess Erna von der Groeben, the sister of the DEF's vice-president, founded an association for shopgirls with financial assistance from the Protestant Association, the Lutheran Provincial Synod, and the provincial government; the new group was christened the Christian Association for Young Girls. Members of the association participated in activities that were intended to build character; the emphasis was on Bible study and good literature. The association also offered stenography courses for members, and maintained a comfortable set of clubrooms where girls could gather to play games, read, or sing. All members were required to attend church services regularly.[53]

In establishing girls' associations for young factory workers and shop-girls, the DEF's primary goal was "to protect and preserve them from the dangerous pleasures [sexual and political] of the big city."[54] Servants' groups, however, were created for somewhat different purposes. Female servants, unlike factory workers and shopgirls, still lived and worked within households; they were not "unsupervised" or morally "endangered." In organizing servants' groups, DEF officers were working in their own interest, since they were themselves employers of servants. Here, the DEF pursued an "ounce of prevention" strategy not primarily in respect to servants' morals, but in order to forestall the unionization of servants by the SPD.

Until 1907, female domestic servants in Hanover were largely ignored by the DEF. Servants could join the small Catholic Maria Association or the Calvinist servants' group, or they might join the Christian Association for Young Girls (although it was not specifically an association for servants). By 1907, however, the DEF was alarmed by the growth (both on the national level and in the city of Hanover itself) of the Union of German Household Employees (Zentralverband der Hausangestellten Deutschlands), which was one of the "free" unions affiliated with the SPD.

DEF leaders objected strongly to the very notion of unionizing servants, and they also rejected the union's overall conception of the relationship between domestic servants and their mistresses. The union argued that servants and housewives had a modern employee-employer relationship, comparable to labor relations in other industries. Consequently, servants were entitled to fixed hours of employment, overtime wages for work performed in addition to those fixed hours, and the elimination of the detested *Dienstbücher* (booklets that listed a servant's past employers and included the former employers' evaluation of her work), which servants were obliged to carry.[55] Mueller and her associates, on the other hand, clung to an older conception of the domestic servant, in which the servant was a member of a patriarchal household, and her relationship with her employer resembled that of a client to her patron. Thus, in her correspondence with a leading member of the Catholic Women's League (the Catholic counterpart to the DEF), Mueller warned that if domestic servants were unionized, "then they will become estranged from the house and family [of the employer]; we ought rather to preserve and promote the patriarchal relationship [between servant and employer]. And what if our maids should seek to gain the upper hand in economic negotiations, or even conduct strikes? . . . a great deal is at stake here."[56] Helene von Fabeck, who would become active in mobilizing local house-wives against the SPD threat, warned fellow clubwomen that the SPD would organize servants not merely so that the party could intervene in the housewife-servant relationship, but also in order to turn servants into "dedicated agents of class struggle," which would strengthen the threat that the SPD posed to the social order.[57] In organizing servants' groups, clubwomen therefore were not just trying to restrict the influence of the SPD among working women in general (the mission of all girls' clubs), but were also directly protecting their own personal economic interests, by attempting to forestall the SPD's penetration into bourgeois households.

The League of Christian Unions of Germany (Gesamtverband der christlichen Gewerkschaften Deutschlands) was also anxious to prevent the organization of domestic servants by the SPD, and in October 1907, the Christian Unions hosted a conference in Cologne to discuss the "servant question." Representatives from the DEF, the Catholic Women's League, the Friends of Young Girls, servants' associations, and other interested organizations were invited. Speakers at the conference proposed some improvements in servants' working conditions and supported the passage of a new federal law on servants, which was to supersede older, illiberal local ordinances on servants. The conference agreed unanimously that unions were an inappropriate form of organization for servants; it resolved to encourage the formation of servants' associations and housewives' associations, and proposed the creation of local commissions that would mediate differences between the two interest groups. As a result of this conference, female servants' groups and housewives' associations were created across Germany.[58]

The Hanover branch of the DEF and its local allies moved quickly to effect the reforms recommended by the Cologne conference. A coalition led by the local Christian Union Cartel, the DEF, and the local branch of the Catholic Women's League established the Hanover Commission on Servants in January 1908. The commission also included representatives from other local women's associations, such as the Reformed (Calvinist) Women's Society, the Jewish Women's League, the Women's Educational Association, and the Patriotic Women's Association.

The commission followed the recommendations of the Cologne conference, and sponsored the foundation of the Hanover Housewives' Association (Hannoverscher Hausfrauenverein), which then sent representatives to sit on the commission. At first glance, the Housewives' Association was a success, since it attracted almost 600 members during its first year; these were almost all "passive" members, however, women who belonged to the DEF or Catholic Women's League who had been persuaded to join the new association. Very few of the women who came to the Housewives' Association meetings were interested in the commission's work; many were suspicious of servants' associations, and feared that the commission would ultimately unionize servants. They tended to reject even the modest reforms proposed by the Cologne conference. DEF organizers tried to counter this fear by pointing out that if clubwomen did not organize servants, the SPD would, but had limited success.[59] The Housewives' Association did fulfill its assigned function, however; it sent representatives to the Commission on Servants, and formally involved housewives in local clubwomen's projects to organize and regulate domestic servants.[60]

The Catholic Women's League was willing to join the DEF in the creation of a confessionally "neutral" housewives' association, but insisted that Protestant and Catholic servants had to be organized separately. The DEF therefore created a new servants' organization, the Protestant Domestic Servants' Association, which sent a representative to the commission; Catholic servants were represented by the Maria Association. With the inclusion of these new members, the commission was complete: it consisted of representatives of both housewives and servants, and allies of each interest group.[61]

The commission's goal was to mediate differences between servants and their mistresses, and thus defuse the issue of the unionization of servants; this was to be accomplished by persuading Hanover housewives to improve servants' wages and working conditions while simultaneously preserving the patriarchal relationship (perhaps "matriarchal" would be more apt, but "patriarchal" was the term used by women leaders) between domestic servants and their mistresses. The commission developed several strategies to influence local housewives. First, it maintained a job referral service for domestic servants, where local housewives could list available positions. An employer who used the commission's referral service, however, was obligated to sign the commission's "model contract," which regulated the servant's working conditions and wages. The "model contract" specified the same wages, days off, and working conditions as those demanded by the "free" servants' union, but it did not provide for a fixed working day or overtime wages (the SPD-affiliated union's contract guaranteed a twelve-hour workday). The commission's referral service, with its attendant contract, was a success; there were never quite enough domestic servants to satisfy local demand in any case, and the commission's service had developed a reputation among Hanover housewives as a source of "quality" domestic servants. The city provided a room gratis to house the referral service.[62]

The relationship between servant and mistress could also be influenced through direct appeals to housewives to act with parental care and firmness toward their maids: this was the Housewives' Association's job. The Housewives' Association was supposed to educate its members about "the responsibility that their position as employers of servants places upon them. The influence that their position gives them over a large segment of our populace, especially over the younger servants, should be employed to educate them [the servants] and to improve their morals."[63] As in their work with factory workers and shopgirls, clubwomen were using the language of gender—here, the promotion of a "maternal" relationship between servant and housewife—to discuss issues of class. The language and imagery of gender in fact replaced the language of class here, so that the awareness of class interests, or class conflict between employers and servants was diffused or suppressed entirely.

The servants' associations were also intended to promote this "maternal" relationship, by acting almost as guardians for servants. The associations were to provide domestics with "wholesome" recreation and companionship, and offer domestic science courses, which would increase their value as employees. In addition, servants' associations were to teach their members "that they occupy a position of trust within the household.

They must learn to recognize that many of their masters and mistresses are benevolent, and that their work as domestic servants is valuable training for their future careers as wives."[64]

The servants' and housewives' associations were thus supposed to promote better labor relations through education, but the commission also established a court of arbitration to resolve intractable disputes between employers and servants. The court of arbitration consisted of equal numbers of housewives and servants, along with two "neutral" jurists. It was intended to be an inexpensive and simple alternative to the police and municipal courts. The arbitration court was a failure, however, since it failed to attract cases.[65]

The Housewives' Association could not meet the commission's expectations, either. The association never really came to life; it did not attract members or volunteers apart from those "donated" to it by the DEF and the Catholic Women's League, and did not become a self-sufficient organization. "Housewives can only be attracted [to meetings] when sociable events are staged," Paula Mueller concluded, "since they are still quite self-centered."[66] A few years after its creation, the Housewives' Association was moribund.

The Commission on Servants was ultimately unable to transform the relationship between domestic servants and their employers. It could not restore the servant to her traditional position as a member of the patriarchal family: the very attempt to do so contradicted the reality of most domestic servants' lives. Domestic servants in Wilhelmine bourgeois households were generally not treated as "part of the family." To emphasize the elevated status of their employers, servants were required to wear clothing and use language that reflected their subordinate status; the use of *"gnädige Frau"* as a form of address is one example. Servants ate and slept in isolation from the families they served, and often had to enter and leave the house through a separate "servants' door." The ideal servant, who faithfully stayed with the family for years, helping to raise the children to adulthood, was very rare: servants usually changed employers every year or two.[67] The Commission on Servants simply lacked the resources and the popular support of servants and housewives needed to transform the prevailing relationship.

Besides its job referral service, the commission's only lasting legacy was the Protestant Domestic Servants' Association, which boasted 200 members by 1913.[68] The DEF, which had created the association, retained control over its activities. Marie Gaster, a DEF member, headed the Servants' Association, and its bylaws specified that at least one officer in the Protestant Domestic Servants' Association had to be an officer from the Hanover DEF branch.[69] Young servants met on their occasionally free Sunday afternoons in the association's rooms to read, play games, hear "educational lectures," or, in summer, take walks together. The associations sometimes hosted "musical evenings," and held classes for members in sewing, tailoring, and infant care.[70] These classes were ostensibly designed to prepare young domestic servants for their future careers as housewives.

Just as it did for its factory workers' group, the DEF was able to secure funding for its work with servants from the authorities. The DEF was able to persuade the city to pay for the rent on the rooms that housed the Servants' Association's headquarters, and it also received subsidies from the *Oberpräsident* of the province of Hanover for this work. In addition, the servants' group was financed by the provincial Lutheran Church.[71]

The Protestant Domestic Servants' Association thus offered its members special services, but it also performed the same functions for members as the other girls' organizations discussed earlier. Schoolgirls' clubs, parish girls' groups, and associations for various categories of working girls all attracted members because they provided sociability and recreation. In practice, these organizations attracted dissimilar social groups: parish girls' groups and girls' clubs had largely lower-middle-class memberships, while servants', shopgirls', and factory workers' associations were explicitly working class.

From the standpoint of clubwomen, the primary function of all of these girls' associations was to articulate and propagate the ideology of moral purity, and hence keep the girls who joined within the social-cultural milieu of the Protestant Church; this also kept them from drifting into the ambit of the socialist labor movement. Working girls' organizations also stressed domestic values, by providing members with domestic science courses. In addition, servants' associations were supposed to promote the ideal of a patriarchal relationship between servant and employer. All of these goals were only one part of the larger agenda of the local women's movement, which was to fight the spread of "social degeneration."

Most of the girls' groups discussed thus far were loosely controlled by the DEF. The local Jewish Women's League did not create any offshoots for young Jewish women. Since less than 2 percent of Hanover's population was Jewish, perhaps the pool of young women available was too small for such an auxiliary.[72] Catholic girls could choose among a smaller number of Catholic girls' parish associations, sponsored by the local branch of the Catholic Women's League in conjunction with local parish priests. The league also established a Catholic shopgirls' association and a club for young Catholic female factory workers. Like the DEF, the league sent its officers to sit on the steering committee of each Catholic working girls' association, and league members led the girls' organizations' meetings. The Catholic Female Factory Workers' Club offered sewing and singing courses to members, while the Catholic Shopgirls' Association held classes in stenography and gymnastics. Both associations hosted expeditions to the Hanover Zoo and hikes through local parks; in both cases, members attended Mass as a group on Easter and other religious holidays.[73]

Like the members of DEF girls' associations, girls who joined the Catholic organizations were probably attracted by the recreation and companionship that these associations offered. Like the DEF, the Catholic Women's League sponsored girls' organizations because they fulfilled the function of symbolizing an ideology of moral purity. Catholic girls' associations had another purpose, however: in a city where Catholics were outnumbered and surrounded by Protestants, Catholic voluntary associations helped to keep their members within the Catholic social-cultural milieu and reinforced their confessional identity. The Catholic Women's League valued the role that voluntary associations could play in preserving members' Catholic identity, and therefore insisted on organizing Catholic servants and female workers separately, although the DEF had proposed the creation of large interconfessional associations for each occupational group.

Both the DEF and the Catholic Women's League also began to organize *gebildete* girls as well after the turn of the century. Clubwomen were not, of course, concerned about the moral purity of upper-middle-class girls (who did not fall through a *Kontrollücke*), but rather were concerned with training successors in the next generation. The Catholic League was unsuccessful at organizing a young women's auxiliary, but young bourgeois Protestant women eventually organized themselves, without any help from older women.[74] This independence was perhaps responsible for the success of the Association of Young Protestants for Social Work (Evangelische Jugendgruppe für soziale Hilfsarbeit). This organization of young women was not led by the DEF or the Committee on Girls in Hanover, but it nevertheless belonged to the local "patriotic" youth movement.

The Young Protestants were founded in 1909 by ten young women in their late teens and early twenties who came from *gebildete* families. A few were students, but the majority were *Haustöchter*, and did not plan to pursue careers. Although they were too young to join adult women's charitable associations, they wanted to spend some of their free time doing social work. The members decided to work as volunteer substitutes in local children's hospitals, creches, day-care schools, and the Frederica Home, thus giving the deaconesses and nurses who worked in these charitable institutions an occasional day off. To prepare themselves for this social work, the Young Protestants ran their own study group, which analyzed the theoretical foundations of social work. By 1913, they had grown to 112 in number.[75] In some ways, this group represented a conservative Protestant version of the contemporary Berlin "Girls' and Women's Groups for Social Welfare Work," which was introducing bourgeois young women to social work in the capital.[76]

The leaders of the Hanover DEF branch would have welcomed the Young Protestants as a junior (and subordinate) auxiliary to the DEF, but the Young Protestants preferred to remain an independent organization. One member recalled later that

> We maintained only a very loose connection with the DEF, [because] we wanted to make our own way, to try for ourselves to reach the goals that we had set for ourselves. . . . we wanted to broaden our knowledge through lectures on civic, economic, and social questions, and through participation in the charitable work of the Inner Mission.[77]

The Young Protestants was therefore different from the other youth organizations discussed in this chapter. The association was spontaneously created by its members, rather than organized from above; it was independent of any adult organization, and members articulated the association's ideology for themselves, which in turn determined and rationalized their activities. The Young Protestants could defend their autonomy vis-à-vis the DEF while other girls' associations could not; this was no doubt largely due to the fact that its members were, on average, several years older than the members of other girls' associations, and that unlike the members of other girls' groups, those in the Young Protestants were the social peers of DEF leaders. Like the *Wandervögel* (another youth organization with a quite different raison d'être which also attracted members from the middle classes), their age and social background enabled those in the Young Protestants to preserve their autonomy.

The Young Protestants was formally independent of the DEF, but shared the DEF's goal of articulating and propagating a particular set of moral and social values. It also tried to contribute to the campaign against the SPD. The Young Protestants worked with groups of working-class children from local *Volksschulen*, helping them with homework and taking them for walks in the local woods. The Young Protestants intended to acquire influence over these children, so that "they [the children] will find the [straight and narrow] path, which most of their parents have forsaken."[78] One of the young women involved in this work wrote a report which expounded upon this goal.

> Loving family life is quite the exception among these children's families, and it is well when they are able to spend as much time as possible outside of these bad circumstances. What they see and hear at home does not set them a good example, and they are given false notions about the propertied classes. One example of this was a child who asked me "Fräulein, what do you do on Sundays? You sleep all day long, don't you?" After I explained to him [in the presence of the other children] that I taught a children's Sunday school class, then eight of the children joined my Sunday school class without my having even suggested it. One can sense the desire for something higher and better in these small souls, and it is our duty to give them what they need.[79]

Like older clubwomen, the Young Protestants used a gendered role, a nurturing, maternal relationship with working-class children, to suppress or defuse class antagonisms.

Beginning with gatherings that were little more than girls' sewing circles, Hanover women's associations had created new recreational and social spheres for girls. Girls' associations became a vehicle by which adolescent girls left their family circles for the companionship of their peers. That these groups were attractive is demonstrated by the fact that 10 percent of the female teenage population joined them, and this included working-class girls. Indeed, clubwomen were more successful at organizing young working women than bourgeois men were at mobilizing their male counterparts.

The girls' groups were perhaps even more important for the local clubwomen, however, than they were for young members themselves, since the organization of these associations provided a training ground for the local movement. In the process of creating these girls' clubs, bourgeois women began to develop strategies and arguments that would surface again in future work. First, the organization of girls' groups led to the formation of an alliance that would provide the bulk of the movement's leadership in the future, a coalition between the DEF, the Educational Association (the local ADF affiliate), and women teachers. On paper, these were separate groups, but in practice, both the membership and leadership of these organizations overlapped heavily. The DEF would tend to function as the leader or umbrella group of this alliance, since it included not only single, professional women (the focus of the other two organizations), but also married women.

In addition, the work with girls' groups marked the beginning of the movement's tendency to depend on public institutions, especially municipal government, for funds, instead of private fund raising. Hanover's city government made rooms available for girls' clubs, or even paid the rent on private rooms. In addition, municipal officials generously financed associations for working-class girls in particular, approving subsidies for these groups and even paying salaries to the clubwomen who led the factory workers' and servants' associations. Besides this public funding, the DEF was able to obtain subsidies from the provincial church to pay salaries for the women who supervised the *Konfirmanden* groups.

Beyond funding and leadership, this period saw the articulation of the themes that would dominate the work of the Hanover women's movement. In justifying the creation of girls' groups, bourgeois women used and joined the contemporary discourse on "social degeneration." In this early work, clubwomen were particularly concerned about the "morality question," the chastity of young working women, but their future work would touch on other aspects of *Verwahrlosung*: alcoholism, prostitution, crime, and the "dissolution" of family life.

In the eyes of bourgeois women activists, immorality among young women was intimately linked to political unreliability, since clubwomen feared that working-class girls would be seduced (literally and figuratively) by Social Democrats. Thus, the movement's work with girls' associations served a dual purpose. On the one hand, this work was a pure expression of spiritual motherhood: clubwomen were sincerely concerned about young working women, whom they saw as alone and unprotected in the city. Bourgeois women created clubs for these girls so that they would have comfortable surroundings and intellectual stimulation in their free time, as well as companionship. But at the same time, these girls' groups served a political function, since they were also created to combat the influence of Social Democracy among young working women and promote political quietism.

The work with girls' groups would be the most overtly antisocialist project that the local movement would undertake before 1914, although its other programs would also use gendered language to mask class interests in more subtle ways. In future social work, the women's movement would carry forward its stress on domesticity and the skills of housewifery, as it began to focus on the families that working girls came from, and turned its attention to working-class mothers and their households. The rationales and techniques that clubwomen developed in organizing working-class girls would be refined and expanded, as the local women's movement began to focus on the working class as a whole, and began to experiment with intervention in working-class families. In the process, clubwomen would expand and redefine spiritual motherhood in ways that would also justify new professional and social roles for bourgeois women.

CHAPTER 4

Fighting the Spread

of "Social Poisons":

Domestic Science and

Social Welfare Work

The creation of girls' associations was only the opening salvo in the clubwomen's crusade against "social degeneration": social work was to pick up where these groups for young women left off. After the turn of the century, local women leaders became concerned not just with the spread of immorality (which had inspired the girls' associations), but broadened their sights to include campaigns against an array of "social poisons": alcoholism, prostitution, criminality, socialism, and the "breakdown" of family life.[1] This sweeping agenda led the women's movement to create a network of social services in Hanover, in which clubwomen acted as proxies for the municipal government in monitoring and assisting the poor. In creating these social welfare programs, the Hanover women's movement was much less explicitly partisan, less overtly antisocialist, than it had been when organizing working-class girls. Instead, clubwomen sought to shore up social stability by furthering the *embourgeoisement* of the working class, attempting to promote *bürgerliche* standards of hygiene, order, child care, and household management in poor households. The social services network created by clubwomen to pursue these goals made up the backbone of the local women's movement; such welfare work was also at the heart of the "moderate" women's movement nationally, in contrast to the issues taken up by the "radical" feminist wing of the movement.[2]

Like the creation of groups for younger women, the Hanover movement's broader programs took place against the backdrop of a highly charged discourse among and between various segments of German society about the causes and consequences of social degeneration. Clubwomen entered an ongoing debate, made use of it, and extended its parameters. Bourgeois reformers offered diverse explanations for the origins of the social degeneration or dissolution [*Kulturverfall*]. The philanthropists and jurists who comprised the German Association for Poor Relief and Charity (one of the chief umbrella groups for charitable organizations) held that the political and economic developments of the 1860s and 1870s—the erosion of the guilds' monopolies, rapid industrialization, and the reform of poor relief laws, which encouraged urbanization—had brought "boundless freedom" to the unprepared masses and thus encouraged restlessness and degeneration.[3] Others argued that the employment of women and children in factories had undermined the authority of husbands and fathers by rendering wives and children economically independent.[4] This weakening of patriarchal authority, in turn, contributed to the state's diminished authority.

Reformers within the medical profession were inclined to attribute the physical misery of the poor to the moral deficiencies of the working class and to the incompetence of working-class wives. The lower classes suffered from poor health, medical reformers asserted, not because they were paid too little, but because they did not spend what they received in a rational fashion. Rather than stretch their budgets to provide humble but nutritious fare, working-class housewives served their families potatoes and coffee, or even wasted money on alcohol. Profligate, unorganized housekeepers, they further undermined their families' health by failing to run their households along hygienic lines.[5]

The women's movement seized upon this aspect of the public debate, in particular, and intensified its focus on working-class mothers and their inadequate housekeeping. All the writers who participated in the discussion about social dissolution and degeneration were haunted by the specter of disorder and social unrest, but for members of the women's movement, this disorder was often conceptualized in terms of poor housekeeping. For bourgeois women, domestic cleanliness, order, and discipline (realized according to the particular standards discussed in Chapter 1) composed the essence of civilized life. The conditions that clubwomen thought prevailed in poor households were thus seen as tantamount to chaos: no properly cooked family meals at the established hours; dirty rooms and soiled clothes; and, above all, children who ran wild on the streets, unsupervised by adults and disrespectful of all forms of authority. Because of the high value that clubwomen assigned to "proper" housekeeping, domestic science would be a leitmotif in the work of the Hanover movement.

Whatever the causes might be, bourgeois reformers agreed that the degenerated lower classes provided a fertile milieu for the spread of "social poisons": criminality, alcoholism, prostitution, socialism, and pornography—the public manifestations of social dissolution. Degeneration had produced the *Lumpenproletariat*, which was lawless and immoral both in public and in private. The bourgeois perception that private immorality was linked to political unrest was reflected in a Hanover attorney's report on a local music hall, which he investigated in October 1910 at the behest of the local women's movement:

> I entered the music hall "*zur Münze*" on a Sunday evening at about nine o'clock. The room was packed with customers; about a quarter were women. Many young girls were present, along with two soldiers and a child. The air was poor, since many of the customers were smoking. All of the skits, etc., were indecent, many exceedingly so. The audience, however, clearly enjoyed the performances. It seems to me that these are the sort of people who, in the event of a riot, are the ones to throw stones at the police . . . such people are capable of any crime.[6]

The reforms bourgeois observers proposed in order to alleviate the lower classes' misery and political unreliability were diverse. Gustav Schmoller and his associates in the influential Verein für Sozialpolitik tended to look to the state as the agent that would reconcile the working class with the rest of society. Schmoller argued that the state could mediate differences between employers and workers through legislation to improve safety in the workplace, to provide workmen's compensation and health insurance, or even to nationalize key industries.[7]

Leaders of the women's movement, along with allies in the medical profession and temperance and abstinence movements, maintained that since the working-class family was the primary forum within which degeneration manifested itself, then the family was also the agency that could resolve the "social question." Intervening in the households of the poor and instilling bourgeois standards of hygiene, order, and morality in working-class families would counteract social dissolution. The chief target of bourgeois women's (and other reformers') campaigns was therefore the working-class housewife, who was held responsible for her family's health and morals. If working-class wives could be taught "rational" housekeeping, then the physical misery of working-class families would be alleviated. Through careful budgeting, the preparation of nutritious meals, and frequent and extremely thorough housecleaning, a woman could safeguard her husband's and children's health and provide a comfortable and attractive home. Ideally, her husband would then prefer his home to the neighborhood tavern, and would rest and be reconciled to the next day's work.

The ideal, a "rationalized" working-class household, was described in a petition submitted by women leaders from Hameln (a town near Hanover) in 1906, which asked for compulsory domestic science training for working-class girls. An extended excerpt is quoted, since this petition perfectly captured bourgeois women leaders' vision:

> A working-class wife, who has completed a domestic science course, would never neglect her household. Accuracy has entered her blood, so that her husband, after a hard day's work, now quickens his step, and looks forward to coming home, where he will find refreshment and relaxation in the bosom of his family. He is greeted by his children, rosy-cheeked and dressed in clean clothing; one can see at a glance that a mother's love cares and provides for them. The husband is grateful for his wife's never-ending diligence. She makes worn-out objects new again, and through rational management of the garden, and a few animals, she earns her grocery money; she provides nourishing, tasty meals and decent clothing. Her husband's wages can then be used to pay the rent and the mortgage on a small piece of property which they are buying in a nearby small town. . . . each child has his assigned chores . . . and does his homework conscientiously each day. In this manner, the children learn the value of time, and are already playing at the jobs life holds in store for them. Where love, peace, loyalty, and harmony rule, in a household that is guided by an experienced woman, there prosperity grows, and even in the smallest humble hut, a pure happiness blossoms.[8]

This fantasy is interesting not only for its nostalgic, implicit rejection of industrialization and urbanization, but also because it incorporates several assumptions about women and their households that were articles of faith for bourgeois women. The most striking is the emphasis on sacrifice. Small feminine sacrifices, small efforts, small savings were enormously significant to genteel women, far beyond the actual economic contribution they might yield. In the households of civil servants or academics, where the family's income might indeed be limited, a wife's thrift and small contrivances were in fact crucial to maintaining an appropriate domestic facade. Even in prosperous households, however, bourgeois women stressed the importance of small sacrifices; women continued to value their mending and knitting, for example, long after small articles of clothing were mass-produced and could be purchased cheaply and easily. Socks knitted by hand for a child or crocheted doilies draped over a chair or piano symbolized a woman's care and love for her family.[9] The cult of the small sacrifice was a central component in the self-image of bourgeois women, and they therefore praised the efficacy of feminine sacrifice in their dealings with working-class women. But the constant round of small sacrifices that were proposed for working-class women added up, in fact, to a systematic pattern of self-denial.

This bourgeois ideal of working-class family life also reflected a striking ignorance of most working-class women's lives. Working-class wives, if they were not already employed full-time in a factory or sweatshop, were expected to contribute to the family income through part-time work as charwomen, by doing piece work, or through taking in more prosperous families' washing and ironing. The income thus earned was crucial to most working-class families' survival. Furthermore, a family might take in boarders to help pay the rent, and boarders meant additional cleaning and cooking.[10] The standard of cleanliness embraced by bourgeois women involved an almost impossible amount of washing and cleaning for working-class women who had little free time or energy, and who lacked running water, help, and the facilities available in bourgeois households. Furthermore, most working-class housewives were already forced to practice extreme frugality, and already strove to keep their dwellings as clean as possible.[11] Lessons from clubwomen in thriftiness were largely superfluous.

A second assumption contained in the petition quoted here is the affirmation that housework must be taught in a formal setting, such as a domestic science course, and would not be simply "picked up" from working-class mothers. Again, this assumption reflects the experience of Wilhelmine bourgeois women, many of whom did not learn to do housework from their mothers. Instead, many girls were sent to stay with a relative or friend of the family after they had finished school, for training in that household, or spent a year at a special boarding school. One woman who grew up in Hanover before 1918 recalled later that "when I was a girl, neither my mother nor the servants ever let me set foot in the kitchen. I simply wasn't allowed to soil my hands with some kinds of housework. As a result, I didn't learn to cook until I was sent to a boarding school in the Harz [mountains], which specialized in teaching domestic science to girls from good families."[12]

The idealized family depicted here also reflected bourgeois women's reverence for thrift. Through thrift and diligence (making "worn out objects new again, and through rational management"), the working-class mother could allegedly supply all the food and clothing for her family, without any assistance from her husband, and without pursuing a job outside the home. In addition, this petition incorporated bourgeois norms on child-rearing, including close supervision of children, teaching them to budget time and maintain regular work habits; embracing these norms, the petition concluded, would lead to upward social mobility. As depicted by clubwomen, the working-class mother was thus a contradictory and unreal figure. On the one hand, she was scapegoated for her family's poverty, yet at the same time, she had enormous potential power: she could single-handedly lift her family out of poverty.

Introducing bourgeois standards of household management into working-class households thus became one of the primary goals of the women's movement. To this end, the Hanover women's movement, supported by the medical profession, advanced reforms that stressed domestic skills and focused on working-class housewives. Bourgeois women, according to this line of reasoning, were the experts in "rational" domestic science. Clubwomen, therefore, were to assert a monopoly over reform programs and services that attempted to intervene in working-class families.

At this point, it is important to note that this analysis of the Hanover movement's programs is concerned more with the intention to intervene in poor households than it is with the reaction of the targeted Hanover housewives and results of this intervention; the sources needed to discuss these latter issues are unfortunately lacking. The reaction of working-class women and girls probably varied according to the methods employed in each program and the resources offered.[13] The services offered by Hanover women's associations that relied on voluntary participation and were popular (such as the legal advice bureau and domestic science courses) obviously met some of their clients' needs, or could be used by poor women for their own purposes. Indeed, some segments of working-class society, along with SPD and union leaders, shared the values of domesticity and respectability that clubwomen prized, which perhaps accounted for the enthusiastic reception of domestic science courses in particular.[14] When clubwomen worked as poor relief or orphans' officers, however, their intrusions into working-class households were doubtless less welcome, and might well have been loathed and thus ineffective. An analysis of the Hanover movement's social work is therefore more useful for what it tells us about the broader political orientation and domesticity ideology of clubwomen than as an example of effective social control.

Although the intention to reform poor mothers' housekeeping and child-rearing strategies was present in other programs developed by the women's movement, it found its purest expression within the domestic science course. By training young working women to bourgeois norms before they married, clubwomen could influence their pupils' future households from their very inception. For this reason, domestic science courses were a thread that ran throughout the Hanover movement's history, and indeed throughout the history of the entire German women's movement. Domestic science classes were offered in Hanover to the members of the groups that clubwomen organized for young working women, and were also offered by the Women's Educational Association and Jewish Women's League; the largest number of pupils were enrolled in the Continuation School, established in 1901. As in other German cities, movement leaders also constantly lobbied local officials to make such courses mandatory for girls in public schools.[15] Even in the 1920s, when the local movement was rent by political polarization and fragmentation, leaders from opposing organizations still agreed about the necessity of offering domestic science courses, the only project the movement could unify behind during this period.

Domestic science courses could trace their roots back to sewing and mending courses organized by bourgeois women's associations during the 1850s in a few industrial towns. By the end of the century, almost all cities whose economies were based on heavy industry boasted domestic science courses for working-class women; usually, these were run by local women's associations and were sometimes financed by religious authorities or local employers.[16] As in Hanover, the sponsors of these courses argued that the chief cause of working-class misery was working-class women's ignorance of housekeeping, which meant that they could not manage on their husbands' salaries. Domestic science courses would improve working-class households' thriftiness and cleanliness, thus increasing workers' domestic comfort and reducing class tensions.[17]

In Hanover, the Patriotic Women's Association had run small domestic science courses since the mid-1890s, but these were restricted to the female employees of a few local manufacturers. The first domestic science school to admit young women from all parts of the city was founded in 1901 by a consortium of women's associations. The alliance consisted of the Society for the Advancement of Female Education, the DEF, the Women's Educational Association, and several local female teachers' organizations. Bertha Harder, a local teacher who was the president of the Society for the Advancement of Female Education, was appointed to head the committee representing this coalition; she turned to *Schulrat* Albert Wehrhahn, who headed the city's Committee on Schools and directed a girls' secondary school, to intercede with municipal authorities on behalf of her committee. The women's alliance was able to obtain rooms for the domestic science courses rent-free from the city, which also provided heat and light, sewing machines and other teaching materials, and an annual municipal subsidy that would steadily increase. Benefiting from so much assistance, the Continuation School for Girls (Fortbildungsschule für Mädchen) opened in November 1901 with fifty-six pupils.[18] The classes met for two hours each day, four times a week, and lasted one year. Each pupil paid three Marks quarterly in tuition.

The goal of the Continuation School, Harder wrote, was to "improve both the girls' training in morality and their diligence at home and at work." The pupils' moral improvement was effected in the obligatory German course, which included "discussions about the questions of daily life with reference to Christian principles." The pupils spent the remaining six hours per week learning to keep household accounts (which stressed thriftiness), sew, knit, darn, cook, iron, and exercise, and one hour per week learning "miscellaneous domestic science."[19] The courses were quickly oversubscribed. In the first three years of operation alone, the women's committee was forced to open five extension branches in different neighborhoods: again, the city obligingly made rooms and equipment available gratis. During these three years, the school graduated more than 800 young women, and the number of graduates continued to grow up through 1914. Altogether, the courses employed twenty women, local female teachers who were thus able to supplement their regular salaries.[20]

The young pupils, who came overwhelmingly from working-class or artisanal backgrounds, were volunteering for a course that took up four evenings a week for a year, and totaled about 400 hours of instruction. Of these, 100 hours were devoted to German classes, which not only aimed at improving their reading and writing skills, but also clearly tried to inculcate a specific (Christian national) *Weltanschauung*. Almost all of the remaining 300 hours were devoted to domestic science, a remarkably large amount of time. Again, the assumption seems to have been that housework could not be simply learned through exposure to and observation of one's mother's housekeeping. This reflected the experience of many Wilhelmine bourgeois women, but it was not a working-class tradition.[21]

These courses indeed implicitly discounted the domestic training a working-class girl received from her mother, substituting instead a model of household management based on bourgeois norms. And the fact that bourgeois women devoted almost 300 hours of training to reach these goals indicates that they were trying to convey a systematic, comprehensive, and specific set of prescriptions.

Why young women from working-class backgrounds would volunteer for (and indeed oversubscribe) these courses is a different question, and one that available sources cannot completely answer. In part, however, the courses must have been so popular because large sections of the working class shared the complex of values that made up domesticity and respectability.[22] In Hamburg, where domestic science was mandatory for *Volksschule* pupils, Karen Hagemann has found that working-class girls differed in their reactions to such courses. The poorest pupils, who often came from larger families, found the rules and principles given in the courses boring and unrealistic, and concluded that this material was not applicable to their households. Their parents, who were more interested in vocational training that would increase their daughters' future income, also did not encourage them to take domestic science seriously. Pupils from the upper strata of the working class, however, tended to like the courses better, since they felt that the approach to housekeeping being taught was compatible with their families' household reality. Their parents were also more positive about the potential value of the course material, since they tended to assume that their daughters would be "only housewives" as adults. One pupil interviewed by Hagemann, whose parents had trained her to prize *Ordnung* and extreme cleanliness, said that she had enjoyed the courses.[23] In Hanover, where the Continuation School was voluntary, it was probably girls from this latter group who enrolled.

Domestic science was a strong theme within the work of the Hanover women's movement from beginning to end; the desire to reform the housekeeping of working-class mothers was also visible in other programs, in which clubwomen entered and inspected poor households. But of course there was more to the movement's network of services than promoting bourgeois styles of housekeeping. Many of the Hanover movement's programs were Janus-faced, attempting to intervene in their clients' lives, but also offering real assistance, or useful services, which accounted for their popularity. The movement's temperance restaurants, for example, fell into this category.

Domestic science courses sought to influence working-class families through training future wives and mothers, but these courses could only affect a part of the working class, those who lived in established households. Unmarried men, or young people of both sexes who had migrated to Hanover seeking work, were beyond the reach of programs that targeted future working-class wives. To influence the diet and life-style of unmarried or "isolated" workers, the local women's movement created a chain of temperance restaurants. The organization that ran these establishments was the Women's Association for the People's Welfare (Frauenverein "*Volkswohl*"), headed by Bertha Duensing (1857–1927). Duensing, an elementary school teacher who had long been active in several local women's organizations, created her People's Welfare Association almost single-handedly in 1904.

Duensing had grown up in a nearby small town, and had been employed in the city's schools since 1892. Energetic, nervous, and excitable, she frequently took leaves of absence from her job because of "nervous weakness" and "stomach pains," but these complaints apparently did not affect a heavy schedule of association-related work.[24] Duensing and her second-in-command, the Calvinist pastor's wife, Maria Eichhorn, drew on their contacts in the DEF and local educational and temperance associations to enlist over 300 "passive" dues-paying members for the People's Welfare organization, and obtained subsidies from the city and local businessmen.[25]

With such financial backing, the People's Welfare temperance restaurants were able to offer "rational" alcohol-free meals at very low prices. By 1911, the association was running three restaurants, which attracted thousands of customers each week. Surviving photographs of the restaurants show large, well-lit, attractive establishments, which maintained a stock of newspapers, journals, and games for the patrons. The temperance restaurants sought to attract the "better" part of the working class, and excluded "suspect elements."

In addition, Duensing's association ran an education program aimed at working-class women. "Mothers' evenings," which featured speakers on topics such as "alcoholism and morality" and "alcohol and nutrition," attracted working-class and lower-middle-class audiences. Duensing also distributed flyers and leaflets among her female audiences that told of accidents, injuries, and divorces, all caused by the influence of alcohol.[26] These popular gatherings created a female space that did not exist in the predominantly masculine pubs, and which indeed stood in opposition to men's "*Wirtshauskultur*."[27]

The temperance restaurants, the Continuation Schools, and other projects of local women's groups (which were largely created by teachers' groups) were complemented by the array of social services offered by the Hanover branch of the DEF. Between 1900 and 1906, the DEF developed a series of projects that constituted a multipronged attack on "social degeneration," programs that often sought to work within existing municipal institutions. The women who headed DEF projects came to stress the necessity of professionalizing their social services, and this approach led to an intertwining, almost a merger, of the DEF and the municipal government in some sectors.

Interweaving of the DEF and the city administration occurred where the DEF was allowed to establish feminine auxiliaries within the poor relief system, as well as other departments. The first department targeted by the DEF was the municipal network of orphans' officers. The city's system for overseeing orphans who lived outside of the orphanage resembled its poor relief network (described in Chapter 2). The city was divided into districts, each with its assigned orphans' officer (*Waisenrat*). Like municipal almoners, orphans' officers were private (male) citizens who were drafted for the job by the city; they were not paid for their work, and an officer who refused his appointment lost his municipal franchise and was assessed municipal taxes at a higher rate. Each orphans' officer was responsible for the welfare of all orphans, foundlings, illegitimate children, and children of widows who had remarried who resided in his district. The orphans' officer, working under the Guardians' Court, nominated guardians for these children. He was expected to inspect regularly the households where these children lived, and to monitor his wards' physical and moral development.[28]

The DEF, asserting that women were better able than men to understand and evaluate children's physical and spiritual needs, persuaded the city to appoint a female orphans' officer for each district in 1903. The new officers were recruited by the DEF; like their male counterparts, they were sworn in at city hall. Female orphans' officers were given special responsibility for all younger children and older girls, that is, the majority of all of the wards in a given district. The DEF volunteers do not seem to have met with any resistance or resentment from their male co-workers. Unlike the men, the women orphans' officers had actually volunteered for the job, and it appears that many of their male counterparts were content to leave most of the work to the women. By 1909, a local observer wrote that the female orphans' officers had assumed the bulk of the work with orphans, foundlings, and illegitimate children.[29] The DEF volunteers, who numbered over 120 by 1906, were supervised by a DEF officer, Johanne Wallmann; she was paid a salary for her work by the city and given an office in city hall.[30]

By 1906, the DEF was able to install female auxiliaries with the poor relief system, as well. Thirty-seven female municipal almoners were appointed by the city *Armenkollegium*; each was supposed to work with several male municipal almoners. The DEF almoners were responsible for the women and children who received poor relief, and all female applicants were supposed to apply to female almoners. As with the orphans' officers, the female municipal almoners were supervised by a DEF officer, who, like Wallmann, was given an office and a salary by the city.[31] Like the orphans' officers, female municipal almoners were accepted by their male counterparts. The tension between male and female almoners that arose in some other cities, including Berlin, was absent in Hanover.[32]

Clubwomen were making use of the fact that many bourgeois social commentators and reformers traced impoverishment and misery to the "irrational," unsatisfactory housekeeping of poor wives and mothers. This emphasis on housework and domesticity proved to be the DEF's best weapon in opening up poor relief work to women, since it logically followed that poor relief officials had to be experts in hygiene and "rational" domestic science—that is, they had to be women. Wilhelm Rothert, a member of the Protestant Association who was active in the local Inner Mission, and an ally of the DEF, put the female almoners' case succinctly in a 1909 survey of local charities:

> Women [almoners] are better able to enter a poor dwelling and take in at a single glance [its] condition, to evaluate the degree of cleanliness and order. Poor women—and these constitute the overwhelming majority [of all poor relief recipients]—will reveal more about their circumstances to another woman than they would to a man. . . . the female almoner's inspection (especially of clothing and the wash) is more thorough, and her evaluation is better. . . . [Women] are better able to exercise an educational [*erziehlich*] influence.[33]

Both female orphans' officers and municipal almoners were expected to monitor the children in the households they visited, and determine if the children were physically or morally "endangered" by a parent's alcoholism, immorality, or brutality. A 1900 reform of the Prussian juvenile welfare laws had facilitated the forcible removal of children from their families (*Fürsorgeerziehung*). Previously, a child had to have broken a law before he or she could be removed into foster care; after 1900, a special court for minors had only to determine that a poor family environment had put the child at risk of being "physically or morally ruined." As a result of the reform, the number of children forcibly taken into foster care both in Hanover and in Prussia as a whole rose steadily; the DEF regularly referred new cases to the local juvenile courts for processing.[34]

The women's movement was also able to persuade the municipal government to make changes in local policies regarding foster children. Children in institutional or foster care in Hanover were placed under the care of a "professional guardianship" agency, which then assigned individual cases to volunteers, who monitored the care of children and represented their interests. Clubwomen were able to persuade the men in charge of this agency to work closely with the movement, and recruited volunteer women guardians.[35] In addition, as more and more children appeared before the juvenile courts for evaluation and disposition after the 1900 reform of juvenile welfare law, the need for a centralized agency to investigate and report to the local juvenile courts became apparent, which led to the creation of the Hanover Foster Care Committee (Jugendfürsorgeausschuss). The Foster Care Committee consisted of representatives from the DEF, the Catholic Women's League, several women teachers' associations, the Protestant Association, and the Young Men's Christian Association. The committee investigated cases referred to it by local voluntary associations, municipal authorities, and the juvenile court, and made recommendations on the disposition of individual children. Although the representatives of the boys' associations attempted to gain control of the committee, they were thwarted by the DEF; female committee members were ultimately able to gain complete control after 1914, when most of their male colleagues enlisted.[36]

In 1904, the DEF was also able to place a member within the police department as a new, salaried "police assistant." Her job was to visit and counsel arrested prostitutes, "those unhappy, seduced young women, who lacked a parent's love and care, which would have prevented them from sinking so deeply."[37] If a prisoner was willing to listen and reform her ways, the police assistant found her a job (usually in a factory, since these women were deemed unsuitable for domestic service) and a place to live. For more than a year after her release, the reformed prostitute was on probation, and the police assistant visited her regularly to monitor her life-style. If the client remained in her new job and dwelling, she was then struck from the police list of registered prostitutes. By 1909, 70 women had passed through this probationary period, and had become, the assistant reported, "diligent, happy housewives, married to orderly men." These 70 women represented only a small fraction of all registered prostitutes, however. During any given year, between 300 and 400 prostitutes were registered with the Hanover police, and the police assistant confessed that she rarely had any success with a woman who worked for a pimp.[38] The salary for this police assistant was originally paid by a local men's charitable association, but after the first few years, DEF officials were able to obtain 2,000 Marks per annum for her salary from the city and the Prussian Ministry of the Interior.[39]

By 1906, the DEF had thus created female auxiliaries (some of whom were salaried) within the municipal government, but it did not stop there. At the same time that its members were entering the city's poor relief system, the DEF was establishing a number of independent social welfare services in conjunction with other women's associations. In so doing, the women's movement acted as a proxy for the city government and in return, its programs received generous municipal funding.

One of the DEF's first independent projects—and its most elaborate and expensive program—was its Home for Unwed Mothers, which was established on the initiative of Countess Selma von der Groeben, the DEF's vice-president. The creation of the home completed a tripartite categorization of "fallen women" that was established within the local women's movement after the turn of the century. The 1900 reform of the Prussian juvenile welfare laws had led to the removal of an increasing number of morally or physically "endangered" girls from their families, and the foster care girls from Hanover and its environs were sent to the Magdalene Home (see Chapter 2). By 1905, the Magdalene Home was thus essentially converted from an asylum for prostitutes to a reform home for young women taken into foster care. The Home for Unwed Mothers, opened in 1903, complemented the Magdalene Home by taking in young women who had moved from the "endangered" category to the status of "first-time fallen women," unmarried women in their first pregnancy. Unmarried women who became pregnant for a second time were not admitted to the DEF's home; they had entered the category of the "completely sunken" and, since the DEF assumed that they were also prostitutes, they were left to the DEF's police assistant.[40]

The Home for Unwed Mothers took in several dozen women each year, women who "before [their pregnancy] had led virtuous lives in every respect, and who showed remorse for their moral lapse."[41] Each had to help with the housework, and participate in regular Bible study sessions with a local pastor, who tried "to help these unfortunates to shed their burdens of sin, and through repentance and atonement to find their way back to the Lord."[42] Although it attracted a growing number of pregnant young women, these never amounted to more than one-tenth of the over 1,000 unmarried women who gave birth each year in Hanover; the strict, religious tone of the establishment may have helped account for this fact.

To finance the home, the DEF raised money from a variety of sources, both public and private. The city donated the first building to house the home and provided an annual subsidy. In addition, the DEF received annual contributions from the agencies that administered Hanover's health and disability insurance funds, and even from the old-age pension fund. The DEF also collected subsidies from two offices in the provincial-level government, that of the *Oberpräsident* and the *Landesdirektor*.[43] Two local physicians, husbands of DEF members, volunteered to care for the home's inmates. By 1912, the home was taking in over seventy women each year, and the DEF was forced to look for new lodgings for the institution. Once again, the city donated land, and contributed 30,000 Marks toward the new home's construction, in addition to defraying the cost of the installation of running water and gas; the provincial-level offices that contributed annual subsidies also helped finance the new building. City Senator Karl Beuermann, who regularly introduced funding resolutions for the DEF in the city council, acted as the DEF's representative in the negotiations with the contractor and helped oversee the subsequent construction. Deputy burgomaster Eyl, a longtime ally, also advised the DEF on how to obtain municipal funding.[44]

To finance such a large project, the DEF also turned to private fund raising. Paula Mueller paid private calls on the mayor's wife, Olga Tramm, and *Landesdirektor* von der Wense; both agreed to join a committee headed by Beuermann, which collected private donations for the home. Over the next six months, the committee raised over 12,000 Marks; the DEF also received donations from local businesses.[45]

Another social service sponsored by the DEF, in cooperation with the Women's Educational Association, was a legal advice bureau for women (Rechtsschutzstelle für Frauen). The Hanover bureau was inspired by a legal advice bureau founded by women's associations in Dresden in 1894, which, although it was greeted with some suspicion by local attorneys, had proved a great success in that city. Provided with rooms by the city, the Hanover bureau opened in 1900; it was staffed by several volunteers from each of the two parent associations and advised women on guardianship law, federal social insurance programs (such as the invalid and old-age pensions), and adoption laws. The bureau also mediated between female clients and their landlords or employers, and helped unwed mothers to collect child support from their children's fathers. The Hanover police cooperated with the bureau by helping its staff track down absconding fathers. The women who staffed the bureau educated themselves in family and social insurance law before they began work, and, in complicated cases, they could consult with a number of local attorneys (several were husbands or fathers of DEF and Educational Association members) who advised the bureau. Altogether, the bureau was one of the local movement's most successful projects: it counseled over 900 women in 1907 alone.[46]

In 1905, the DEF inaugurated yet another project, a program to provide nursing and housekeeping services for poor married women who had recently given birth. Care for poor women who had given birth was the traditional province of the Childbed Association (see Chapter 2); by 1905, however, the caseload had increased to such an extent that the Childbed Association could no longer meet all applications. The Hanover *Regierungspräsident*, the chief Prussian administrator for the Hanover metropolitan area, asked DEF leaders to enter the field. Fifteen DEF members volunteered to supervise a corps of about two dozen lay nurses, who cared for their clients during their convalescence, as well as taking care of the client's housework and family. In the course of their work, the lay nurses were also expected to evaluate their clients' households and, along with the DEF volunteers, educate them about hygiene and "rational" domestic science. The DEF's program covered about two to three hundred families each year; the office of the *Regierungspräsident* helped to defray some of the project's costs, while the city contributed grants, which rose from 1,000 Marks in 1906 to 2,500 Marks per annum in 1912, to pay for the lay nurses' training.[47] The DEF also received financing for this work from the provincial *Oberpräsident*, as well as from the agencies that administered the disability and pension insurance funds.[48]

The last large social service established by the DEF in Hanover was a shelter for homeless women, which opened its doors in October 1906. The shelter had been badly needed; prior to its creation, homeless women had the choice of spending the night in a police lockup, trudging out to the asylum in the neighboring village of Kleefeld, or sleeping in unoccupied dwellings or in the train station's fourth-class waiting room. The situation of homeless men was not much better. They, too, could sleep in the police station, or seek lodging in a shelter for men run by the (men's) Association against Begging and Homelessness (Verein gegen Hausbettelei und Obdachlosigkeit). The city had been under pressure for some time to set up a larger public shelter for both sexes, but municipal administrators avoided doing so, arguing that it would cost too much.[49]

In 1906, DEF vice-president von der Groeben, who had long urged the creation of a shelter for women, persuaded the provincial Association for Newly Released Prisoners to form a commission consisting of representatives from the city, provincial government, church, and police to study the problem of female homelessness. This commission persuaded the city to donate a house for a women's shelter, and arranged for the shelter to receive regular donations from public and private sources; it was then turned over to the DEF.[50]

The shelter took in women referred to it by a variety of sources: the DEF's own municipal almoners; the police, who picked up and delivered homeless girls who were felt to be "morally at risk" (the shelter had a direct telephone line to police headquarters); the Association of Female Friends of Young Girls (see Chapter 2), which referred women found at the train station; and the DEF police assistant, who sent women who were in the "probationary period" of leaving prostitution. Several hundred women and children were received each year; the number rose to almost 1,000 by 1912. Each woman could stay as long as she actively sought work, and the average stay was ten to twelve days. The shelter was crowded from the start, and by 1913, the DEF petitioned the city for a new, larger building. Once again, Senator Beuermann spoke on behalf of the DEF, and the city financed the move into a new, nineteen-room house. Thanks to the lobbying of Senators Beuermann and Merten, the mayor's office also formally committed itself to paying the 3,500 Marks annual rent on the new building for the next ten years, plus an additional annual subsidy of 2,500 Marks.[51]

The city funded the DEF shelter because in this case, as in other instances, city administrators believed that women's associations were appropriate and inexpensive proxies for the city government. "Charitable women's associations," Burgomaster Tramm declared in one city senate debate over funding decisions, "are much better able to handle questions regarding women correctly, and this also relieves the city's finances."[52] Even though the city was now donating tens of thousands of Marks to clubwomen's projects each year, it was still cheaper than establishing corresponding municipal social services, since the women's movement could draw on volunteer labor and contributions from the private sector. Table 4.1 reflects the ultimate outcome of this policy, summarizing the DEF network of social services and the number of paid and volunteer workers that these programs involved.

Local officials depended on the unpaid volunteers of the women's movement to run these programs because this strategy was easy and inexpensive. Clubwomen relied on authorities for funding for similar reasons: the authorities had the resources, and the easiest way to get the money was simply to petition the state. Almost all the programs created by the Hanover women's movement before World War I would primarily rely on the state for financing. Private fund raising was rarely resorted to, because it took too much time, energy, and money (bazaars

Table 4.1. DEF Social Services Network, 1906

Social Service Workers	Year Begun	Volunteers	Salaried
Placement Bureau for Social Workers	1900	Unknown	Unknown
Legal Advice Bureau	1900	6	0
Leaders of Girls' Associations	1900	16	2
Orphans' Officers	1903	126	1
Home for Unwed Mothers	1903	0	2
Police Assistant	1904	0	1
Nursing/Housekeeping for Women in Childbed	1905	15	22
Municipal Almoners	1906	37	2
Shelter for Homeless	1906	0	2
Total		200	32

Sources: *Evangelische Frauenzeitung* 6 (1905–6): 62, 65; 7 (1906–7): Beilage to May issue, 1; ADEF, H 1a, 1906 annual report of the Commission for Children's Protection and Youth Groups; ADEF, CC 2, annual reports of the Legal Advice Bureau. The totals are higher than the actual number of women involved, since some women worked in more than one program.

and balls, for example, had built-in overhead costs), whereas public subsidies could be obtained simply by petitioning and lobbying, and were almost guaranteed to be renewed annually. The DEF was the biggest single beneficiary within the local movement, and on the DEF's tenth anniversary, Paula Mueller voiced her satisfaction over this relationship by giving a public speech to thank officials: "the authorities have always displayed a friendly attitude toward us," she said, "and in many ways have come more than halfway to meet us [in our requests]."[53]

Because financing could be obtained relatively easily from the state, clubwomen had little incentive to lobby for political rights for themselves or to build up a partisan political presence in local politics, which might have otherwise been used to secure influence. Indeed, in Hanover's antidemocratic political structure, a mass political organization of women would have been next to useless, since officials were insulated from popular pressure. Gaining personal influence with officials was easier (since women leaders were often connected to these men already) and more effective. In 1919, after Hanover's municipal constitution had been reformed and democratized, DEF leaders looked back nostalgically at the prewar period. Before 1918, they wrote, "the officials were the ones who essentially controlled the details of public policy. . . . [Thus] the work of the DEF primarily depended upon winning influence with important officials and leaders. This method often brought us success."[54] This strategy also left the women's movement almost completely financially dependent on the state, but before 1918 this did not appear to be a disadvantage.

Starting from the twin premises that contemporary society was degenerating and that bourgeois women were particularly suited, by virtue of their maternal and domestic qualities, to counteract this trend, the Hanover women's movement had thus developed a network of social services, which were partly public and partly private. These services were complemented by institutions created by the local Patriotic Women's Association. The association had expanded its programs dramatically during the 1890s. It tended to focus its attentions on medical intervention in the lives of the poor. By 1908, the association, in conjunction with the provincial Red Cross, administered a local medical empire, which included an outpatient clinic for poor relief recipients, a home for the handicapped, clinics for children, an asylum for tuberculosis patients, and a training school for nurses. The creation of these institutions was made possible not only by municipal and provincial subsidies, but also by the new state social insurance funds, which paid for workers' medical care.[55]

The Patriotic Women's Association's most significant attempt to reform working-class family relations was its set of infant care clinics (Säuglingsfürsorgestellen). It opened three between 1906 and 1910. These clinics were part of a national network of infant care clinics run by Patriotic Women's Associations across the German Empire, which were organized in response to the high levels of infant mortality prevalent in working-class families. Governmental authorities and bourgeois social commentators alike viewed the high number of infants who died before their first birthdays as a loss to the nation: a loss of future workers and soldiers, who might have contributed to Germany's economic and military strength. Infant mortality was largely attributed to poor mothering by working-class women (another aspect of social degeneration) and especially to the practice of bottle feeding. The infant care clinics would help reverse this trend by persuading women to breast-feed their children and by educating them about other aspects of hygienic infant care.[56]

As in other cities, the Hanover infant care clinics found it difficult to persuade many working-class women to breast-feed their infants. Many were simply unable to nurse at regular intervals because they were expected to contribute to their families' income. The clinics were only really successful after they began to pay small "nursing premiums" to mothers who breast-fed their babies and who were willing to submit to regular inspections to prove that they were still nursing. Women who were unable to nurse their infants—and as the flyer reproduced here shows, the clinics put some pressure on such women at least to try to nurse—were given bottled cow's milk at a reduced price. During their visits to the clinics, mothers were counseled by nurses or physicians on "rational" child care, but there is no evidence that the advice was taken to heart. A working-class mother often could not adjust her schedule to feed her child precisely at three hour intervals (as physicians recommended), or put up with the infant's screaming if he or she was hungry, and the appointed hour had not yet arrived. Yet even if many of the mothers preferred to follow their own instincts, the nursing premiums, cheap milk, and free treatment of infant diseases constituted a powerful attraction: the number of infants brought to Hanover clinics rose from 1,200 in 1907 to almost 1,900 in 1911, comprising about one-third of all children born in the city.[57]

Clubwomen were most interested in infant care, but they made attempts to influence the upbringing of older children as well. A coalition of women's associations distributed leaflets and pamphlets to the mothers of schoolchildren, with advice and tips on proper child-rearing. A leaflet for the mothers of first-graders, for example, prescribed a set routine for each schoolchild's day, advising mothers on the most minute details. This flyer recommended what time the child should get up in the mornings, and when he or she should go to bed; the precise order and method for washing each part of the body each morning; proper diet and menus for each meal; the best method for cleaning the child's bedroom; a schedule for washing children's hair, and cutting their fingernails and toenails; and rules for homework and play. This leaflet even advised on how a mother could induce regular bowel movements in her child. "Make sure that the child visits the toilet before going to school; such habits help to regulate the digestion. Impress upon your child, that he should only use the toilet at school as an exception, not the rule. Thus you can strengthen the nascent sense of decency and modesty in your child, which can be lost if your child uses the toilet in the presence of other, older pupils."[58] This advice, which stressed cleanliness, a regular timetable for each child's day, close supervision of children's free time, and the imposition of a regi-

Merkblatt des Hauptvereins für Volkswohlfahrt in Hannover, Maschstraße 10.

Verfaßt von Kreisarzt Dr. Dohrn in Hannover.

Mütter, stillt Eure Kinder selbst!

Flaschenernährung – englische Krankheit – Tuberkulose.

Der Segen der Brusternährung.

Frau Schulze nährt ihr Kind selbst. Sie ist nämlich eine vernünftige Frau und sagt sich, daß die Nahrung, welche die Natur dem Kinde bestimmt hat, die einzig richtige ist. Außerdem kostet es nichts. Wenn sie manchmal etwas Stiche im Rücken hat, so tröstet sie sich: meinem Manne tut auch der Buckel in seinem Berufe weh.

Der Jammer eines Flaschenkindes.

Frau Müller gibt ihren Zwillingen gleich von Anfang an die Flasche. Sie hört mehr auf die kluge Nachbarsfrau als auf den Arzt und die Hebamme. Diese sagen, daß jede Frau ihre Kinder stillen kann, wenn sie nur alle 3 Stunden richtig anlegt und nicht gleich mit der infamen Flasche dazwischen fährt. Frau Müller meint aber, sie hätte keine Nahrung. Außerdem hat sie auch keine rechte Lust und Zeit. Schließlich hat sie's auch dazu, um sich eine Wartefrau zu halten.

This pamphlet was distributed to new mothers who came to Hanover's infant care clinics. It describes the fates of two babies, one of whom was breast fed, while the other was given a bottle. The bottle-fed baby is always ill and dies young. The breast-fed child becomes a healthy and successful worker and soldier, fulfilling the fondest hopes of pronatalists. (Landeskirchliches Archiv der Evangelisch-lutherischen Landeskirche Hannover E2 112)

½ Jahr.

Der kleine Schulze gedeiht an der Mutterbrust trotz aller Armut recht schön. Er ist stets zufrieden, schreit nicht und macht allen Freude.

Die beiden Müllers nehmen anfangs auch gut zu. Im Sommer aber bekommt der eine Darmkatarrh, weil die Milch sich in der Hitze zersetzt hat.

Das arme Kind erleidet einen qual-vollen Tod. Der andere Müller wird zwar dick und aufgeschwemmt, er ist aber stets quarig, hat viel Erbrechen und leidet an Verstopfung.

1 Jahr.

Der kleine Schulze bekommt rechtzeitig seine Zähne und läuft auch schon am Ende des ersten Jahres.

Müller liegt wie ein dicker Kloß im Wagen und mag nicht laufen, weil er zu weiche Knochen hat. Er hat infolge der Flaschenernährung, wie so viele andere Flaschenkinder, die gefürchtete englische Krankheit bekommen. Der Arzt geht im Hause ein und aus und kostet viel Geld, ebenso auch die Medizin.

mented, "rational" discipline upon the child's body and bodily functions, reflected bourgeois values.

In establishing their programs for working-class women and children, women leaders were espousing a particular vision of motherhood, an ideal that reflected bourgeois views about family life and maternal duty. Clubwomen saw their work as tending to improve and strengthen moth-

3 Jahre.

Schulze springt im Garten umher und kann schon den Vater von der Arbeit abholen.

Müller wackelt mühsam an der Hand der Wärterin umher. Er hat O-Beine, weil die weichen Knochen die Last des Körpers nicht tragen können. Auch leidet er an Krämpfen, wie wir sie oft bei Flaschenkindern sehen.

8 Jahre.

Schulze lernt fleißig in der Schule, weil er frisch und gesund ist. Er hat auch feste Zähne und kann gut kauen und verdauen.

Müller mit dem Wasserkopf fällt das Lernen sauer. Er ist schwach und muß oft fehlen. Die Zähne sind weich und angestockt, weil der kräftigende Kalkgehalt der Muttermilch fehlt. Arzt und Zahnarzt kosten eine Menge Geld.

14 Jahre.

Müller muß ins Bad geschickt werden. Die weichen Knochen des Brustkorbes haben sich verbogen. Er hat eine Hühnerbrust und auch einen Buckel. Auch leidet er oft an Husten.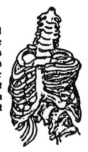

Schulze wird ein flotter Schlosserlehrling. Kein Hammer ist ihm zu schwer.

ers and motherhood; they argued that expanded maternal influence over children, and in society as a whole, was the key to "saving" Germany. At the center of their efforts stood the working-class housewife, who was simultaneously scapegoated for her family's "decline" and yet also assigned enormous potential power.

In light of these aspirations and this ideal of motherhood, it is ironic

20 Jahre.

Der stramme Schulze wird Gardist und ist ein Stolz seines Vaterlandes. Er kommt auch sonst gut vorwärts, denn in einem gesunden Körper steckt auch ein gesunder Geist.

Müller, das Flaschenkind, wird wegen seiner O-Beine zurückgestellt. Auch scheint sich der verderbliche Tuberkulosekeim in der engen Brust eingenistet zu haben.

25 Jahre.

Der flotte Schulze kriegt eine schöne, reiche Frau. Er läßt auch später alle seine Kinder stillen. Sie bleiben alle gesund, und daher ist auch die Familie so groß und stark geworden.

Der engbrüstige Müller ist von der Schwindsucht befallen. Er kommt ins Krankenhaus, aber da ist nichts zu retten. Er stirbt, und damit ist ein Teil der Familie Müller ausgestorben.

that the effect of some of these programs was to undermine the position of real-life mothers by weakening their influence, while empowering the clubwomen who ran these programs. Domestic science courses, for example, implicitly attempted to prevent working-class girls from modeling their future household management on their mothers' strategies. The day-to-day domestic arrangements of poor mothers were subject to scrutiny and criticism by DEF municipal almoners and orphans' officers; even those women not on poor relief were monitored by DEF lay nurses, if they asked for assistance when giving birth. New working-class mothers were the target of a campaign by the Patriotic Women's Association, which actively sought to supplant the influence and advice a woman received from her own mother and neighbors about child-rearing; instead, the infant care clinics hoped to remold new working-class mothers in clubwomen's image. Mothers of older children received unsolicited advice about the most intimate details of child-rearing.

How much success clubwomen had, if any, in recasting poorer women's housekeeping and child-rearing is difficult to assess, as are the responses of these programs' clients. In some cases, poor women could not avoid and probably resented the intrusion and advice of clubwomen; poor relief and medical care during childbirth, for example, were difficult to obtain without the mediation of bourgeois women's associations. Services that relied on voluntary participation and were popular, such as the temperance restaurants and infant care clinics, offered real attractions (subsidized meals or milk), or offered advice that could be used by clients for their own purposes, or simply ignored.

Services offered by the women's movement to poorer women could be exploited, gladly accepted, ignored, or resented, but there were few other alternatives to these programs. By 1906, local women's associations, especially the DEF and the Patriotic Women's Association, had assumed responsibility for the bulk of all the "open" public and private programs that served poor women and children; they were excluded only from the "closed" forms of poor relief, institutions that served incarcerated clients, such as sanitoriums and orphanages. Clubwomen were able to stake out these new jurisdictions successfully because of three factors. First, bourgeois public opinion had reached a consensus about the spread of "social poisons" and "social degeneration," and the threat that these posed to the Wilhelmine social order. Second, women's associations were able to use accepted sexual stereotypes and the doctrine of "spiritual motherhood" to persuade their contemporaries that bourgeois women's maternal qualities and domestic expertise made them particularly well qualified to combat "social degeneration," by working with, and exercising authority over, working-class women and families. Third and last, clubwomen were able to persuade local authorities to fund their projects because Hanover authorities saw women's associations as inexpensive proxies for the municipal government; as a result, the movement came to rely on the state. Hanover clubwomen owed their success not only to their hard work and political skills, but also to the fact that their proposals came at the right time, and augmented existing institutions and power relations.

The women's movement was attempting to expand and revise contemporary gender roles for bourgeois women, giving them a more active, albeit maternal, role in community affairs. At the same time, however, these same women were developing programs that underwrote a more rigid, segregated sexual division of labor for working-class women than for bourgeois women. Not surprisingly, municipal authorities found these goals laudable, and worthy of support.

The political context of these programs was subtle, and not overtly partisan. The overall goal was to further the *embourgeoisement* of the German working class: to promote *bürgerliche* values, habits, and lifestyles among working-class families. More directly, the clubwomen who ran these programs argued that a "rational" working-class housewife, trained to bourgeois standards, would raise her family's standard of living, and thus pacify her husband (as the petition regarding domestic science classes made clear). In an indirect fashion, clubwomen thus intended that this would shore up bourgeois social and cultural hegemony.

The irony, of course, was that much of the working class had already accepted the values of domesticity and order that clubwomen were trying to promote. That was why the movement's domestic science courses were oversubscribed, and why its clubs for working-class girls were successful. The specific styles and standards of household management that the movement was trying to inculcate were specific to the bourgeoisie, but the overall acceptance of domesticity and gender role polarization was not.

Hanover's clubwomen had not invested so much time and energy in creating these social welfare services solely because they were concerned about the spread of "social degeneration," however. Women leaders had another motive in establishing this new sphere of authority, one that also received their peers' support. In creating social services as a field, clubwomen were trying to establish social work as a career, a profession that would be dominated by women. Social work, moreover, was to be only the first in a series of "maternal" professions for single women.

CHAPTER 5 The Gendered Workplace:

Women, Education, and

the Professions

By 1906, the Hanover women's movement had created a small empire of social services, largely staffed by volunteer workers, but the leaders of the women's movement never intended that these programs should be permanently run by amateurs and volunteers. Eventually, all social services were to be taken over by trained, professional social workers. Social work as yet hardly existed as a career, but women leaders intended to change this; the Hanover women's movement, along with women's associations across the German Empire, created professional social work as a vocation for bourgeois women.

Social work was not the only career that Hanover clubwomen wanted to open to bourgeois women, however. The drive to broaden women's education and to open new professions to women was one of the local women's movement's most pressing concerns; this campaign rivaled and sometimes merged with (for example, in the case of social work) the crusade against "social degeneration." The means adopted by local women's association leaders in their campaign to open specific professions to women were versatile and often imaginative, and they were rewarded with significant successes.

Hanover clubwomen relied on two arguments in their public and private appeals for expanded educational and professional opportunities for women. First, they claimed that there was a "surplus" of women in Germany, especially bourgeois single women, who were forced to find employment. Second, women leaders asserted that women's innate attributes could work to their advantage, and society's, in certain vocations.

Women leaders' perception that Germany suffered from a surplus of women (dubbed the *Frauenüberschuss*) was widely shared by their contemporaries. Women did in fact slightly outnumber men in imperial Germany (by 17 million to 16 million), and bourgeois observers claimed that "surplus" women were especially numerous among the educated classes, because nuptuality rates in these circles were held to have declined since the beginning of the nineteenth century. In Hanover, and in Germany as a whole, leaders of the women's movement and social commentators concluded that many of the women in the "better classes" (the estimates ranged from 25 to 50 percent) were unable to marry.[1]

The specter of thousands of genteel spinsters provoked anxious discussion over how to secure the financial and social status of these women, who were sometimes left without sufficient means of support after their parents' deaths. Gentlewomen looking for "suitable" work (*standesgemässe Arbeit*), work that was not socially degrading, had few options. Across Germany, thousands of women found themselves in the same position as Amalie Sieveking, the daughter of a Hamburg senator, who was obliged to earn money secretly, doing needlework at home after her father's death.[2] The destitute, genteel spinster was a powerful symbol for bourgeois parents, and supporters of improved education for girls were able to use this image effectively. Hedwig Kettler, one of Hanover's earliest advocates for the creation of girls' college preparatory schools, wrote pamphlets entitled "One Million Women Too Many!," and "What Will Become Of Our Daughters?," which exploited parents' fears.[3]

There is little evidence, however, to support the women's movement's claims. A look at Hanover's vital statistics reveals that in fact the city's nuptuality rates increased slightly between 1890 and 1910. During the Wilhelmine period, approximately seven out of every eight adult women in Hanover eventually married (see Table 5.1). If we assume that few women are likely to marry after the age of forty, then the absolute number of confirmed spinsters (never-married women older than forty) in Hanover grew steadily between 1890 and 1910, but their share of all women over forty actually decreased slightly. There was indeed a modest surplus of women in Hanover, and Hanover men were slightly more likely to marry than women, but the overwhelming majority of women could expect to marry.

Wilhelmine social commentators acknowledged that most working-class women eventually married, but argued that there were strong class differences in nuptuality rates, and that women from better-off families were less likely to marry. "Over 40 percent of the adult women in our

Table 5.1. Unmarried Men and Women over Age 40 in Hanover, 1890–1910

| Year | Total Unmarried over 40 | | % Population over 40 Unmarried | |
	Men	*Women*	*Men*	*Women*
1890	1,325	2,763	8.2	13.5
1900	1,893	4,030	7.9	13.3
1910	2,749	5,634	7.7	13.1

Source: Statistisches Amt, *Statistisches Jahrbuch*, 1st ed., 7.

country are unmarried," DEF leaders declared in 1899, "and since the poor marry much more frequently and easily, this means that less than 50 out of every 100 girls from the higher classes will find their lives' work in marriage."[4] It is difficult to test this claim, since little work has been done on class differences in nuptuality rates in Wilhelmine Germany. Available evidence indicates that although bourgeois women may have married less frequently than their working-class sisters, there is no proof that the percentage of spinsters among the "higher classes" ever reached such spectacular heights as 40 or 50 percent.[5] It seems more likely that, as Martha Vicinus concluded in her analysis of the British "woman surplus," that "the conviction shared by all middle class commentators that the number of unmarried middle class women was steadily increasing was due to their increase in absolute numbers and their increased visibility, brought about in part by their acceptance of paid work and in part by the public discussion of their plight."[6]

In addition, social commentators were probably deceived about the number of unmarried bourgeois women since most of these writers came from the *Bildungsbürgertum*, which perhaps did contain a higher percentage of spinsters. Families in the *Bildungsbürgertum*, squeezed by the increases in the cost of living during the last half of the nineteenth century, were increasingly unable to dower their daughters sufficiently, and thus were often unable to marry them off. This problem was not shared by the bourgeoisie as a whole, however.[7]

Still, the perceived reality was that many German bourgeois women were destined to remain spinsters, and the Hanover women's movement shared and benefited from this perception. Local women's associations also relied upon contemporary sexual stereotypes in their efforts to create new jobs for bourgeois women. The Hanover women's movement targeted careers in which women's "maternal" nature would be an asset. Clubwomen focused on opening professions that required sensitivity, tact, compassion, or other feminine virtues. As social workers, doctors, teachers, and nurses, bourgeois spinsters would use their innate maternal skills to serve society. The use of sexual stereotypes in lobbying for expanded vocational opportunities will be discussed on a case by case basis, but the common denominator was the extension of traditional notions of gender.

Hanover women leaders relied upon sexual stereotypes in other endeavors, but their campaign to open new careers to women is the clearest example of how they adeptly used perceived gender differences, rather than equal rights feminism, in setting and pursuing their goals. The Hanover women's movement targeted careers for bourgeois women that were compatible with contemporary sexual stereotypes; it did not ask that women be given the right to enter all professions on equal terms with men. This choice of strategy offered certain advantages, since local clubwomen could use their contemporaries' consensus that women were more compassionate and sensitive than men. The emphasis on gender differences also imposed certain constraints on local clubwomen, however, such as the need to frame women's professional work in terms of service to the community, rather than as a matter of personal choice.

In short, Hanover clubwomen argued that bourgeois women were forced by economic circumstances to pursue better education and careers, and that their crusade would not threaten existing gender roles. In accepting the narrowed definition of the woman question formulated by liberals during the 1870s, which referred only to the plight of genteel, unmarried spinsters, clubwomen were committing themselves to the pursuit of economic rights for bourgeois women, rather than political rights for all women. Leaders of women's associations repeatedly emphasized that they were not radical *Emanzen* ("libbers"), who sought political reform, that women professionals would in fact work to shore up the Wilhelmine social order and the nuclear family. They spoke of women's natural capacity for self-sacrifice in the service of others, and of duties, not rights. Paula Mueller reassured DEF members that "The world need not fear that a free woman will be like a slave who breaks his chains; instead, she will demonstrate the truth of the words spoken by our great poet, 'freedom is responsibility.' . . . [Women will] work to make our society healthier and purer."[8] Because clubwomen accepted traditional gender roles and confined themselves to an agenda of economic advances for women, they would win the support of bourgeois public opinion, especially from liberals from the *Bildungsbürgertum*, who shared women leaders' definition of the woman question.

One of the first steps Hanover women took to broaden women's education was the creation of the Society for the Advancement of Female Education (Verein zur Förderung weiblicher Bildung), which was founded in 1892. Initially, the society did not sponsor explicitly vocational education, but rather offered an array of lecture series and seminars, which were open to any adult woman. Some of these courses could be taken for diversion or edification, such as the lecture series on "Florentine Art during the Renaissance." Others, such as the foreign language and bookkeeping courses, were useful to teachers or secretaries who wanted to improve or polish their skills. The society also sponsored advanced academic courses for women, such as Latin and higher mathematics; until the Hanover Girls' Gymnasium opened in 1900, the society's Latin and mathematics seminars were the only courses in these subjects available to Hanover women.[9]

The city provided the society with lecture halls and seminar rooms free of charge, and the society hired upper-form teachers from local boys' secondary schools and professors from the University of Göttingen and the Hanover Polytechnical Institute as instructors. Instructors' salaries were paid out of membership dues; the society was supported by contributions from "passive members," who paid three Marks per annum, and by "active" members, who paid twelve Marks each year (or eight Marks, if they were teachers) for the right to attend twenty lectures. Tuition for seminars ranged from twelve to thirty Marks. At these prices, it will be seen that although the society's courses were formally open to all women, in practice only bourgeois women could have afforded to enroll, since twelve Marks represented about a week's wages for a working-class woman.[10]

The society resembled the Women's Educational Association (discussed in Chapter 2) in that it attracted single women as both members and officers: it was run for the most part by and for single women. Of the fifteen women who served as officers in the society between 1892 and 1910, eleven were single; this constituted a higher percentage of unmarried leaders than any other women's association in Hanover.[11] Three of the fifteen women were teachers, which explains why the society made special efforts to attract teachers to its courses by offering a discount in tuition for teachers and sponsoring courses of special interest to teachers.

Mathilde Drees (1862–1938) was one of these teachers; her seat on the executive committee of the society was just the first of many leadership positions she would hold in Hanover women's associations. Born and educated in nearby Oldenburg, where her father was the headmaster of a boys' school, Drees had received the same education as other female teachers of her generation. She attended a girls' secondary school (*höhere Mädchenschule*) and a two-year seminar for women teachers. After graduation, Drees worked as a governess for five years, and then taught for eight years at the girls' secondary school in Oldenburg where she had been a pupil.

In 1897, she left Oldenburg to audit university courses in Berlin, where women were now permitted to prepare for the state examination for upper-form teachers (*Oberlehrerinnenprüfung*). Drees passed the examination for upper-form French teachers, and in 1900, at the age of thirty-eight, she arrived in Hanover as one of the city's first *Oberlehrerinnen* (a female upper-form teacher).[12] Drees was an energetic, determined woman, possessing both humor and tact, who quickly became an officer in several local women's associations, and a leader among Hanover's women teachers. Politically liberal, she was a member of the "moderate" wing of the BDF, and became closely associated with moderate leader Helene Lange. Drees eventually rose within Lange's German General Association of Female Teachers to a position on the national steering committee. On the local level, she was popular with many members of the women's movement.[13]

Drees was persuaded to join the Society for the Advancement of Female Education by her friend Bertha Harder, another *Oberlehrerin* who sat on the society's executive committee, and who was the head of the movement's domestic science Continuation School; eventually, Drees herself taught in the Continuation School. The society offered courses that broadened the range of educational opportunities open to women in Hanover, but, by itself, the society could not produce professional women like Mathilde Drees and Bertha Harder. Professional training for women would be provided by other Hanover women's associations, which set their sights after 1900 on effecting substantial reforms in women's education. Before turning to these educational reform associations, it is necessary to briefly review the state of girls' education in Hanover prior to 1900.

Like Mathilde Drees, most middle- and upper-class girls in Wilhelmine Germany attended a girls' secondary school. Girls' secondary schools were not overly burdened by state supervision or regulations, because graduation from these schools brought no entitlements, such as boys' schools offered their pupils. Girls' schools did not prepare their pupils for the *Abitur*, the entrance examination for German universities, nor were their graduates allowed or expected to pursue higher educations.[14] The only institutions that offered professional training to secondary girls' school graduates were the female teachers' seminars, which prepared women to teach in the girls' secondary schools or in the *Volksschulen*.

In Hanover, as in Germany as a whole, therefore, the only profession open to bourgeois women before 1900—lower-form teaching—did not require higher education and was not particularly lucrative. Female teachers at Hanover's public girls' secondary schools worked without an established pay scale or pension plan for years; in 1892, when the city finally granted a teachers' petition to fix a pay scale, female secondary school teachers were assigned salaries that corresponded to those earned by *Volksschullehrerinnen* (female elementary school teachers). Female teachers' annual salaries started at 1,000 Marks, and rose gradually to reach a ceiling of 2,100 Marks after twenty-one years of service. These salaries fell far short of what was required to maintain a bourgeois standard of living for a single woman, and many teachers were forced to tutor pupils privately, during their hours off. Female teachers at the city's girls' secondary schools repeatedly asked for higher salaries, but the city council turned a deaf ear to these petitions, however, and it became clear that female teachers could only increase their wages dramatically if they obtained higher education and taught upper-form classes, a preserve of male teachers.[15]

Whether women ought to be allowed to teach upper-form classes in girls' secondary schools was the subject of a lively debate in turn-of-the-century Germany as a whole. The question had first been raised in 1887 by a group of Berlin mothers and female teachers, led by Helene Lange (who helped found the BDF). This group petitioned the Reichstag to assign women a greater role in teaching the upper grades of girls' secondary schools, especially the classes in religion and German. They also asked the state to establish institutions in which women could be educated for these assignments, as it was recognized that the female teachers' seminars did not provide sufficient preparation. In an accompanying pamphlet, which became widely known as the "yellow brochure," Lange set forth the women's movement's rationale for these reforms.[16]

Lange and other movement leaders argued that girls' education was not geared toward preparing pupils for university study, which necessarily included classical languages and mastering a great deal of other material, such as mathematics. Instead, Lange pointed out, girls' schools were intended to prepare women for social and familial roles, to foster certain accomplishments and types of behavior, and to make them morally and intellectually self-sufficient. The formation of a moral, maternal personality was thus just as central to girls' education as the material learned.[17]

To Lange and her associates, it was self-evident that maternal qualities in pupils could only be fostered by a teacher who possessed these qualities, that is by a woman teacher. The upper grades, in which girls were perceived to be at the most critical stage (puberty and adolescence), and especially religion and German classes (which taught ethical and social values) were felt to be the forums most urgently in need of women teachers' maternal influence. Lange's conclusion, that "women must be raised by women," became the rallying cry of women's educational associations, and had many supporters among Hanover's clubwomen. A powerful argument was thus created for opening a new profession (upper-form teaching) to bourgeois women, but this argument was made not on the basis of women's rights to equal education and opportunities, but rather as a way to serve the community, by providing schoolgirls with a proper, maternal socialization.

In order to compete with university-trained male upper-form teachers for positions in girls' secondary schools, Lange and other leaders of the German women's movement realized that female teachers had to be adequately educated for the job. In 1888, private groups in three university towns—Berlin, Königsberg, and Göttingen—established continuing-education courses for female teachers designed to prepare women to teach upper-form classes.[18] In 1894, the Prussian government introduced a state examination for women who had completed the courses; those, like Mathilde Drees, who passed were officially certified as *Oberlehrerinnen* (upper-form teachers).[19] Women's organizations in several German cities created university preparatory schools for girls during the 1890s, but those who graduated had to attend Swiss universities, since German universities did not yet admit women. Until 1908, when women were allowed to study in some departments of Prussian universities, the only path to a career as an *Oberlehrerin* for women who could not afford to study outside of Prussia was the continuation course and special state examination for female upper-form teachers.[20]

No evidence remains to tell us by what means Hanover municipal administrators were persuaded that the admission of women into upper-form teaching was desirable, but it is clear that a number of key officials were converted to the position of the women's movement. By 1898, only four years after certified *Oberlehrerinnen* became available, the city was actively seeking to hire female upper-form teachers for Hanover's public girls' secondary schools. In an 1898 city council debate over the issue of hiring *Oberlehrerinnen*, Burgomaster Tramm declared that female upper-form teachers were necessary since "the education of the female sex can and must be improved and made more profound, in light of the recent enormous development of our culture." Deputy Burgomaster Eyl concurred, affirming that "no matter how one may feel about this issue, one will not be able to get around the necessity of hiring *Oberlehrerinnen*."[21]

Hanover municipal officials were perhaps persuaded not only by ideological considerations, but also by the fact that academically trained male teachers were increasingly hard to come by. A surplus of male upper-form teachers and university-educated professionals of every kind during the 1880s had induced the Prussian government to restrict university admissions; as a result, by 1900, Germany suffered from a shortage of qualified professionals in many fields, including teaching.[22] Since the salaries and job titles given to male upper-form teachers at girls' secondary schools did not compare to those enjoyed by teachers at boys' secondary schools, the shortage of university-trained teachers was particularly acute at girls' schools. By hiring female upper-form teachers, Hanover administrators could please local leaders of women's organizations and, at the same time, fill positions that could not otherwise be filled, with teachers who would work for lower salaries. Between 1898 and 1904, the city hired ten new *Oberlehrerinnen*.[23] Almost all of these women would fill leadership roles in the local women's movement.

Once they had introduced women into higher-level positions, the clubwomen also began to work to broaden the influence of women in the school system as a whole. In 1907, the DEF and teachers' associations approached the city about including women in the municipal *Schuldepu-tation*, a committee appointed by the city council to formulate municipal educational policy. Clubwomen were supported in their campaign by their perennial ally, Deputy Burgomaster Eyl, and were ultimately successful in having women teachers and association leaders appointed to the *Schuldeputation*.[24] Some of the new upper-form women teachers were included.

Hanover's first ten *Oberlehrerinnen* included Drees, Harder, and others whose work within the local women's movement will be discussed in the next chapter. These women were a homogenous and fairly tight-knit group. All had been born between 1862 and 1876; their average age at appointment was thirty-two.[25] Several of the *Oberlehrerinnen* lived together. Drees, for example, shared rooms for over twenty-five years with another upper-form teacher who became active in the local women's movement, Anna Ramsauer (1871–1945).[26] Hanover's *Oberlehrerinnen* joined the same women's associations, and several local organizations— such as the Society for the Advancement of Female Education—counted more than one upper-form teacher among their officers. In 1906, the *Oberlehrerinnen* founded their own separate association, a local chapter of the League of Academically Trained and University Educated Female Teachers (Verband akademisch-gebildeter und studierter Lehrerinnen). Ramsauer was elected to head the new chapter.

Leaders of the national and local women's movement were aware, however, that producing upper-form teachers who had won their positions through special examinations was only a transitional method for opening new professions to women. In order to compete with male upper-form teachers for comparable salaries, titles, and positions, women would ultimately have to acquire the same educational credentials, that is, attend *Gymnasien* and universities. By 1900, however, young women were permitted to take the *Abitur*, and those who passed could enter universities in Baden, and later Bavaria, Saxony, or Württemberg.[27] The idea of establishing *Gymnasien* for girls had been debated in the press and within the women's movement for over ten years, and its influence had reached even Hanover.

Women leaders now advanced an additional reason why some young women ought to be given an education comparable with their brothers', one that found some public support (especially in Hanover): the women's movement wanted to produce female physicians, as well as *Oberlehrerin-*

nen. Medicine, they argued, was a natural extension of women's traditional nurturing and healing functions. Educational reformers were greatly assisted here by public opinion, which was inclined to view the treatment of female patients by male doctors, especially the treatment of "women's diseases," as an injury to feminine modesty and chastity.

Many German men and women agreed with one (male) supporter of female physicians, who wrote that a male doctor who examined a female patient without witnesses made "a mockery of right, modesty, and morals."[28] The public's sympathy for this line of reasoning no doubt helped account for the fact that over 40,000 women and 15,000 men signed a petition circulated during the early 1890s, which called for "female physicians for women's diseases."[29] Men who supported this demand may have had an additional reason to do so, since husbands might have preferred that their wives not be examined intimately by a male physician.[30] In effect, the issue was framed as the question of a female patient's right (or her husband's right) to choose her physician, rather than a woman's right to choose her career.

Once the issue was framed as a question of patients' rights, an 1899 drive to establish a girls' *Gymnasium* found support in Hanover. The catalyst in this instance was the presence of Hedwig Kettler (1851–1937), who had moved to Hanover from Weimar in the late 1890s. Kettler came from a civil servant's family and was artistically talented. She received advanced training as a painter, and later wrote novels, marrying one of her cousins, Julius Kettler, relatively late in life. They had two daughters. After her marriage, Kettler turned her attention to agitating for new careers for women. She created a periodical, *Frauenberuf,* which publicized efforts to improve women's education. Like other leaders in the women's movement, Kettler argued that industrialization had "emptied" the household of many of its former productive functions (which had provided employment for unmarried women in the homes of their relatives), and "stranded" many single bourgeois women, who were now "surplus," and in need of professional training.[31]

In Weimar, Kettler founded the Women's Association "Reform" (Frauenverein "Reform"), a national organization that had established the first full-fledged German girls' *Gymnasium* (not just *Gymnasial* courses, as in Berlin) in Karlsruhe in 1893. Kettler was adept at attracting members to her association and at organizing pressure group tactics, such as petitions, public appeals, and fund-raising drives. Unfortunately, she was also difficult and domineering. Kettler's unwillingness to compromise and her tendency to act without consulting her associates soon alienated them, and by 1897 the other officers of "Reform" ousted her from the association's executive committee altogether.[32]

Kettler made a new beginning in Hanover, where she created a local organization in 1898, the Association for the Reform of Women's Education (Verein "Frauenbildungsreform"). The new association's declared goal was to found a girls' *Gymnasium* in Hanover. As in Weimar, Kettler threw herself into the work of attracting new members and soliciting funds. She successfully lobbied the Prussian Ministry of Culture for official permission to establish *Gymnasial* courses for girls in Hanover, but failed to convince the city government to assume responsibility for the courses.

The new *Gymnasial* courses were therefore organized privately, and Kettler created several subassociations to generate financial support. A thirty-two-person board of patrons, consisting of local notables, was enlisted to lend the new enterprise respectability and monetary support. Each patron donated a substantial sum to the association, ranging from 50 to 500 Marks, and lent the use of his or her name to public appeals and circulars. A seventy-person "Committee to Assist the Girls' *Gymnasial* Courses" contributed lesser sums, while the parent association itself attracted literally hundreds of more humble citizens as passive members, who each contributed two Marks a year in dues.[33]

A perusal of the lists of the girls' *Gymnasium* patrons and association members makes it clear that while Kettler provided the initial impulse for the *Gymnasial* courses, she tapped into a wellspring of support for a girls' *Gymnasium*, which must have existed before her arrival on the scene. The patrons ranged from the wife of the arch-conservative Prussian Field Marshall Alfred Count von Waldersee (the former chief of the General Staff) to the wives of leading local National Liberal politicians, including the publisher of the National Liberals' Hanover newspaper. All of these women would join the DEF after its creation in 1899. Hanover's leading Jewish notables were also well represented among the patrons; six of the thirty-two patrons were either married to or were themselves leading Jewish bankers and manufacturers. With the exception of the Guelph families and the city's few prominent Catholic citizens, almost all of the subsets of Hanover's bourgeoisie—"Prussians," National Liberals, Jews, businessmen, officers, civil servants, and professionals—were represented among the supporters of the girls' *Gymnasium*.[34]

The girls' *Gymnasium* drew supporters from many quarters, but anonymous letters sent to Kettler reflected the fact that other Hanoverians were skeptical or even hostile toward the proposed school. City administrators were therefore tentative in their support for the *Gymnasial* courses. As mentioned, the city refused to set up municipal *Gymnasial* courses, and initially refused Kettler any financial subsidies. As it had for other projects of the women's movement, the city did, however, make rooms available in a wing of one of the public girls' secondary schools, and provided heat and light gratis.

The *Gymnasial* courses for girls opened at Easter 1899, with ten pupils. For several years, Kettler's association could not afford to hire full-time teachers for the courses, and the faculty consisted of upper-form teachers from local boys' secondary schools who were sympathetic to the cause of higher education for women, and who were therefore willing to "moonlight." After 1902, the city began to contribute yearly subsidies to the school, which reached 6,000 Marks by 1906. The passage of time, along with the fact that all of the *Gymnasial* school's graduates passed the *Abitur* and went on to successful studies at German universities, gradually increased public acceptance of the school. In 1907 the city assumed responsibility for the courses, which now included seventy pupils.[35]

Only a handful of the school's original patrons and other supporters sent their own daughters to the *Gymnasial* courses; clearly, most patrons saw the new institution as intended for *other* families' daughters, genteel families forced to provide for their daughters. No doubt some of the patrons would have sympathized with the mother of one future female teacher, who supported higher education for some women, but resisted her own daughter's studies right up to the end, arguing that her daughter had no financial need to work. Her daughter completed her course work in spite of this opposition. The night before her daughter's certification examination, the mother prayed for hours on her knees that her daughter might fail the test, and thus avoid shaming the family by working. Her daughter's prayers, however, were evidently more effective, since she passed the examination.[36]

Most of the *Gymnasial* courses' pupils came from far less prominent families than those represented by the patrons. Of the eighteen young women who entered the new institution's first two classes, only four had fathers who had themselves attended universities. Eight of the eighteen fathers were merchants, and the remaining six fathers included a *Volks-schule* teacher, a farmer, and a master carpenter.[37] Clearly, the courses' first pupils included not only girls from distressed genteel backgrounds, but also girls whose families sought upward social mobility for their daughters through the traditional conduit for sons: higher education. True to Kettler's promise that the courses would produce female doctors and teachers, all but one of the eighteen graduates chose university majors in either medicine or a field that led to teaching.[38]

After 1900, then, the combined efforts of the local women's movement (which had sponsored the *Gymnasial* courses) and the national women's movement (which had pressed the Prussian government to provide cer-tification examinations for *Oberlehrerinnen* and to open universities to women) made it possible for Hanover's young women to pursue careers as physicians or upper-form teachers at girls' schools. In practice, how-ever, these professions were an option for only a few. Not many parents were willing, or able, to invest in their daughters' prolonged education. Preparing a daughter for the university meant not only paying tuition for ten years of a girls' secondary school, but also the fees for five additional years of *Gymnasial* courses, which cost 240 Marks per annum (equal to about six months' rent for a bourgeois family's apartment).[39]

Furthermore, once a young woman had passed the *Abitur*, she would be forced to leave home to attend a university; bourgeois parents were generally unwilling to sanction an unmarried daughter's move to a strange city. Finally, although the new professions were made more ac-ceptable by the fact that they were supposedly compatible with women's "maternal" nature, there was no escaping the fact that the new upper-form teachers and female physicians were entering careers that were not traditionally feminine, and which brought them into direct competition with men. This fact alone was enough to damn the new professions in the eyes of many parents.

Although they supported women's rights to become upper-form teach-ers and physicians, DEF leaders were also developing another set of "maternal" professions for bourgeois women, that of the social worker and allied careers in the social service sector. These vocations did not involve the stumbling blocks inherent in achieving a position as an *Ober-lehrerin* or physician. Professional training could be obtained locally, without taking the *Gymnasial* courses or attending a university. Far from conflicting with the established sexual division of labor, these careers grew directly out of one of genteel women's traditional duties, charitable work. Best of all, professional social work was a new creation, and hence the women entering this career would not compete with men.

The female municipal almoner and orphans' officer were to be replaced by trained, full-time social workers, but these jobs represented only the tip of the iceberg of new positions for women envisioned by the leaders of the Hanover women's movement. The DEF ran a placement bureau for social workers of all kinds, and its leaders foresaw a future when each large business hired a private social worker to counsel and oversee female workers, when government and the private sector appointed an army of social workers to care for infants and children in special centers, and when courts and administrative bodies employed "socially trained" women to work with female clients, applicants, or prisoners.[40] The key to realizing all of these goals, DEF leaders believed, was professional training.

As in the arguments for *Oberlehrerinnen* and female physicians, the rationale for the professionalization of social work stressed service, not rights. Women ought to be allowed to become *Oberlehrerinnen* and doctors, it had been maintained, in order to provide needed services to, respectively, pupils at *höhere Mädchenschulen* and female patients. Social workers, however, were to work not merely for the good of their clients but would serve society and state as well. A women's historian has observed that the first female professionals hid their ambition from themselves and society "under the cloak of self-sacrifice,"[41] and this disingenuousness was nowhere more apparent than in the field of professional social work.

"Woman has been driven to help relieve the distress of entire classes within our population," Adelheid von Bennigsen wrote in 1905, "and she has had to develop her work without any training, almost even without any guidance. The understandable mistakes committed due to this lack, the obstacles that have sometimes been put in her way, prove that a thorough, well-planned course of preparation is needed."[42] Since 1900, the DEF had received municipal grants to sponsor periodic lecture series on "The Principles of Charitable Work," which were held in conjunction with the Society for the Advancement of Female Education.[43] In 1905, the DEF took the next step, and opened the Christian Women's Social Seminar in Hanover (Christliches-Soziales Frauenseminar, hereafter referred to as the Social Seminar); apparently, it was the first professional school for social workers founded in Germany.[44] The Social Seminar offered a one-year course (later expanded to two years) that combined theoretical instruction with practical training in local charitable institutions.

Its founders intended that the Social Seminar should train women from the educated classes. The school's first prospectus specified that pupils had to come from *gebildete* families and had to have completed a secondary girls' school; the tuition, moreover, was a substantial 400 Marks per annum (about six months' rent for a "better" bourgeois apartment). The first pupils were in fact drawn from genteel families. The women who graduated from the first five classes were almost all the children of officers, professionals, and high-level civil servants; only a few listed their fathers' profession as "merchant" or "landowner."[45] The first women to enroll in the Social Seminar came, by and large, from much more prestigious families than the first graduates of the girls' *Gymnasium*.

The Social Seminar was fortunate in its director, Adelheid von Bennigsen, who used her personal political connections to the school's benefit. Her father was one of the leading National Liberal politicians of his generation, and Bennigsen was on good terms with local National Liberal officials such as Burgomaster Tramm and his deputy, Hans Eyl. Tramm, Eyl, and Leon Wespy (who headed one of the municipal girls' secondary schools and sat on the city's school commission), consistently spoke for the seminar in the city senate's deliberations, and ensured that the school received steadily increasing subsidies. They were also regular guests at receptions and galas hosted by the seminar.[46] Thanks in part to its strong ties to local government, the Social Seminar eventually developed an almost complete monopoly over local professional social work. Through the end of the 1930s, almost every woman employed in social work in Hanover or neighboring cities, whether public or private, was a seminar graduate.[47]

The Social Seminar's curriculum, unlike many other schools for social workers, stressed religious values and formal training in religion. Table 5.2 presents the 1917 schedule for the theoretical segment of the curriculum, which included two religious courses, as well as a course on the women's movement. This course of study formed a contrast to Alice Salomon's Social Women's School in Berlin, which was a leader among schools for professional social work; Salomon's curriculum contained nei-

Table 5.2. Curriculum of the Christian Women's Social Seminar, 1917

Lecture Title	Number of Hours Given per Semester
Political Economy	36
Social Policy	24
Recent History of Our Allies and Enemies	12
Constitutional and Administrative Law	24
Municipal Governments: Their Laws and Social Responsibilities	18
History of the Church and Canon Law	12
Religious and Moral Aspects of Christianity	18
Introduction to Philosophy	24
Educational History	18
Guardianships, Juvenile Courts, and the Removal of Children into Foster Care	12
The Position of Women Under Civil Law	6
The Women's Movement	6

Source: STAH XV Gb 150 vol. 1.

ther religious training nor courses on the women's movement.[48] The Hanover seminar's courses were usually taught by local pastors, professors, or lawyers. The course on the German women's movement was taught by Drees's life-long companion, *Oberlehrerin* Anna Ramsauer; other lectures on topics of special interest to the women's movement were frequently given by local women's association leaders, including Paula Mueller and Drees herself.[49]

In the years between 1905 and 1914, the DEF and the Social Seminar increasingly stressed the need for professionally trained social workers, and placed an ever growing number of seminar graduates in positions within local government, large businesses, and charitable institutions. This success was accompanied by a growing insistence by DEF leaders on the redemptive value of work for the individual female professional and on the sacrifice and selflessness inherent in professional social work. For decades, women leaders had routinely congratulated themselves and their peers on their charitable work with the poor; the traditional term for such activities is revealing—*Liebesarbeit*, or works of love.

The rhetoric that accompanied the professionalization of social work, however, carried this tendency even further in its unremitting claim that social work represented self-sacrifice and service for the common good.

These claims were in fact essential to a campaign that saw social work as a manifestation of the doctrine of spiritual motherhood, since the movement (and German culture as a whole) defined maternity as consisting largely of self-sacrifice, service, and succor. A pamphlet written by Bennigsen in early 1914 is a good example of this line of argument; its assertions echoed those which could be found in dozens of other articles and pamphlets written by DEF leaders and other women active in developing social work:

> We [women] must become seekers of duty, rather than seekers of happiness. Only then can our efforts and our entire beings be of service in our own communities and in society as a whole. And only that [service] can preserve us from the bleak fate of being unfulfilled. In fulfillment, we will find happiness. . . . The profession [of social work] is unique in that the training period and the subsequent career both include a continuing succor, service to others in the truest sense of the word. . . . She who does not have real love for the work, who does not possess a complete willingness to sacrifice and the strength to practice self-denial, ought to refrain from social work.[50]

Emphasizing the fact that social work involved real sacrifice for the greater social good not only helped women get support for professional social workers, it also undoubtedly helped to ease the sting of having a genteel daughter or sister who was forced to seek paid social work.

The women who entered the new "maternal" professions were supposed to come from the educated classes. This was the intention of local clubwomen, although, as we have seen, not all of the girls' *Gymnasium* graduates came from genteel families. Lower-middle-class women—the daughters of lower-level civil servants, white-collar employees, and small businessmen—did not enter into association leaders' calculations at all for many years, except as potential members of girls' organizations. After 1905, however, the local women's movement became aware of the increasing employment opportunities for women in clerical work, and women's associations began to offer vocational training for lower-middle-class girls.

Office work for women was a by-product of the enormous expansion in the service sector of the Wilhelmine economy, expansion that would continue after World War I. Both the public and private sectors employed an increasing number of women in sales, accounting, and clerical work of every description. In the eyes of many young women from Hanover's petit bourgeois families, the new white-collar jobs promised a certain amount of status and independence from their families. One woman who grew up in these circles recalled later that "many of the girls were eager to become a *Fräulein vom Amt*. . . . [One young woman] wanted to take training so that she could get a job as a telegraphist—*das war 'was!*—but her father [a lower-level, white-collar employee of an insurance company] forbade it. He said that no daughter of his would rest her feet under someone else's desk. She was especially disappointed because some of her school chums were allowed to work at such jobs."[51]

Young women seeking vocational training for office work could join one of the dozens of stenography clubs, which offered beginners' courses, or enter any one of the city's numerous small, private "business schools," which taught stenography and typing. Too many of these schools, however, were what one local girls' vocational teacher called "crammer schools"; their pupils, he declared, became "mere stenographers, those poor creatures who must sit at their typewriters year after year, and thereby ruin their nerves, becoming unfit to advance in their professions."[52]

To provide lower-middle-class girls with better vocational training, the alliance of women's organizations that ran the Continuation School for Girls expanded its curriculum to include a trade school in 1905. The trade school, which required a commitment of twenty-seven hours per week for one year and cost 100 Marks quarterly (and was therefore not accessible to working-class girls), included courses in accounting, business correspondence, stenography, typing, business English, and German. Within a few years, the trade school was receiving more applications than it could handle and was obliged to set up a second set of courses. The city had given the Continuation School an extra subsidy for the trade school from the time it opened and financed the additional rent for classrooms for the new trade school courses. From the beginning, the school received more requests from local businesses for graduates than it could fill, and its pupils quickly found employment.[53]

The strong demand for clerical workers was the trade school's primary justification. In petitions for municipal funding or public appeals, women's associations had relied heavily on traditional conceptions of gender and gender roles to justify opening "maternal" professions to women or to intervene within working-class families, but this rhetoric was completely absent in the case of the trade school. Women's associations, which for years had maintained that many bourgeois women were unable to marry, could not use this line of reasoning in appeals for the trade school; the school was intended to educate young women from the lower middle class, a class that was not supposed to suffer from a serious "woman surplus." Possibly, women leaders saw little need to put forward any detailed rationale for the trade school. It filled a manifest niche in the local economy and had the support of local businesses, and perhaps that was sufficient.

Once the trade school was established, the steering committee that directed the Continuation School invited a representative from the Commercial Union of Female Salaried Employees (Kaufmännischer Verband weiblicher Angestellter) to help supervise the trade school. A local chapter of the union, a national organization, had been founded in 1903; except for the contact with the Continuation School, the Hanover chapter held itself somewhat aloof from the activities of other local women's organizations. The Commercial Union did not fit into any recognized niche in the local women's movement. Its members, most of whom were saleswomen or clerical workers, came from petit bourgeois families, and thus were not the social peers of most members of other women's organizations. On the other hand, the union's members were too independent and too well-off to adopt a subordinate role vis-à-vis leading bourgeois women's organizations, as had the DEF's affiliated servants' and factory workers' groups. The relative independence of this occupational group had indeed frustrated the DEF's efforts to organize shopgirls.[54]

The Commercial Union therefore kept largely to itself. It had a central *Vereinshaus*, which contained a small library, a newspaper room, and an employment referral bureau, and it offered members courses in foreign languages, accounting, typing, and stenography. It also maintained a small unemployment insurance fund. The association hosted frequent lectures and small dances for its members. Its annual *Stiftungsfest* (founders' day celebration) was apparently an elaborate production, with skits, singing, dancing, and poetry recitals; the festivities usually went on long after midnight.[55]

With the exception of a female telegraphists' association, all other women's professional organizations founded in Hanover before 1914 that have left traces in local archives were teachers' associations. Far from being aloof, these organizations played an important role in the local women's movement, sharing its leadership with the DEF and the Educational Association. As we have seen, leaders of teachers' associations were active in the creation of the committee that founded the Continuation School, and in the organization of the People's Welfare Association. Teachers' organizations also assisted the DEF in creating its chain of girls' clubs, and its legal advice bureau for women. Women who led teachers' associations were also officers in the Women's Educational Association, the Society for the Advancement of Female Education, and the Association for the Reform of Women's Education, which had founded the *Gymnasial* courses.

The first female teachers' organization was a local chapter of the Association of Prussian Female Elementary School Teachers (Landesverein preussischer Volksschullehrerinnen), founded in 1897. The leader of the Hanover chapter, Anna Dörries (1853–1936), provides a good example of the overlap in membership and leadership between teachers' associations and other women's organizations. The daughter of a pastor, Dörries worked as a governess for several years after finishing a female teachers' seminar. She was then obliged to go to work in an elementary school, because her widowed mother and invalid sister needed her to live with them, and contribute to their support. Dörries joined Kettler's association to create a girls' *Gymnasium*; she and her mother belonged to the DEF. Dörries was an active DEF member, and ran the DEF schoolgirls' club that was attached to her school for many years. In the course of representing the teachers' association, and the movement as a whole, she developed an excellent relationship with several officials who oversaw the city's schools, especially Senator Grote, who assisted the DEF in many matters. Grote saw to it that the city paid for Dörries's trips to the national conventions of the Prussian Female Elementary School Teachers. When clubwomen carried their point and won the inclusion of women in the *Schuldeputation*, she was one of the first women appointed.[56]

The creation of Dörries's elementary school teachers' chapter was followed over the next ten years by the creation of a string of other female teachers' associations: one for lower-form teachers at the girls' secondary schools; one for music teachers; one for teachers of needlework and knitting; one for kindergarten teachers; and, as we have seen, one for the new *Oberlehrerinnen*. Altogether, 332 female teachers belonged to these associations by 1908. All of these associations belonged to the national umbrella organizations for female teachers' groups, the German General Association of Female Teachers (Allgemeiner Deutscher Lehrerinnenverein).[57]

Hanover's female music teachers' group, founded by Agnes Hundoegger (1858–1927), was in fact nationally known for pioneering new forms of teaching. Hundoegger, the daughter of one of Hanover's leading physicians, possessed a self-disciplined, self-sufficient personality. At the age of sixteen, she was sent alone to Berlin to study at the Hochschule für Musik, graduating with degrees in piano and song. She returned to Hanover and began a career as a pianist. Hundoegger was also active in the local women's movement and helped to found the women's legal advice bureau.[58]

Hundoegger loved to travel, and during a 1896 visit to England she became acquainted with the Tonika Do method of teaching; the new technique taught children to sing by learning to sight read, rather than just parroting back what was played to them.[59] Hundoegger was converted to the new system, and returned home determined to popularize it in Germany. In 1909, she founded the Tonika Do League to teach the new method. She was successful in popularizing the system among female music teachers, but had little success with men; Tonika Do was not introduced into public schools, although female teachers who gave private lessons used it widely.[60] Hundoegger's Hanover association became one of the leading women music teachers' groups in Germany. Hundoegger herself worked with other leaders in the local women's movement on several projects and was on the executive board of the Women's Club, discussed in the next chapter.

From the time that teachers' associations were created until the end of World War I, they functioned more as sociable organizations than as labor groups. Teachers' associations hosted sociable events for members and worked to advance members' professional skills and training. The music teachers' association, for example, held occasional courses for members on Tonika Do theory and on new methods of instruction. For years, the only contact that teachers' associations had with the city government was when the organizations requested the use of public auditoriums for their annual congresses, or asked for small subsidies to finance continuing-education courses for members.[61]

Teachers' associations did not attempt to represent female teachers as a whole during negotiations over teachers' pay scales; indeed, a historian who perused only the records relating to teachers' salary negotiations might be forgiven for supposing that there were no female teachers' associations in Hanover. Female teachers frequently petitioned the city for increases in their pay, housing allowances, or pensions, but they always presented themselves in petitions as small groups of individuals, never as associations. Appreciation for the fact that teachers' associations did not act as collective bargaining units was expressed by Burgomaster Tramm on the conclusion of a series of negotiations that raised all teachers' pay scales in 1906. He thanked the teachers for "refraining from any sort of agitation in the press or in their associations; they have conducted themselves with tact, as befits administrative decisions in this area."[62]

During the 1920s, women's professional associations would begin to function as collective bargaining agencies, but in Wilhelmine Hanover, "persuasion," "connections," and "caution" were the watchwords of women leaders. Most would have agreed with Paula Mueller that the aim of the women's movement was not to break down barriers indiscriminately, but rather to permit women to fulfill their own potential, based on an essentialist understanding of gender roles. In a society where each woman could choose her own career, Mueller claimed, "*a [sexual] division of labor which reflects the natural strengths and talents [of each sex]*" would arise of its own accord.[63] This was a gendered version of Adam Smith's "invisible hand"; in reality, the professions in which bourgeois women gained a foothold in Hanover were not determined by an invisible hand but, at least in part, by the visible activities of the local women's movement.

In their drive to open new educational and professional opportunities to women, women's associations had chosen their targets carefully and had been fortunate in their timing. They had pursued an economic rather than a political agenda, which gained the support of local liberal notables. In addition, the women's movement proposed careers for bourgeois women that were compatible, or could be presented as being compatible, with established notions of gender: "maternal" professions. In the case of professional social workers, the movement was able to build upon concerns about social unrest and poverty that were already present in the German middle and upper classes. The women's movement also targeted professions, such as upper-form teaching and clerical work, that suffered from a shortage of workers and where women could more easily obtain positions than might otherwise have been the case.

Market forces, carefully planned campaigns, and a "surplus" of women thus combined to determine which careers would be opened to women. As we have seen, the "surplus" of women is not well documented, but the women's movement could rely upon the fact that social commentators believed that such a surplus existed. This agreement was crucial to the movement's success. Public opinion was too firmly persuaded that a married woman ought not hold a job for new professions to be opened to all women, and therefore the new careers were presented as alternatives for single bourgeois women only. The "surplus" of single women then became a necessary component in the women's movement's argument, since only the "surplus" made single women a significant enough group to warrant new schools and legal reforms prerequisite to the new careers.

Single bourgeois women were thus the chief beneficiaries of the creation of the maternal professions, and single women would go on to create their own forums for recreation and companionship. The local women's movement as a whole, however, consisted primarily of married or widowed women, women who had been mobilized and organized, by and large, around the issues of fighting social degeneration, improving social services, and opening new professions to bourgeois women. By 1906, the women thus organized numbered in the thousands, and it is to these women as a whole, to the entire local women's movement as a single network, that the next chapter turns.

Behind the numerous projects of the Hanover women's movement—the girls' *Gymnasium*, the shelter for homeless women, the legal advice bureau for women, or the chain of temperance restaurants—stood the machinery of club life, the routine activities that kept the sponsoring associations going. Behind the leaders of the movement—Paula Mueller, Anna Dörries, Bertha Duensing, or Mathilde Drees—stood the rank-and-file association members, whose dues and donated time turned their leaders' proposals into concrete achievements. The minutiae of club life and the activities of average clubwomen were seldom mentioned in the newsletters, correspondence, and pamphlets generated by local women's associations; they were nevertheless essential.

An examination of clubwomen in the mass, a social profile of women's associations, belongs in a history of the Hanover women's movement as much as the profiles of the movement's leaders and accounts of its large projects. An investigation of the movement's social profile reveals where all the new clubwomen who joined associations after 1890 came from, and how the women's movement was able to mobilize women from social groups it had previously ignored. In addition, analyzing the activities of individual, average clubwomen gives us a sense of how associational work fit into their daily lives and demonstrates how ties between individual clubwomen helped weave separate women's associations into a unified women's movement.

It can be difficult to read between the lines of sources to discover how local women's organizations handled the day-to-day machinery of club life and how conflict within associations was resolved or muted. Few sources discuss the details of club life; most give accounts of meetings that apparently were run in a spirit of almost delirious harmony. This stilted, formulaic style, used in reports of meetings, was in fact so common in

German associational life that it has been dubbed *Vereinsdeutsch*.[1] The following report on a DEF meeting of national officers and *Ortsgruppe* (local chapter) leaders gives an example of the determined tone of collegial goodwill.

> That the meeting was inspiring and valuable for all participants could be seen in the reports of [each woman's] experiences and in the exchanges of opinion, which continued to be lively right up to the end. The active involvement [of participants] in the debates testified to the growing interest and the deeper understanding which our members have for the questions of the day. Many of the *Ortsgruppen* representatives expressed this belief in their assurances that they were returning home with renewed joy and love for their work.[2]

In Hanover, and across Germany, clubwomen who were starting large projects learned to use bureaucratic modes of operation, conducting their organizations' work according to written statutes; as one observer of Hamburg women's associations put it, the women learned to be *vereinsfähig* ("capable of running associations").[3] This learning process was reflected in a set of DEF guidelines for new chapters, which stressed that association work must be conducted in a "businesslike fashion": officers should keep account books carefully, along with copies of incoming and outgoing letters and minutes of past meetings. Meetings should "not carry the stamp of a social occasion, with a babylonian confusion of voices, but rather are to be conducted in a parliamentary fashion from the very beginning. A bell must be kept at hand, in order to halt any overflowing river of talk." Parliamentary forms were to be observed without regard to considerations of age or social status.[4]

Although the details were rarely mentioned in associations' annual reports, all organizations had to manage the machinery of club life: collecting dues, cajoling "passive" members to attend meetings, attracting new members, and finding places to meet. This last item posed a more difficult task for women's groups than for their male counterparts. Bourgeois women were limited in their access to public places; they could be seen in churches, shops, and restaurants, but not in taverns, the favored meeting place for many men's associations. Small groups could meet in a member's home, but larger women's organizations, unless they were wealthy enough to build their own headquarters, sometimes had to hunt for meeting places. A handful of women's organizations had ties to sympathetic hotel owners, who allowed the use of their facilities, or to larger male associations, which made their own meeting halls available. The DEF, for example, often used the meeting hall of the Protestant Association. Just as they turned to the city for funding, clubwomen often relied on the city for meeting space as well. The city maintained one large municipal auditorium, which was often made available to women's associations, especially teachers' groups. The city also allowed women's organizations to use municipal rooms when local chapters hosted the national conventions of their associations.

In general, however, space limitations worked to discourage frequent meetings of large women's groups, which was perhaps one reason why most of the city's larger women's associations held general membership meetings only once per month. The DEF, the Catholic Women's League, and the Patriotic Women's Association, for example, held monthly "members' meetings," which included a public report on the association's recent work and a presentation (*Vortrag*) on a topic that might have popular appeal. The presentations often discussed the association's annual national convention, to which the speaker might have been sent by the local chapter, or the national conventions of other women's groups, such as the BDF. Presentations delivered to Hanover DEF members during 1906, for example, included lectures on "Women's Professions," "Our Goals in the Women's Movement," and "The Juvenile Welfare Courts." These meetings demanded little involvement from most members; one Hanover woman recalled later that "my mother belonged to the local chapter of the Patriotic Women's Association, but all that really meant was that she occasionally attended a presentation on 'Infant Hygiene,' or some other lecture of this sort."[5]

"Passive" members were women who paid their dues, occasionally attended a lecture, and lent the use of their name to public appeals. Taken individually, their contributions were modest; but since there were so many of them, their combined support was essential. Mathilde de Haen can be taken as an example of this type of clubwoman. The daughter of a forestry official, she married Eugen de Haen in 1862. Eugen de Haen was a chemist and founded a chemical factory that ultimately became one of Hanover's most successful enterprises. Both of the de Haens were born in the province of Hanover and moved to the city during the 1860s; by 1871, the de Haens could afford to build an enormous villa in Hanover's best neighborhood. Their grandson later recalled that the de Haens lived "according to the style of the rich *Bürgerfamilie* before 1914, a style that today would seem impressive. With all personal modesty, [I can say that the household] was run on a grand scale and was well funded."[6] The de Haens had a box at the Hanover Theater, and kept a carriage with a fine span of horses.

Mathilde de Haen did not join any of the women's associations that existed in Hanover before 1890. Perhaps, as a newcomer and a woman who was not from an educated family, she would not have felt comfortable in one of the "older style" women's associations; perhaps her children—she had ten, three of whom died young—took up too much of her time. After 1900, however, free of maternal obligations and long established as one of Hanover's wealthier matrons, de Haen joined several of the newer women's associations, focusing on the causes of women's education and temperance. She became a passive member of the Women's Educational Association, of a society that ran a day nursery, of Bertha Duensing's temperance Women's Association for the People's Welfare, and of the organization that founded the girls' *Gymnasium*. Mathilde de Haen contributed money to these societies and attended meetings, but she never served as an officer.[7]

The bulk of most women's associations' work was done by association activists, women who made a commitment to donate time to an organization's projects. Activists included not only association officers, but also the women who sat on an organization's advisory board (*Beirat*), women who worked on subcommittees, and women who volunteered for jobs like that of the parish almoner, municipal almoner, and the orphans' officer.

Ella Oppler was an activist, primarily within Jewish women's organizations. Oppler was a contemporary of Mathilde de Haen; she was born in Hanover in 1843, and married Edwin Oppler in 1866. Oppler moved in quite different social circles than de Haen, however. Mathilde de Haen's father was a lower-level civil servant, and she married a man who became a wealthy businessmen only after some years; Ella Oppler, on the other hand, was born into a family of Jewish professionals—her father was a physician—and married a fashionable and successful architect. She was on the executive committees of several Jewish charities: an association that ran a retirement home for Jewish female teachers; a group that oversaw a local Jewish boarding school; and an organization that raised money for the dowries of poor Jewish brides. Ella Oppler was also active in secular women's associations. She belonged to the Women's Educational Association and to the society that founded the girls' *Gymnasium*; she was also on the executive committee of the Women's Club, discussed later.[8]

Many of the Hanover movement's activists were teachers. Maria Mühry (1855–1937), whose father had been a high-level forestry official, was the vice-president of Hanover's DEF chapter. Mühry supported her widowed mother by teaching at a private school run by another prominent member of the local women's movement from 1886 to 1905, and then applied for a position at a municipal girls' lyceum. *Schulrat* Wespy, who frequently assisted the DEF in its dealings with the city, and who knew Mühry from his work with the DEF, supported her application. "She is a refined lady, who is a master of the social forms, comes from a very good family, and enjoys respect and considerable influence among her fellow teachers and within Hanover society as a whole," he wrote.[9] Thanks to Wespy's intervention, the normal rules were waived, and Mühry was given credit (in terms of her placement on the pay scale and retirement benefits) for the twenty-one years she had taught in private schools, and started at the relatively high salary of 2,300 Marks. In 1911, she was appointed the head of a new school (a *Frauenschule*), created by the city to train lyceum graduates in domestic science and kindergarten teaching. Mühry was conservative, both in a partisan political sense and within the women's movement; in 1912 (after the BDF's "turn to the right"), she wrote with satisfaction that "the time of the exaggerated drive for emancipation is over; those who think and work more calmly have clarified and deepened [the woman question]."[10] Besides her work in the BDF, Mühry also belonged to Duensing's temperance association and headed a private disability insurance fund created by Hanover women teachers.

Toni Eicke (1863–1935) was another teacher activist, although her personal connections and social background were not as grand as Mühry's. Eicke was one of four sisters orphaned at a young age; she did not have the money for a teachers's seminar, and instead trained as a needlework instructor at the school run by the Women's Educational Association. She and her sister Ella, who was also an elementary school teacher, supported two other sisters who lived with them. Eicke pieced together a living for years, working part-time for the city, and part-time in private schools; in 1906 she finally obtained a full-time position at a municipal elementary school. In addition to her job, Eicke carried a full load of association-related work. She was the head of the local association for "technical" women teachers, that is, needlework and physical education teachers, who had less education, lower salaries, and less status than regular elementary teachers. Eicke also belonged to the DEF and worked as a DEF orphans' officer. Her sister Ella belonged to Duensing's temperance association.[11]

The Eicke sisters were not the only examples of pairs of relatives active in local associations. Clubwomen shared ties of blood and marriage, and many women in confessional, professional, and social welfare organizations were officers in more than one association. Familial relationships between members of different associations, or overlap in leadership, tended to draw women's organizations together into a single network. Johanna Woltereck, a merchant's widow, was an example of these links between organizations. She was on the executive committee of both the Women's Educational Association and the organization that founded the girls' *Gymnasium*, while her daughter-in-law, Fanny, sat on the steering committee of the Women's Club.

Julie von Hugo was also an activist, although on a more modest scale. Born in 1852 into an old Hanover family with a tradition of military service to the Guelph dynasty, her family belonged to a stratum of Hanover society that held itself aloof from the circles frequented by Jewish women like Oppler or parvenus like de Haen. Julie von Hugo was a woman of independent means and never married. Her brother later wrote that "she was able to make intelligent, correct judgments . . . and possessed a sometimes astounding knowledge of human nature."[12] These qualities were of some use in her associational work; she volunteered for many years as her neighborhood's *Armenhelferin*.

Julie von Hugo did not live with family members, as did Mühry and Eicke. At age twenty-six, she established a household with a girlhood friend, Baroness Hedwig von Minnigerode; they lived next door to Julie von Hugo's brother and his family. The two women shared a home together for thirty-four years. In 1908 they moved to Cassel, where von Hugo died in 1912.[13]

Many other single clubwomen chose the same life-style. Anna Ramsauer and Mathilde Drees shared a set of rooms at the Women's Club, which they furnished together, for over twenty years. Dozens of other association members, moreover, were listed in the city directory as sharing a apartments with other clubwomen.[14] The decision to live together with another single woman, often for decades, was common among unmarried genteel women before World War I, in Germany and elsewhere; in the United States, such relationships were dubbed "Boston marriages." National BDF leaders like Helene Lange and Gertrud Bäumer, or Anita Augspurg and Lida Heymann, also cohabited for most of their adult lives.[15] A DEF member, writing in the association's magazine, celebrated these "female friendships," asserting that single or widowed women could save themselves from a lonely old age by establishing a household with another woman.

> Where two women live together [she wrote], in true comradeship, there is a real home. In it, one can feel secure. . . . warmth and harmony fill it. Female friendship—anyone who has experienced it, knows that he [*sic*] has drawn a good lot in life. . . . And—I add this, so that I will not be seen merely as an idealist—such female friendships are good also in a pecuniary sense. A lone woman may barely make ends meet, but if two pool their money, then they have a quite serviceable income.[16]

Some of these "Boston marriages" were undoubtedly real marriages—sexual and romantic unions, as well as domestic partnerships. In the case of the Hanover clubwomen discussed here, it is impossible to say which, if any, of these relationships between single women were romantic, or if they were sexually consummated. The sources necessary for such a judgment (letters or diaries) are unavailable. What is clear, however, is that many Hanover spinsters were each other's companions, helpmeets, and financial partners: in some instances, for decades. Many women joined associations together with their roommates, or belonged to associations that were allied with organizations their roommates had joined. Like the familial ties between clubwomen, the links between association members who were also neighbors, or who cohabited, helped weave the separate women's organizations in Hanover into a single local women's movement.

Ties between clubwomen from different associations were also reinforced by participation in the Women's Club (Frauen-Klub), which was the city's leading women's recreational association. The Women's Club had been founded in 1900. The club was originally proposed by a group of women's associations led by the Society for the Advancement of Female

Education. The leaders of these associations enlisted a committee—composed of the wives of local notables—to raise funds and outfit the new club. The wife of Hanover's burgomaster, Olga Tramm (who had helped raise funds for the DEF), took a prominent part in this new project and sat on the club's executive committee. The city donated a large, well-situated building (the Tramms' former official residence) to house the club, and private donations ensured that the club was elegantly furnished. The buffet in the dining room alone cost 1,000 Marks, about a year's salary for a beginning elementary school teacher. Besides the dining room, the club boasted a library, a reading room, a large salon, rooms for women's associations to hold committee meetings, and sitting rooms and bedrooms to board "single ladies."[17]

The club was intended to be "a meeting place for educated women, where single professional women, in particular, can feel at home, and find refreshment, intellectual stimulation, and sociability."[18] Some of the leaders of women's associations mentioned in previous chapters, such as Mathilde Drees and Anna Ramsauer, lived at the club, while many others took their meals there. The *Bürgertum* of Hanover, having reached a consensus that bourgeois single women ought to be able to pursue certain careers, had decided to provide recreational facilities for these new professional women.

The Women's Club was created for single women, but it soon attracted married bourgeois women to its events. The club hosted "literary afternoons," special teas, lecture series, and frequent hiking expeditions for women. Women who were prominent in Hanover society attended these events, especially the teas; Olga Tramm, one of the club's patrons, occasionally sang as part of the entertainment.[19] The club became the sociable center of the Hanover women's movement. The club was also displayed to movement women from other cities; it was used to host parties and receptions when local associations hosted the national conventions for their organizations.[20]

Some of the club's events, such as its annual women's *Fasching* (Mardi Gras) celebration, were so popular that the club had to rent a hotel to accommodate all of the members who attended. Like other clubs and associations, the Women's Club adopted special themes for its *Fasching* masquerades, but the club differed in that all roles were apparently played by women. The centerpiece of the 1909 *Fasching* party, which was organized around the theme of a "peasants' wedding," was the bridal procession, which had just come from church; [it] made an enchanting picture with its musicians, bridal pair, the parents and relatives of the bride—which included many fine peasant figures—the bridesmaid with her admirers, and the village schoolmaster with his pupils. After the father of the bride had greeted the guests with a humorous speech, a peasants' roundelay took place, followed by solo dances, and comic presentations of all sorts. The scene was enhanced by the appearance of curious tourists from the city, gypsies, peddlers, and military officers, who were in the midst of holding a military exercise.[21]

The choice of a wedding as the celebration's theme, by a club dominated by single women, is interesting. Some of the leading roles in this masquerade were played by local actresses, who often donated their services to the club's entertainments; presumably, however, many of the parts were played by club members. The women of the club were using *Fasching*, which traditionally includes donning masks to conceal identity and permit role-playing, to cross not only social boundaries, such as those between the urban bourgeoisie and rural peasants, but also to exchange sex roles. The leaders of the local women's movement threw themselves into these roles with gusto; over 300 women attended this *Fasching* masquerade, which was proclaimed a great success. The Women's Club *Fasching*, moreover, was not unique. Women's associations in other cities also hosted recreations in which members played roles and cross-dressed. The Berlin Association of Female Artists and Female Friends of Art, for example, hosted an annual all-female ball at which some members dressed as men, and even led out members in women's clothing onto the dance floor; the ball was counted one of the more important events in the Berlin Season.[22]

The Hanover Women's Club was a social magnet; it provided not only common ground for women in the local women's movement, but also a forum that drew women's associations together. Leaders of women's associations met there socially, and some lived there together. The network of sociability that revolved around the club reinforced the familial and, in the case of women teachers, collegial relationships that bound local clubwomen together, and contributed to the growth of consensus within the women's movement.

The Women's Club was a meeting place for association activists, but, like other organizations, most of the women who came to its events were "passive" members. Women like Ella Oppler or Julie von Hugo, who were willing to contribute their time, were sometimes in short supply within the local women's movement; the Catholic Women's League in particular often complained that the bulk of its social work fell upon relatively few shoulders.[23] Women's associations sometimes had difficulty in finding volunteers because social work was often unpleasant, as Paula Mueller confessed in a letter to an associate:

> Do you think, dear Frau Steinhausen, that I do poor relief work because it is my personal inclination to do so? I must confess to you that actually each visit to the poor requires an effort on my part, that for my part, I have no real love for the poor. Often, I find them positively disgusting, and the bad air [in their dwellings] makes me feel ill. Left to myself, I would never visit the poor, but I do it out of love for God, and because I have the strength to be of use to my fellow man.[24]

Other activists were inspired to volunteer by precisely the same conditions that revolted Mueller. Frieda Duensing, a relative of Bertha Duensing, began her career in social welfare work after she visited the Hanover women's poorhouse in 1892. Frieda Duensing shared many of Bertha's characteristics; she was excitable, moody, idealistic, and compassionate. Duensing was horrified by the women's poorhouse: "Seven mothers with their children were crammed there into a single room, a large, whitewashed, disgustingly filthy room. . . . I could see how a woman would steadily sink in such a poorhouse."[25] Duensing began to volunteer for social welfare work; later, she left Hanover to study for a degree in law. Duensing eventually became a leader in juvenile court work and was one of the first to write and speak out on the issue of child abuse.[26]

Although association work was sometimes unpleasant, women's organizations were able to recruit enough activists to staff their programs, and by 1906 the number of activists alone far outnumbered the entire pre-1890 combined memberships of older women's associations. Table 6.1 gives a list of local women's associations founded between 1890 and the beginning of 1906, along with membership figures. When the membership figures of the new organizations are combined with the number of women who belonged to the "older" organizations in 1906 (given in Table 6.2), the enormous expansion of the local women's movement is thrown into relief. Altogether, local women's organizations recruited at least 3,394

Table 6.1. Women's Organizations Founded in Hanover, 1890–1906, with Membership Figures from 1906 to 1908

Organization	Year Founded	Membership
Association of Former Female Pupils of the Synagogue Religion Class[a]	1890	not available
Association of Christian Women Teachers	1891	54
Society for the Advancement of Female Education[a]	1892	n.a.
Association for the Outfitting of Poor Jewish Brides	1892	n.a.
Association of the Female Friends of Young Girls	1895	n.a.
Association of Prussian Female Elementary School Teachers, Local Chapter #1[a]	1895	80
Association of Prussian Female Elementary School Teachers, Local Chapter #2[a]	1897	120
DEF[a]	1899	562
Association for the Reform of Female Clothing[a]	1900	133
Society for the Establishment and Maintenance of Day-Care Schools[a]	1902	86
Commercial Union of Female Salaried Employees[a]	1903	334
Female Auxiliary of the Zion Lodge[a]	1904	88
The *"Frauenwohl"* Association[a]	1904	52
Association of Hanover and Linden Female Teachers[a]	1905	61
Catholic Women's League	1905	196
Tonika-Do League (music teachers' association)[a]	1905	117
German Women's Navy League	1905	n.a.
Women's Association for the People's Welfare[a]	1906	328
League of Academically Trained and University-Educated Female Teachers[a]	1906	63

Sources: STAH, XV Gb 171, *"Geschäftsbericht für die Jahre 1905/1906 und 1906/1907 des Frauenvereins 'Volkswohl'"*; ADEF, Akten der Ortsgruppe Hannover, 1906 annual report; ADEF, FF 1, *Listen der dem Nationalen Frauendienst angeschlossenen Vereine*; *Die christliche Frau* 4 (1905–6): 402; Kaiserliches Statistisches Amt, *Statistik der Frauenorganisationen im Deutschen Reiche*, 10–64; Altmann-Gottheimer, *Jahrbuch der Frauenbewegung*, 12–62, 74–81.

Note: This list includes organizations founded between 1890 and the first half of 1906; it excludes short-lived groups and girls' groups (discussed in Chapter 3). Unfortunately, membership figures for all associations were not available for any single year, and the above membership figures date from 1906 to 1908; where figures for all three years were available, I have given the figure for 1906.

a. Joined the *Bund Deutscher Frauenvereine* between 1900 and 1914.

Table 6.2. Membership Figures in 1906 for Women's Organizations Founded before 1890

Organization	Membership
Childbed Association	not available
Association of the Day-Care School of the Inner City of Hanover	n.a.
Frederica Association	31
Women's Association for the Care of the Indigent Ill of the *Vorstadt* Neighborhood of Hanover	n.a.
Jewish Women's League	n.a.
Women's Division, Gustav Adolf Association	n.a.
St. Elisabeth Society	n.a.
Patriotic Women's Association	480
Magdalene Society	171
Women's Educational Association	298
Dorcas Society	n.a.
Maria Society	n.a.
Boedeker Creche Society	58
Association of Christian Spinsters	n.a.
Reformed (Calvinist) Women's Society	30

Sources: STAH Schulamt 2357, Jahresbericht für die Boedekerkrippe, 1907; Kaiserliches Statistisches Amt, *Statistik der Frauenorganisationen im Deutschen Reiche*, 10–68; LKAH, S 3d 114, 1906–7 annual report of the Magdalene Society and S 3d 226, 1906 annual report of the Frederica Association; *Adressbuch der königlichen Haupt- und Residenzstadt Hannover*, 1906 ed., part II, section 10, listings for voluntary associations.

Note: One association, the Magdalene Society, had "passive" male members; I have included only female members in its membership figure. Except for the Jewish Women's League, the organizations for which membership figures are unavailable were all small groups that did not publish membership lists.

members by 1906, and since membership figures are not available for all the associations listed in Tables 6.1 and 6.2, in reality the number was somewhat higher.

Of course, many of these organizations, especially those with largely "passive" memberships, had overlapping memberships, and thus the number of women who joined (as opposed to the number of membership cards issued) was much smaller. The combined membership of all local women teachers' associations which were affiliated with the Allgemeiner Deutscher Lehrerinnenverein, for example, was 441 in 1908, but the leader of one teachers' association estimated that the total number of women who belonged was 332.[27] It is impossible to determine exactly how much smaller the actual number of women was, since membership lists are not available for all women's associations, but it is possible to make an educated guess by using a sample of women who belonged to local women's organizations.

A catalog containing the names of 1,090 women who belonged to Hanover women's organizations during the years 1906–8 was compiled for this study, a sampling of the local women's movement.[28] Women's names were taken from membership lists and, where lists were not available, from sources that mentioned the names of officers and activists in a given organization. The catalog is weighted toward several subgroups: toward Protestant women, since complete membership lists for Jewish and Catholic women's organizations were not available; toward activists, because activist women were more likely to be mentioned in source materials; and toward educational, confessional, temperance, and social welfare organizations, since complete membership lists for women's professional associations have not survived.[29]

The 1,090 women in this sample represented a total of 1,621 membership cards in local women's organizations; they averaged 1.5 memberships per woman. Using this ratio as a guideline, the actual number of women behind the 3,394 members listed in Tables 6.1 and 6.2 was probably about 2,000, a conservative estimate of the number of bourgeois women in the Hanover movement in 1906. Of the 1,090 women in our sample, 668 were activists.

An analysis of the marital status of these 1,090 women shows that the local women's movement tapped into a reservoir of single adult women during the course of its expansion between 1890 and 1906. Table 6.3 gives a breakdown of the marital status of the entire sample and of selected subgroups. Almost half of the 1,090 women were single; this represented a considerable increase over the percentage of women involved in associations before 1890 who had been single (27 percent), and a much higher percentage than the proportion of all adult women in Hanover as a whole who were unmarried in 1906.

Unmarried women also represented a plurality of all women among the activists; 315, or 47 percent of the 668 activists were single. Single women were especially well represented among DEF activists and educational activists. Married women could only be found in proportions reflecting their real percentage of the population among temperance activ-

Table 6.3. Marital Status of Members of Selected Associations, 1906
(in percentages)

Category	Married	Single	Widowed
All Hanover women over 21	55.9	28.8	15.2
Entire sample of 1,090 women	40.2	47.1	12.7
Activists total	38.2	47.2	14.6
DEF activists	29.0	52.4	18.6
Educational association activists	27.3	59.1	13.6
Temperance association activists	52.9	35.3	11.8
Members of pre-1890 associations	38.5	46.2	15.3
Total membership DEF	38.2	50.8	11.0
Educational associations	35.3	45.4	19.3
Temperance associations	49.3	37.3	13.4

Note: Membership lists for professional women's associations are not available, but their members can be assumed to have been overwhelmingly single. For a discussion of the sources and methodology used, see the appendix. In this table, as in subsequent tables in this chapter, the following definitions apply: "Members of pre-1890 associations" refers to women who had joined the older women's associations (discussed in Chapter 2) between 1890 and 1906; "Educational associations" includes the memberships of the Association for the Advancement of Female Education, the Women's Educational Association, and the various organizations that were founded to support the *Mädchengymnasium*; and "Temperance associations" includes the members of the Women's Association for the People's Welfare and the German League of Abstinent Women.

ists. The "older," pre-1890 women's associations also reflected this trend toward an increase in the number of unmarried members: whereas only 27 percent of the women who belonged to the organizations listed in Table 6.2 during the 1880s had been single (see Table 2.2), by 1906 these same organizations, overall, had memberships wherein 46 percent of the women were single.

Several factors contributed to this growth in the number of single clubwomen. First, the number of unmarried women in the entire sample was boosted by the members of professional associations, which had been absent in Hanover before 1890, and which by definition consisted almost exclusively of single women. The creation of women's professional organizations, which constituted some of the largest associations in both Hanover and in the BDF, dramatically shifted the membership of the local and national women's movement toward single women.

Other types of associations also registered an increased number of single members, however. The high percentage of unmarried members in educational associations perhaps reflected the fact that single women, who were especially responsive to the symbol of the impoverished, genteel spinster, were likely to be sympathetic toward groups that sought to improve women's educational and professional opportunities. The fact that the percentage of single activists in social welfare organizations also grew is an indication that the movement's chief argument, that the spread of social degeneration required bourgeois women's work with poor women and children, also justified the increased involvement of unmarried women in the public sphere. In addition, the work the DEF and other welfare groups were taking on demanded a greater commitment of time than the limited projects of the older women's organizations; single women (if they did not have to work for a living) presumably had more time to devote to social welfare work.

Single clubwomen grew in numbers after the turn of the century, but they did not entirely account for the growth of the local women's movement. The Hanover women's movement had expanded not only through attracting more unmarried women, but also by mobilizing women from social circles that had been largely ignored by the older women's associations. Table 6.4 presents a breakdown on the social profile of the entire sample of 1,090 women as a whole and of selected subgroups. Even a perfunctory analysis of this table reveals that the local women's movement had a much broader social base by 1906; the number of women from the bottom rungs of the *Bürgertum* had grown dramatically. Whereas only 5.1 percent of the 98 members of the "older" women's associations discussed in Chapter 2 had been wives or daughters of shopkeepers, artisans, lower-level civil servants, nonacademic professionals, or white-collar employees, by 1906 20.6 percent of the 1,090 members of associations were drawn from these groups. Conversely, the percentage of members from the more prestigious strata of bourgeois society, the *Gebildeten* (the wives and daughters of academic professionals or high-level civil servants), had declined. Although 40.8 percent of the 98 women discussed in Chapter 2 had come from these groups, by 1906, their share was down to 24.8 percent.

Of the subgroups presented in Table 6.4, the DEF was by far the most socially inclusive. Although its officers were drawn from elite social circles, its activists were not; 14.4 percent of the total DEF membership came from the lower middle class, as did an impressive 25 percent of its activ-

Table 6.4. Occupational Background of Husbands and Fathers of Members of Selected Women's Organizations in Hanover, ca. 1906 (in percentages)

Occupation	All 1,090 Women	Old Organizations (1880s)	Old Organizations (1906)	DEF
Academic professionals	12.2	14.3	18.4	10.9
Businessmen	3.8	7.2	8.7	1.4
Higher-level civil servants	12.6	26.5	17.4	14.2
Officers	7.7	11.2	15.7	8.7
Landowners	1.9	—	2.0	1.4
Managers	2.2	—	3.0	2.4
Lower-level civil servants	6.4	1.0	2.0	5.8
White-collar employees	1.5	—	—	0.1
Shopkeepers	7.1	3.1	3.9	5.5
Artisans	3.7	—	—	1.2
Nonacademic professionals	1.9	1.0	1.0	1.8
Pensioners	4.8	6.1	3.9	4.2
Occupation unknown	34.2	29.6	24.0	42.4
Total petite bourgeoisie	20.6	5.1	6.9	14.4
Total *Gebildete*	24.8	40.8	35.8	25.1

Note: Old organizations are those organizations founded before 1890 and discussed in Chapter 2; the figure given for Old Organizations (1880s) represents members who belonged to these organizations during the 1880s (see Table 2.2), while Old Organizations (1906) refers to the occupational background of women who joined these groups between 1890 and 1906.

For a discussion of sources and the methodology used, see the appendix. "Petite bourgeoisie" was derived by adding the percentage for Lower-level civil servants, White-collar employees, Shopkeepers, Artisans, and Nonacademic professionals. "Total *Gebildete*" (the "educated classes") represents the combined figures for Aca-

DEF Activists	Educational Organizations	Educational Activists	Temperance Organizations	Temperance Activists
11.3	15.9	18.3	21.6	35.3
0.8	8.7	2.9	11.0	5.9
8.9	22.7	22.8	19.5	11.8
8.1	8.7	4.6	4.1	—
3.2	0.5	—	—	—
1.6	1.9	2.9	1.4	—
14.5	3.4	2.9	4.1	5.9
0.8	1.0	—	—	—
6.5	5.8	4.6	2.7	—
2.4	0.5	—	2.7	—
0.8	1.0	—	—	—
6.5	4.3	4.6	—	—
34.6	25.6	36.4	32.9	41.1
25.0	10.2	7.5	9.5	5.9
20.2	38.6	41.1	41.1	47.1

demic professionals and Higher-level civil servants. "Academic professionals" were men in the so-called *freie Berufe*, professionals such as doctors, lawyers, and architects, who had attended institutions of higher learning. "Higher-level civil servants" were those who had also attended universities, while "Lower-level civil servants" were those who had not. "Nonacademic professionals" were professionals such as apothecaries and photographers, who had some sort of professional training but who had not attended a university. "Businessmen" owned factories or large businesses, while "Shopkeepers" were small businessmen. "Managers" were high-level executives in large businesses.

ists.[30] Other women's associations varied in their degree of exclusivity. As we have seen, the women's associations founded before 1890 conformed to the pattern of increased percentages of single members, but in 1906 these organizations were still attracting women from the same social groups that had provided them with members during the 1880s: academic professionals, high-level civil servants, and officers. Educational associations and temperance organizations were also fairly exclusive; 38.6 percent of all educational association members and 41.1 percent of all temperance society members came from *gebildete* families. Overall, the members of temperance associations closely resembled the 1880s members of the "older" women's associations, both in the high percentage of married members and in the elite social profile of the membership.

The fact that the DEF, instead of another organization, attracted the most members from lower-middle-class backgrounds is a clue to why the local women's movement became more socially inclusive. The DEF, after all, was primarily concerned with social welfare work and required an increasing number of activists to realize its programs. The sheer scale of these projects forced DEF leaders to recruit members from new social circles. In addition, of all the projects undertaken by local women's associations, the DEF's social welfare programs were the most familiar to the wives of shopkeepers, artisans, and lower-level civil servants. Women had formed the majority of all parish almoners (*Armenhelferinnen*) in Hanover since the 1880s (see Chapter 2), and substantial numbers of lower-middle-class women had been included among these almoners from the beginning. The role of municipal almoner or orphans' officer probably did not seem so strange to a social group that was already providing women for work as parish almoners.

Furthermore, the DEF was in many ways the most accessible and inclusive women's association in Hanover. Most other women's groups would not have been so attractive to lower-middle-class women. The associations founded before 1890 were generally exclusive, recruiting from narrow political or occupational groups. Women's professional and educational associations, on the other hand, tended to attract women from the higher-status *Bildungsbürgertum*, which supposedly suffered from the greatest "woman surplus," and whose members were thus more passionately interested in women's professional opportunities. Female professional organizations, moreover, were largely closed to married women. Any woman who was a Protestant, however, could join the DEF, and

Table 6.5. Marital Status of Jewish, Catholic, and Protestant Activists, ca. 1906

Confession	Number	Percent Married	Percent Single	Percent Widowed
Hanover total		55.9	28.8	15.2
Protestant	535	38.3	46.7	15.0
Catholic	24	25.0	70.8	4.2
Jewish	27	55.6	22.2	22.2

Note: For a discussion of sources and methods, see the appendix.

most Hanoverians were Protestant; the DEF, therefore, was the closest thing to an umbrella association that the local movement had. DEF chapters may have served the same function in other predominantly Protestant Prussian cities, which was where the women's movement found most of its membership.

The social profile and distribution of marital status varied greatly among women from different confessional groups. Not surprisingly, Catholic and Jewish women were drawn largely from the families of businessmen and academic professionals, rather than from those of high-level civil servants; Catholics and Jews were discriminated against in the civil service, and thus underrepresented in that occupational group. What is unexpected, however, is the difference in marital status distribution between Catholic, Protestant, and Jewish clubwomen (see Table 6.5). These figures must be approached with caution, since complete membership lists for Jewish and Catholic women's associations were not available, and thus names and personal data could only be located for Catholic and Jewish activists. The absolute number of Catholic and Jewish women analyzed in Table 6.5 is therefore low: our sample included 24 Catholic activists and 27 Jewish activists. Bearing this in mind, the differences in the percentages of single, married, and widowed women are nonetheless interesting. In 1906, Jewish women still conformed to the older pattern of a high percentage of married members, with 55.6 percent of all Jewish activists married, and only 22.2 percent single. Catholic women, on the other hand, represented the opposite extreme: 70.8 percent of all Catholic activists located for this study were unmarried.

The absolute number of Catholic and Jewish activists represented in Table 6.5 is small; this is due not only to gaps in source materials, but also to the fact that there were in fact many fewer Catholics and Jews than Protestants in Hanover. As we saw in Chapter 1, the city's population was overwhelmingly Protestant: in 1910, 87 percent of all Hanoverians were Protestant, as opposed to the 10.3 percent who were Catholic and the 1.7 percent who were Jewish.[31] Yet, although Protestant activists far outnumbered Catholic and Jewish activists, the membership figures for the DEF —the city's chief Protestant women's association—did not overshadow the number of members in the Jewish Women's League or the Catholic Women's League to the same degree. The number of women in the DEF in 1906 was 562, while the Catholic Women's League boasted 196 members; no exact membership figures are available for the Jewish Women's League, but sources suggest that the combined membership of the two local organizations that were affiliated with the national Jüdischer Frauenbund was probably between 200 and 300 women.

Thus, although only 1.7 percent of all women in Hanover were Jewish, the chief Jewish women's associations attracted almost half as many members as the leading Protestant women's group. Similarly, although Catholics were also very much in the minority (and, as we have seen, those Hanoverians who were Catholic were largely working class), a bourgeois Catholic women's group was able to enlist almost 200 members. These figures suggest a high degree of organization among women from the two minority confessional groups. Perhaps specifically confessional associations had more appeal for Catholic and Jewish women, who were surrounded and outnumbered by Protestants. For some, confessional organizations probably helped to define and preserve their confessional identity.

Different women's associations, then, attracted substantially different memberships, both in terms of social background and marital status. It would be gratifying to be able to trace neat correlations between an association's membership profile and its work or policies, but this is only possible in a few cases. The empirical reality of the Hanover women's movement was too jumbled to permit such tidy or clear analysis. If women's association leaders were aware of the differences between women's organizations' membership profiles, this is not recorded in our sources; Hanover clubwomen habitually spoke of the entire local women's movement as being simply *bürgerlich*.

In a few cases, however, a link between an association's membership profile and its activities is discernible. As discussed earlier, many of the

DEF's programs involved work that was familiar to women from lower-middle-class families, a fact that helps account for that organization's high percentage of petit bourgeois members. In addition, Hanover's feminist and nationalist clubwomen (as we shall see) came from social backgrounds that were particularly compatible with their associational work.

Analysis of the movement as a whole, then, reveals that different women's associations attracted different memberships, and that the overall social profile of the women's movement changed between 1880 and 1906. The women's movement became more inclusive, drawing women from every stratum of the city's bourgeoisie. These women were mobilized to found women's associations, to attend meetings, and to do volunteer work for their organizations. The bulk of Hanover clubwomen was motivated by two prime concerns: the need to fight the spread of "social degeneration" and a desire to create new professions for single bourgeois women. These were the two bread-and-butter issues of local women's associations, and they were sufficient to call a large and vigorous women's movement into being.

By the eve of World War I, the local women's movement had made considerable progress in these two, all-important areas. Hanover women's associations had created a girls' *Gymnasium* and a school for professional social workers, to train women for new careers. The movement had established a network of social services to combat social degeneration and had persuaded the city to fund a great deal of this network's activities. Women leaders had organized one-tenth of the city's young women into auxiliary girls' groups, a preventative measure against immorality and an attempt to train the next generation's clubwomen in their own image.

These activities represented an explosion of organizational energy, but Hanover's clubwomen were not unique in this respect. The growth in the number of Hanover women's associations was only one local example of a larger, national trend in Wilhelmine Germany: an enormous increase in voluntary organizations of every kind. Voluntary associations, clubs, and societies had proliferated among all social groups and in every geographical region in Germany.[32]

Hanover clubwomen's male counterparts were included in this trend; Table 6.6 presents a breakdown of the number of voluntary associations in Hanover in 1906. A comparison of the number of women's and men's organizations makes it clear that, although local women's associations had grown substantially since 1890, their numbers were still dwarfed by Han-

Table 6.6. Voluntary Associations in Hanover, 1906

Type of Association	Men's	Women's	Mixed
Charitable/social service	37	17	2
Professional	120	10	—
Sports	60	—	4
Hobbies	31	—	—
Sciences	6	—	—
Arts	5	—	2
Stenography	31	10	1
Educational	6	3	2
Musical	76	—	5
Political	15	1	—
Neighborhood (*Bürgervereine*)	34	—	—
Veterans'	35	—	—
Health reform	8	1	3
Miscellaneous	10	—	—

Source: *Adressbuch der königlichen Haupt und Residenzstadt Hannover*, 1906 ed., part II, 180–225.

Note: Confessional associations are listed by type: for example, a Catholic merchants' association would be listed under "professional" associations. "Charitable" excludes *Stiftungen*; funeral and savings societies are also excluded, as are provincial-level umbrella *Verbände* that had seats in Hanover. "Health reform" groups sought to reform diet, dress, or medical treatment and included the Vegetarian Society and the Homeopathic Association.

over's masculine organizations, which numbered in the hundreds. In Hanover, as in other cities, local observers were aware of the almost excessive proliferation of associations. The editors of one of Hanover's leading newspapers asked rhetorically in 1909, "what are we to say, when educated people found an association, complete with a set of statutes, solely in order to gather once a fortnight to eat potato pancakes, or to smoke a given number of pipes. . . . [This] has led to the often heard joke, 'is there no Association against the Proliferation of Associations?' "[33]

In comparison with local men's organizations, Hanover women's associations were limited not only in number, but in variety, although women had made some progress in reducing this disparity since 1890. The city boasted men's associations of every stripe, whereas women's groups were largely limited to professional or social service organizations. With the exception of the Women's Club, female recreational associations—musical, sporting, or hobbies groups—were almost nonexistent. A few local women's choral and athletic associations were founded during the Wilhelmine period, but these always went under within a year or two; none was functioning in 1906. Women's recreational groups only achieved continuity and success as auxiliaries to men's sporting or musical groups: the "mixed" organizations (as associations or meetings that included both men and women were called) listed in these categories in Table 6.6 were all large men's groups that had feminine subdivisions.

Women apparently had less success in the recreational sphere of club life. Why this was so is unclear. It is true that bourgeois women were generally not encouraged to pursue athletic activities in Wilhelmine Germany, which doubtless contributed to the failure of women's sporting associations, but singing was not regarded as unfeminine, and women's choral societies were socially acceptable. Women had modeled many aspects of their social service and professional organizations on men's associational life, and masculine models for successful recreational groups were not lacking; still, Hanover's young women could not establish a successful women's bicycling or choral society. Instead, the bulk of women's organizational energy was directed toward social service associations. Women were autonomous and successful in the sphere of service, but not in creating their own formal recreational associations.

Perhaps social service was feminine, whereas recreation was not. Women, after all, were expected to spend their leisure and recreational time with family members, especially their children; playing with children was a duty as well as a form of recreation.[34] Women were able to escape their families (at least temporarily) and function effectively in the public sphere so long as they appeared to be serving or helping others, an extension of their traditional familial roles. In a service capacity, they received their peers' approval and support. A women's recreational association, on the other hand, would have been manifestly self-serving and would have taken time away from domestic duties. Only the Women's Club, which was ostensibly for single professional women (who presumably had no or fewer domestic duties), was openly and purely recreational.

Hanover clubwomen had, by and large, chosen to restrict themselves to social service and were successful within that sphere. Women leaders had reason to be satisfied with their choice of strategies and were optimistic about their movement's future. By 1906, they had secured a niche within the local political structure and had influence over municipal policies that concerned women and children. The movement's goals had found widespread support among the city's *Bürgertum*. Women leaders believed that women's rights would continue to advance slowly but steadily, as they had for the past twenty years.

To continue to flourish, the movement relied on the state, especially on municipal and provincial authorities, who provided the ideal environment for clubwomen's programs. While local officials supported and funded the movement's projects, they did not wish to take on responsibility for this work, to "nationalize" social work. The movement thus enjoyed public funding for a sphere that it controlled almost entirely. The Hanover women's movement was secure, but only so long as the local political structure, which had nourished the women's movement, remained unchallenged.

CHAPTER 7

The *Kasernierung* Campaign:

Alliances and Rivalries in the

Fight against Social Degeneration

and Prostitution

By 1906, the leaders of the Hanover women's movement had had many successes; they had created a comprehensive network of social services and other programs designed to fight "social degeneration" and to promote new opportunities for bourgeois women. They had achieved all of this using private strategies, relying on personal connections with local officials and notables for financial support, rather than public agitation for reform. The women's movement was united, acting in coalitions and alliances that were based on a firm consensus among clubwomen. In 1906 all of this came to an end. The unified front that the movement presented to the public was exploded from within, and clubwomen turned to public agitation when they launched a campaign to combat a proposed change in the legal regulation of prostitution. This crusade would lead clubwomen to debate questions of morality and state policy in public for the first time. This campaign was one of the most important and certainly one of the noisiest battles in the movement's larger war against social degeneration. It divided the Hanover movement and gave birth to a new feminist wing.

Beyond this, the 1906 debate was important because it differed substantially from contemporary campaigns against the regulation of prostitution mounted by feminists in other German cities and abroad. It became a clear example of how various wings of the women's movement could handle the same issue quite differently. Hanover clubwomen shared a belief in gender difference and spiritual motherhood with feminists in Hamburg and Bremen, but they did not approach the question of prostitution in the same way. Rather than attacking men and identifying with prostitutes, as did feminists in other cities, Hanover women leaders were constrained by their close connections with bourgeois men and developed an approach that combined feminine values with class interests.

This approach was considerably to the right of the feminist, or "radical" wing of the national German movement, which was reaching the apogee of its influence nationally at about this time. The BDF had been founded in 1894 at the initiative of the leaders of the moderate Allgemeiner Deutscher Frauenverein and was dominated by ADF leaders until after the turn of the century. Under this leadership, the BDF pursued a limited agenda which resembled the ADF's: one that focused on obtaining increased economic opportunities for women while shunning political controversy. The power of the feminist or radical wing of the BDF had been growing steadily on the national level since 1898, however. German feminists, like their "moderate" opponents, believed that men and women had inherent emotional and psychological differences, but argued that women were nonetheless entitled to equal social and political rights. Feminist rhetoric was generally based on the tenets of classical liberalism; feminists themselves tended to support German progressive liberal parties.

BDF feminists were thus reviving a line of reasoning that had first been articulated by Luise Otto, but had been downplayed within the national women's movement since the 1860s; this school of thought emphasized the pursuit of political rights for women. Moderate leaders within the BDF, on the other hand, did not demand equal rights for women per se, but rather claimed particular rights for women (such as the right to work as an upper-form teacher), which were justified by specific gender differences. They argued that women's suffrage would represent the "capstone" on all reforms and advances for women; it was a right that would be won only after women had realized many other goals and would not be achieved for decades. For the present, moderates asked only that women be allowed to vote in local elections.[1]

Moderate leaders like Helene Lange represented the majority within the German women's movement and dominated the BDF until the turn of the century.[2] For years, the moderate leaders had focused on increasing women's educational and professional opportunities, and rejected proposals that the BDF espouse women's suffrage or other political rights for women. Frustrated by their lack of success within the BDF, the radicals created a new umbrella association for German feminists in 1899, the Union of Progressive Women's Associations (Verband Fortschrittlicher

Frauenvereine). The associations which led this union were the abolitionists, who opposed state regulation of prostitution, which was seen as unfairly penalizing prostitutes and not their customers; the Women's Welfare Association (Verein *"Frauenwohl"*), which agitated for political and social rights for women; and (after 1902) the German Union for Women's Suffrage (Deutscher Verband für Frauenstimmrecht). After 1904 the radical wing of the women's movement also included the League for the Protection of Motherhood (Bund für Mutterschutz).[3]

BDF leaders initially rejected the Progressive Union's agenda and the union's attempts to persuade the BDF to adopt the same positions; the balance of power shifted, however, after 1900. Some of the most influential moderates, like Auguste Schmidt, who had led the ADF for decades, retired around the turn of the century. A few of the radical's arguments (especially the abolitionists' demands), moreover, began to attract widespread support within the BDF. The feminists' breakthrough came at the 1902 BDF congress, which endorsed abolition and women's suffrage; in addition, Marie Stritt was elected to the BDF's presidency. Stritt was inclined to sympathize with feminist positions and organizations, and gave the radical wing space in the BDF's journal, as well as support within the BDF's executive committee.[4]

Under Stritt's aegis, the BDF began to support abolitionism and women's suffrage. A 1907 program issued by the BDF called not only for abolitionism and suffrage rights, but also for higher education for women, the reform of those sections of the Civil Code that regulated marriage, and an end to restrictions on female employment.[5] Besides lobbying within the BDF, feminists founded new organizations to effect change, including the German Union for Women's Suffrage, established in 1902. In 1906, the union was reaching the peak of its strength and influence, with most of its branches founded between 1906 and 1908.[6]

Abolitionism was at the core of the radicals' efforts, and was part of a larger international campaign launched by bourgeois women against state regulation of prostitution. Abolitionists sought to abolish laws such as the Contagious Diseases Acts in Britain, or paragraph 360 of the German penal code (the term was also intended to echo the use of the word "abolitionist" by earlier reformers who had worked to end slavery). These laws were passed by European governments trying to contain the spread of venereal disease in the nineteenth century; officials blamed prostitutes as the source of infection and tried to ensure a supply of healthy prostitutes for male clients through police regulation and medical supervision of prostitutes. Regulation laws allowed for compulsory medical examination of all women suspected by the police of being prostitutes. They also mandated that prostitutes be incarcerated in prison hospitals if found to have venereal disease, and authorized the administration of painful and sometimes lethal "therapies" for these diseases.[7] Male clients of prostitutes were neither examined nor treated. After their release from prison hospitals, these women were registered as prostitutes with the police and forced to submit to regular medical examinations. In Germany, local police departments regulated the lives of registered prostitutes, specifying those streets and areas where prostitutes could live and work. In some cities, such as Hamburg, the police established a system that gave a monopoly over regulated prostitution to brothel owners.[8]

Abolitionists, who created a variety of organizations across fin-de-siècle Europe to oppose this system of regulation, developed varied critiques of regulation; all of their attacks focused on the victimization of women by men. Indeed, abolitionists' arguments were based on a schema of sexual victimization, which operated on different levels, affecting diverse groups of women in different ways. Frequently, abolitionists argued, innocent young women were victimized by male seducers, who robbed virginal girls of their "honor," caused them to "fall," and then abandoned them (sometimes pregnant, or infected with venereal disease), often leaving these girls no alternative except prostitution. Abolitionists also argued that prostitutes were treated unfairly by the double standard embodied in regulation, which mandated forcible treatment for women but not for men. Another group of women victimized by regulation were the falsely accused; abolitionists wrote frequently of respectable women and girls who were taken for prostitutes by police, and then humiliated by an invasive medical examination. Sometimes, these women were even registered as prostitutes and had their reputations and livelihoods destroyed.[9]

Abolitionists argued that the system of legalized, regulated prostitution also victimized the wives of men who visited prostitutes. Regulation encouraged men to visit prostitutes because it offered a false sense of security from venereal disease and (especially in areas where brothels were legal) made prostitution more accessible. But since regulation did not end the spread of disease, male clients were often infected; in turn, they infected their wives, and even unborn children.[10]

Most nineteenth-century European abolitionists argued that prostitution should not be regulated by the state, but rather be ignored by officials. Prostitution, they argued, could be eliminated through educating young men to practice self-restraint, encouraging early marriages, and providing poor women with economic alternatives to prostitution. Since abolitionists opposed outlawing prostitution, they generally did not receive any support from religious conservatives, who viewed prostitution as a sin, warranting punishment.[11]

The abolitionist movement began in Britain with the creation of the Ladies' National Association, led by Josephine Butler, who became the movement's best-known leader. The British abolitionists' analysis included all of the different kinds of victimization just discussed. Judith Walkowitz, who has studied the British movement, argues that British abolitionists were so angry over prostitutes' victimization that they ultimately developed "a powerful identification with the fate of registered prostitutes." Their empathy and identification with prostitutes eventually led them to develop a sexual political analysis that criticized the sexual victimization of "respectable" women and prostitutes alike.[12]

Butler's is still the best-known abolitionist group, but the movement was not confined to Britain. Butler herself traveled across Europe, encouraging the formation of an international abolitionist network.[13] Movements in France, Italy, Britain, Germany, and other nations differed in the aspects of women's sexual victimization that were emphasized, but all of the women active in these movements wrote angrily of victimization.[14]

In Berlin, abolitionist leader Anna Pappritz evoked the entire schema of victimization outlined here in a pamphlet tellingly entitled *Herrenmoral*. Pappritz wrote that by refusing to "restrain" themselves, and by insisting on regulation to ensure a healthy "supply" of prostitutes,

these men systematically make women into the sexual slaves [*Lustsklaven*] of men. . . . regulation must remain useless so long as it includes only a minority of the infected, the prostitutes, while the much more dangerous man goes free, and is able to spread the disease further. The man is more dangerous because it is he who creates prostitution by creating the *demand*, and so he seduces previously innocent individuals and infects them, and in this way spreads the disease to circles which would naturally be quite removed from prostitution, that is, the circles of working women; these unhappy victims are often forced into prostitution through their infection while the man finally spreads the infection to his own wife and children.[15]

In Bremen, abolitionists mounted a campaign that also stressed women's victimization. Bremen feminists developed a sophisticated sexual political analysis of the women's position. These abolitionists came to see prostitution as being at the heart of the "woman question." They were passionately concerned with the fate of young women who could be arrested and forcibly examined by police and physicians, and even killed by murderous "treatments" for venereal disease (which sometimes involved dosing women with derivatives of mercury or arsenic), while the men who had seduced or infected these women went free. In 1909, the Bremen women's movement united against this legal harassment to submit a petition to the city authorities, which spoke angrily of the humiliation and degradation of women unjustly accused of prostitution and subjected to humiliating medical examinations. They also argued that regulation promoted white slavery.[16] In Hamburg, radical feminist Lida Gustava Heymann led a similar crusade against the victimization of prostitutes by police and brothel keepers in 1904 and 1905.[17]

Sexual victimization thus became the leitmotif of abolitionist campaigns led by radicals in other cities, and these women did not hesitate to accuse and confront men, especially the police and male-dominated state. In Hanover, however, such an approach would have been out of character for women leaders. In Hanover, clubwomen saw prostitution as yet another "social poison," a symptom of degeneration, and preferred to rely on their personal connections with officials, rather than public confrontations. The movement's work was done discreetly, and seldom came to public notice. Women's alliances flourished in the world of the committee meeting room, which was closed to the public. Women leaders had learned to rely on persuasion, connections, and consensus among women's associations, rather than on public debate and agitation. Above all, the Hanover movement presented a united front to the public, and this excluded open debates or controversy between clubwomen.

The movement's united front was exploded from the inside, however, at the end of 1906, when the festering issue of the regulation of prostitution was brought to the fore in public debates. In their work on other projects designed to combat social degeneration before 1906, clubwomen had enlisted the city government's support for programs that were intended to foster moral behavior among Hanover's working-class families. During the debate over the regulation of prostitution, however, women leaders tried to persuade the municipal government itself to enforce moral behavior; in effect, clubwomen attempted to force the city government to live up to their standards. Instead of enjoying the support of municipal authorities and men's organizations, the women's movement now had to oppose the local men's associations and politicians. Public controversy represented a departure from earlier tactics for local women leaders, and it ultimately led to fissures within the city's women's movement.

The social foundation for the 1906 controversy (and for abolitionist campaigns elsewhere) was the explosive growth of prostitution in Wilhelmine Germany and across Europe. This growth was a by-product of rapid urbanization and of the frequent economic contractions that characterized urban economies. Young women who were drawn to the cities often found only low-paid or seasonal work. They turned to prostitution when other work was unobtainable or, occasionally, prostituted themselves in order to supplement low wages or to support themselves when they were between jobs. Thus, for most of these young women, prostitution was often the best of a bad set of economic options; it was usually a temporary, pragmatic choice. The creation of a large market in prostitution was noted by many observers, some of whom estimated the population of prostitutes to be in the tens of thousands.[18]

The legal foundation for the 1906 debate lay in the contradictions within the penal code's regulation of prostitution. The federal laws that applied to prostitutes were not only impossible to enforce, but also enshrined a double standard of morality for the sexes and ignored religious values; as such, they inevitably became the subject of political controversy. Hanover was only one of many cities to witness local political struggles over the issue of prostitution. In every case, the roots of the conditions that aroused reformers' ire were traced to paragraphs 180 and 361 of the German penal code.

Paragraphs 180 and 361 provided the legal framework for German local authorities to regulate prostitution. Paragraph 361 protected prostitutes registered with the police from arrest, so long as they obeyed prostitution ordinances issued by local authorities and submitted to regular medical examinations. The other paragraph, 180, outlawed pandering, which was defined as "Regularly or for profit facilitating . . . or furthering fornication."[19] Since this broad definition could (and frequently was) interpreted to include renting to prostitutes, police were put in an awkward position. They were required to register and regulate prostitutes under paragraph 361, which implicitly guaranteed registered prostitutes the right to work unmolested by police. At the same time police departments that took paragraph 180 seriously would be obliged to prosecute those who rented to prostitutes or otherwise facilitated a prostitute's conduct of business.

A variety of local systems of regulation emerged within this contradictory framework. Local authorities could rely on voluntary registration by prostitutes, or they could track them down and compel them to register. Once registered, prostitutes could be allowed to work on any street not designated as forbidden, or (conversely) compelled to work only on certain streets, or forced to work only within brothels (as was the case in Hamburg).[20] A system of brothels sanctioned by the police, with a local monopoly on prostitution enforced by police, obviously came much closer to infringing upon paragraph 180 than any other system of regulation. Hanover authorities rejected licensed brothels, and instead relied upon a system of enforced registration of women identified by the police as prostitutes, with registered prostitutes forbidden access to specified streets and areas.

Although Hanover's regulations were more humane than Hamburg's brothel system, they still imposed a severe set of constraints on prostitutes; those who structured their lives in accordance with police regulations would have been invisible and isolated. They were forbidden to enter restaurants, cafés, theaters, circuses, and other places of amusement, forbidden to live with men or with other prostitutes, and forbidden to go outside after dark. They were not allowed to live or solicit on a long list of streets, or on any street near a church, school, hospital, or home of an "executive police official."[21] Over the years, many streets that had been legally accessible to prostitutes were successively placed on the forbidden list, after neighbors complained that prostitutes had "invaded" the neighborhood. Indeed, so many streets were forbidden to prostitutes that by 1902 a physician employed by the city complained that "sometimes it is really difficult for the girls to get from one street to another without crossing a forbidden area; if things continue as they are, soon . . . the girls will have to employ an airship" to report for their twice weekly medical examinations.[22] In practice, no prostitute could conform completely to regulations for very long. During the year 1900 (when 421 women were registered as prostitutes with Hanover police), prostitutes were arrested 1,831 times, usually for being caught on forbidden streets or for being out after dark.[23]

Until they moved, married, or found gainful employment, and could thus escape registration, the prostitutes who were on the police list were hemmed in by extensive regulations, subject to frequent harassment and arrest, and liable to hospitalization and dangerous "therapies" for venereal disease if they failed to pass a twice weekly medical examination. Regulation, however, was the fate of only a minority of Hanover's prostitutes. For every registered prostitute, it was estimated that there were three to five "free" prostitutes, women who had escaped police observation and registration.[24] Women who worked as prostitutes only occasionally to supplement low salaries (especially those in seasonal occupations), women who prostituted themselves but who could show that they were employed as barmaids or waitresses, or full-time prostitutes who were skillful at eluding police observation could all escape registration.[25] The system of registration thus trapped a minority of prostitutes, circumscribing their lives and probably contributing to the high turnover among registered prostitutes, but it did not deter the larger group of "free" prostitutes. Contemporaries estimated that approximately 1,000 women worked as unregistered prostitutes full- or part-time in Hanover around the turn of the century.[26]

There was a strong sentiment among some police officials, however, that there were not enough prostitutes, that Hanover in fact suffered from a shortage of prostitutes. In a series of meetings within the police department and between police and city officials held in 1901 and 1902, the police argued that "in relation to the number of inhabitants there are too few prostitutes in Hanover," especially too few "better" or "more respectable" prostitutes. This shortage had been caused by an overly strict enforcement of registration and of vice regulations, which had induced many prostitutes to leave Hanover. A "better class" of prostitutes had to be persuaded to return to the city; otherwise, police claimed, the number of crimes of indecent assault and sexual harassment of women would rise. The current situation was "untenable."[27]

Implicit in these internal debates between police and city administrators was a model of sexuality, especially male sexuality, that Martha Vicinus has characterized as the "energy-control model." This model "always defines sex as something to be released, or controlled; if controlled, it is sublimated or deflected or distorted."[28] According to this view, prostitution provided a necessary safely valve for male sexuality, which, if deprived of this "safe" outlet, might assume a more threatening, asocial form. Unfortunately for the police, this model of male sexuality contradicted religious norms, and the conclusion to which this view led them—that the city suffered from a "shortage" of prostitutes—would have outraged many of the town's leading citizens. Thus, the police could hardly proclaim their assessment of the situation publicly, and the need to act discreetly limited their attempts to lure more prostitutes to Hanover, since any substantial reform of vice regulations would attract public notice. In the end, the police settled for easing up on the enforcement of vice regulations in general.[29]

Whether the lax enforcement of regulations produced the desired increase in the number of prostitutes is impossible to say, but it certainly led to an increase in complaints lodged by neighborhood associations, demanding tighter police control of prostitution. Between 1903 and 1906, the police received petitions from churches, individuals, entire neighborhoods, and property owner associations claiming that their streets were "infested" with prostitutes: because prostitutes frequently shared apartments, police were tolerating brothels.[30]

The police were placed in a quandary, caught between the perceived need to ensure a steady supply of prostitutes and the difficulty of finding a place to put them. The situation came to a head in 1906 when several local businessmen, with the support of police officials, petitioned for the right to establish one street as a center for prostitution. The backers of this plan modeled their proposal on Bremen's Helenenstrasse, a walled-up, dead-end street containing twenty houses, each with opaque windows, within which all of Bremen's registered prostitutes were required to live. All of the buildings on Helenenstrasse were owned by one landlord, who was permitted to charge exorbitant rents, but whose stewardship was otherwise closely supervised by the police. Hanover police officials who supported the plan did not openly base their arguments on the need for a larger supply of prostitutes, and so stressed the plan's potential for bringing venereal disease under control through regular medical examinations of the confined prostitutes. This attempt to isolate prostitutes physically and geographically, and to regulate their medical treatment was called *Kasernierung* (literally, "putting them into barracks").[31] Initially, the plan was backed by police officials, who viewed it as a way to solve the irksome problem of how best to regulate prostitution and put an end to the chronic complaints lodged by the citizenry.

The attempt to pacify public opinion proved to be a serious miscalculation. The businessmen backing the plan were indiscreet, and word leaked to the press about the proposal before all of the buildings on the targeted street had been acquired. Newspaper accounts of the planned *Kasernierung* soon led to more controversy than the police had ever faced under the old system, as public opinion became polarized by the plan. For the next five months, hardly a week went by without a public assembly, a petition to the authorities, or an exchange of editorials in the press either for or against *Kasernierung*, as large numbers of men and women in Hanover were mobilized by two coalitions, one supporting and one opposing *Kasernierung*.

Although the coalition working against *Kasernierung* attracted some support from men (primarily from the clergy and the Association for the Improvement of Public Morals), it was essentially a coalition of women's organizations. Initially, the anti-*Kasernierung* alliance, which consisted of twenty-three women's associations, resembled other women's coalitions that had gone before it. It was led by the DEF and consisted of the same organizations that had worked together on other issues: the Catholic Women's League, several women teachers' associations, the Society for the Advancement of Female Education, the Female Friends of Young Girls, the Women's Educational Association, and others.[32]

There was a newcomer within the anti-*Kasernierung* alliance, however, an association that would ultimately challenge the DEF's domination of the 1906 coalition. The first protest meeting and petition against *Kasernierung* was organized by local feminists, a small group of women who did not belong to the "mainstream" organizations allied with the DEF; these feminists created a Hanover chapter of the International (Abolitionist) Federation—the organization that had been created by Josephine Butler and other English abolitionists.[33] The Hanover federation chapter was headed by Bertha Duensing and Adele Lessing. Lessing was the wife of a local physician; her son Theodor would become a well-known journalist and philosopher. Theodor Lessing supported his mother's activism and served as a speaker at one of the first federation meetings. The fact that Duensing, a temperance activist, was the only established local movement leader to join Lessing is not surprising; in other cities, such as Bremen, the two movements (abolitionism and temperance) also had overlapping membership. In Hanover, Bertha Duensing would become the chief spokesperson for the Abolitionist Federation.

The Hanover abolitionist chapter was founded about two weeks after knowledge of the *Kasernierung* became public by the same women who had established the Women's Welfare Association a year earlier: the city's small band of feminists. The welfare group was a local branch of Minna Cauer's organization, a leading association within the radical wing of the national movement. Before the *Kasernierung* debate opened, Hanover feminists had restricted themselves to discussing issues of the day that pertained to women within the Women's Welfare Association. They lacked the resources to launch any larger projects; compared to the DEF and other, more conventional women's associations, the Women's Welfare Association was small and lacked the personal connections to local politicians that could have helped feminists to obtain municipal funding for their proposals. In addition, feminist leaders lacked ties to more powerful, mainstream local women's associations; leaders of the Women's Welfare Association and other feminist organizations did not sit on the executive committees of local women's educational, charitable, or confessional associations.[34]

Besides being somewhat isolated, Hanover feminists, like all German feminists, also suffered from limitations that arose out of the very nature of the reforms they promoted. Most feminist goals, such as women's suffrage and the reform of the German Civil Code, could not be realized by work at the local level, but rather required the support of a majority within the Reichstag, a development that was very unlikely. The announcement of the *Kasernierung* plan thus came as a windfall for Hanover feminists; it gave them a concrete local question around which they could organize, an issue that would be decided locally and which Hanover feminists could therefore hope to influence.

The Abolitionist Federation was soon joined by the rest of the local women's movement, twenty-two women's organizations, including the local DEF; in this new controversy, DEF leaders were not inclined to abdicate leadership to local feminists. Together, the DEF and the federation led a broad coalition of women's organizations, which held mass meetings attended by hundreds of women, and which circulated and submitted several petitions to city officials.

The chief objection advanced by women's organizations against the *Kasernierung* of prostitutes (and indeed against the entire system of registration and regulation of prostitutes) was that the acceptance of prostitution as a "necessary evil"—which the police proposal (and paragraph 361) implicitly acknowledged—endorsed a double standard for men and women by ensuring men continued access to prostitutes. DEF leader Paula Mueller questioned "how we women are to understand the fact that . . . [conduct] which in one sex is seen as a natural, excusable weakness, in the other sex is condemned as vile depravity? And how are we to understand it when the state builds a protective wall around this vice . . . and itself sanctions and organizes vice?"[35] In a petition submitted to the city authorities, the women's coalition argued that the state and society must uphold a single, chaste standard of behavior for both sexes; the current system of regulation, they asserted, led to the "confusion of the people's conscience."[36]

The Hanover women's movement used the language and standards of religion, rather than those of the law, because the latter were not available to them, and perhaps not congenial. Under the German penal code, prostitution was legal, but German churches still regarded it as a sin. The leaders of the Hanover movement could therefore invoke religious support for their position when they could not obtain the support of the law. Moreover, religious terrain was probably more familiar and comfortable to these women than the language of the law.

The women's coalition also argued that *Kasernierung* would not halt the spread of venereal disease, because the majority of prostitutes were not regulated. Thus, they would continue to operate outside of the "controlled" area assigned to prostitutes and would not come under medical scrutiny. Finally, leaders of the women's alliance (primarily the feminist leaders of the federation) objected to *Kasernierung* because it would worsen the prostitutes' situation. In a petition written by federation leaders, the alliance argued that "the girls who are put in the brothels are branded as lost souls, and experience has shown that once a girl is interned in such a house, she cannot be influenced for the better, and return [to 'respectable' society]."[37] Petitions and memorandums written by DEF leaders showed less concern for the prostitutes. In speeches and petitions put forth by the united women's coalition, the denunciation of a state-sanctioned double standard and the denial of the efficacy of registration in controlling disease were always mentioned first, and stressed at much greater length than the negative impact of *Kasernierung* on prostitutes.

Thus, like abolitionists in Bremen and Hamburg, Hanover activists opposed regulation. The Hanover coalition's reasons and rhetoric resembled the analysis of abolitionists elsewhere, but only up to a point. Hanover women leaders, like abolitionists in Bremen and Hamburg, demanded that a single chaste standard of behavior be applied to both sexes. Like other abolitionists, the Hanover coalition showed some concern for the oppression of prostitutes that regulation entailed, although they did not identify with prostitutes as much as other abolitionists did.

However, the Hanover women's alliance could not, and did not, extend its criticism to men. It chose not to make use of the elaborate schema of sexual victimization developed by abolitionists elsewhere in Germany and in other nations. Unlike other abolitionists, the leaders of the Hanover movement did not argue that men were the cause of prostitution, that men ruined innocent girls, that prostitution was the sexual victimization of women by men. Compared with the abolitionist campaigns of radical feminists in Bremen and Hamburg, the theme of prostitutes as victims of men's lust and regulations played an insignificant role in the Hanover coalition's rhetoric.

Indeed, rather than accusing men of victimizing prostitutes, they instead complained that the police defense of prostitution as a "necessary evil" was an insult to men; it reflected, the women's alliance wrote, "a shameful estimation of men."[38] This final argument in fact turned the usual image of male sexuality presented in abolitionist rhetoric elsewhere on its head: rather than asserting that male sexuality was brutal or uncontrolled, Hanover women were (perhaps disingenuously) insisting that men were not as immoral as the police assumed.

The fact that Hanover abolitionists did not stress prostitutes' sexual victimization under regulation, and—linked to this—that they did not express anger toward men because women were being victimized, led to other contrasts between the Hanover coalition and abolitionists in Bremen, Hamburg, Britain, Italy, and France. Hanover women also chose not to use the other themes and images of sexual victimization that were staples in abolitionist rhetoric elsewhere: the "roundups" of innocent young girls by police officials who mistook them for prostitutes and forcibly registered these innocents; lives ruined by unfounded accusations; and married women infected with and destroyed by venereal disease, which their husbands acquired through contact with prostitutes.

Some of the themes that the Hanover movement ignored were not just abolitionist rhetorical devices; they spoke of actual threats to women, even to respectable bourgeois women. "Respectable" women, were, after all, sometimes falsely accused by police, and some married women were given venereal disease by their husbands.[39] Hanover abolitionists, however, did not speak of these very real threats in their campaign.

In addition, they omitted one of the most successful and lurid devices developed by their counterparts in other cities: the image of the young, virginal, lower-class girl, lured unwittingly into a life of prostitution with the complicity of police officials, and offered up to wealthy men as a "maiden tribute." The intersection of female victimization and class conflict contained in this image of the sexual exploitation of working-class girls by upper-class men proved especially explosive and useful in Britain; British abolitionists were able to use it to build alliances with working-class men in their repeal campaign, appealing to these men to work with middle-class women to protect "their" women.[40] Although there was no "maiden tribute" scandal in prewar Bremen, abolitionists there were also able to use this issue to build alliances with the SPD.

Abolitionists elsewhere used these images of victimization and class exploitation even though they knew that the working-class girls involved were not always virginal victims. Katharina Scheven, a leading Berlin abolitionist, realized that there often was no hard and fast boundary between promiscuity and transient prostitution. Many women, after all, had sex outside of marriage and even benefited materially from these relationships (in the form of food or clothing, for example), and yet did not consider themselves to be prostitutes. Scheven argued, however, that regulation trapped these young women, and thus did victimize them: "the state is degraded to the status of a chief procurer, because it uses forcible measures to turn women who have occasionally strayed, who were seduced or fell, into full-time prostitutes."[41] Abolitionists thus knew that the "maiden tribute" image was not, strictly speaking, always accurate. They nevertheless considered even "promiscuous" working women to be victims, and thus were willing to use this rhetorical device to gain support for their cause.

Hanover's women leaders could not use the "maiden tribute" theme as a means of winning allies, however, because this would have meant an attack on men of their own class. The clients of prostitutes were of course drawn from all social classes, and it would have been impossible to launch a critique of male clients that targeted only working-class men without also including bourgeois men who sought out prostitutes. Indeed, using the "maiden tribute" theme would have meant singling out wealthier men and exploiting class tensions. If the Hanover women's movement had pursued its attack against the men who frequented prostitutes, using all the levels of female sexual victimization caused by regulation as rhetorical weapons, its campaign ultimately could have led to a kind of rhetorical war between the sexes, similar to the all-out attacks launched by abolitionists elsewhere.[42] Bourgeois men could not have been excluded from such a campaign.

The Hanover women's movement had too many connections with, and received too much support from, the male politicians who ran the city: such an attack was apparently unthinkable. It would have disrupted the close ties that the movement's leaders had cultivated with local politicians, which ultimately might have threatened the many social welfare projects that the city was funding. In practice, moreover, alliances with working-class organizations over this issue would almost certainly have meant working with women and men from the socialist labor movement, and socialism was yet another "social poison" that Hanover's bourgeois women leaders shunned.[43] Thus the language of class, so eloquent and useful in abolitionist campaigns elsewhere, was silenced in Hanover. Instead, prostitution was analyzed almost exclusively within the framework of "social degeneration."

The Hanover women's movement was thus constrained in its discussion of prostitution, yet it still could not ignore the issue entirely, and certainly could not have overlooked the proposed *Kasernierung*. The women's leaders were deeply concerned about the spread of social degeneration and what they perceived as an increase in public immorality, and they simply could not countenance the creation of an established red-light district. Caught, therefore, between two imperatives—the need to work with local male leaders and the need to fight "immorality"—the Hanover movement developed arguments against *Kasernierung* that strikingly differed from the abolitionist movements in other areas that have been studied by historians.

The fact that Hanover abolitionists (unlike their counterparts in Bremen and Hamburg) did not see prostitution as merely the ultimate expression of female sexual victimization, and thus a paradigm for the position of all women, also made a difference in how they viewed the prostitutes themselves. In their speeches and writings, prostitutes were not depicted as unwilling victims, eager to be saved. Rather, the reclamation of prostitutes was admittedly disheartening work, which usually produced little in the way of results, since few prostitutes apparently *wanted* to be saved, at least by these bourgeois women. The Magdalenium run by the local movement, the only option offered by bourgeois women to prostitutes, was after all an institution that stressed hard labor and strict (even moralistic) religious reeducation. Paula Mueller had to remind her followers repeatedly that no matter how sparse the results, such *Rettungsarbeit* could not be abandoned; in a passage that hints at the unenthusiastic reception women in her organization received, she wrote hopefully that "perhaps a conversation that appears to make no impression [on the prostitute] will later exert an influence, just as many a half-forgotten passage from the Bible can work wonders, years later."[44] In private, Mueller was even more cynical about the prostitutes; in an internal memorandum, she complained about "the insolent behavior of the registered prostitutes."[45]

The fact that Hanover abolitionists did not identify with prostitutes, but rather wanted to promote chastity, was also reflected in the women's coalition's counterproposals for police policy. These proposals were less concerned with protecting prostitutes' (or suspected prostitutes') civil rights and physical integrity than they were with persuading the police to enforce a single, chaste standard of public behavior for both sexes. "In our opinion," Mueller and von der Groeben wrote the authorities, "the individual's morals cannot be regulated by police, who rather are obliged to safeguard *public* order and morality. . . . [We therefore urge] the most stringent punishment possible of all offenses against public order, decency, and morality, including those offenses committed by men as well as by women."[46] If the police had followed the women's alliance's proposals, prostitution would have been technically legal (since Hanover women could not single-handedly repeal paragraph 361 of the German penal code) but in practice impossible to pursue as an occupation in Hanover.

The police might not have agreed entirely with Mueller's proposals, but they evidently felt that it would be wise to consult with the DEF. Since the *Kasernierung* proposal had been announced in October, Mueller and other DEF leaders had been meeting in private with police and city officials, attempting to convince the authorities to negotiate a compromise. The police, surprised and disarmed by the controversy that their plan had aroused, were eager to find a more acceptable solution.[47] By December, they dropped their original plan and proposed instead merely to "localize" prostitution, restricting prostitutes to certain streets. This would have reversed the current rules; instead of being prohibited to live or work on some streets but permitted access to all others, prostitutes would have been permitted access only to designated streets and forbidden all others.[48] Even the localization plan, moreover, was subject to amendment and negotiation with the DEF.

The fact that Mueller and other DEF leaders were able to demand, and get, meetings with the chief of police, and the tone of these meetings—both sides repeatedly expressed their trust in each other, and sympathy for the other's position—reflect the extent to which the bourgeois women's movement had become intertwined with the local (masculine) political structure. As a part of these exchanges of opinion (and perhaps as a show of good faith), the chief of police had even turned over to Mueller copies of police internal records and memorandums. Meetings like these between radical abolitionists like Lida Gustava Heymann and the chief of the Hamburg police would have been simply unthinkable; indeed, Heymann engaged in repeated legal battles with the Hamburg police.[49] In Hanover, on the other hand, close cooperation between the women's movement and the police was the rule.

The police were not only troubled by the women's coalition, however. They were also coming under pressure from the opposing camp, a coalition of men's organizations that argued that the *Kasernierung* of prostitutes was precisely what was required to protect public order and decency. The pro-*Kasernierung* alliance was led by the Hanover Home and Property Owners' Association, the local chapter of the Society to Combat Venereal Diseases, and several neighborhood associations. This coalition claimed to speak for a large group of prosperous male citizens who, weary of the recurring problem of where to house prostitutes, saw *Kasernierung* as a good solution. Like their opponents, the pro-*Kasernierung* forces organized a series of public assemblies, at which they agitated for increased police regulation of prostitutes and passed resolutions urging city authorities to implement the proposed new system.[50]

In framing their arguments, leaders of men's organizations used the same model of male sexuality that police officials had implicitly relied upon in internal debates, the view that prostitution provided a "safety valve" for male sexual energy, which might otherwise assume asocial forms. The Property Owners' Association went even further in this line of argument, deducing that if men "naturally" needed access to prostitutes, then a certain percentage of women were "naturally" born to be prostitutes (3 percent was the figure mentioned, but the association did not cite any sources for this percentage). The Property Owners' Association accused women's organizations of ignoring the fact that "women born with an unalterable disposition to become prostitutes will inevitably, using a hundred excuses, desert good jobs, a steady income, and family ties in order to satisfy their sexual impulses and thereby serve the *necessary* function of protecting the purity of our daughters from seducers." Prostitutes were simply women who had been "born hot."[51]

Other members of the pro-*Kasernierung* coalition were not prepared to support this theory publicly, although many tacitly endorsed it. Police officials certainly had some sympathy (in private) for this line of reasoning; one vice-commissioner noted in an internal report that "sensual predisposition, reinforced by inadequate childhood training," rather than poverty, led to the choice of prostitution as a vocation.[52] However, police officials apparently felt that airing this conclusion in public would stir up too much controversy. In public, therefore, other leaders in the pro-*Kasernierung* alliance stressed only the need to control the spread of venereal disease.

The local branch of the Society to Combat Venereal Diseases, which was especially active in the pro-*Kasernierung* coalition, was particularly insistent on this point. The doctors who headed the society stressed repeatedly (in spite of evidence to the contrary) that they *could* correctly diagnose venereal disease in accused prostitutes, and that their "therapies," when forcibly applied to the *kasernierte* prostitutes, would stop the spread of venereal disease. These physicians ignored the women who challenged their authority by pointing out that treating women, while ignoring the disease in men, was futile; the public health problem posed by men who spread venereal disease was never addressed by the pro-*Kasernierung* alliance.

The venereal disease argument, unfortunately, was a rather weak reed to fall back upon. Women's organizations, as discussed already, could and did attack the efficacy of *Kasernierung* and regulation in this respect. The anti-*Kasernierung* alliance sponsored a public meeting (attended by over 1,000 men and women) at which a well-known physician discussed why regulation could not check the spread of sexually transmitted diseases, and how the proposed new system would even worsen the situation.[53]

A secondary argument advanced by *Kasernierung* supporters was the need to protect "decent" women from sexual harassment by men who might mistakenly take them for prostitutes by separating prostitutes from other women.[54] Leaders of the anti-*Kasernierung* alliance rejected this protection repeatedly and vehemently; "a true woman can take care of herself on the street," an abolitionist declared at a women-only mass meeting to "thunderous applause."[55] This was a rejection of the victimization motif at every level: Hanover abolitionists were asserting that they did not even need to be protected from men who mistakenly took them for prostitutes. The solution to this issue, the women were insisting, was to eliminate prostitution, rather than to segregate it.

Prostitutes themselves, however, apparently accepted the necessity of distinguishing themselves from "respectable" women; at least, they perceived that this necessity was one of the reasons why they were coming under pressure. In a petition sent by "several prostitutes" to the chief of police, they proposed that instead of *Kasernierung*, prostitutes should simply be allowed to walk the streets between 11 P.M. and 3 A.M. only; "in our opinion no respectable lady would then ever be molested again," they wrote, "since such a woman would never go out late at night without an escort." In practice, this proposal would have been an improvement: instead of being hemmed in by regulation about "restricted areas," they would have been given the freedom of the streets for at least a few hours each night. Furthermore, this would have put prostitutes on a schedule, or "clock," that was the precise inverse of the hours when "respectable" women were permitted to go outdoors. The city would have been formally divided, geographically and temporally, to reflect a dualistic view of women. In any case, the petitioners asked for a clear resolution to the currently ambiguous situation, "because we are human beings, too, and at times do not know where we are to lay our heads down."[56]

Unfortunately for the prostitutes, the debate over regulation of prostitution could not be resolved so easily. As months went by and ever larger public meetings were held on the subject, both sides began to cast aside conventions of dignity and politeness. Opponents attended and disrupted meetings held by the other camp, challenging speakers. The open expression of anger in public meetings and the face-to-face confrontation between men and women in debates were unique in the history of the Hanover women's movement, and unusual for German bourgeois political culture.[57]

Both sides came to vent their anger in the form of satirical humor as well as in formal debate. Supporters of *Kasernierung* singled out unmarried leaders of women's organizations, sarcastically naming them "benefactors of the world [*Weltbeglückerinnen*]" and urging them to seek success "in other areas where they may better find happiness and joy . . . remembering the [scriptural] Word: 'it is not good that man should be alone!' "[58] In the other camp, *Kasernierung* opponents targeted male clients of prostitutes. One speaker urged ironically (at a women's-only meeting) that if prostitutes were indeed eventually interned in a dead-end street, then police should be required to take the names of all men who entered. Another group in the anti-*Kasernierung* coalition announced in the press that it had begun taking photographs of all men entering known houses of prostitution on a certain street; "the photographs give a good likeness of the clientele [they wrote] . . . and will be forwarded to the police."[59]

By January 1907, anger, confrontation, and public meetings—especially "mixed" meetings attended by both men and women where questions of sexuality were discussed—created fissures within the women's alliance. DEF leaders were increasingly uncomfortable with the tone of the anti-*Kasernierung* campaign and attempted to head off further public debate. In addition, in their meetings with local officials DEF leaders had promised the chief of police that, in return for changing his proposal from *Kasernierung* to localization (and for delaying even localization, subject to consultation with DEF leaders), the DEF would try to limit public debate.

Mueller could not cite this reason in her discussions with feminist federation leaders, however, since DEF negotiations with the police had been conducted in secret. Instead, in private meetings with Bertha Duensing, Mueller somewhat disingenuously objected that in mixed meetings women were apt "to overstep the boundaries of decency beyond which they ought not to go [in public]" and thereby made a bad impression upon men. The DEF's objections were dismissed by Duensing, who countered that "the comingling of men and women in such meetings has a moralizing effect" and that in any case "we cannot handle this matter with kid gloves."[60] The federation proposed to continue holding public meetings, with or without DEF support. Mueller and von der Groeben kept their promises to the police; after January 1907, the DEF worked to minimize public debate and unrest, gradually withdrawing from the leadership and organization of public meetings, and eventually from the women's coalition itself. With the loss of the DEF and other mainstream women's organizations, the women's coalition fell apart.[61]

Despite the wishes of mainstream women leaders, however, the federation continued to hold public meetings on the topic, inviting well-known feminists from the radical wing of the national movement, such as Anita Augspurg, to speak in Hanover. By March, Mueller began to attack this continuing publicity in meetings of her own organization. In April, this split surfaced in the local press. In an exchange of letters to the editor, Paula Mueller criticized the abolitionists' tactics, repeating the DEF's claim that women ought to limit their discussion of moral issues in "mixed" meetings. "Given the current situation in Hanover," she concluded, "it can serve no further purpose to discuss these issues in public." Hanover abolitionists declared in response that they would continue to hold public assemblies. "We view the goals and purposes of the [Abolitionist] Federation from far too lofty a standpoint," they wrote, "for [our] dignity to be injured by any possible inappropriate comments made by members of the audience."[62] After this exchange, all cooperation between the DEF and local feminists was at an end.

This split did not lead to the defeat of the women's alliance, however. In the end, police did not implement even the plan to localize prostitution, and the entire debate sputtered out in a stalemate between the two opposing coalitions. Prostitutes in Hanover continued to live and work under the old system. This outcome was due to several factors: divisions between the organizations in the pro-*Kasernierung* coalition, advantages that the DEF had in dealing with the police, and the unwillingness of police to provoke additional opposition and debate.

The head of the police department, fearful that additional uproar might cost him his job, had made it clear in his meetings with DEF officers that he would only authorize localization if his subordinates could propose streets where the neighbors would not object to living next to prostitutes. Not surprisingly, no such street could be found. The pro-*Kasernierung* neighborhood and property owners' associations, united in their support for some kind of geographical segregation of prostitutes, each rejected the idea of locating prostitutes in *its* neighborhood. The neighborhood associations soon began to bicker among themselves over which neighborhoods were to be "sacrificed."[63] Faced with the certain prospect of even more publicity and protest if they continued with their plan, police ultimately dropped all new proposals. Although the old system of regulation had definite drawbacks, keeping it was easier than forcing the introduction of a new system.

The anti-*Kasernierung* alliance had also contributed to the final, stalemated outcome. By generating publicity and petitions against *Kasernierung*, the coalition had helped make any change too costly for police to consider. The DEF had contributed in more subtle ways, drawing on its value to the city and its ties to top city and state officials in order to influence the police and local administrators. Their opponents recognized this fact. By February 1907, property owners' associations lamented openly that women leaders had been able to influence the *Regierungspräsident* against *Kasernierung*, which doomed the proposal.[64]

Ultimately, even the DEF had only enough resources to stave off *Kasernierung* and localization. The system of registration and regulation of prostitutes was never seriously challenged in Hanover; it was based on a federal law (paragraph 361), which women's associations were not powerful enough to have repealed. Even so, local women's associations were able to prevent the introduction of a much more repressive system of regulation. Furthermore, Hanover was not the only German city in which women's organizations were able to influence local systems of vice regulation; after 1902, the women's movement was able to prevent the introduction of the brothel system into any additional German cities.[65]

Throughout the *Kasernierung* campaign, women's associations from different wings of the local movement, both the feminist federation and the more conservative DEF and its allies, were unified in their analyses and proposals. They agreed on the causes of prostitution, advanced the same objections to regulation and *Kasernierung*, and jointly supported an agenda that would have sought to eradicate prostitution entirely. Even the Hanover branch of the federation (the national abolitionist organization, which frequently used the rhetoric of victimization, and which was affiliated with Butler's association) rejected a campaign based on a schema of victimization.

The Hanover women's alliance split ultimately not over principles but over tactics. Serious differences emerged during the course of the *Kasernierung* campaign between feminists and other women's associations over issues of political style and strategy. The leaders of the DEF and their allies within the women's coalition had trained themselves to function within the world of "nonpartisan" local politics. Rather than join a political party or agitate publicly for their goals, leaders of mainstream women's organizations preferred to apply quiet pressure on the established local political structure: they pulled strings and worked with officials whom they knew through their earlier projects and through familial ties. Their goal was the creation of a women's sphere within local politics, a nonpartisan realm within which bourgeois women had jurisdiction over all issues concerning women and children.

Hanover feminists, on the other hand, embraced a political style that stressed work within the public sphere rather than pressure applied behind the scenes. Open debate and agitation, they argued, would serve to educate the public and, if enough followers were attracted, would eventually force the authorities to yield to feminist demands. The feminist political style was willing to court public confrontations with opponents and was not "neutral" in party politics: local feminists would eventually ally themselves with Hanover's progressive liberals. The overall difference between feminists and other women's associations in political style and organizational tactics was reflected on many levels, but is perhaps best captured in one small detail: although the DEF, Catholic Women's League, and Patriotic Women's Association never advertised their meetings in advance in the press, preferring to mail individual invitations to members, the abolitionists and the Women's Welfare Association regularly advertised, and their announcements usually invited "all interested persons" to attend.

The mainstream of the local movement would carry forward its position in the 1906 campaign, by continuing to crusade against immorality, social degeneration, and socialism; women leaders would also continue to work in private, using their connections with officials. Over time, the DEF and other women's groups developed a variety of social programs that, drawing upon the city government's support, employed both coercion and persuasion to regulate and reform the sexual behavior of their fellow citizens.

One example was the work of the Cartel to Combat Public Moral Decay, which the DEF founded in 1908 in conjunction with a men's morality association and many of the other women's associations (especially women's teachers' groups) that had been involved in the anti-*Kasernierung* coalition. The cartel was initially created to oppose the spread of "trashy literature" (*Schund- und Schmutzliteratur*), but its jurisdiction grew steadily. It was tireless in its surveillance of public morals. The cartel tried to persuade local booksellers not to display suggestive or trashy publications, and its definition of "trashy" was broad and vague, including not only periodicals such as *Simplicissimus* but also ten-Pfennig Buffalo Bill westerns and popular romances. The cartel also collected newspaper advertisements for abortionists (who advertised as masseuses or fortune-tellers); packets of such clippings were sent to local newspaper publishers along with threats to organize subscriber boycotts if these advertisements continued to appear. This tactic was usually successful, but the cartel did not hesitate to call on allies within the police department and city government to pressure recalcitrant booksellers and newspapers. It also maintained a file on local cinemas that admitted children, with an eye to developing a municipal ordinance which would restrict the admission of minors to some types of films. No item was so small that it was beneath the cartel's notice: it sent representatives to local art exhibitions to ascertain whether all of the pictures on display were suitable for children, and checked the books on the shelves in the train station's waiting rooms.[66]

The 1906 campaign thus had several consequences for the local women's movement. It became a focus for the mobilization of Hanover's bourgeois women, but it was also a fulcrum that divided the women's movement over tactics. The *Kasernierung* debate led to the establishment of local chapters of explicitly feminist organizations, such as a suffrage group, but these associations remained a tiny minority within the local women's movement. For the bulk of the local movement, the 1906 campaign was part of a series of programs that tried to suppress all forms of extramarital sexuality. This was a natural result of the women's alliance's arguments, which had avoided criticizing bourgeois men and the victimization of women by regulation: from the beginning, the movement had been more concerned with the spread of vice and social decay than it had been with the sexual exploitation of women.

In contrast to the crusades mounted by the radical wing of the women's movement in other cities, the Hanover campaign for the abolition of regulation was not fueled by anger at the sexual victimization of women by men; Hanover women were constrained from accusing men because of their long-standing ties to a bourgeois male political establishment. Instead, their analysis was articulated as part of a larger agenda that sought to preserve bourgeois hegemony through combating social decay and the spread of immorality. Hanover clubwomen developed a distinct sexual political analysis of the relations between men and women that was heavily influenced by the fear of social degeneration and the growth of socialism. In the campaign against men's regulation of prostitution, however, this analysis conflicted with, and was constrained by, feelings of class solidarity and previously existing alliances with bourgeois men. It is possible that in this respect, the Hanover women's movement was representative of local women's movements in other German provincial cities; the DEF archive has records of other abolitionist campaigns that resemble the Hanover debate more closely than they do the struggles in Hamburg or Bremen.[67]

The difference in tactics that emerged during the *Kasernierung* campaign between local feminists and mainstream clubwomen was carried over into the Hanover women's movement as a whole after 1906. Local feminists such as Bertha Duensing and Adele Lessing would go on to found chapters of other feminist organizations, including an association for women's suffrage. In their new organizations, they continued to use the tactics employed during the 1906 debates: publicity, public education, and debate. These tactics had seemed to work once (there is no evidence that the federation ever learned of DEF meetings with police) and were employed repeatedly in support of other goals. Later feminist organizations, however, never enjoyed as much support or success as they had achieved during the *Kasernierung* campaign; feminist groups constituted only a tiny fringe of the local women's movement after 1906.

In the eyes of DEF officers and the leaders of other mainstream women's associations, on the other hand, the *Kasernierung* debate had confirmed the efficacy of working within the local political structure; they never collaborated in public debate or protest again. For feminists, the 1906 campaign was supposed to be only the first of a series of local projects that would further the feminist agenda. For the bulk of the city's clubwomen, however, the *Kasernierung* controversy had only been one battle in the larger crusade against social degeneration. It had been a successful battle, but it had led to divisions within the local women's movement, a fissure that would deepen over the years.

T he *Kasernierung* campaign gave Hanover feminists a taste for activism, and between 1906 and 1910 they founded local chapters of other feminist organizations. They created a feminist wing within the Hanover women's movement and allied themselves with progressive liberal men. During the same period nationalist women created their own local associations, antithetical to feminist organizations. At first glance, feminists and nationalist women would seem to have little in common: their demographic profiles and their goals were almost mutually exclusive. Nationalist women and feminists, however, developed similar political styles. Both groups chose to work publicly, and both allied themselves with men's organizations. In so doing, they broadened the political spectrum of the local women's movement, and constituted its right and left wings.

The movement's left wing emerged first. By mid-1907, local feminists had begun to consider other projects besides abolitionism. Once it became clear that the police were indeed going to retain the old system of vice regulation, the local abolitionists lost momentum, met less frequently, and ultimately dissolved the Hanover abolitionist chapter; the same women moved on to other causes. Local feminists shifted to work within the Hanover League for the Protection of Motherhood (Bund für Mutterschutz), and in 1910 created a chapter of the German Union for Women's Suffrage (Deutscher Verband für Frauenstimmrecht). The feminist wing of the local movement now included three organizations: the Women's Welfare Association, the League for the Protection of Motherhood, and the suffrage group.

Hanover feminists continued to rely on publicity, public education, and debate in order to achieve their goals. Local feminists were unable to attract the publicity and audiences that they had drawn during the *Kasernierung* debate, however, because they were unable to find another local issue that related to feminist concerns and goals. In addition, they were unable to attract recruits from the rest of the local women's movement, because feminists had broken with other women's organizations over the issue of public debate during the *Kasernierung* campaign. Feminists' estrangement from the mainstream of the local movement was reflected in the 1907 report of the Women's Welfare Association to its national leadership; it claimed defiantly that "our association, in spite of many difficulties that arise from its isolated position [in Hanover], has continued to work to spread progressive ideas."[1]

It was in fact difficult for Hanover feminists to translate these ideas into any praxis locally, which might have attracted new members. The Suffrage Union, for example, aimed at a goal—votes for women—that could only be realized through success at the national level, within the Reichstag. Within Hanover, local feminists concluded that all that could be done was educational work. Hanover Suffrage Union meetings, therefore, hosted speakers who laid out basic arguments in favor of women's suffrage and gave encouraging reports on other nations where women had already won the right to vote.[2]

The Hanover chapter of the League for the Protection of Motherhood, which was founded as an auxiliary of the local Women's Welfare Association, was also limited in its scope; its modest projects were a far cry from the ambitious program of reform envisioned by the league's national leaders. The national League for the Protection of Motherhood had been created in 1904 when a splinter group of radical feminists, alienated by the growing influence of Anna Pappritz and other abolitionist moderates, had seceded from the national Abolitionist Federation. The league espoused ideas that the "moderate" wing of the women's movement could not stomach. It asserted that women, like men, ought to be free to pursue sexual and emotional fulfillment, both within and outside of marriage. The league supported women's right to abortion, contraception, and extramarital sexuality; it argued that unwed mothers ought to be assisted by the state and treated as the social equals of married mothers. The league called its vision of sexual relations the New Morality (*neue Ethik*); its program established it as one of the most radical organizations within the German women's movement.[3] Its ideas drew frequent attacks from more conservative women's groups, especially the DEF.

Besides educating the public about the New Morality through its journal and assemblies, the concrete work of the league consisted of assisting unwed mothers, whom the league saw as victims of outmoded prejudice. League volunteers worked with unwed mothers, advising them or even providing them with lodgings and financial support. Most of the projects that assisted pregnant single women were undertaken by provincial chapters of the league while the Berlin national headquarters focused on propaganda, disseminating the principles of the New Morality. The Hanover chapter, for example, was unable to establish a permanent home for unwed mothers (such as the DEF's), but did offer advice to pregnant single women.

Within a few years, this division of labor had created a split within the organization. Members of many provincial league branches saw the work with unwed mothers as the league's raison d'être and resented the negative publicity stirred up by the activities of the Berlin office. Some of the league's national leaders, on the other hand, claimed that provincial leaders ignored the ideas behind the New Morality; they feared that chapters outside of Berlin were in danger of degenerating into mere social welfare associations.[4]

The league, a radical organization within the larger German women's movement, was thus itself divided between radicals and moderates. This split mirrored developments within other German feminist associations. The radical wing of the women's movement was generally held to consist of the Abolitionist Federation, the Women's Welfare Association, the League for the Protection of Motherhood, and the Suffrage Union, and yet each of these organizations contained moderate and radical factions.

The moderate faction within the Abolitionist Federation, led by Berlin abolitionist Anna Pappritz, eventually gained the upper hand in that organization. Lida Gustav Heymann and Anita Augspurg, who had led the Hamburg abolitionist radicals in a fierce and controversial campaign against that city's brothel system between 1900 and 1905, were gradually outmaneuvered and outnumbered by Pappritz and her followers. Most of the radicals withdrew from the Abolitionist Federation and devoted themselves to work within the League for the Protection of Motherhood and the Suffrage Union after 1908.[5]

The Suffrage Union, too, was divided; it ultimately fissured into no less than three separate organizations. The first splinter group demanded universal suffrage for all adult men and women. The second, more conservative, wanted to retain the property requirements that limited citizens' suffrage rights in many areas of the German Empire, but sought to extend the franchise to women who met these requirements. The third organization sought to bridge the gap between these two positions.[6] Taken as a whole, the radical, feminist wing of the German women's movement was divided and weakened by 1908, and had lost the commanding position within the BDF it had enjoyed only a few years earlier.

In the case of each association just discussed, Hanover feminists could be ranked with the moderate feminists. The local abolitionist chapter advanced arguments that matched Anna Pappritz's willingness to employ police coercion against prostitutes, a position vehemently rejected by the radical Hamburg abolitionists. The Hanover chapter of the League for the Protection of Motherhood was oriented toward social welfare work with unwed mothers and not propaganda. There is in fact evidence that some of the Hanover league officers explicitly rejected the New Morality ideology of the Berlin organization. The Hanover branch never joined the national league directly, but instead was affiliated with the local Women's Welfare Association.[7] Finally, after the national Suffrage Union had divided into splinter groups, the Hanover chapter affiliated with the more conservative organization, which did not demand the abolition of the Prussian three-class suffrage system.[8] Hanover feminists may have seemed radical to the rest of the local women's movement, but they were moderates within the context of the national feminist wing of the BDF. Just as the Hanover "radicals" were more moderate than nationally known feminists such as Anita Augspurg, so too the Hanover movement overall stood to the right of the BDF national leadership, which was dominated by the radical wing before 1908.

Hanover feminists thus could not be compared with radical feminist leaders like Lida Gustav Heymann and Helene Stöcker, but this fact did not placate local DEF leaders, who consistently sought to undermine the city's feminists after 1907. The DEF's main target was the Hanover League for the Protection of Motherhood. Paula Mueller and her associates saw the city's league chapter as the local embodiment of the New Morality, a set of proposals that was anathema to the DEF. Since the local league was an auxiliary of the Hanover Women's Welfare Association, the welfare group also came under attack by the DEF. The DEF distributed pamphlets denouncing the New Morality, and Mueller gave public lectures assailing the league and all its works. In addition, the DEF saw to it that the Women's Welfare Association was prevented from joining the Cartel to Combat Injuries to Public Morals, because it was

Table 8.1. A Social Profile of 18 Hanover Feminist Activists, ca. 1906

Marital Status	Confession	Husband's/Father's Occupation
Married: 11	Protestant: 5	Academic professional: 7
Single: 4	Jewish: 3	Businessmen: 2
Widowed: 3	Catholic: 2	White-collar employee: 2
	Unknown: 8	Military officer: 1
		Unknown: 3
		Female professional: 3[a]

Note: For a discussion of sources and methods, see the appendix.
a. A teacher, a dentist, and a *Naturheilerin*.

affiliated with the league, even though the latter was in the process of leaving the national League for the Protection of Motherhood. In the eyes of DEF leaders, any cooperation with local feminists, even over issues where they shared a common analysis, was simply out of the question.[9]

The DEF campaign against local feminists helps to explain feminists' social profile. Hanover's feminist associations are examples of organizations in which the membership profiles were clearly influenced by the associations' policies. In the case of local feminists, their memberships were influenced in a negative sense by their work, since their rhetoric and agenda ultimately made them the target of a campaign to discourage civil servants' wives or daughters from joining.

An examination of the Hanover feminists' social profile makes it clear that they were bourgeois but lacked the plentiful ties to civil servants and politicians that characterized the members of mainstream women's associations. At any given time between 1906 and 1908, between 40 and 75 women belonged to the three local feminist groups discussed here, a tiny percentage of the approximately 2,000 women who belonged to local bourgeois women's associations; only 18 women held positions as feminist leaders during these years. A social profile of these eighteen feminist activists is given in Table 8.1.

Hanover's feminists were generally drawn from the "better classes" and were dominated by *gebildete* women. Three of the women were professionals in their own right, and seven of the remaining fifteen were the wives of doctors or lawyers (that is, "free" professionals, without ties to the state). Local feminists were also predominantly women who were or had been married; only four of the eighteen were single, forming a strong contrast to the high percentage of unmarried activists in more mainstream organizations. The feminists' social profile resembled that of local temperance activists; both groups consisted largely of women from the educated bourgeoisie who were or had been married.

In fact, several of these feminist activists also belonged to Bertha Duensing's protemperance Women's Association for the People's Welfare. The overlap between feminist and temperance activists was not unique to Hanover; Elisabeth Meyer-Renschhausen has found that the same affinity existed in Bremen. This was because many temperance activists were motivated by a conviction that men's consumption of alcohol (women generally did not drink) led many husbands to abuse their wives and children, and to waste money on drinking while their families suffered. In some cities, temperance leaders were led by this analysis to also denounce domestic violence and even marital rape. For many women, temperance was thus a way to fight a form of masculine injustice, and some of these activists would have also been predisposed to join other women's groups that fought male oppression, namely, feminist associations.[10]

Apart from the links to temperance organizations, Hanover's feminists were largely isolated from the mainstream of the local movement; these eighteen activists were not part of the overlapping, criss-crossing network of memberships that characterized the bulk of Hanover's clubwomen. The only exceptions were two Jewish activists, Toni Bensey and Bertha Friedenreich, who also belonged to Jewish charitable associations; perhaps Jewish clubwomen were more tolerant of feminist affiliations than DEF members.

The religious affiliation of ten of the eighteen women could be ascertained, and only five of these were Protestant. The remaining five consisted of two Catholics and three Jewish women—Adele Lessing, Friedenreich, and Bensey—who held most of the top leadership positions in the local Women's Welfare Association and Abolitionist Federation.

In contrast to more established women's associations, none of the eighteen came from civil servants' families; this meant that Hanover feminists lacked the personal ties to local government that the DEF and other mainstream groups enjoyed, and exploited. The DEF itself was probably partially responsible for this fact. Its public attacks on the league and its parent organization, the Women's Welfare Association must have gone far to lower the reputation of local feminist associations in Hanover's elite circles, which included the families of high-level civil servants. This campaign against local feminists was reinforced in 1908, when a small group of high-level civil servants (probably prompted by Paula Mueller) began to discourage the wives of civil servants from joining the league or the Women's Welfare Association.[11] So far as can be determined, they were successful: in Hanover, civil servants' wives and daughters did not join feminist groups.

The DEF's animosity toward the local League for the Protection of Motherhood was only one part of its larger campaign against the entire radical wing of the BDF. On the national level, the DEF worked within the BDF to minimize the influence of German feminists; indeed, the DEF had joined the BDF in 1908 primarily in order to strengthen the BDF's moderate wing and to undermine the radicals. In 1909, the DEF was instrumental in securing the rejection of the national League for the Protection of Motherhood, which had applied to join the BDF; this mirrored the rejection and isolation of the league chapter within the Hanover movement. The rejection of the league's application was a turning point in the history of the BDF; it ultimately led to the resignation of BDF president Marie Stritt, who had been sympathetic to feminists, and her replacement by the more conservative Gertrud Bäumer. The accession of Bäumer marked the completion of the BDF's turn to the right. Now, the Hanover movement no longer stood to the left of the national movement's leadership; instead, the BDF's executive committee now reflected the rhetoric and style of the movement at the grass-roots level in Hanover.[12]

The DEF did not comment on the emergence of another group of women's associations, created around the same time that local feminist organizations were established: nationalist women's groups. In Hanover, nationalist women's associations were created as auxiliaries to two masculine nationalist organizations, the Navy League and the German Colonial Society.

Nationalist women's associations were allied with, but not at the heart of the world of Wilhelmine patriotic societies, which Roger Chickering refers to as "the German-national public realm—a realm defined by consensus on a broad range of issues and a commitment to defending a common set of national symbols."[13] These issues and symbols included support for military preparedness, a naval buildup, the pursuit of empire, the preservation of the language and ethnic identity of Germans living outside the empire, and a broad defense of "national interests," which incorporated vehement antisocialism. Besides the Navy League and the Colonial Society, the German-national public realm during this period included the Pan-German League, the German Army League, the German School Association, the German Language Association, and the Eastern Marches Society.

The men in these organizations generally opposed women's public activism, but many of them came to see the usefulness of women's auxiliaries to their associations. Women, after all, could pay dues, buy tickets to public lectures that might otherwise go unsold, and recruit their male relatives for the cause. Over time, the German-national realm expanded to include a limited role for women, and a subordinate one, consisting largely of charitable work. It was nevertheless a toehold for women in a domain, national defense and foreign policy, that was supposed to be the proper concern of men alone.[14]

In some of these organizations, the work that women did was an extension of conventional charitable work. The chief focus of the women's auxiliary to the Eastern Marches Society, for example, was to provide relief for sick, orphaned, or impoverished Germans in the eastern provinces of Prussia. Women in western chapters raised money through teas, dances, and other conventional means; the funds were then distributed by the women in the eastern chapters.[15]

In Hanover, only two patriotic organizations established successful women's auxiliaries: these were the Women's Navy League (Flottenverein deutscher Frauen) and the Women's Division of the Colonial Society (Frauenbund der Deutschen Kolonialgesellschaft). Both associations had membership profiles that were just the opposite of those of feminist groups. While feminist groups (thanks in part to the DEF) were in disrepute among civil servants' families, nationalist women's groups, although they were more aggressively partisan and were much smaller than mainstream women's associations, were still respectable.

One dozen women activists from these nationalist organizations were identified from surviving sources; almost all were wives or daughters of high-level civil servants or officers. Seven of these activists were single, while three were married and two were widows.[16] The presence of civil servants' wives and daughters among nationalist activists, and their absence among feminists, reflected the fact that jingoism, even when it came from women, was more *salonfähig* than feminism. These membership profiles, moreover, mirrored those of their masculine counterparts: this was hardly surprising, since many women members were wives or daughters of members of masculine patriotic groups.

Unlike feminist activists, moreover, these nationalist leaders were linked to the mainstream of the local movement through overlapping memberships with other organizations. Four of these nationalist activists were also members (and, in some cases, officers) of women's charitable associations; three belonged to local women's educational associations, while two more were active in (Protestant) confessional associations. The overlap between nationalist women and the local movement also included some overlap with organizations that were affiliated with the "official" women's movement, the BDF.

One woman who exemplified the overlap between the "official" women's movement, the broader local mainstream movement, and the world of nationalist clubwomen was Elsbeth Spiegelberg, a banker's wife. Head of the local Women's Navy League, she also sat on the executive board of its national organization. At the same time, Spiegelberg belonged to the local DEF and a women's group that ran a day-care center, and was an officer of the Women's Club; the DEF and Women's Club were affiliated with the BDF. Spiegelberg was also one of the patrons of the local girls' *Gymnasium*. One of her fellow officers in the day-care group—part of the local movement's mainstream—was Ida von Kortzfleisch, who also belonged to the Women's Division of the Colonial Society. Kortzfleisch later became a nationally known advocate for the emigration of German women to African colonies, and founded a school to help train women for the colonies.

The Women's Division of the Colonial Society pursued goals that—although not charitable—could be seen as falling within the proper sphere of bourgeois women, but which still gave members a whiff of adventure, since they forged a connection between stay-at-home women and the "untamed wilderness." The Women's Division was created in 1910 to match young women who desired to emigrate to South West Africa with respectable colonial families that needed female servants; in a sense, this was thus an extension of the organized servant recruitment that clubwomen already were engaged in at home. The division paid for a young woman's passage if she committed herself to a minimum stay of two years.

The goal in supplying these servants was twofold. First, the division hoped by supplying German nurses and nannies, it could minimize the contact that settlers' children had with African servants, so that the children would be raised according to German customs and values, preserving their national identity. Second, the majority of these women, it was hoped, would marry German settlers, and thus prevent widespread intermarriage between male settlers and African women; "racial mixing" was viewed as an abomination, and something that could be averted by the presence of an appropriate supply of German women. The division's masculine counterpart, the German Colonial Society, fully approved and supported this agenda.[17]

For the women at home, this work had several rewards. Membership in the Women's Division was socially respectable, since it carried the imprimatur of patriotism; the goals of the division transcended traditional charity, although they were still conventionally feminine; and members were given the illusion that they were connected to the colonial experience. In lectures and publications, members were told how the women whom they sent to South West Africa created "German households . . . under the open skies."[18]

Hanover's chapter of the German Women's Navy League, founded at the end of 1905, had a more problematic relationship with its masculine counterpart. Other women's patriotic associations were able to complement their masculine affiliates by pursuing charitable activities, or (as in the Colonial Society) goals that were still an extension of bourgeois women's accepted role. The women affiliated with the Navy League, however, wanted to reach a "great goal": to raise enough money to finance the building of a warship for the German Navy. In order to reach this goal, each member of each chapter was given a small savings bank, shaped like a warship, into which she was to deposit part of her household allowance each month; in addition, local chapters held fund-raising teas, dances, and plays.[19] In effect, this group was attempting to broaden the sphere of public activism allowed to women in the German-national public realm.

Raising enough money to pay for a warship was deemed unrealistic and undesirable by the men's organization; indeed, the sum required could never have been raised by the women. The leaders of the Navy League repeatedly urged the Women's Navy League to confine itself to educating working-class women to be patriotic. If the Women's Navy League insisted on raising money, Hanover Navy League leaders urged that the women finance the outfitting of a hospital ship; hospital ships were a much more suitable interest for women than warships.[20]

The leaders of the Women's Navy League rejected this suggestion with some heat and persisted in their plans to finance their own warship. In effect, they were rejecting a sexual division of labor in patriotic activism. Their persistence earned them considerable ridicule in the local press; the pro-Guelph *Deutsche Volkszeitung* was especially sarcastic in its reports on the women's league, predicting that "the present generation will hardly live long enough to see the realization of this project. . . . this warship, which is currently located up on the moon, will not be fetched down from there until A.D. 3000 or 4000."[21]

The Women's Navy League staged numerous fund-raising events to raise money for the warship, including the production of a play. "Hail Germany's Fleet!" which had been written by a league member. One of the city's leading newspapers, the *Hannoverscher Anzeiger*, printed a review of the play that reflected the patronizing tone that characterized most newspaper reports on the Hanover league chapter. "It must be admitted," the reviewer wrote, "that the authoress brought intentions quite worthy of praise and a very respectable patriotic fervor to her task, which was to impress deeply upon her audience, who already all knew it, the necessity of a strong German fleet, the importance of the colonies, the duty of German women to help Germany rise to greatness, and many other [similar] sentiments."[22] The league also hosted teas to raise money, where members sold portraits of the kaiser and pictures of the German fleet on maneuvers.[23]

In the long run, the league was unable to raise the sums required; its national leadership voted to devote the money raised by all chapters to building a convalescent home for sailors. The fact that the league worked for years to fund a warship, however, in the face of opposition from nationalist men and ridicule from the bourgeois press, demonstrates the ambiguous role that nationalism played in bourgeois women's lives. A small number of clubwomen were able to use the power and the social respectability of patriotic symbols to justify their presence and contributions in a sphere—the German-national public realm—that was previously closed to them. Within this realm, most of them pursued goals that could be seen as an extension of conventional feminine work, but a few went beyond this, to try to create an expanded role for nationalist women.[24]

The Women's Division of the Colonial Society and the German Women's Navy League were not large or powerful organizations within the local political environment, but by their very existence, they filled two functions. First, they acted as feminine complements and counterparts to larger masculine nationalist pressure groups; in addition, they extended the political spectrum of the local women's movement. By 1910, the Hanover women's movement had grown and expanded far beyond its 1906 boundaries, not only in numbers, but in terms of the range of women's associations. In 1906, the local women's movement had lacked a feminist wing, especially in comparison with the national women's movement. By 1910, however, the city's women's organizations ranged from the League for the Protection of Motherhood and the Suffrage Union, through the bulk of the professional, educational, and social welfare associations in the middle—which saw themselves as part of the larger sphere of nonpartisan local politics—to the nationalist women's groups.

The emergence of a right and left wing within the local women's movement was made easier by the 1908 reform of the Prussian Law of Association (*Vereinsrecht*). The old Law of Association, which was passed in reaction to the political upheavals of 1848, had forbidden women to attend meetings at which political questions were discussed. The law, which included a broad, vague definition of "political matters," could have been construed to prohibit many of the meetings hosted by mainstream women's professional and social welfare groups before 1908; it certainly should have applied to the public debates over *Kasernierung* staged by the Hanover women's movement. In practice, however, bourgeois women generally were allowed to attend and sponsor political meetings after the turn of the century without police interference. The law was used instead to prohibit socialist women's meetings, and to prevent women of all classes from formally joining political parties. After the law was reformed in 1908 to permit women to participate in party politics, feminists joined progressive liberal parties in increasing numbers; Hanover feminists joined disgruntled National Liberals to found the city's branch of the Progressive People's Party (Fortschrittliche Volkspartei) in 1911. Nationalist women would affiliate with the Conservative Party a few years later. The overall effect was to further politicize both ends of the spectrum within the women's movement. Terms such as "left" and "right" were now definitely applicable to some Hanover clubwomen. Feminists were now firmly associated with progressive liberals on the left end of the party political spectrum, whereas conservative women were linked to right-wing partisan groups.[25]

Women's nationalist and feminist associations appeared at about the same time in Hanover, and shared several important characteristics. Both nationalists and feminists worked within an explicitly political sphere, to accomplish political goals. Neither set of associations made any pretense at political neutrality; both were affiliated with masculine political pressure groups. These two groups differed in their relationship to the rest of the local women's movement, since feminists were largely isolated from the mainstream, whereas nationalist women were part of clubwomen's network of overlapping memberships. Nevertheless, feminists and nationalist women shared the distinction of having established a toehold for clubwomen within masculine partisan politics. After 1914, nationalist women in particular would build upon this beachhead.

Nationalist and feminist associations had strong partisan affiliations after 1908, but they represented only a minority of the women who were mobilized by the city's women's movement. In 1910, the majority of the women who worked within Hanover's bourgeois women's associations were still primarily interested in improving women's economic and professional opportunities and in combating social degeneration, and pursued a strategy of political party "neutrality." Although local feminists and nationalist women were comfortable working within the sphere of party politics, most of the movement's activists were not. The leaders of the bulk of the city's women's associations aspired only to be skilled administrators of a sphere of "women's politics," a jurisdiction that would include all issues concerning women and children, and an area of competence that would be funded and protected by the state. This goal, a politically "neutral," professional women's sphere, was a feminine analogue to the ideal of local government cherished by male notables: nonpartisan professional administrators, who would provide "neutral" good governance.

Women leaders believed that they could achieve this goal by working within established local political structures, and that involvement in the world of masculine party politics was not merely unnecessary, but undesirable. Most of them continued to assert this through 1914, and beyond. War and revolution would force them to reevaluate their position: clubwomen would become politicized and divided, as a large section of the local movement moved decisively into the German-national public realm.

W orld War I transformed the women's movement in Hanover; it drastically increased the scope of local clubwomen's work and had an enormous impact upon their day-to-day lives. The war was anticipated and prepared for by local women's associations, and it initially unified women's associations that had been estranged. The war in fact marked the movement's high-water point, in terms of the scope of its work and its influence in local government, as the women's movement assumed responsibility for much of the enormous load of social work generated by the war. As the war progressed, however, clubwomen were increasingly divided as, politicized by war and revolution, they joined different and competing masculine political parties. This outcome was presaged even before the war by a drift toward the right in the national women's movement, and by the beginnings of partisan political divisions among women leaders.

The groundwork for political divisions within the women's movement had been laid by the 1908 reform of the law governing public assemblies and organizations, discussed in the last chapter. After 1908, women were free to join the political parties of their choice, although initially only the Social Democrats and the Progressive Liberals welcomed female members enthusiastically. Women from the radical wing of the movement, including Hanover feminists, soon joined chapters of the Progressive People's Party, or other local left liberal groups. The other bourgeois political parties, which were hostile to many of the goals of the women's movement, were less eager to recruit women leaders; eventually, however, most parties established women's auxiliary groups. The Conservative Party was the last to do so; in 1913, Paula Mueller and other DEF leaders formed the Conservative Women's Union, which the Conservative Party grudgingly accepted as an auxiliary. The union was independent of the DEF, and Mueller somewhat disingenuously stressed that within it she acted as a private person, not as the head of the DEF.[1]

Although movement leaders were entering partisan politics, however, the BDF still had to maintain its *Überparteilichkeit*, or partisan neutrality. "Neutrality" was one of the cornerstones of BDF policy, enabling it to unify women from different political backgrounds, and giving legitimacy to its claim to speak for all organized bourgeois women. But as Bärbel Clemens points out, once prominent women leaders joined antagonistic political parties after 1908, it became difficult for the BDF to take any detailed positions on issues of interest to women, since specific stands would inevitably be closer to some political parties' positions than others; thus, the BDF would be vulnerable to accusations of having violated the precept of neutrality.[2] As a result, the BDF was constrained in many ways. Where member organizations did take specific stands on political issues, as in the suffrage movement—which had to decide whether to work against three-class suffrage—the result was division and recriminations.[3]

Not surprisingly, this partisan politicization led to tension within the BDF during the last few years before the war. Gertrud Bäumer and other women from the moderate wing of the BDF (who replaced radicals within the leadership of the BDF in 1910) allied themselves with Friedrich Naumann and his National Socialist liberals; under Naumann's influence, they were increasingly strident in their support for an imperialist foreign policy. This nationalist attitude led the BDF to resist the efforts of the International Council of Women (an umbrella group which fostered cooperation between the various European and the American national women's movements) to advance peace initiatives.[4] The BDF's aggressively nationalist stance further alienated leaders of the movement's radical wing, like Lida Gustav Heymann and Anita Augspurg, who were involved in the pacifist movement.

The BDF's drift to the right was reinforced by pressure from the DEF. The DEF had never supported some of the BDF's goals, especially the demand for women's suffrage, but before 1911 the DEF had agreed to remain "neutral" on the issue in internal BDF debates, by abstaining from votes within the BDF on policies relating to women's suffrage. However, once DEF leaders were formally affiliated with the Conservative Party, which strongly opposed women's suffrage, they came under pressure to abandon this neutral position. Mueller began to criticize the BDF's support for women's suffrage, violating her organization's agreement to remain neutral on the issue, and demanded that the BDF moderate its position. Bäumer and the rest of the moderates, fearful that the DEF would leave the BDF, made concessions, modifying the BDF's policies to pacify Mueller.[5]

In 1913, against this background of growing nationalist sentiment within the women's movement, and alarmed by increasing international tensions over the Balkans, the DEF began to prepare for the outbreak of hostilities. In correspondence with the Patriotic Women's Association, the DEF negotiated a division of labor between the two organizations in the event that war was declared; in addition, the DEF compiled lists of women in various cities who volunteered in advance to assist in the mobilization of the army and the economy.[6] At the same time, conservative women's organizations began to prepare their members for war by celebrating the vital importance of women's work in wartime. One example was a 1913 celebration organized by the Hanover DEF chapter to commemorate the 100th anniversary of the liberation of Germany from Napoleon's occupation. The evening included songs, a slide show, heroic tableaux vivants, and a speech by DEF vice-president Countess Selma von der Groeben, who reminded her audience that

[German] heroines, who joined in the struggle and risked all they had . . . gave everything, their entire feminine selves [*Frauentum*] as a *single* sacrifice for Germany's honor. . . . these women remembered their Fatherland and persevered. . . . they asked nothing for themselves, but everything for their children, Germany's sons. . . . and should the time for weapons come again—and how soon it could—you [women] will be ready.[7]

The evening concluded with the declamation of a poem written by a DEF member, a poem that was read aloud at meetings of other Hanover women's associations that year:

It was in the year '13.
The nation was bleeding . . .
What was it, that kept the entire people from collapsing, bleeding?
[It was] Germany's women, who with firm and gentle hands
    bandaged the wounds of all of who had been wounded in the field.
Then many a husband learned to rely upon his wife's loyal care.
Death came near many, who then returned to life.

In simple and plain clothing, her countenance transfigured with pity,
never had Woman's beauty seemed so gracious or precious to Man.

Subsequent stanzas related how German women taught their children
piety during their fathers' absence, which enlisted Providence on the
Germans' side and ensured victory. The poem concluded with a warning
to German women to be ready to take the same roles again if another war
should come.[8]

These texts sounded the same themes that clubwomen had stressed in
earlier discussions about women and social work. In the years after 1900,
women leaders had asserted that feminine sacrifice would save the German people from social degeneration, and that in engaging in professional social work, German women were working not for their own
benefit, but for society's. Now, women's services would help save the
nation from foreign, as well as internal, enemies. In each case, clubwomen
assumed that women would be effective if they followed the twin precepts of morality and service.

The themes stressed in these texts—feminine selflessness, sacrifice, and
transcendence of the self through service to the *Volk*—were renewed
and elaborated upon after the declaration of war in August 1914. Like
their contemporaries, leaders of the women's movement experienced the
"spirit of 1914" as a *"Rausch der Volkseinheit"* (intoxicating feeling of
national unity). Marianne Weber (the wife of Max Weber and a prominent BDF moderate) wrote that the declaration of war led to the "convulsion of my soul . . . [caused by] the submersion of my individual ego in the
great current of unity."[9] No less than their male counterparts, leaders of
women's associations were euphoric and eager to participate. "A beautiful
unity prevails amongst our ranks [i.e., women's associations], as well as a
desire to act," wrote Paula Mueller shortly after the war's outbreak. "We
have reached out over the barriers of confession, political orientation, and
the different wings of the German women's movement to clasp each
other's hands."[10]

Unity among women's organizations found tangible expression in the
foundation of the National Women's Service (Nationaler Frauendienst),
which the BDF established in August 1914. The Women's Service represented a women's version of the *Burgfriede* (domestic political truce),
which all of Germany's political parties and pressure groups had entered
into after the outbreak of hostilities. The National Women's Service in-

cluded women from across the political spectrum: not only the associations that made up the BDF, but also the Catholic Women's League, women's nationalist organizations, and leading female Social Democrats. Gertrud Bäumer presided over the service's national executive committee.[11]

Paula Mueller assumed leadership of the Hanover section. The Hanover Women's Service incorporated over thirty local women's organizations, including Jewish, Catholic, Protestant, feminist, and conservative women's associations. Unlike Women's Service branches in some other cities, the Hanover Service did not formally incorporate a socialist women's group; in 1914, there was no socialist women's organization in Hanover. The leadership of the Hanover Women's Service reflected the composition of the pre-1914 movement. Officers from the DEF, teachers' organizations, and Women's Educational Association held almost all of the key positions in the Hanover Women's Service hierarchy.[12] Throughout the city, clubwomen abandoned much of their peacetime association work in order to focus on the war effort.

The Patriotic Women's Association and the Red Cross assumed responsibility for nursing and caring for soldiers in the field while the Women's Service staked out the home front as its jurisdiction. It was just as well that the women's movement acted to seize this territory, since some organization was needed to assume responsibility for the women and children left at home: in August 1914, the home front was in a state of disarray. The German army had planned only for a rapid, overwhelming attack, such as the Franco-Prussian War had been; consequently, the government had not developed any schedules for the mobilization of the economy, nor given thought to the effect that a drawn-out war would have on the population.[13] The result was economic chaos, as the army's mobilization deprived millions of families of their chief wage earners. Many more families were made destitute when shortages of raw materials (caused in part by the Allied blockade of German ports) and conversion of the industrial sector to wartime production led to the closure of factories and workshops, as well as the loss of other jobs in the service sector. Women were especially hard hit by unemployment, since many of the peacetime industries that had to restrict production, such as textile manufacturing, employed largely female work forces.[14] In Hanover, over 2,500 women were thrown out of work within the first few weeks of the war: many had been textile workers, waitresses, and barmaids.[15]

The Hanover Women's Service assisted both the families of soldiers and those indirectly affected by the war. Soldiers' dependents were entitled to a minimum income from the federal government, but this support did not begin to cover the actual cost of living. In the winter, for example, wives of soldiers received twelve Marks a month, plus six Marks a month for each child under the age of fifteen.[16] Hanover, along with many other cities, chose to supplement the support that soldiers' families received. Care for soldiers' dependents was administered under the auspices of the municipal War Welfare Office (Kriegsfürsorgeamt), which the Women's Service supplied with volunteer workers. Women's Service officers headed up the internal departments of the War Welfare Office, and the service held two seats on the municipal committee that oversaw all of the city's wartime welfare programs. The number of women involved in wartime welfare work was unprecedented. One hundred eighty Hanoverian women alone worked in the division that verified information given in the applications for support, which had been submitted by over 12,000 soldiers' families. After support had been approved for soldiers' dependents, women volunteers from the Women's Service continued to "supervise these families, both to care for them and to check up on them."[17]

The Women's Service also established a network of social services independent of the city, which cared for those who had been indirectly affected by the war, such as unemployed textile workers. The service fed thousands of hungry people, found homes for war refugees, employed women to sew clothes for the military, and established a special unemployment office for unemployed women.[18] In general, the service gathered together social services which had been previously offered by separate women's associations under a single central control, and then expanded the scale of these services.

After mid-1915, when unemployment ebbed and the initial economic upheavals caused by the war had subsided, the Women's Service turned its attention to enlisting German women in the war effort. The new programs included recruiting women for munitions production and other vital industries, and providing support services such as dormitories for single women workers and day care for the children of married women workers. In addition, the service tried to educate all German women on Germany's war aims, the necessity of recycling and conserving scarce resources, and other ways of contributing to the war effort.[19]

In mobilizing women for the war, the Women's Service followed patterns established before 1914 by the women's movement. The service continued to defend the prewar principle that social services that catered to women and children should be administered and controlled by women. As a result, the women's movement alone was responsible for the mobilization of Hanover women during the first two years of the war.

The areas of competence claimed by the Women's Service were carryovers from prewar work. Fund raising, job referrals, soup kitchens, and the supervision of welfare recipients were all familiar jobs for women's associations. Only the scale of these services was new, as was the accelerated integration of women within the municipal welfare bureaucracy. In the eyes of women leaders, however, the Women's Service's work was urgently important in a way that women's associations' activities before 1914 had not been, because the service made a vital contribution to the war effort. Women leaders reminded the public that the military front was dependent upon the maintenance of the home front by women, which in turn was made possible by social services. Marie-Elisabeth Lüders, one of the leading organizers in the women's war effort, stressed this connection later when she observed that

> The private personal lives of women became a matter of war policy, and its formulation and execution was just as important as every other question connected with offense and defense. Replacing men called up for service with women workers was dependent upon the nurseries' work [which freed mothers for work]; the transport of munitions hinged upon the kindergartens and day-care centers; bombing raids were prepared for [by establishing] dormitories for single women workers, and machine gun fire made possible [by the work of] welfare offices and [female] factory personnel officers [Fabrikpflegerinnen].[20]

Further, Women's Service leaders were well aware that only the women's movement could have supplied the nation and the government with so many women who were trained to lead and organize social services. They reminded men that without the services of the women's movement, German women could never have been enlisted in the war effort so quickly or easily.[21]

As the war continued, the home front for many German women was literally shifted into their homes, especially into their kitchens. By 1916, when the Allied blockade led to unforeseen shortages of raw materials, German women were increasingly preoccupied by the time and effort it took simply to keep their household economies running. Merely obtaining a minimum of foodstuffs and fuels for heating and cooking required initiative and resourcefulness. In addition, housewives had to contend with the government's attempts to intervene and regulate their household economies. Lüders later recalled that by 1916:

> The compulsory aspects of the economy [*die Zwangswirtschaft*] were expanded week by week. In the end, the production and distribution of all materials and objects that one needed for daily life were regulated by laws and decrees. . . . our economy of poverty and necessity was characterized by confiscation, prohibitions regarding the sale and use of materials, by collection drives, and by attempts to save or produce substitutes for raw materials.[22]

She listed "war-related materials" that were collected, processed, and recycled—coffee grounds, fruit pits, gramophone records, wine corks, and women's hair—all the detritus of domestic life.

The Hanover Women's Service developed an array of services to help keep individual household economies afloat. Housewives could attend classes that taught women how to cook with substitutes for eggs, butter, flour, and meat, or how to wash clothes and dishes without proper soap. The service also offered courses on how to repair shoes, and, when leather became impossible to obtain, how to make straw soles for worn-out shoes.[23] In the winter of 1915, the service sponsored the foundation of a new Housewives' Association (it replaced the moribund organization discussed in Chapter 3), which opened three cooperative stores where housewives could buy food directly from local rural housewives. These cooperatives were supposed to undercut food speculators and middlemen, and thus hold down the price of food. Ultimately, the Women's Service hoped that the control of speculators and retail prices would help fight the effects of the Allied blockade by ensuring an equitable distribution of scarce foodstuffs.[24]

Although the women's cooperatives did a brisk trade in whatever rural housewives brought to market (an ever declining amount), there were limits to how far the Women's Service could counteract the Allied blockade. During the last two years of the war, many foods could only be obtained through barter or, infrequently, for exorbitant prices on the black market. There were also limits to how far the Women's Service could mobilize German women for work in industries that were vital to the war effort. After 1916, the service's autonomy came to an end; the government, acknowledging that the war would continue indefinitely, established a Central Work Office for Women (Frauenarbeitszentrale or FAZ) within the War Ministry to recruit women workers for wartime production. The government appointed Marie-Elisabeth Lüders to head the new department.[25]

Since women were exempt from compulsory national service, the FAZ was established to persuade women to volunteer for work in industries critical to the war effort; Lüders and her assistants were placed in charge of the entire women's war effort. Besides locating women workers and assigning them jobs where they were most needed, the FAZ provided social services that would facilitate the expansion of the female labor force. This entailed the creation of an array of support services, including running day-care centers for the children of women workers, establishing dormitories for single female workers, and training a division of female factory inspectors, who monitored women's working conditions.[26] For many reasons, the FAZ was not able to mobilize as many women workers as the government had hoped for, although many women were driven to take jobs outside of the home by inflation and the inadequate support paid to soldiers' families.[27]

Poverty and need may have been effective recruiting agents, but they were not calculated to inspire patriotic sentiment. Beginning in 1915, and especially after the *Hungerwinter* of 1916–17, German women in other cities staged food riots, and participated in wildcat strikes. In Munich, crowds of women stormed the city hall in 1916 when a reduction in the bread ration was announced, and this attack was only the first of many demonstrations over food shortages.[28] In Hanover, women did not stage food riots, but shortages of food, clothing, and coal, combined with the deaths of sons, brothers, husbands, and fathers, began to produce war-weariness in the mass of Hanoverian women. Before the war ended, over 13,000 Hanover men, or 8 percent of the city's male population, would fall in battle. Their wives and daughters, increasingly demoralized, were less and less able or willing to make the sacrifices demanded of them.[29]

War-weariness was beginning to appear among Hanover clubwomen, as well. The number of women volunteers for social work began to decline; the Women's Service was forced to issue repeated appeals for volunteer workers for the War Welfare Office after 1917. The leadership of the service felt compelled to remind those women who continued to work of "the necessity . . . especially in our private contacts with others, of keeping morale up."[30]

The shortage of volunteer workers, the lack of professional training of many of those who did volunteer, and the continuing expansion of municipal welfare services led to an increase in the number of professional social workers and female office personnel hired by the city after 1916. The city also absorbed some of the private social services that the Women's Service had founded, such as the job referral service for women. The women who administered these programs now worked directly for the city.[31] This professionalization of social services and absorption of private programs mirrored the creation of Lüders's FAZ on the federal level.

Paula Mueller and other women leaders simply could not understand the decline in the number of women volunteers, and they were appalled by the war-weariness that they saw around them. Furthermore, relatively minor lapses on the part of Hanover women, such as declining enthusiasm for volunteer work, were only the tip of the iceberg. Mueller and her fellow DEF officers suspected that many Hanover women were derelict in their most basic duties as wives and mothers, duties that were closely linked to clubwomen's traditional ideal of "feminine honor," a concept that conservative women's organizations had further refined during the course of the war.

As we have seen, the women's movement before 1914 championed a definition of feminine honor that was a slightly revised version of the contemporary notion of feminine respectability and duty. In the popular mind, feminine honor was equated with chastity, and with moral behavior in a broad sense. Women had a duty to embody the principle of morality within their families, and to exercise a virtuous influence over their husbands and children. The women's movement had expanded this definition of femininity, and had successfully argued that women had a duty to embody and advance morality in society as a whole, not merely within their families; this argument had justified the movement's network of social services and its broader fight against "social degeneration."

If women were charged with advancing morality and combating social decay, then men had a duty to provide leadership and protection. Men, DEF leaders argued, had been created as "leaders and defenders in all matters [outside the family]."[32] With the coming of World War I, the protective duties of men assumed new importance. As soldiers, men were now responsible for the military front, which protected women. The Hanover

Women's Service praised the "strength and firmness [with which] they [soldiers] endure hard assignments to ensure the [physical] security of women and children, and the inviolability of home and hearth."[33]

The war had also heightened the importance of women's duties toward their families. The Women's Service stressed this duty in flyers and speeches:

We women, do we not have a great responsibility? We have been entrusted with the care of all that our men have left behind, the responsibility for their property and for their beloved children. . . . [When our men return] they should be able to survey their children with satisfaction, children who, under mother's guidance, have been good and have not forgotten how to obey.[34]

In the absence of fathers and husbands, women alone could uphold standards of order and good conduct inside the family, and thus uphold the home front. If they did not maintain familial order, Women's Service leaders feared that the breakdown of private order would lead to social collapse, and the collapse of the war effort itself.

In addition, the Women's Service redefined and expanded the concept of feminine honor and duty outside of the family. In wartime, women were not only obligated to suppress public manifestations of immorality, but were also called upon to promote sobriety (in its broadest sense), diligence, and patriotic behavior, behavior "befitting the seriousness of our times."[35] In Women's Service literature, simplicity and chastity became inextricably linked to patriotism. One of the many areas in which gravity and sobriety could be expressed was women's clothing. Leather and wool were scarce resources, not to be wasted on high boots or pleated skirts. The Women's Service urged women to conserve these materials and, beyond that, to wear clothing that was an outward manifestation of the wearer's sense of patriotism and modesty. Flamboyant or suggestive clothing was denounced as a

brazenly immoral [style] of women's clothing which is completely un-German, which even in this serious time can be seen on the street, and which is tragic proof of the superficiality and thoughtlessness of those women who wear it. . . . It is a sign of the worst type of degeneration. . . . German femininity consists of personally reflecting, in dress and in attitude, the seriousness of our times.[36]

Women's Service literature thus put forth a model of feminine honor and conduct in wartime in which women contributed to the war effort in their work, were frugal with scarce resources, controlled and disciplined their children, and, in general, behaved in a sober, patriotic fashion. Even their clothing was freighted with public significance, since dress was supposed to reflect and support a somber, determined atmosphere.

The service gave special attention to groups of women who might have a hard time living up to this ideal. Female factory workers, thrown out of work by the war, were supposed to be especially liable to moral degeneracy; the service developed special outreach programs, including lessons in cooking and *Bürgerkunde* (citizenship) for these women. Because participants were provided with free meals, these courses did not lack for students. Barmaids, *Animiermädchen* (women who, paid by tavern owners, encouraged men to order extra alcohol in bars), dancers, and prostitutes posed a special problem; many had been thrown out of work by the call up of their customers. Some had attempted to find new work by volunteering at the Red Cross to work as nurses, "but of course were sent away."[37] The DEF toyed with the idea of establishing labor camps (*Arbeiterinnenkolonien*) for these women after the war but, so long as the war continued, settled for demanding that they be kept under strict control by the police.[38]

Increasingly, however, leaders of the Hanover women's movement perceived that not just barmaids, but also many Hanover families led lives that fell far short of the Women's Service's expectations. Youths, brought into factories to replace departing soldiers, earned adult wages, and were tempted to spend too much on alcohol and amusement. Their mothers were often too preoccupied with the struggle to make ends meet to supervise their children closely. The Women's Service rebuked mothers for the ensuing "roving about of youths in the streets and parks, [for their] noise and laughter does not accord with the gravity that ought to prevail in wartime."[39] Local military authorities had proclaimed a curfew for teenagers, and restricted their access to bars and other places of public amusement, but police did not strictly enforce these ordinances. Groups of youths were often out after dark, patronizing taverns, cinemas, and coffeehouses.[40] Mueller concluded that "again and again, we must remind women of their duties . . . [especially] their duties in caring for their children."[41] Perhaps working mothers resisted this advice, which after all was being offered by single, well-to-do women: the childless are rarely seen as credible authorities on child-rearing by parents.

Women's Service leaders argued German women were even more seriously derelict in their duties when they transgressed in their behavior toward other men while their husbands were away. Women's Service leaders feared that many women had begun adulterous relationships with other men, or might even display an inappropriate interest in prisoners of war. One service flyer reminded Hanoverian women that

> The moral purity of German women was once the glory of the German people, and what has become of it now? There are German women . . . whose conduct is so revolting, that they must conceal [it] and there are even some so lost to shame that they make public the ugliness of their lives. Such women sin against the Fatherland, and a people that tolerates such immorality must begin to die.[42]

Feminine licentiousness was the most terrible breach of women's honor and patriotism, a lapse that deeply disturbed the officers of the Women's Service.

Taken together with the decline in volunteers for Women's Service projects and the growing problem in maintaining morale even among clubwomen, the failure of many Hanover women to fulfill their duties toward their families (as the service defined these duties) led the DEF activists within the Women's Service to become increasingly disillusioned and disappointed with their fellow women. Service leaders compensated for other women's lack of enthusiasm by stressing their own boundless willingness to sacrifice (their *Opferbereitschaft*). The optimism and euphoria that had been palpable in the service's earlier proclamations were now replaced by grim determination and by a hard-line insistence on German war aims.

After 1917, Women's Service leaders worked in concert with male nationalist groups such as the Committee for Agreement on War Aims, which urged that Germany annex wide stretches of central Europe in the event of a victory; the service also hosted assemblies for women, which featured nationalist speakers, lectures entitled, for example, "To Persevere Is Not Enough: To Win Is."[43] President Wilson's Fourteen Points speech, delivered in January 1918, and the American diplomatic efforts that followed the Allied victories of August 1918, were rejected out of hand by the service. As late as October 16, Mueller declared publicly that members of the Women's Service, "rather than bow helpless before [Wilson's demands] with bound hands, would sacrifice everything, suffer anything."[44]

This uncompromising attitude did not accord well with the somewhat opportunistic tack that was taken by the liberal leaders of the BDF during the last two years of the war. Like the DEF, BDF leaders rejected Allied demands and insisted on holding out until the bitter end. However, the BDF expected a concession from the government in return, to wit, suffrage rights for women as a reward for women's war contributions.[45] The DEF had never supported female suffrage, and DEF leaders found the BDF's wartime agitation for the franchise intolerable. Throughout the last half of 1917, Mueller resisted demands from within the DEF that the association leave the BDF, but by 1918 the rift between the two organizations had widened even further, and the DEF officially withdrew from the BDF. In Hanover, some local DEF officials agonized over the break but supported the national organization.[46]

By leaving the BDF, the DEF had drawn back from the organized women's movement on a national level; in Hanover and in other cities, however, the DEF continued to work with other women's associations. On the local level, the meaning of the DEF's break with the larger organization was thus largely psychological or symbolic. It signified that the DEF, alienated by the liberal wing of the BDF, had ceased to define itself primarily as a part of the women's movement, and was in fact drawing closer to male conservative groups. Alice Bensheimer, a leading BDF moderate, noted that after its split with the BDF, the DEF began recruiting members who had been unwilling to join while it had been part of the official women's movement, "people whose ideas are the opposite of freedom and self-determination."[47] To replace the BDF within the world of organized Protestant women, leaders of Protestant women's groups created the Vereinigung Evangelischer Frauenverbände Deutschlands (the Union of German Protestant Women's Leagues, or VEFD). The VEFD, an umbrella organization, was intended to serve as a conservative alternative and rival to the BDF.[48]

The intoxication of national unity had drawn the women's movement together in 1914, and papered over political tensions that had been mounting since 1908; it had led the movement to new heights during the war. In the long run, however, this heady solidarity had been unable to overcome divisions between liberal and conservative women leaders. *Überparteilichkeit* had worked for the BDF to a certain extent in formulating policies on women's issues, but members of the women's movement also held divergent opinions on issues that lay outside of the sphere of women's politics: Germany's imperial policies, its war aims, and whether suffrage rights ought to be based on property qualifications. Leaders of the women's movement, although they might be united on some issues affecting women, were also—as individuals—part of a partisan political spectrum established by men, and the tensions generated within that spectrum ultimately found their way into the women's movement.

On the local level, the truce between women's organizations held a bit longer. The women's movement in Hanover had found its own version of *Überparteilichkeit*, defining its work as being for the common good, and apart from partisan politics, although in a broad sense, the movement supported bourgeois interests. Even before the war ended, however, some leaders within the Hanover Women's Service were beginning to question the patriotism and honor of their fellow clubwomen. The partisan politicization of the Hanover movement could not be held back much longer, and the dam began to burst at the end of 1918. The German Revolution, and the events following the war, weakened and divided the local movement, as antagonistic political parties began to compete for clubwomen's loyalties.

CHAPTER 10

The Women's Movement Adrift:

Revolution, Inflation, and Collapse,

1919–1923

The Hanover women's movement fell quickly from the pinnacle it had reached during the war: between 1919 and 1923, the movement confronted financial, existential, and spiritual crises. The German Revolution unleashed a wave of partisan politicization among local women leaders, introducing tensions within Hanover women's associations that mirrored those that had plagued the BDF for years. This politicization was the by-product of an important advance for women; thanks to the revolution, clubwomen were of course now able to vote and to run for office. In Hanover, as across Germany, leaders of women's associations took advantage of this opportunity, and well-known clubwomen won municipal, provincial, and national elections. But the organizations that these women came from declined, even as some leaders rose. Women's associations faced first an existential crisis, as they groped for a new raison d'être, and then a financial crisis; in the process, entire sections of the Hanover movement collapsed.

The German Revolution initiated this period of crisis. Conservative Hanover women, such as DEF activists, experienced the revolution and German's military defeat as a loss of national honor; they felt shocked and betrayed. The collapse of the German military front, the male "outer" front that protected the home front of women and children, signaled more than just military defeat. It implied the collapse of the entire model of sex roles that the Women's Service had codified in its wartime propaganda. In writing about the events of 1918–19, DEF leaders chose words that would have been applicable to a betrayed woman, which thus reflected their own identification with the nation: Germany's defeat represented her "defilement" and "shame," while the Treaty of Versailles was seen as a "rape," entailing a loss of "honor."[1] The collapse of established sex roles, along with the new republic's proclamation of female suffrage, eased and accelerated conservative women's entrance into public political spheres that had been previously closed to them. Frightened by the prospect of a socialist republic, Paula Mueller traveled to Berlin in November 1918. Working with other conservative women activists, Mueller quickly made plans to mobilize bourgeois women voters in support of the right-wing bourgeois parties; she also worked out the details of the DEF's alliance with the Deutschnationale Volkspartei (the German National People's Party, or DNVP, the successor to the old Conservative Party). She herself joined the DNVP, along with other DEF activists, and was elected to the Reichstag in 1919 as a DNVP deputy, changing her name to Mueller-Otfried.[2]

Not all of her associates could make the transition that Mueller-Otfried accomplished with such ease. Formally entering the realm of male-dominated public politics, competing against and working with male colleagues, was difficult for many conservative women. Even those women who had led and organized in the women's movement were accustomed to operating out of a "women's sphere" of influence, a political style that relied on connections within the masculine political structure to obtain what it required. The new political order demanded different tactics, and some conservative women could not envision themselves operating within it. "Frau Rötger is still quite hesitant in regard to all of these questions [the mobilization of bourgeois women to support the DNVP]," a DEF activist wrote Mueller-Otfried, referring to a leading member of the Women's Service. "She can hardly accustom herself to the idea of women exercising the right to vote, and says that she is quite unversed in political affairs."[3] Frau Rötger had had years of education and experience in dealing with public policy questions within the women's movement, but she found it hard to revise her self-image to include participating in masculine party politics.

Many women had difficulty adjusting to the reality of women's suffrage because it had come as a result of Germany's defeat and revolution. Marianne Weber, a leading BDF moderate expressed this view in an article she wrote for a newspaper in December, 1918:

> What we women have worked for decades to achieve—the political equality of our sex—has come upon us like a thief in the night, in the

dark hour of destiny which we have lived through with our people.... It is unbearably painful that our political freedom should be born first out of the collapse of our national hopes and, secondly, through the shattering of our state's form of being.[4]

The circumstances that attended the birth of women's suffrage, then, ensured that many bourgeois women would view the right to vote with ambivalent feelings.

Many conservative women, such as Paula Mueller-Otfried, were nevertheless able to adjust to the new circumstances and make the leap into masculine public politics; the closer ties between conservative women's organizations and masculine nationalist circles that resulted were one of the legacies of World War I. The new umbrella organization for Protestant women's groups, the VEFD, did yeoman work for the DNVP in the 1919 elections. Officers of Protestant women's groups created electoral committees in each city, and did door-to-door work, distributing pamphlets and getting out the vote. In all, the VEFD and DEF contributed substantially to the DNVP's electoral totals, bolstering the tendency of new women voters to choose center or right-wing parties.[5]

A chapter of the German Women's League (Deutscher Frauenbund), another right-wing women's organization, was also established in Hanover at the end of 1918. An offshoot of the prewar Imperial League against Social Democracy, the German Women's League had been founded in 1909. Its work was largely oriented toward propaganda, to promote "patriotic" and nationalist sentiment among German women, largely through public lectures and teas. The league was anti-Semitic; its statutes prohibited Jewish women from joining.[6]

Clubwomen were being mobilized politically on the left, as the right. Women leaders entered into party politics across the political spectrum, and on all levels, from the Reichstag down to the local city council. In Hanover, most candidates for municipal offices did not belong to the same parties that existed at the national level (there were no DNVP candidates for city council, for example), but rather were divided after 1919 into tickets that chose names such as the *Bürgerliche Mitte*, *Demokraten*, and the *Ordnungsblock*. Until 1929, the SPD, Communist, and Center parties were the only national-level parties to run candidates in local elections.[7] Women who had been active in women's associations before 1918 were soon incorporated into the leadership of local voting blocks, and several women's association leaders, including Anna Ramsauer and Mathilde Drees, became active in the new liberal Deutsche Demokratische Partei (German Democratic Party, or DDP). Other local activists, who were married or related to National Liberal Party members, joined its successor party, the Deutsche Volkspartei (German People's Party, or DVP); this group included Olga Tramm and Mathilde Drechsler-Hohlt, who would become a prominent leader in the local movement during the 1920s. The German Revolution thus transformed many women's association leaders into professional politicians, and narrowed the gap between "women's sphere" politics and party politics.

The absorption of local activists into antagonistic political parties began to generate political tensions within the women's movement almost at once. During the early 1920s, these struggles were primarily played out within the new Hanover Women's City League (Frauenstadtbund). The City League was the successor organization to the wartime Women's Service; women leaders had agreed during the war that a permanent, formal union of women's associations was superior to the prewar ad hoc coalitions that the movement had generated, and had decided to convert the Women's Service into a peacetime City League once the war was over. A constitution was drawn up in advance, and it was agreed that Mathilde Drees would replace Paula Mueller-Otfried as head of the organization once the conversion took place.[8]

In November 1918, Drees and her allies moved abruptly to effect the conversion and to place Drees in charge. Without giving other women leaders the customary warning about new resolutions, liberal activists passed a resolution at a Women's Service meeting that put the new name and constitution into effect. Mueller-Otfried and her conservative allies were caught off guard and could not muster enough votes to stop the conversion. In protest, the DEF, along with moderate or conservative allies such as the Catholic Women's League, the Women's Division of the Colonial Society, and others, resigned from the City League. Drees had to negotiate with and placate Mueller-Otfried before these associations agreed to return to the fold.

Over the next few years, the DEF and other conservative women's groups would withdraw, rejoin, and withdraw again from the City League. At first, the DEF considered withdrawing because its officers refused to serve with women who belonged to the SPD. Later, the DEF did withdraw because the City League affiliated itself with the BDF, although the DEF and its allies later rejoined the City League again. Throughout this period, Mueller-Otfried and her allies tried to gain admission to the City League for the right-wing German Women's League, but Drees was able to sustain majorities against this because of the German League's statutory anti-Semitism.[9]

Even within the DEF, partisan political differences were beginning to cause trouble. Mueller-Otfried's announcement at a DEF meeting at the end of November 1918 that she was joining the DNVP unleashed a storm of criticism within the local chapter. Guelph partisans within the DEF accused Mueller-Otfried of violating the organization's neutrality; several Guelph officers came close to resigning. Internally, DEF officers ended up compromising on a new stance that combined "political neutrality" with support for center or conservative bourgeois parties. On the local level, this was easily implemented; the DEF simply urged its members to vote for the *Bürgerblock* (the name used in several elections by a coalition of center-right parties) in local elections. On the national level, this translated into support for parties that espoused "nationalist" and religious values, such as the DVP, the DNVP, and the Guelphs.[10]

This compromise began to disintegrate after 1920, when the DVP was included in governing coalitions on the national level, which made the DVP part of the Weimar "system" in the eyes of DNVP supporters. Discord within the DEF grew after 1923, when DVP representatives served in ruling coalitions alongside the SPD. Mueller-Otfried and the DNVP members within the DEF began to attack the government in terms that were also a thinly veiled assault on the DVP. The dispute within the DEF reached a climax in late 1924, when Mueller-Otfried used the DEF's newspaper to denounce

the miserable way in which German dignity and honor are being betrayed by the current possessors of political power . . . individuals, who consider themselves politically sophisticated, and use the word *Realpolitik* to conceal their lack of principles. . . . we must be not only passively, but actively nationalist and keep our distance from those wretched weaklings, who take lessons from the French on [German] war guilt. . . . [Such leaders] are not lifting us up, but rather are leading us deeper and deeper into the morass.[11]

DVP members within the DEF, led by Drechsler-Hohlt, correctly interpreted this as an attack that included the DVP and its leader, Gustav

Stresemann, and Drechsler-Hohlt wrote to local newspapers, denouncing Mueller-Otfried's violation of the DEF's "neutrality." The entire affair led to heated debates within the DEF, as well as Drechsler-Hohlt's resignation. In the aftermath, the DEF resigned yet again, and permanently, from the City League; Drechsler-Hohlt was a prominent member of the City League, and Drees and her friends appear to have supported Drechsler-Hohlt in the dispute.[12]

Yet at the same time that the women's movement was experiencing bitter partisan political divisions, individual women leaders had new opportunities, due to the changes in both local and national politics and laws introduced by the Weimar Republic. On the surface, these changes should have worked to the movement's benefit, as well. Reforms that feminist leaders had thought years away were granted under the Weimar constitution, which guaranteed female equality in marriage and in civic life, and opened all civil service offices to women.[13] The Weimar Republic also undertook reforms that realized the agenda of more moderate women leaders, by establishing an extensive network of state welfare services, staffed by professional female social workers.

Many of these changes did not work to the women's movement's advantage, however, or even benefit women as a whole. The article of the Weimar constitution that guaranteed women's equality stated that women and men had "basically the same rights and duties," a qualification that was later used to restrict women's civic rights in some areas.[14] In addition, equality within marriage could only be secured through a revision of the marriage provisions of the German Civil Code, which was not undertaken. The Reichstag did not follow up with legislation that would have put the new constitution's provisions regarding women into effect; the promise of equality was thus only partially fulfilled.

Other political changes introduced in the new republic actively worked to the local women's movement's disadvantage. Municipal democratic reform in Hanover pulled the rug out from under the movement, by abolishing local elites' complete control of the city's government, and thus ending the movement's special relationship with municipal officials. In addition, the city now assumed much of the social work that women's associations had hitherto carried out, depriving the women's movement of many of its functions. The women's movement did not adapt well to these changes in the local political environment and was unable to find new projects, or a new raison d'être.

When the new municipal political system was introduced in 1919, however, it was not immediately apparent that reform would work to the disadvantage of the women's movement; indeed, the new rules permitted women leaders to enter political parties and run for office, and several did so successfully. The early 1920s witnessed the peak of many local activists' political influence and achievements. Mathilde Drees was elected to the lower house of the city parliament (Bürgervorsteherkollegium), along with Margarete Willig, a Guelph partisan who had headed the DEF's corps of female poor relief almoners, and conservative Auguste Jorns, who succeeded Adelheid von Bennigsen as director of the Christian Women's Seminar. In addition, Anna Ramsauer, Drees's old friend and roommate, was elected to the municipal school board. Paula Mueller-Otfried, as befitted the city's most important woman leader, achieved the loftiest position of all, being elected to the Reichstag.[15]

The municipal government these women leaders entered had undergone substantial changes as a result of the revolution. Unnerved by the unrest and upheaval that was spreading throughout Germany in November 1918, the Hanover city council had accepted Burgomaster Tramm's resignation on November 10; Robert Leinert, who represented the SPD in the Prussian Landtag, was elected as his successor, and two other local SPD leaders were appointed as city senators. This swift capitulation to the SPD, and the fact that SPD representatives were legally elected under the existing municipal constitution, calmed political tensions in Hanover, and hindered the emergence of more radical political groups.[16]

The city's two legislative houses also approved important changes in the municipal constitution. Universal adult suffrage in municipal elections was introduced in January 1919. The upper chamber (Magistrat) was reformed, and made more responsive to the will of the lower chamber, the city council. Municipal senators were now elected directly by city council members, and served twelve-year terms, instead of lifetime appointments. The burgomaster (now called the *Oberbürgermeister*, or mayor) still retained considerable executive powers, however.[17]

In the local and national elections held during 1919, the SPD was supported by a plurality, although not a majority, of local voters. The city's *bürgerliche* political parties were divided, however. Three bourgeois groups—a progressive liberal coalition, a pro-Guelph party, and an alliance consisting of local DNVP and DVP politicians—gained seats in the city council, but were unable to work together until 1924. Until 1924, then, the SPD had the single largest delegation in the city council; together with the progressive liberals, the SPD had an absolute majority, and controlled the mayor's office.[18]

In 1924, the bourgeois parties united to form a "coalition for order," which held a majority in the city council, and which elected a new mayor, Arthur Menge. The SPD gained an absolute majority in the council in the elections of 1929, but was unable to force Menge's resignation, or place SPD senators in the upper chamber. From 1929 until the Nazis took control, local government was caught up in a tug of war between the SPD on the one hand, and Menge and his supporters on the other.[19]

Although leaders from the bourgeois women's movement had done well in the first elections after the war, they played a diminishing role within this new municipal political system thereafter. A handful of former clubwomen served among the seventy-four city councilors, but most held office for only a few years, and none was ever advanced to the upper chamber. Even in the city council, bourgeois women were outnumbered by women representatives from the SPD and Communist Party. Five bourgeois women were elected to the city council between 1919 and 1933, while eight women represented the SPD and the Communists.[20]

Almost all of the women who sat on the city council were concerned with municipal welfare services, which were reformed in 1922. During the war, the city had run the War Welfare Office independently of the municipal poor relief system, which relied on a network of male and female volunteer almoners. The War Welfare Office, with its staff of professional social workers and nurses, had compared favorably with the older poor relief system and proved itself able to handle unprecedented numbers of applicants. The War Welfare Office's caseload swelled even further after 1918, when demobilization and the transition to a peacetime economy dislocated thousands of workers. Wilhelm Schickenberg, a city senator who headed the War Welfare Office, proposed in 1919 that all municipal assistance programs, including the poor relief system, be merged into a single new Welfare Office (Wohlfahrtsamt), which would be better organized, more efficient, and professionally staffed.[21]

Schickenberg's proposal accorded with federal social welfare legislation that was being prepared by the Weimar government. Indeed, one of the hallmarks of the new regime was its concern with social welfare policy, and its far-reaching proposals for new social services. The SPD, which dominated the Weimar government during its first years, intended that the republic should be a *Sozialstaat*. During the early 1920s, the Weimar Reichstag passed a series of laws regulating and extending the social services and financial assistance offered to various groups. It also approved legislation in 1924 that provided the organizational framework for the administration of these social services, the *Reichsverordnung über die Fürsorgepflicht* (Federal Law on the Responsibility to Provide Social Welfare Assistance), which merged local war welfare offices with previously existing poor relief systems.[22] Most of the administrative responsibility for these social services, and much of the cost, were given to municipal or communal governments; the federal government thus assigned local governments additional duties and expenses without increasing their revenues.

Hanover anticipated the 1924 federal law with its new Welfare Office, which was created in 1922. The Welfare Office united services that had previously been distributed between the War Welfare Office, the poor relief system, and several private charitable organizations, including some women's associations. Its subdivisions dealt with minors (especially orphans or "endangered" youths), all persons who qualified for assistance under the new social legislation, alcoholics, and "morally endangered" or homeless women. The city was divided into social welfare districts; in each, a committee consisting of a professional social worker, a doctor, a teacher, and four volunteers evaluated and monitored individual cases.[23]

The new social welfare system thus included volunteer workers (the city could not afford an entirely professional force of social workers), but the new volunteers were drawn from more diverse social groups than the prewar municipal almoners and played a much less important role in the administration of social services. The legislation establishing the Welfare Office specified that at least half of the volunteers had to come from the working class, and that at least half had to be women. The requirement that half of the volunteers should be working class reflected the determination of the Hanover SPD (like SPD locals in other areas) to wrest control over social assistance programs from the bourgeoisie. This resolve was embodied by the Workers' Welfare organization (Arbeiterwohlfahrt), created by the SPD in 1919 to promote the involvement of the organized working class in social welfare programs.[24]

In theory, the clubwomen and bourgeois men who had worked as volunteer municipal almoners could have made up half of the volunteers in the new welfare system, but very few chose to enter the welfare district committees. In the years before 1919, approximately 800 *bürgerliche* men and women had worked under the old poor relief system as municipal almoners or orphans' officers, as well as in other positions. The new welfare system cut the number of volunteers to 328, and the new regulations specified that of these, only half, or 164 could come from *bürgerliche* backgrounds. The city, however, could not recruit even this low number of volunteers out of the ranks of the old municipal almoners: only 34 men and women who had been active in local poor relief before 1918 chose to volunteer under the new system. Male almoners had been compelled to work before the war, under penalty of forfeiting their municipal franchise and being forced to pay higher taxes; many no doubt gladly gave up the job, now that it was no longer compulsory. The clubwomen, however, had been volunteers. Now, some were too old to continue this work, while others had been hard hit by the inflation of the early 1920s and needed to find gainful employment; perhaps some refused to work on district committees that included SPD volunteers.[25]

At any rate, the role of volunteers under the new system was limited. Most of the work of visiting the recipients of aid, advising them, and evaluating their progress fell on the shoulders of the social workers. Figures published in the late 1920s and early 1930s indicate that over 85 percent of all visits to aid recipients were made by the social workers.[26] The old system, under which poor relief recipients were visited, monitored, and admonished by better-off neighbor/almoners, was gone.

On the surface, the new welfare system was what the local women's movement had sought for years: social work was turned over to a staff of professionally trained bourgeois women, who handled all issues involving women and children. In reality, however, the new system fell short of the movement's vision in several crucial respects. Clubwomen had agitated for a social welfare system that would be led by women. The new Welfare Office, however, was headed by Schickenberg, and most of the supervisory positions were also filled by men. The social workers who dealt with the actual recipients were not allowed to make decisions regarding levels of aid, or control the dispersal of other types of financial assistance, because women were regarded as too softhearted. Schickenberg argued that the social workers who handled individual cases should not decide questions of money because women, "who are so strongly influenced by their hearts, [would] attack the structure of laws, ordinances, and other regulations, and with true feminine shrewdness, always find holes in the bureaucratic wall [and disperse too much money]."[27] This was not the role for social workers that the local women's movement had envisioned. The professionalization of social work in Hanover in fact reflected the warning issued by national leaders in the field, Alice Salomon and Marianne Weber, who noted that professionalization and bureaucratization of social work often led to the "alienation" of social workers, whose field was so rationalized that much of the humane character of their work was lost.[28]

The women's movement was not in a position to do much about these shortcomings, however, or even to maintain its own programs. One by one, local women's associations closed or turned over to the city the institutions that the women's movement had founded and nurtured before World War I. In many cases, the inflation of 1923 forced the closure of projects or institutions that were already weakened.

The municipal government did not ask to assume proprietorship of the movement's projects. Financially strapped by the social services that national legislation assigned to local governments, Hanover municipal officials would have been glad to leave some institutions to the women's movement. Many local women's associations could no longer afford to support their projects, however. Charitable organizations in Hanover and across Germany were in a precarious financial position during the early 1920s. Economic upheaval, followed by the inflation of the early 1920s, had reduced or destroyed their endowments, and the social groups that had previously been a source of donations were also hard hit, no longer able to contribute as much to local charities.[29]

The DEF was forced to turn over its shelter for homeless women to the city in August 1920; the shelter needed to be renovated and expanded, and the DEF could not even afford to pay the current operating costs. The DEF's decision was echoed by the Women's Educational Association, which asked the city in 1921 to take over its school, which trained women to teach domestic economy and other subjects in the public schools. After turning over its school, the Educational Association, one of the oldest women's associations in the city (and the local branch of the ADF, the General German Women's Association) was forced to dissolve itself. Its sister organization, the Society for the Advancement of Female Education, took over the Educational Association's work in running the movement's legal advice bureau, but was forced to give up the work in 1923; the women who ran the bureau no longer had the time to do so, since they had to find paying jobs. The Committee of Hanover and Linden Women's Associations closed down its Continuation School for girls, which had included a trade school to prepare women for work in the business world. The women who ran the school argued that public schools now offered the same kinds of courses, which made the Continuation School unnecessary.[30] Taken together, these actions constituted the dissolution or surrender to the city of some of the oldest and most important institutions created by the local women's movement.

The DEF lost other programs besides the shelter for homeless women. Its network of female municipal almoners and orphans officers had been abolished and replaced by the new municipal welfare system. Its program of home care for poor women who had recently given birth was also made redundant by the Welfare Office. The DEF was able to maintain its home for unwed mothers, although Schickenberg—irritated by the DEF's tendency to run the home as it pleased without regard for his advice— repeatedly asked the municipal government not to subsidize the home. He was unsuccessful. The DEF obviously retained enough influence within local government to secure this remaining subsidy.[31] Still, its work during the 1920s was limited when compared with its array of welfare services before World War I. Overall, the network of social services created by the Hanover women's movement before 1914 was dissolving; parts of it were taken over by the city, while other programs disappeared entirely.

Local women's associations were unable to replace those projects which had been nationalized with new programs, new agendas. The local women's movement had been overtaken by events: the admission of women to professions previously closed to them, their accession to new political rights (particularly the right to vote), and the creation of a state welfare system realized most of the movement's prewar agenda, which meant that the movement had worked itself out of a job. In addition, the movement had come to rely heavily on the state (especially municipal authorities) for funding, and this dependence was now coming back to haunt women leaders. After the city government was taken over by the SPD, women leaders were unable to gain local officials' support for new projects, and they had few other sources of funding.

The loss of a raison d'être was not confined to the Hanover movement. At the beginning of the Weimar period, women activists across Germany were at a loss when faced with the question of what the movement's role should be in the new republic, where so much of the BDF's prewar agenda was now realized. Minna Cauer, a well-known liberal feminist, viewed the attainment of women's suffrage as a kind of conclusion to the "woman question." "The old women's movement is done. . . . I consider that my tasks in the women's movement are completed, now that women have achieved citizenship." She ceased publication of the periodical that had been the voice of the radical wing within the BDF, *Die Frauenbewegung*.[32] On the right, the DEF also struggled to find a new purpose; Mueller-Otfried was forced to reassure the Hanover chapter that the DEF still had work to do and a reason to exist. In the future, she said, the organization could focus on tasks that derived from the "German" part of its name, now that most of the "women's" problems were solved.[33]

Across Germany, many organizations within the women's movement struggled with a kind of malaise during much of the 1920s. The problem was most acute for specifically feminist groups, such as the ADF; its local chapter in Hanover had been the now defunct Educational Association. Unlike women's confessional and professional associations, which had core identities and missions to fall back on, feminist organizations lost their footing in the new republic, where the "woman question" was ostensibly solved.

The ADF, for example, had focused before the war on promoting women's work in municipal government, and on trying to gain municipal political rights for women. When these rights were granted in 1918, the ADF struggled for several years to find a new mission. Some members resigned in 1919, because they argued that gaining the right to vote meant that "the task of the women's movement has been fulfilled." The entire local chapter in Brunswick left the ADF and converted itself into a housewives' organization.[34] After several years of floundering, the ADF was rescued by the World League for Women's Suffrage and Women Voters, which offered to take the ADF as its German branch. The ADF accepted, and changed its name to the League of Women Citizens (Staatsbürgerinnenverband).[35]

At the same time that it was groping for a new role in the republic, the German women's movement as a whole also had a *Nachwuchsproblem*, a problem attracting younger women to carry the movement forward into the next generation. Younger women during the 1920s tended to see the women's movement as "a collection of elderly female teachers, who wore their hair done up in buns."[36] BDF leaders were acutely aware that the movement as a whole was aging. Many younger women saw the movement as old-fashioned and unnecessarily antagonistic toward men. Such women felt that the struggle for formal, legal equality was won, and they were more interested in expressing emancipation through their personal lives, and through building companionate relationships and marriages with men, where the partners could be "comrades."[37] Gender struggles were in fact passé during the Weimar period.

The Hanover movement experienced the same problems and the same malaise that inflicted the national movement. Leaders of many local women's associations noted that their memberships were aging, that younger women and new members were not attracted to their meetings. The Women's Club was one example. Before 1914, the club hosted literary evenings, teas, hiking excursions, enormous Mardi Gras celebrations, musical performances, and other sociable events, but it grew quiet during the 1920s. In 1925, a local newspaper noted that "in its first years, the club provided a common ground for all women's associations, and attracted . . . [members of] fine society. . . . Now, it is more a meeting place for older women, especially retired professional women."[38] In the Hanover of the 1920s, young bourgeois women had a greater choice of socially acceptable leisure time activities; new forms of commercial mass entertainment—including increasingly popular motion pictures, jazz bands, and afternoon tea dances—competed with associations for women's free time.[39]

Women leaders were unable to replace their old goals with new visions, and a new agenda, that might have attracted younger members. Furthermore, even if the Hanover movement had come up with a new set of proposals, it could not have found funding. The city, which had encouraged and subsidized the movement's efforts before World War I, was no longer in a position to do so. Throughout the 1920s, the Hanover municipal government struggled to meet its obligations as a part of the Weimar social welfare system, while seeking to limit municipal debt; as a result, the city constantly sought to cut costs wherever possible, and was not in a position to finance new projects.[40]

Even if the city government had not been financially strapped, it is doubtful whether women's associations could have secured support for ambitious new proposals from an administration wherein SPD politicians had a strong voice. The women's movement had lost much of its influence within municipal government when Burgomaster Tramm had been forced to resign, and his associates replaced in part by SPD leaders. This was especially true through 1924; during this period, the SPD controlled the mayor's office, while the municipal welfare system was being reorganized and expanded. Thus, clubwomen's influence reached its nadir during the years when the movement urgently desired to have a voice in welfare reform.

The movement's diminished influence was illustrated by the municipal government's reaction to its petitions regarding the city's social workers. During the 1920s, the City Women's League petitioned the city several times to appoint a woman to supervise all female social workers; in addition, the Women's League asked that social workers be made permanent civil servants (*beamtet*), instead of being given year-to-year contracts. Even though the Women's League was supported by Schickenberg, the city did not grant these petitions until 1929, after years of lobbying. Even then, social workers were not given the status of permanent civil servants until they had served for ten years.[41] Women activists would regain some of their contacts in local government after 1924, when conservatives reclaimed the mayor's office. By that time, however, the projects that the movement had used its influence to further, and to gain municipal financing for, were largely gone.

By 1923, then, the Hanover women's movement had lost much of its influence in local government and its sense of mission, along with many of its functions; in addition, it was weakened by partisan political divisions. The hyperinflation added to these problems by plunging the movement into a severe financial crisis. Women's associations, already on shaky financial ground due to the steady inflation that had continued since the war's end, became almost moribund. Many were unable to hold meetings because no money was available for renting rooms, or to pay for heating.

Unable to pay the rent on its rooms, the Housewives' Association was forced to rent part of the Women's Club in 1922. Until October 1922, the association ran a cooking school for servants, which provided meals for the women who lived in the club, such as Drees and Ramsauer. This operation nearly led to the bankruptcy of the association during the hyperinflation, and it was forced to discontinue its cooking course, and move into still smaller rooms.[42]

As early as 1920, the local DEF chapter was having difficulty collecting dues from members, even though clubwomen whose income had suffered were charged a lower rate. By 1922, the DEF was forced to close one of its few remaining programs, which took poor children to the countryside during the summer; the group could no longer even afford to send out postcards to members, announcing meetings. Between May and November of 1922, the DEF could not hold any meetings at all. The association faced financial collapse during 1923, but was rescued in part by generous donations from a women's club of German immigrants in Peru; its Home for Unwed Mothers was kept going by donations from American Quakers.[43]

In addition, although the DEF now received little money from the city, it was still able to obtain subsidies at irregular intervals from provincial-level officials, who were somewhat insulated from the SPD's increased power in local and national government, and whose tenure predated the Weimar period. DEF leaders were apparently still able to make use of their contacts in these circles. As before the war, DEF projects received subsidies from the office of the *Oberpräsident* of Hanover, from the Landesdirektorium, and from the provincial agency that administered workers' old-age and disability insurance funds.[44] These grants were modest, however, compared with the total support received from public bodies by the DEF before the war. In the long run, the only important institution that the Hanover DEF was able to maintain was the Home for Unwed Mothers, which was rescued by a 1924 federal law that required the authorities to shoulder the cost of caring for the home's inmates.[45]

It was not only women's associations that struggled financially during this period: clubwomen themselves fought to survive hyperinflation. Many older women, preoccupied with the struggle to support themselves, were no longer able to spare time for association projects and meetings. Like Martha Richter, who had served as the unpaid director of the Women's Educational School for over twenty years, many clubwomen had lost their fixed incomes or annuities to the inflation of the early 1920s. Richter petitioned the city for financial assistance in 1925, explaining that she had lost her sources of income in the hyperinflation of 1923, and had been forced to move in with relatives. "With the help of some pensioners' social assistance [*Kleinrentnerfürsorge*] and constant needlework [which she sold], and by being extremely frugal," she wrote, "I have been able to pay for my own food and other necessities, and thus have not been a burden to my relatives, who have their own problems. But now there is less demand for needlework products, and my health is failing." In view of her long service to the Women's Educational Association School, which was now run by the city, the municipal government granted Richter a pension of

800 Marks a year.[46] This was very little to live off of, but it was still more than many of Richter's fellow clubwomen were left with after 1923.

Those women's organizations that were able to shifted focus after 1922 to helping *Kleinrentnerinnen* such as Richter; for the first time, clubwomen began to dispense charity to women of their own class. The Housewives' Association and the DEF collected food and clothing for distressed gentlewomen. The DEF also offered advice to these women and spent much of the money from Peru on them.[47] The local women's movement simply no longer had the resources, or the institutions, to undertake large-scale projects to help women like Richter; instead, it was only able to mount projects that involved home visits and distributing food, reminiscent of the work done by charitable groups before 1880. Indeed, the work for *Kleinrentnerinnen* was the only substantial new project undertaken by the DEF during the 1920s.

By the mid-1920s, charitable, educational, and social welfare organizations, which had formed the heart of the prewar Hanover women's movement, were declining or disappearing. Their functions had been largely taken over by the city or state, and they were unable to find a new mission, new projects. Other parts of the movement, however, were not hit as hard. Professional and confessional organizations had core identities to fall back on, and did not suffer as badly during the 1920s. Furthermore, conservative women's groups experienced substantial growth during the 1920s. Partisan conflict had been suppressed before 1908, and muted thereafter, especially during the war. But the political changes brought by peacetime opened the door to overt politicization within the local movement, and as the 1920s wore on, more and more bourgeois women were mobilized by groups on the right. "Neutrality," which had meant a broadly shared commitment to the "common good," and to bourgeois interests, was largely abandoned by the Hanover movement during the Weimar period. Instead, the strategy that Paula Mueller-Otfried had offered to her association in 1919—substituting "German" issues for "women's" issues—would be adopted by other clubwomen, as a broad section of the movement redefined its politics to embrace aggressively nationalist policies.

CHAPTER II

Growth on the Right:

Housewives and Nationalists,

1923–1933

While social welfare and educational organizations within the local women's movement suffered from malaise and decline during the 1920s, other sections of the Hanover movement were stable, or even grew. Professional organizations, in particular, had a core identity to fall back upon even after the "solution" of the woman question, and these associations continued to flourish. Indeed, by the late 1920s, the "official" women's movement in Hanover (those organizations affiliated with the BDF) consisted primarily of professional organizations. But these associations were also turning inward during the 1920s, increasingly concerned with providing professional representation for members. Professional groups presented themselves as the champions of bourgeois women as a whole less and less, and no longer provided strong leadership for the Hanover movement. Increasingly, the most vocal, articulate segment of the local women's movement was its right wing, comprised of nationalist organizations that experienced a rebirth or revival during the 1920s. The number of overtly politicized, right-wing women's organizations in Hanover grew during the Weimar period, and these groups explicitly rejected not only the "New Woman" and other social changes of the period, but also the entire democratic Weimar "system."

One of the targets of nationalist women was the growing number of professional women workers, although nationalist women did not attack professional women's associations openly. The fact that Hanover was home to thousands of female professional and white-collar workers during the 1920s was a reflection of Hanover's role as an administrative center, but it was also a testament to the efforts of the prewar women's movement, as was the fact that women were heavily concentrated in the

Table 11.1. Professional and White-Collar Women in Hanover, ca. 1925

Category	Number
Teachers	753
Musicians	61
Painters and sculptors	28
Physicians	12
Pharmacists	57
Nurses	991
Social workers and kindergarten teachers	274
Dentists	4
Dental technicians	10
Bookbinders	76
Chemists	25
Photographers	34
Telegraph or postal workers	896[a]
Clerical workers, salesgirls, or other office workers employed by local businesses	1,681[a]

Source: Statistisches Amt, *Statistisches Jahrbuch*, 2d ed., 106, 137.
Note: These figures are taken from a special survey that included only those women employed in "dependent" positions, thus excluding self-employed women or women who worked in supervisory positions. In the case of such professions as social workers or nurses, these figures probably include almost all women employed in Hanover, since most women in these categories worked under male superiors. In the case of the so-called free professions, which included physicians and dentists, the figure given probably excluded many of the women in these professions, since physicians and dentists sometimes had their own practices.

a. This figure is valid for 1928.

"maternal professions," as Table 11.1 demonstrates. This increase in the number of female professionals and white-collar employees fueled the expansion of women's professional organizations. The number of women in the Commercial Union of Female Employees, for example, rose from 332 in 1906 to 1,681 in 1928, while the number of members in local branches of women teachers' organizations grew from 495 in 1906 to 1,393 in 1922. In addition, new female professional associations, such as a chapter of the German League of Social Workers, were founded after the war.[1]

The growth of professional organizations did not strengthen the local women's movement as much as might have been expected, however. Women's occupational associations—especially teachers' groups—had been the backbone of the local women's movement before 1914, along with the DEF and the now defunct Women's Educational Association.

Now, professional organizations were no longer primarily interested in working with other women's associations to push for social reform. Teachers' associations continued to belong to the City Women's League, but that body was undermined from the start by internal divisions. Instead, women's professional associations began to function as collective bargaining groups, although they did not refer to themselves as unions. Teachers' associations, which before 1914 had left petitioning the city about salaries and pensions to individual members, began to lobby the city about raises and benefits after 1919; teachers' associations began to see themselves as the proper representatives of individual teachers in wage disputes. This development represented a considerable change in the self-understanding of teachers' associations.[2]

Besides the professional organizations, the only other segment of the local women's movement that expanded during the 1920s was that of women's right-wing associations. The right wing of the local women's movement was initially led by the DEF, but it grew to include new organizations, especially a revitalized and enormously expanded housewives' association. In part, their popularity was due to the fact that nationalist women's groups articulated the fear and anger that some bourgeois women felt over the social and political changes of the 1920s. Like the leaders of the DEF, many *bürgerliche* women experienced Germany's defeat and subsequent revolution as a profound dishonor, something that had shamed Germany, and broken down the "natural" boundaries between the "outer [military] front," protected by men, and the "inner front," the home front, which was women's responsibility. Nationalism was a way of clinging to the remnants of Germany's honor, to the God-given German values and culture with which Protestant bourgeois women identified. Thus, nationalist women tried to mount what they perceived as a last line of defense against foreign enemies by struggling to preserve German culture, or *Deutschtum*.[3]

The struggle to preserve *Deutschtum* took two forms within nationalist women's associations. First, right-wing women's groups worked in a broader sense to promote nationalist sentiment among bourgeois women, by articulating the same grievances and making the same attacks on the Weimar "system" as their masculine counterparts. Nationalist women's associations in Hanover, such as the anti-Semitic German Women's League, called protest meetings against the "peace of shame" (*Schmachfrieden*) imposed by the Treaty of Versailles, the loss of Upper Silesia, and the French occupation of the Ruhr. The Ruhr occupation, where the French used black troops from North Africa, drove bourgeois nationalists almost to a frenzy, since fraternization between black French troops and local German women embodied both sexual and national dishonor. Paula Mueller-Otfried experienced actual physical distress upon hearing of German women who transgressed by consorting with the enemy. She wrote a friend that "it makes me so very much ashamed, when I hear repeatedly that German women and girls in the occupied areas throw themselves into the arms of the enemy, and in their disgraceful coquetry and flirtation ignore the fact that they are of German descent and ought to uphold German honor. [These reports] make one feel so weak, so completely ill."[4] For Mueller-Otfried, the occupation was thus analyzed through women's experiences, and women's sexual honor (or lack thereof) was equated with national honor.

Right-wing women thus voiced the same grievances about German foreign policy as nationalist men, although they often conceptualized these issues in terms of feminine honor or shame. In addition to such complaints, they also tried to preserve *Deutschtum* by defending the German family. Before 1914, the promotion of a specific style of household management (mediated especially through domestic science courses) had been used to counteract "social degeneration" by clubwomen. Now, however, the rhetoric about familial dissolution escalated to a new level, and the "defense" of a specific type of family structure became nationalist women's primary strategy to preserve *Deutschtum*.

Nationalist women's arguments regarding family structure should be seen within the context of a national debate in Weimar Germany regarding immorality and the endangered family.[5] The decline of the German birthrate had occasioned concern and discussion before 1914, but the loss of life during World War I, the continuing decline in fertility after 1918, and changes in gender roles during the 1920s rendered this discussion almost hysterical, especially on the right.[6] For the right wing, discussion about population policy was articulated in debates about immorality and the preservation of the family and segregated gender roles.

Many Protestant bourgeois women saw the entire postwar period as a time of dissolving boundaries, erasing lines of secure demarcation between men and women, parents and children, rulers and ruled. Magdalene von Tilling, the head of the VEFD, expressed her dismay over this "chaos" by mourning the disappearance of "the orderliness [*Ordnung*] of life, within which we lived so securely."[7] Proposals by progressive liberals to reform divorce law, or liberalize access to abortion, were perceived by nationalist women (and the right as a whole) as further assaults on the family, and on basic social boundaries.[8] Nationalist women thus participated in this national debate on immorality and the family, and nationalist women's associations tried to repel these "assaults" on the family by encouraging bourgeois women to uphold German "morality," preserve "traditional" (polarized) gender roles, and increase average family size.

The DEF was the first Hanover women's organization to articulate both forms of nationalism: the form expressed in the rejection of Germany's foreign policies and the form expressed in the debates over the family. As early as December 1919, DEF leaders had decided to give up the principle of "political neutrality" completely in order to emphasize aggressive nationalism. DEF officers justified this abandonment of political neutrality by arguing that in the past, the DEF had been able to gain what it wanted by lobbying individual government officials, and by relying on personal connections. Now, however, it would be necessary to influence political parties. The DEF's new 1920 program stated that in the future, the DEF's work would reflect the "German" part of its name as much as it would women's issues. Mueller-Otfried explained to the Hanover chapter in the spring of 1919 that the DEF would not ally itself with any single party, "but the word 'German' [in our name] includes a political orientation, and the representation of interests that stand above parties." She listed such interests: the rejection of many of the provisions being negotiated at Versailles, the return of forfeited German territory, preserving the unity of church and state, and securing the right of the emperor to return to German territory.[9] In practice, this new program meant working for the conservative *Ordnungsblock* coalition in local elections, and urging members to vote for the DNVP, DVP, or Guelphs in national elections. The DEF was particularly fervent in its support of President Hindenburg.[10]

The DEF was only the first Hanover women's organization to reformulate its policies in more explicitly nationalist terms; it was not the largest, or most successful association to do so. The largest, and most active right-wing women's organization in Hanover during the 1920s was the local chapter of the National League of German Housewives' Associations. The Hanover Housewives' Association was founded under the auspices of the local Women's Service in 1915, and worked during the war to distribute scarce foodstuffs equitably and to educate housewives about their duties during wartime.[11] After 1918, however, the association's membership declined, and it almost collapsed during the hyperinflation of 1923. The Housewives' Association was revived and steered to the right by Bertha Hindenberg-Delbrück, who joined the Hanover chapter in 1925 and quickly came to dominate it.[12]

Hindenberg-Delbrück was a member of the right-wing German National People's Party, and was determined to split her association off from the City Women's League (which she regarded as too liberal, and a product of the detested revolution).[13] She also intended to purge her group of Jewish members, whom she later called "a vanishingly small racially alien part of the *Volk*," who should not enjoy the same rights as "German-blooded" members.[14] Finally, she wanted to lead the Housewives' Association to support conservative goals; she argued that all DNVP women ought to try to infiltrate and win influence within "neutral" women's associations. "That is the only way," she wrote, "to counteract successfully the pacifistic-democratic influence [of liberal women in the movement]."[15] Through astute maneuvering, and because her world view resembled that of many other clubwomen, she would succeed on all counts.

The Housewives' Association was still officially politically "neutral," like the DEF; the group nevertheless stressed broadly nationalist themes, without endorsing any specific political party. The association's newsletter regularly denounced the Treaty of Versailles, for example, and attacked German women's organizations that maintained contact with British or French women. The association also ran "Buy German" campaigns, which sought to persuade German housewives to boycott imported goods. The parent organization of the Hanover chapter, the National Federation of German Housewives' Associations, also cultivated close ties with industry and supported protectionism, although it was formally a consumer group. In local politics, the Housewives' Association invited speakers from the *Ordnungsblock* to address its members before elections, and vehemently denounced the influence of the SPD in local government.[16] Hindenberg-Delbrück in fact worked diligently to cultivate close relations with the members of the *Ordnungsblock* and was aided in her attempts to gain support from the city government by her close relationship with Mayor Menge's sister.[17]

In addition, the Housewives' Association attacked contemporary changes in gender roles and sought to defend its version of the German family. Hindenberg-Delbrück particularly loathed the alleged rapid increase in the number of professional women and working women, whom she felt undermined the German family by their supposed aversion to childbearing and housekeeping. Thus, clubwomen's fear of familial decline, a strong theme in the movement's prewar work, was broadened and updated: the fight to preserve the family now included not only teaching domestic science and improving housekeeping standards (a leitmotif in the movement's work before 1914), but also attacks on working mothers and wives, a topic that women leaders had ignored before the war. In addition, the Housewives' Association revived and expanded the movement's prewar attacks on the SPD.

Hindenberg-Delbrück and her colleagues were bitter over the fact that the housewife was increasingly seen as old-fashioned, and less important to the national economy; Hindenberg-Delbrück herself angrily compared housewives to Cinderella, neglected and despised, while the new professional women (Cinderella's stepsisters) got all the attention from society at large, and the government.[18] The Housewives' Association argued that these professional women were disastrous wives and mothers. Hindenberg-Delbrück wrote that

It is one of the regrettable trends of our time that so many German women, out of ignorance of housekeeping and child-rearing, seek to avoid the happiness that a healthy woman receives from [bearing] a child. When one observes today's woman, who is externally masculine, with short hair and cigarettes, and a tired, indolent facial expression, one might well fear for the future of the German people. . . . [Such women are responsible] for the destruction of unborn life [abortions], which are performed in such numbers that these losses now exceed all the deaths in the Great War. . . . [Housewives] must wish that their fellow women would not work in offices so much, but rather should be trained for their real profession as housewives and mothers.[19]

The Housewives' Association entered into a close alliance with the local Bund der Kinderreichen (League of Large Families) to promote the "proper" form of family life, and to combat the growth in the number of mothers working outside the home. The Housewives' Association and the league together denounced the idea that a "normal" family had "only" two or three children. By the early 1930s, the Housewives's Association joined the right-wing campaign against *Doppelverdiener* (working couples), and applauded a new law that would permit the firing of married female civil servants.[20] By the end of the Weimar period, the Housewives' Association even came to combine this preoccupation with eugenics. In its newsletter, the organization called for the passage of a law to tax the childless in order to benefit "child rich" families (a *Familienlastenausgleich*); this would enable "hereditarily sound" (*erbtüchtige*) married couples to afford more children.[21]

Hindenberg-Delbrück's enmity against single working women in fact went so far that she attacked the growing trend toward addressing all women, married or not, as *Frau* in the workplace or public settings. Hindenberg-Delbrück claimed that this title should be reserved for married women exclusively, and tried to persuade her colleagues in the national DNVP to propose legislation to outlaw the practice. She was unsuccessful.[22]

Besides using these general policies and attacks on working women to appeal to potential members, the Housewives' Association also attracted women by promoting an updated image of the housewife. The association proposed to restore the status of housewives by modernizing the housewife's image and adapting her role to fit within the new *Wohnkultur* (domestic life-style) of the 1920s.[23] For example, the organization presented its members as educated and trained consumers, who carefully evaluated the new domestic technology (electrical appliances, new types of domestic architecture and decoration) and incorporated these items selectively into their households. In 1927, the National League established an office in Leipzig that tested domestic appliances and other products, and issued purchasing recommendations for housewives based on these tests. Products which the league passed on were entitled to carry a copy of the its symbol, a stylized sun, in their advertisements and labels, as a seal of approval. In its newsletters and propaganda, the Housewives' League reminded its members to look for the sun symbol when making their purchases.[24] Another way in which the Hanover Housewives' presented itself as a force for modernization was its support for the "rationalization" of housework and of the household, reflected in its work with architects.

The Housewives' Association thus successfully combined old and new values to attract members: broadly nationalist policies and the defense of a particular vision of the family, along with a claim to represent a modernized, professionalized style of housewifery. Under Hindenberg-Delbrück's leadership, the Hanover chapter grew rapidly, from about 500 members in 1925 to 1,050 in 1928, more than double the size of the largest prewar bourgeois women's association.[25] The Housewives' Association was an unprecedented success. Hindenberg-Delbrück used this membership, along with contacts in local government (more easily available after conservatives regained partial control of Hanover's administration in 1924), to promote specific programs that reflected this right-wing combination of new and old.

First, the Housewives' Association vigorously attempted to influence Hanover's municipal housing policy, in order to promote the "rationalization" of the household.[26] Hindenberg-Delbrück began her campaign in this area by attempting to win an appointment for a member of the Housewives' Association to the municipal Buildings Committee (*Bandeputation*). This would have given the association direct influence and input over the city's building policies. The composition of the committee was determined by law, however, and did not permit the inclusion of representatives of voluntary associations. Mayor Menge, who was elected when the conservatives gained control in 1924, therefore was forced to turn Hindenberg-Delbrück's request down; he softened his refusal, however, by offering to include her in the municipal architectural prize commission, which judged local architects' proposals for model floor plans for apartment houses. The proposals selected for prizes then served as guidelines for municipally subsidized housing.[27] Through voicing her opinions in these prize commissions, Hindenberg-Delbrück could hope to influence the floor plans and overall design of new housing developments. Hindenberg-Delbrück was in fact included in several subsequent prize commissions, such as a 1926 commission that evaluated 146 proposals.[28]

Through work in these commissions, Hindenberg-Delbrück was able to establish contact with men who were leading architects or who were active in the municipal buildings department.[29] The Hanover Housewives' Association was able to further its access to these circles by holding a special public meeting at the beginning of 1927 on "Housewives and Architects." At this meeting, which was attended by representatives from the leading architects' association, builders, the mayor, and the municipal buildings department, the Housewives' Association presented its wishes concerning new construction in the city.[30]

The specific suggestions that members of the association stressed when working with local architects and builders emphasized the arrangement of the kitchen, the main focus of the national movement to "reform" and rationalize housework. In particular, Hindenberg-Delbrück and her fellow members pushed for the introduction of modern kitchen sinks, with hot and cold running water, along with other details to create the new, small *Arbeitsküche*.[31] The Housewives' Association thus pursued its vision of a "modern" household and housework. The association appears to have had some success in influencing local architects and the city, particularly in the building of new apartment houses in Kleefeld.[32]

The Housewives' Association also promoted its vision of housekeeping and architecture in a series of exhibitions staged in 1928 and 1929. In the first exhibition, members of the public could see a model apartment, set up especially to demonstrate the association's version of the new *Wohnkultur*. It featured several rooms with examples of the latest styles of furniture, along with a host of appliances using the modern "magic maid," electricity: new sorts of ovens, washing machines, refrigerators, vacuum cleaners, and irons.[33]

These exhibitions contained a mixture of both old and new styles of domesticity, and reflected the broader political agenda of the association and the conservative women who led it. The model apartment, for example, included both old and new concepts of design. The decoration of the apartment followed the modern style of the 1920s *Wohnkultur*; the curtains were light, to let in sunlight and avoid trapping dust, and the wallpapers were also in light colors. Much of the floor was covered with linoleum. In choosing the furniture for the apartment, the association selected modern, sleek designs, influenced by the Bauhaus.[34]

But this model apartment also contained much that reflected prewar domesticity and conservative conceptions of the family. In a period when live-in domestic servants were fast disappearing from bourgeois households, this apartment contained a maid's room, which reflected the association's struggle to uphold class distinctions. Furthermore, the association emphasized that it promoted the use of electric labor-saving appliances and modern domesticity *not* in order to free wives from housework, or to make it possible (or easier) for mothers to work outside the home, but rather to give them more time to serve their husbands and children. In the opening speech for the first exhibition, Hindenberg-Delbrück explicitly rejected the idea the new household technology should lead to the "liberation of women and the rationalization [of the household]"; she regarded this as "mindless Americanization." "In spite of rationalization," she argued, "the German woman wants to remain the person who cares for and guards the home, and wants to stay a wife and mother."[35] Housewives needed labor-saving devices, Hindenberg-Delbrück argued, so that they could devote themselves more intensively to their children, and have even more children. The model apartment was designed for a family with five children, because (as the guide to the exhibition explained) "in our opinion, the future of the German *Volk* rests with the family, and indeed only with the large family."[36]

The Housewives' Association also focused on the old problem of domestic servants, which had occupied its predecessor, the prewar Housewives' Association. Hindenberg-Delbrück and her association lobbied vehemently against a proposed new federal law on servants, which would have replaced the old law on servants rendered obsolete by the revolution. The Housewives' Association objected to almost every provision of the draft presented by the government to the Reichstag, including the stipulation that servants be given nine hours rest at night; Hindenberg-Delbrück wrote that any attempt to regulate the number of hours worked by servants was "impractical." The association especially objected to the provision that unmarried pregnant servants could not be simply tossed out onto the street, but rather were entitled to the normal notification period. If pregnant servants were not dismissed, then they were entitled to four weeks rest before their due dates, a provision that Hindenberg-Delbrück also rejected. Instead, she demanded the right to fire pregnant servants without warning, "for moral reasons, and because children are present [in the household], and to secure the public reputation and security of the family."[37] The association's stand on this question showed once again how flexible a concept "morality" was: for progressives, it could be used to justify solidarity with "fallen" women, but in the hands of conservatives, it could be used quite differently.

Overall, the Housewives' Association rejected the entire proposed law as "socialist." It was unnecessary, and was only proposed "so that Marxism can complete its work on and in the family, and carry its destructive struggle and moral barbarism into the family."[38] If housewives were forced to comply with the law, Hindenberg-Delbrück wrote, they would cease to employ servants, which would promote the type of servantless household found in America, "and we know that there is in fact no family life in America and no domestic culture, which our German lives and hearts require."[39] A strong family life rested on the work of servants.

Instead, the Housewives' Association proposed to regulate the relationship between servants and employers, and to end the decline in the number of servants in bourgeois households, by implementing a *hauswirtschaftliches Pflichtjahr* (a year of mandatory domestic science training) for all working-class girls. Hindenberg-Delbrück argued that working-class girls needed such training in order to learn to care for their own families; bourgeois girls, she claimed, picked up such knowledge at home, and could therefore be excused from formal courses. This argument carried forward the Hanover movement's prewar lobbying for obligatory domestic science training for working-class women. The Housewives' Association, in coalition with the DEF and other conservative women's groups, proposed that all female *Volksschule* graduates should be compelled to take one year of domestic science courses, followed by a one-year "apprenticeship" in the home of an experienced bourgeois housewife. Only through such training, members of the coalition wrote, "can our women reach competence in domestic science and the role of the *Hausmutter*, which will lead to the economic, physical, and moral healing of family life, and will counteract the serious problems and dangers that threaten our entire *Volksleben*."[40]

These proposals had two purposes. First, they furthered the Housewives' Association's goal of presenting housework as a modern profession, one that required professional training by a "master" housewife, similar to other careers. In addition, the *Pflichtjahr* also would have served to alleviate the shortage of domestic servants in bourgeois homes. As the expanding service sector offered working-class women an increasing number of jobs, it became more and more difficult for bourgeois housewives to find domestic servants. In addition, the economic upheavals of the early 1920s had left many bourgeois families unable to afford servants. An "apprenticeship" that induced or compelled young working women to be "trained" for low or even no wages would have solved the bourgeois "servant problem," reinforced class distinctions, and shored up the status of middle-class housewives. It would have also represented the ultimate "civilizing" of working-class girls by bourgeois women.

Through intense lobbying of those politicians whom they knew personally, the members of Hindenberg-Delbrück's coalition were able to win support from local bourgeois parties for at least a one-year course in domestic science. The SPD delegation in the lower house of the municipal parliament, however, was able to block the plan's adoption. The SPD did not object to the idea of domestic science training, but demanded that the courses should be voluntary, not mandatory, and should be given within the public schools; the bourgeois women's coalition was unwilling to compromise, and so the proposal died. The Housewives' Association was able to convince the city to begin to offer domestic science courses at the local girls' vocational school, but these attracted only a few hundred pupils during the 1920s. Later, the Housewives' Association was also able to persuade the municipal employment office to force unemployed women to take a four-hour course in sewing as a condition for receiving unemployment support.[41]

Frustrated by the SPD's opposition to a *Pflichtjahr*, women leaders fell back upon the idea of offering private domestic science courses, as they had before the war; the new classes were called "motherhood courses," and were supposed to promote "rationalized," "modern" child care. The conservative coalition created by Hindenberg-Delbrück was joined in this effort by the liberal and professional women's groups that made up the Women's City League, headed by Mathilde Drees.[42]

Like the domestic science training offered by the Women's Educational Association before 1914, the "motherhood" courses were successful, attracting many more applicants than the women's movement could accommodate, since rooms and funding were found for only 75 to 100 pupils per year. Available sources cannot tell us why these courses were so popular, but in Hamburg, where "modern" domestic science courses were also oversubscribed, the pupils were drawn largely from "better off" working-class families or from the lower middle class. These young women could expect to afford the appliances and household style promoted by the courses, and were enthusiastic about domestic "modernization." Poorer women, who could not afford the consumer goods or standard of living presupposed by these courses, tended to be more skeptical about household "rationalization."[43]

The fact that these courses were the only project that all leaders of local women's groups could agree to support speaks volumes about the state of the women's movement in Hanover during the 1920s. Before the war, the women's movement had presented a united front on one issue after another, and had created coalitions to work on a variety of women's interests, including improving women's education and professional opportunities. Now, however, movement leaders came together only to promote "motherhood" courses, which explicitly supported a traditional, although now "rationalized," sexual division of labor.

The Housewives' Association was the largest and most visible conservative women's group in Weimar Hanover, but it was not the only such organization. By the late 1920s, the Housewives' Association was joined by several other nationalist women's groups. Together, these organizations formed a coherent movement within the splintered local women's movement, maintaining close contact with each other and working together.

The DEF was an ally of the Housewives' Association, as one might expect, but beyond that, the VEFD served to coordinate the work of nationalist Protestant women. Nationally, the VEFD ran a school to train conservative Protestant women as public speakers; in conjunction with the DNVP, these women were then sent to address Protestant women's groups on topics such as the treatment of Germans in Poland, the occupied Ruhr, and the necessity of preserving *Deutschtum*. *Deutschtum* in fact became a code word used by nationalist women and the DNVP to designate Protestant bourgeois values, the preservation of bourgeois economic status, domesticity, and a corporative social structure.[44] As in other cities, in Hanover the VEFD and DEF together created courses for Protestant women for "political training," which combined education about the new civil rights gained by German women with a broader conservative political orientation.[45]

Of all the women's associations in Hanover, the Women's Division of the Colonial Society should have faced a crisis regarding its raison d'être, since Germany no longer had colonies, but in fact the group flourished during the late 1920s. It had almost collapsed during the hyperinflation of 1923, but thereafter grew steadily. From a low point of less than 100 members, the Hanover chapter grew to 322 members by 1930, gaining 82 new converts in 1929 alone, which made it one of the fastest-growing chapters in Germany.[46]

The society worked to support German settlers who remained in former German colonies, raising money to finance German schools in East and South West Africa, and sending books to German reading circles there. The group also arranged for the children of settlers to travel to Germany and receive a higher education. The society hoped to preserve the *Deutschtum* of settlers by giving their children a German-style education and to minimize the children's contact with British colonists and authorities. As before the war, the group also continued to recruit and send servants and brides to German families in Africa. The availability of German servants, it was hoped, would reduce the number of German children being raised by African servants, so that colonists' children would be taught "German customs and *Heimatart*." German brides were to avert the "danger of mixing [the races]."[47]

The anti-Semitic German Women's League also continued to grow during the 1920s, and became one of the most articulate nationalist women's groups in the city. The league's main purpose was to promote nationalist, patriotic sentiment among German women, in order to mobilize female voters to work for "a nationalist government, which will finally raise the name of Germany among nations to a position of honor and respect."[48] Like other right-wing women's groups, the league's work combined mainstream nationalist rhetoric with concern for the German family and German morality. The league promoted "patriotism" by hosting public assemblies in which topics such as "England's policy of encirclement" were discussed, or patriotic poetry recited. The league also sent aid to ethnic Germans in Poland. To protect German morals, the league also worked in the local film censorship board and spoke out against alleged white slavery in the occupied Ruhr. It became one of the larger women's organizations in the city and maintained cordial relationships with other center and right-wing bourgeois women's associations.[49]

Although the overt nationalism of the German Women's League was a development of the Weimar period, its style and methods were similar to those of prewar women's associations; the league's propaganda was often done within the context of afternoon teas, and the overall tone of their meetings was fairly genteel. This provided a contrast to the style of the most militant nationalist women's group to emerge during the 1920s in Hanover, the Queen Louise League. Named after the queen who rallied Prussia during Napoleon's invasion, the Louise League was closely affiliated with the nationalist paramilitary *Stahlhelm* organization. The Louise League also was founded in order to promote nationalism among bourgeois women, but its style was distinctly militarist, as a description of one of its elaborate annual celebrations of Louise's birthday makes clear:

> The *Stahlhelm* opened the meeting by playing the "Cuirassier's March," and then, to the sound of the "York March," the flags of patriotic associations were carried in, and grouped around the bust of Queen

Louise in the front [of the hall]. The league's president, Frau Hölscher, gave a speech which pointed out how Louise's time was similar to our own, since "misery, distress, bondage and the chains of slavery oppressed our poor *Volk* then, as now." . . . The singing of the league's anthem was followed by a gripping and beautiful drill ceremony with the flags . . . finally came a short play by Lienhardt, "the baker of Winstein," . . . its content showed that in spite of French rule in those days [during Napoleon's rule] German nature triumphed. . . . The meeting ended with the flags being carried out to another march.[50]

At another meeting, a speaker discussed the "war guilt lie" and the stab-in-the-back theory of the German Revolution. In keeping with the quasi-military tone of the league, members of the group referred to one another as "*Kameradin*."[51]

By the mid-1920s, Hanover's "patriotic" women's associations began to draw closer. They sent representatives to each other's meetings and exchanged greetings on holidays and anniversaries. Joined by the local Patriotic Women's Association (Red Cross), these nationalist associations began to form a movement within the women's movement. The Louise League, the German Women's League, the DEF, and the women's auxiliary of the Colonial Society allied themselves with the Housewives' Association to press for the domestic science *Pflichtjahr*. They made up the original alliance that sponsored the "motherhood" courses, and were only later joined by the BDF-affiliated Women's City League in this work.[52] In addition, nationalist women's organizations worked closely with their masculine counterparts, such as the local chapter of the Association for *Deutschtum* Abroad.[53]

At the same time, however, most nationalist women's groups continued to maintain ties to associations that were still affiliated with the BDF; thus, right-wing associations came to form a movement within the movement, yet most were still linked to the "official" women's movement represented by the BDF and the City Women's League. The fact that these links between nationalist and BDF-affiliated groups still existed was reflected in the same formal expressions of "friendship" exchanged between nationalist women's groups. Nationalist and BDF-affiliated groups still sometimes notified each other in advance of their meetings, and sent representatives to each other's annual assemblies; they exchanged greetings on the occasions of the anniversary of each association's foundation; and in their own records, they kept lists of "friendly" or allied associations that included both sorts of groups.

The list of "friendly" organizations kept by the Housewives' Association, for example, included not only other conservative or nationalist groups such as the DEF, the VEFD, the German Women's League, and the Louise League, but also the BDF-affiliated City Women's League, the Association of Technical (needlecraft) Female Teachers, the League for German Women's Culture (a "life-style reform" group), and the Association of the Friends of Young Girls. The 1926 annual assembly of the local German Women's League included not only representatives from the DEF and the Patriotic Women's Association, but also emissaries from the Women's Club, the Housewives' Association, and the women's auxiliary of the Colonial Society, which all still belonged to the BDF. As late as 1931, when the world of Hanover clubwomen was becoming severely strained by partisan polarization, the Women's City League was still sending representatives to celebrations organized by the German Women's League.[54]

While the right wing of the movement was growing and consolidating, forming a new locus within the broader local movement, one new women's association did try to carry forward the prewar tradition of *Überparteilichkeit*, or political "neutrality." After the collapse of the old ADF affiliate in Hanover, the Women's Educational Association, the old Society for the Advancement of Female Education, now renamed the Staatsbürgerinnenverband (League of Women Citizens), became the local ADF branch. It was led by Mathilde Drechsler-Hohlt. The Women Citizens would prove to be the only important organization within the Hanover movement to strive for a centrist position; instead of succeeding in unifying the movement, however, the Women Citizens would only earn the enmity of the right.

Drechsler-Hohlt had begun her career in the Hanover movement as an officer in a women's temperance association just before the war, and she became active in the National Women's Service after 1914. Immediately after the revolution, she sided with the DEF in rejecting the new Weimar system, but moved toward the center thereafter, drifting away from Paula Mueller-Otfried. She became the head of the local DVP women's caucus, and eventually became a defender of the government once her party joined the ruling coalition; at the same time, she became a champion of equal rights for women.

Drechsler-Hohlt argued that a League of Women Citizens was necessary in order to educate women about their new role as citizens, and to mobilize them to attain complete equality. The various political parties could not be relied upon to do so, she claimed, because each pursued its own interests. Only an independent, nonpartisan women's group could rise above separate interests to see "what is necessary for the state, and [to see] in all purity the laws that govern the workings of the state. That such a standpoint is possible must be the conviction of a League of Women Citizens, otherwise it has no reason to exist." Political parties pursued interest group politics, she concluded, while the League of Women citizens would support a *Staatspolitik*. Mathilde Drees, a close ally of Drechsler-Hohlt, also reflected this belief in a politics that could transcend political parties in order to unite women, when she wrote that partisan differences "can have no place in women's organizations. There is one *Weltanschauung* that can and should bind together all women, and that is the law of morality [which lives] in our hearts." This view of a "women's politics" would guide the Women Citizens and the Women's City League almost to the very end of the Weimar period.[55]

Drechsler-Hohlt intended that the Hanover chapter should become an "*überparteilicher* gathering point for the political education of women."[56] To this end, the group sponsored a series of public lectures on such topics as "the geographic underpinnings of politics" and "the development and positions of the political parties." For its members, the league ran a series of small reading groups, which studied and discussed various political treatises.[57] Like the rest of the ADF, however, the Hanover chapter confined itself primarily to educational work, and was unable to translate its principles into concrete local political practice. Indeed, this would have been almost impossible: adopting specific stands on local issues would have ultimately meant violating political "neutrality," since such specificity would inevitably have brought the league closer to some parties than others.

The ADF's strict partisan neutrality ruled out any close alliance with the Housewives' Association and other conservative groups, although the Women Citizens were closely allied with liberal Mathilde Drees and the Women's City League. Indeed, as tension grew between the Women Citizens and right-wing women's association, Drechsler-Hohlt openly criticized strident nationalism within the Hanover women's movement, writing in the local newspaper that women ought to reject a rigid nationalism that tends to excess and fanaticism. In domestic politics, [this is expressed] by attacks on everything *Rassenfremd* (anti-Semitism) and in foreign politics, it panders to the popular desire to threaten force through gestures and phrases. . . . Germany needs [a rational nationalism], bowing one's head [to necessity] while balling the fist and gritting the teeth. . . . [We need] responsible nationalist policies, not speeches, the waving of flags, and oaths.[58]

This was a clear repudiation of the style and rhetoric of local nationalist women's associations, especially the German Women's League and the Queen Louise League.

By the late 1920s, tension between the Housewives' Association and the rest of the Women's City League was growing. Hindenberg-Delbrück was uninterested in working with the city's older educational and professional women's associations, which were affiliated with the more liberal BDF; she was determined that the Housewives' Association should pursue its own course. At the same time, women's professional associations were becoming collective bargaining groups and were less involved in the City Women's League. The two most vital sectors of the local women's movement thus had little common ground, especially as the criticism of working women by the Housewives' Association became more vocal. The tension between housewives and women's professional organizations was also mirrored on the national level, in the growing divisions between these groups' parent organizations.[59]

In addition, personal rivalries between Hindenberg-Delbrück on the one hand, and Drees and Drechsler-Hohlt on the other, were also growing. Hindenberg-Delbrück resented Drees's claim that because she was the head of the City Women's League, she was therefore the head of the local women's movement, and spoke for all associations that belonged to the league, including the Housewives' Association. Hindenberg-Delbrück felt that Drees's public pronouncements in her role as leader of the league were too liberal, and emphasized women's rights too much; increasingly, Hindenberg-Delbrück came under pressure from local nationalists who felt that by belonging to the league, the Housewives' Association was tacitly endorsing Drees's (that is, liberal, DDP) politics. Hindenberg-Delbrück was apparently alienated, for example, by a speech given by Drees at the fiftieth anniversary celebration of the local Patriotic Women's Association (Red Cross), in which Drees claimed that the organizations of the City League were active members of the BDF. Afterwards, Hindenberg-Delbrück was approached by a conservative local politician who asked her "if we [the Housewives' Association] were really *Frauenrechtlerinnen*," which embarrassed her.[60] Most of the other nationalist women's associations that the Housewives' Association worked with did not belong officially to the BDF or to the City League (although they were still on friendly terms with BDF affiliates), and Hindenberg-Delbrück was concerned that her organization's reputation in local nationalist circles was suffering because of its affiliation with the City League. In addition, she claimed that the members of her association were also alienated by Drees and the BDF, arguing that "we cannot tie our entire membership to the one-sided women's rights program of the City League."[61]

Drees and the organizations that made up the City League had founded the Housewives' Association during the war, and the National League of German Housewives still belonged to the BDF, but Hindenberg-Delbrück was determined to break with Drees, the City League, and ultimately the BDF. In 1928 she found a pretext to do so. Drechsler-Hohlt and the Women Citizens borrowed a copy of the Housewives' Association membership list in order to obtain names for a pool of female jurors to be given to the city; later, the list was also used (without asking Hindenberg-Delbrück) to issue invitations to a lecture given by BDF leader and liberal politician Gertrud Bäumer to a meeting of the Women Citizens. Hindenberg-Delbrück then forced the resignation of the member of her association who had given the membership list to the Women Citizens (a friend of Drechsler-Hohlt). When Drees sided with Drechsler-Hohlt in this matter, the Housewives' Association resigned from the City League with no warning or discussion.[62]

When Drees, Drechsler-Hohlt, and their allies in the Housewives' Association submitted a resolution at a subsequent meeting of the Housewives' Association calling for the association to rejoin the City League, Hindenberg-Delbrück did not permit it to come to a vote. Instead, she delivered an astonishing forty-five-minute polemic, denouncing Drees, Drechsler-Hohlt, the City League, and the entire BDF; she then declared the meeting adjourned. When her opponents counterattacked and threatened to bring up the matter at future meetings, Hindenberg-Delbrück responded that if the resolution was not dropped, that she would begin a public campaign to discredit the Women Citizens, in which she would accuse the Women Citizens of attempting to infiltrate and dominate the

Housewives' Association. Hindenberg-Delbrück's nationalist allies—the DEF, German Women's League, and others—promised to join this attack, which would have constituted a public civil war within the women's movement. Appalled and taken aback, Drees and Drechsler-Hohlt agreed to drop the matter.[63]

Hindenberg-Delbrück had now achieved almost all of her goals. She had broken with the City League, and purged her own association of members who were sympathetic to Drees and Drechsler-Hohlt. In addition, the affair had the added bonus (from Hindenberg-Delbrück's standpoint) of reducing the number of Jewish members in the association, since many of the members who resigned in protest over Hindenberg-Delbrück's actions were Jewish. She wrote later to an associate that

> to our joy, after this struggle almost all Jewish members resigned from our chapter. Since then, I have emphasized the Christian aspects of our work in our newsletter, for example, publicizing our Christmas celebration, so that Jewish women would not feel comfortable in our group, and therefore do not seek to join. . . . The entire national organization [of housewives] should have done the same, in my opinion.[64]

Once free of the restraint imposed by membership in the City League, the Housewives' Association became more vehement in its attacks on the BDF and the international women's movement. In 1929, the Housewives' Association joined other nationalist women's groups, in Hanover and nationally, in denouncing the National League of Women Citizens for hosting the 1929 World Congress of the World League for Women's Suffrage and Citizenship, because this conference included representatives from Britain, France, and the United States. In the Hanover chapter's newsletter, Hindenberg-Delbrück wrote that the Women Citizens should be ashamed "to greet women from the nations that [wrote] the Treaty of Versailles with celebrations on German soil. . . . [Patriotism] forbids the public show of friendly cooperation with women from the victors' states as long as our *Volk*, our brothers and sisters in occupied areas are ground into the mud by these nations."[65]

By the end of the 1920s, a vigorous right wing had thus emerged within the Hanover women's movement. Many organizations within this right wing still maintained links to associations affiliated with the BDF, but by the end of the 1920s, the nationalist wing was also increasingly hostile to the "official" movement represented by the Women's City League. The

Depression would only intensify these rivalries. After 1929, unemployment skyrocketed in Hanover; by the end of 1932, almost one-third of the city's labor force was receiving unemployment insurance, and more were on shortened workweeks. Parallel to this development, Hanover's political spectrum began to polarize and fragment, as happened across Germany. Between 1919 and 1929, Hanover had been an SPD town; the party was united internally and dominant in local elections as in few other German cities. Between the national elections held in 1928 and 1930, however, the SPD's share of the local vote declined slightly, from 51 to 45 percent; during the same period, the percentage won by the National Socialists increased from 2 to almost 21 percent. By July 1932, the SPD had sunk to 37 percent of the vote in Hanover, while the Nazis received over 40 percent.[66]

The rise of the National Socialists should have provoked a strong reaction from the women's movement, since the Nazis proposed to drive women out of public life and restrict them to the home. While some members of the movement struggled to find an effective response to the National Socialists, others allied themselves with the Nazis: none actively resisted the National Socialist takeover. The League of Women Citizens and the BDF as a whole tried to warn German women against the Nazis, but were fatally hampered by their most basic principle, *Überparteilichkeit* or partisan neutrality. Attacking the National Socialists directly and by name would have violated the precept of political neutrality. In addition, such an attack would have offended the two nationalist housewives' leagues that still belonged to the BDF, and would have provoked an open split within the organization. Thus, until the housewives' leagues left the BDF in 1932, its leadership had to be deliberately vague in its warnings.[67]

In Hanover, even those local women leaders who belonged to the BDF, like Mathilde Drees, Anna Ramsauer, Mathilde Drechsler-Hohlt, and Bertha Duensing, also belonged to the German People's Party or the German Democratic Party, which had both drifted to the right during the late 1920s. These groups did not resist the imposition of rule by emergency decree in 1932, even before the National Socialists came to power.[68] Bound to their parties as much as to the Women's City League (the local embodiment of the BDF), Drees, Drechsler-Hohlt, and the others were unable to mount an all-out, effective campaign against the Nazis.

From the time the Depression began until the two housewives' leagues left the BDF in late 1932, the BDF, the Hanover City Women's League, and the local Women Citizens issued appeals to women voters before elections that certainly intended to warn against the National Socialists (among others), but which were deliberately vague. During the period before the autumn 1930 elections, the Women Citizens supported "parties that will preserve the state." A few months later, its leadership urged women "to form a front against radicalism. . . . we must support peace, order, justice and reason against [the forces of] revolution, hate, and blind passion."[69] This statement could be read as an appeal against a range of parties, including the National Socialists.

Almost two years later, before the critical elections of July 1932 (when the Nazis' share of the national vote rose from 18.3 percent to 37.3 percent), the Women's City League reprinted a BDF appeal to all parties to respect women's political rights, including the right to serve in legislatures. The BDF recommended that female voters keep this right in mind when casting their ballots.[70] This was much more clearly a criticism of the National Socialists, since they did not nominate female candidates for any positions, but it did not name them. Considering the threat that the Nazis posed to women's political rights, the BDF could have mounted a much more spirited critique, but it was hampered by the need to appease the two large housewives' leagues. Only after these two leagues had left the BDF, before the very last free election, held in March 1933, did the BDF launch a more pointed, direct attack on the National Socialists. Its March 1933 appeal to women voters still did not name the Nazis, but called upon women to vote "against the suppression of women in political life . . . against the exclusion of women from the law-making process . . . [against] the incitement of popular passions, and radicalism that will destroy our people."[71] But this relatively forceful statement came too late to have much effect. The "official" women's movement had been unable to rally clubwomen to resist the National Socialists.

There were even hints that some members of the Women's City League were sympathetic to National Socialism, or at least did not reject it as sharply as did the national BDF leadership. The ADF seemed to be shifting to the right during the early 1930s. Drechsler-Hohlt resigned as head of the Hanover Women Citizens in 1931 and, after an interim, was replaced in 1932 by a nationalist attorney named Maya Hering-Hessel; after 1933, Hering-Hessel would have a very successful career in the National Socialist Frauenschaft. Hering-Hessel organized at least one meeting of the Women Citizens, which featured a speech by her (presumably a sympathetic one) on "the position of women within National Socialism." She also invited a local Nazi functionary to speak before the group.[72] Other rank-and-file members of the Women's City League were perhaps also intrigued by the Nazis, or at least the Nazis themselves assumed so: a National Socialist–affiliated white-collar women's organization advertised at least one meeting in the City League newsletter. On the national level, then, the BDF leadership mounted veiled attacks on the Nazis; on the local level, however, the line between the women's movement and National Socialism was not so sharply drawn.

Bertha Hindenberg-Delbrück, Paula Mueller-Otfried, and the other leaders of local nationalist women's groups, such as the German Women's League and the Queen Louise League, belonged almost to a woman to the DNVP. The DNVP had no intention of resisting the National Socialists, and indeed entered into an electoral alliance with the National Socialists in late 1931, dubbed the Harzburg Front; it was formed in order to increase the vote for the entire "nationalist opposition" and to undermine the government. At the same time, the women's organizations affiliated with the Harzburg Front began to coordinate their work and policies: on the national level, the National Socialist Frauenschaft, the Queen Louise League, the women's committee of the DNVP, and the Ring of Nationalist Women (a right-wing umbrella group) began to work together.[73] From this point on, Hanover's nationalist women's organizations were openly and actively committed to bringing down Weimar democracy, by virtue of their affiliation with the Harzburg Front.

Even before the creation of the Harzburg Front, the DEF was relentlessly attacking the Weimar government. In July 1931, for example, the DEF supported the DNVP's rejection of Chancellor Brüning's acceptance of the Young Plan and subsequent negotiations with the Allies to amend the plan; the DEF responded by calling on all its members to protest the Young Plan by boycotting all foreign-produced goods. At the same time, the Hanover Housewives' Association was also launching its most vigorous "buy German" campaign to date.[74]

During the same week in October 1931 that the women's Harzburger Front was created, the BDF was holding its annual congress. At this assembly, BDF representatives passed a resolution supporting an international disarmament conference to be held in Geneva the following year. This support for disarmament brought vehement attacks from the women's organizations affiliated with the Harzburg Front, even though nationalist women who still belonged to the BDF (such as Leonore Kuhn) had approved earlier drafts of the BDF resolution before the creation of the Harzburger Front.[75]

The attack on the BDF resolution led to the final break between right-wing women's organizations and the BDF; conservative women now openly decided to side with the "national opposition" against the organized women's movement. The BDF resolution also proved to be the catalyst for the decision of the two housewives' leagues, the National League of German Housewives and the farm women's National League of Agricultural Housewives, to leave the BDF. The two leagues made their decision jointly, and within the urban National League of German Housewives the move to leave was led by Hanover's Hindenberg-Delbrück, who had acquired considerable influence within the national association.

Hindenberg-Delbrück initially claimed that resignation from the BDF was necessary due to financial demands on the National League, but this argument was indefensible, since only a few hundred Marks per year were involved. Later, Hindenberg-Delbrück and her allies (who included DEF vice-president Selma von der Groeben, who also belonged to the Housewives' Association) shifted to the argument that the organization should resign because nationalist women tended to classify the housewives' league as a "left-wing organization" due to its affiliation with the BDF. Hindenberg-Delbrück asserted that housewives had little in common with the professional women who made up the bulk of the BDF's membership; her description of the role of the housewife, Hiltraud Schmidt-Waldherr notes, bore a distinct similarity to the ideal role for women set forth in the National Socialist Frauenschaft's first manifesto.[76]

In the Hanover chapter's newsletter, Hindenberg-Delbrück justified the housewives' separation from the BDF in even more politically explicit terms, which showed how far part of the movement had shifted to the right during the 1920s. "In the near future we will see," she predicted, "which group of women leaders possessed more insight and foresight." The housewives' leagues had left the BDF, she wrote,

> not because the goals of the housewives' movement are too narrow, but rather because they are broader and aim higher than those of the BDF. . . . The BDF concentrates on *women*, on their importance, their

rights, and their national and international "solidarity." The housewives' movement has concentrated from the very beginning on the *family*, the *Volk*, and the *nation*, within which the housewife takes her place as an achiever, a producer, and a servant; she does not approach [these institutions] with demands. On the one side [the BDF, the goals determined by] the individual, gender, and freedom (in the sense of liberalism)—on our side, organic incorporation into a natural, higher community life [*Gesamtleben*].[77]

The Housewives' Association had now moved very near to the imagery and substance of the National Socialists' rhetoric on women.

With the exception of the German Women's League, nationalist women's organizations in Hanover did not openly espouse anti-Semitism or other forms of racism (although the Housewives' Association had managed to drive out Jewish members using subtle forms of discrimination), but much of their rhetoric overlapped with that of the National Socialists. They prepared bourgeois women for the Nazis' message in many ways: in their distaste for women who worked outside the home; in their espousal of a rigidly "traditional" sexual division of labor; in their hostility toward the SPD; in their aggressive concern for the "oppression" of ethnic Germans who lived outside of Germany; and in their insistent, repeated attacks on both the Treaty of Versailles and on the attempts of Weimar statesmen to come to grips with Germany's postwar circumstances (such as the Young Plan). Not all of these women were happy with the Nazis' plans to exclude women from public life; DEF leaders, for example, in internal memorandums deplored this "new movement's" desire to confine women to the home.[78] But even those who were uneasy about some of the National Socialists' proposed gender hierarchy did not allow their misgivings to keep them from working loyally for the Harzburg Front, and thus for the NSDAP's ascent.

After the Nazi seizure of power in 1933, the DEF's misgivings proved to be well founded. Almost all bourgeois women's organizations in Hanover, and across Germany, were forcibly dissolved or dissolved themselves in 1933, including the umbrella group that bound the bourgeois women's movement together, the BDF. The Hanover Women's City League dissolved itself two weeks after the BDF's demise, in May 1933. Hindenberg-Delbrück joined the National Socialist Party, and her Housewives' Association became affiliated with the National Socialist Frauenfront. The

Women's Colonial Society was permitted to continue to operate until 1936, and then it, too, was dissolved. Only the DEF, the Catholic Women's League, the Jewish Women's League, and a handful of other religious groups were allowed to continue operation independently, and even then under strict limitations.[79]

Hindenberg-Delbrück and the Housewives' Association had only purchased a short respite, however; in 1935, the association was dissolved altogether, and its former members joined the Deutsche Frauenwerk, created by the new *Reichsfrauenführerin*. The women from the Housewives' Association who entered the Frauenwerk were ruthlessly subordinated to the female National Socialist leadership, and some were later purged and relegated to obscurity, including Hindenberg-Delbrück. The new Nazi state had no room for an independent women's movement, and no place for independent women leaders, even nationalist ones. Almost all of the organizations that had made up the bourgeois women's movement were gone by 1936, and the few that remained were subordinate to Nazi women's organizations. The "first" women's movement had been destroyed, in Hanover and across Germany.

Conclusion

In the end, many of the leaders of the Hanover women's movement embraced political partners who proved fatal to the movement's autonomy and very existence; women leaders had done better with their prewar strategy of remaining "above" partisan politics. In fact, partisan "neutrality" served the Hanover women's movement well before 1914. Clubwomen were able to use this stance to combine a vision of gender difference with class interests, in order to create an ideology that united women from different strata of bourgeois society, and which even occasionally transcended confessional divisions. At the national level, standing "above party" also helped the BDF to weld together disparate groups. After 1919, however, this strategy began to fail. Even the belief in spiritual motherhood and policies based on gender difference, which was shared by women from across the political spectrum, could not transcend partisan political differences. The women's movement clung to the idea of partisan neutrality to overcome these divisions, but this choice only served to hamper some movement leaders' attempts to combat the rise of National Socialism.

As this study has shown, however, the movement's decision to remain "neutral" never meant that bourgeois clubwomen were indifferent to the conflicts and interests that shaped masculine politics, even before 1914. Although some of the national movement's leaders sincerely embraced partisan neutrality for its own sake, the movement as a whole did not choose neutrality freely. Instead, it was forced on the women's movement before 1908 by the laws that regulated women's participation in voluntary associations in much of the German Empire. Many women leaders nevertheless were interested in party politics, and after the law was reformed in 1908, some joined men's parties, while continuing to work in the women's movement. Between 1908 and 1914, partisan political differences began to manifest themselves at the national level within the movement, as the BDF was forced to make concessions to keep the conservative DEF within its ranks, and as the suffrage movement split over the issue of three-class suffrage. After 1919, this politicization only accelerated.

In Hanover, at least, these differences had been latent within the movement even before 1914. The Hanover women's movement shared BDF leaders' belief in spiritual motherhood, and used this argument to gain access to higher education for women, to open new professions for women, and to develop a network of social welfare services. The movement's agenda was grounded in essentialism, although few clubwomen were as articulate about this as BDF national leaders; only Mueller-Otfried, Groeben, Kettler, Drechsler-Hohlt, and Hindenberg-Delbrück left behind a body of extensive writings that detailed their beliefs. But Hanover clubwomen's programs were not based solely on a vision of gender: their work also reflected class consciousness.

Although the Hanover movement was "above political parties" before 1914 in terms of local partisan politics (as indeed even municipal officials were expected to be), clubwomen pursued an agenda that did incorporate class interests. Their programs represented a shared consensus between bourgeois men and women about the threat posed to bourgeois society by "social degeneration" and socialism, and how to defuse that threat. As a result, themes emerged within the movement, projects that used the rhetoric of spiritual motherhood to bolster the hegemony of bourgeois values and norms. One of the most important of these themes was an attempt to promote the *embourgeoisement* of the German working-class family. The insistence that the housekeeping of poor or working-class German women was catastrophic, and that domestic science education could solve the nation's social ills, provided a strong line of continuity within the Hanover movement, from beginning to end.

Another persistent theme in the Hanover movement was fear of and hostility toward the SPD. Clubwomen tried to combat the influence of the SPD before 1914 by organizing young working women into confessional associations, where they would be protected from the labor movement's milieu. In a more subtle way, the programs that tried to promote working-class *embourgeoisement* were also antisocialist, since clubwomen argued that reversing the "degeneration" of poor families would chip away at the social conditions that nurtured the party. The movement's hostility toward the SPD became most visible in its work on the "servant question," which affected bourgeois women's personal interests. Clubwomen fought the SPD's attempts to unionize servants and (during the 1920s) to reform servants' working conditions; this theme provided another strong line of continuity within the movement, from beginning to end.

Because its programs were based on a shared consensus about "social degeneration" and supported bourgeois interests, while still remaining "neutral" in bourgeois partisan politics, the Hanover movement was able to secure broad support from local notables. Before 1900, a few women's associations obtained funding and support from masculine voluntary associations or from individual notables, but, thereafter, most of the movement's work was funded by local authorities. Teachers' groups, the Educational Association, temperance organizations, and especially the DEF were able to secure regular subsidies from the city government. In addition, provincial-level officials donated substantial sums to the movement's projects. Movement leaders obtained this financing in part because local authorities shared their analysis of the "social question," but also because they shared sociable and familial ties with leading officials.

The effect of these connections became visible during the 1906 debate over the *Kasernierung* of local prostitutes, the most controversial and public dispute in the movement's history. In other nations and, indeed, in a few other German cities, radical feminists had argued that prostitutes were sexually victimized by both their clients and state regulation; feminists' identification with these victimized prostitutes fueled their anger and criticism of a male-dominated state. In Hanover, however, movement leaders analyzed prostitution primarily as one part of the broader problem of immorality and social degeneration. They did not view prostitutes as victims, nor did they attack men with the anger and vehemence that feminists did elsewhere: Hanover women were constrained from accusing men because of their long-standing ties to a bourgeois male political establishment, which subsidized much of their work. Their analysis and rhetoric, therefore, diverged sharply from those of radical feminists who worked on this issue.

After 1919, when local government was reformed, and city authorities were elected on a democratic basis, the Hanover movement lost some of its connections to municipal officials; this was especially true while the SPD dominated the city government between 1919 and 1924. During this period, much of the movement's work was taken over by the city. When bourgeois political parties regained partial control over city hall after 1924, some movement leaders were again able to cultivate ties to local officials. Since most of their programs had been lost before 1924, however, women's associations were much less dependent on the city for funding, and needed these connections less.

During the Wilhelmine period, then, the Hanover women's movement remained "neutral" in terms of bourgeois party politics, but pursued an agenda that reflected clear class interests, which helped women leaders to gain male notables' support. After 1908, however, when legal reforms permitted women to join masculine political parties, clubwomen began to join or affiliate with different political parties. Local feminists began to assist progressive liberals in their local campaigns, while moderate and conservative bourgeois women cultivated ties with the National Liberal and Conservative parties. This partisan divergence did not affect the internal solidarity of the Hanover movement before 1914, or cause overt political tensions; a shared agenda based on spiritual motherhood and bourgeois cultural hegemony still united Hanover clubwomen.

The bitter national divisions created by war and revolution, combined with the granting of suffrage rights to women, opened the floodgates to politicization and partisan disputes within the movement after 1919. The Women's City League, the umbrella organization for the local women's movement, tried to uphold a policy of partisan neutrality, but the league itself was divided between liberals like Mathilde Drees, and conservative nationalists like Bertha Hindenberg-Delbrück and her allies in the DEF. Partisan political struggles took place even within previously united individual groups, such as the DEF and the Housewives' Association. While organizations that had been at the core of the movement withered or disappeared, like the Educational Association and the Women's Club, new strident nationalist women's associations grew rapidly. Under these circumstances, "neutrality" was an unsuccessful strategy for the City League, but movement leaders were unable to find a new agenda that would reunify clubwomen. As a result, the Hanover movement was unable to launch any major new joint projects during the Weimar period.

Divided internally, the Hanover women's movement was unable to develop an effective response to the threat posed by the National Socialists, and here the local movement mirrored events at the national level. The BDF tried to use "neutrality" during the last years of the Weimar Republic to avoid a split between liberal professional women and the conservative housewives' associations. In the end, however, the housewives' organizations did leave the BDF, and joined the Harzburg front; some of the most vigorous proponents of this split and shift to the far right, as we have seen, came from Hanover. Even the local ADF drifted to the right and, by 1932, was under the leadership of a woman who later rose to a high position within the Nazi Frauenschaft.

In fact, different wings of the women's movement, and various national women's organizations, reacted differently to the National Socialists' rise. It is this divergence that has complicated historians' attempts to assess how, if at all, the movement contributed to (or could have resisted) the Nazi seizure of power. Claudia Koonz, Renate Bridenthal, and others have argued that similarities between the movement's vision of gender and family and the Nazis' family ideology predisposed some segments of the movement to accept National Socialism, and that some organizations within the BDF "even welcomed the Nazis eagerly."[1] Koonz in particular concludes that many organizations within the BDF did not resist the Nazis at all because these associations "subscribed to an ideal of motherhood shared by Hitler and his followers, and their nationalism made women susceptible to a dictatorship that promised a restoration of order."[2]

These conclusions have been hotly rejected by other historians, including Ann Taylor Allen, Elisabeth Meyer-Renschhausen, and Irene Stoehr, who have stressed the potentially radical aspects of the movement's embrace of gender difference. These scholars deny that there is any connection between the movement's embrace of spiritual motherhood and gender difference, on the one hand, and the fact that many bourgeois women's associations accepted National Socialism, on the other. Indeed, they argue that the women's movement did not acquiesce in the Nazi seizure of power at all.

Stoehr argues that the movement's decision to continue to uphold a policy of political "neutrality" during the Depression, even as the Nazis became a more serious threat to women's rights, derived from a broader "indifference" toward all masculine political parties. Stoehr asserts that the leaders of the BDF, alienated by a system in which they had little or no stake, turned their backs on male-dominated parties and the government during the Depression, instead adhering to an alternative "women's politics." This "indifference," Stoehr concludes, which persisted through March 1933, was still "one of the worst forms of resistance [that the movement could have offered], especially toward the Nazis."[3] Meyer-Renschhausen makes a similar argument about Bremen feminists.[4]

Allen asserts that although some Nazi programs resembled those of German feminists, "the similarity to feminist ideas was more apparent than real." While the National Socialists did use similar metaphors and language, she claims, their real meaning was quite different from that of

BDF leaders; she concludes that, in so doing, "the Nazis provided the classical example of the organization of power through the appropriation and redefinition of language."[5] She does not, however, explain in depth what these differences in real meaning were, nor attempt to prove that the agenda of the BDF as a whole differed from the Nazis in substance, if not in rhetoric.

These scholars are persuasive in their claim that spiritual motherhood and gender difference could provide a basis for a socially critical feminism, but their work is most compelling when they discuss the early women's movement, or the radical feminist wing that emerged after 1900. They are less persuasive when they acquit the mainstream of the women's movement of nationalist tendencies, especially for the Weimar period. As this study has shown, in assessing any overlap between the ideas of the women's movement and the National Socialists, and the attitude that bourgeois women's organizations took toward the Nazis, a more nuanced, detailed approach is required, one that notes changes over time and distinguishes between different segments of the women's movement.

Professional women within the BDF leadership such as Dorothee v. Velsen and Else Uhlig-Beil, national leaders of the Women Citizens' League who were affiliated with the progressive liberal DDP throughout much of the Weimar period, were undoubtedly opposed to the National Socialists, and were appalled by the Nazis' proposal to exclude women from public life. The extent to which they could work openly against the Nazis within the movement was limited, however, by the policy of partisan neutrality, which forbade attacks against specific parties. Within the Women Citizens' League, therefore, leaders could only warn members against parties that would "tend to interdict women's political rights."[6] Liberal BDF leaders were constrained from more open attacks by the presence of the conservative housewives' associations within the BDF, which would have objected strongly to an anti-Nazi campaign by BDF leaders. Only after the departure of these groups in late 1932 was the remaining BDF leadership free to speak more openly against the National Socialists, and even then, the tradition of political neutrality muted their voices.[7]

Other moderate or right-wing women's organizations—some of which belonged to the BDF, and some of which did not—did not oppose the National Socialists; indeed, some of the leaders of these associations entered into electoral alliances with the Nazis. Many of the leaders of the urban National League of German Housewives' Associations and the Union of Rural Housewives' Associations (respectively, the largest and third-largest organizations within the BDF) were also active in the DNVP, which was allied with the Nazis in the Harzburg Front after late 1931. Some of these women, such as Countess Margarethe Keyserlingk and Lenore Kuhn, were even on the BDF's executive committee. The Women's Division of the Colonial League, which was closely affiliated with nationalist men's groups, also still belonged to the BDF. Other associations, such as the DEF, had left the BDF, but were still part of women's movement in a broader sense. Together, the DEF and its sister organization, the VEFD, influenced Protestant bourgeois women to vote for the DNVP and, by extension, the Harzburg Front, which strengthened the Nazis' hand.

Other nationalist women's organizations, such as the Louise League or the anti-Semitic German Women's League, had never belonged to the BDF, and indeed cannot be said to have been part of the national women's movement; on the local level, however, these groups were active within the world of clubwomen, exchanging tokens of friendship and working together with associations that did belong to the BDF, such as the Women's Club and the Housewives' Association. As we have seen, nationalist women's groups shared overlapping memberships with mainstream women's associations, and even demonstrated some overlap in leadership, embodied by such women as the Navy League's Elsbeth Spiegelberg and the ADF's Maya Hering-Hessel. Nationalist women's groups threw themselves into the Harzburg Front enthusiastically, working energetically for an end to the Weimar system.

All of these centrist and right-wing associations stressed themes that would become part of the National Socialist message: to the extent that their arguments did overlap with those of the Nazis, they helped to prepare bourgeois women for the National Socialists' propaganda. The center and nationalist wing of the Hanover women's movement trumpeted several of the positions that would become staples in National Socialist rhetoric: championing of "traditional" gender roles; an insistence that these gender roles were being undermined, leading to a decay of the German family; attacks on wives and mothers who worked outside of the home; contempt and hostility toward the SPD; aggressive concern for the "oppression" of ethnic Germans who lived outside of Germany; and insistent, repeated attacks on both the Treaty of Versailles and on the attempts of Weimar statesmen to come to grips with Germany's postwar circumstances (such as the Young Plan). These women did not, however, overtly support the Nazis' racial theories and agenda, although one women's association excluded Jewish members, and at least one other group discouraged Jewish women from joining.

Nevertheless, because of the themes that they stressed in public, and the work that they did as part of the Harzburg Front, the right wing of Hanover's women's movement and its leaders shared at least some culpability for the National Socialists' success. The women's movement can only be completely exonerated if one defines the movement narrowly, focusing primarily on the liberal, professional women's associations that made up the rump of the BDF after October 1932. The distinction between those who opposed the Nazis and those who cooperated is clearer, moreover, at the national level; national leaders of the liberal professional associations generally did not also belong to a variety of center and right-wing organizations. On the local level, where the leadership overlapped substantially between women's associations, where nationalist and mainstream women's groups were sometimes closely allied, and where the women's movement as a whole stood to the right of the BDF leadership (as was the case in Hanover), these distinctions are much more difficult to make, and culpability was more broadly shared. Certainly, it is clear that many of Hanover's clubwomen must have voted for the Nazis in 1932 and 1933.

That the Hanover movement pursued clear class interests even before World War I and that many of the city's clubwomen shifted far to the right during the Weimar period are proof of how politically flexible the concept of gender difference could be. Although the first generation of the German movement had used a model of gender difference to construct an analysis that was socially critical, and although radical feminists in later generations also used "women's values" as a basis for a critique of male dominated institutions, the history of the Hanover movement shows that gender difference cut both ways. "Morality," "spiritual motherhood," and "women's values" were malleable concepts, which could also be incorporated into a broader conservative social analysis, one that sought to preserve bourgeois political and cultural hegemony. After 1919, this model of gender difference was carried forward within the Hanover movement and put to the service of extreme nationalism.

The case of the Hanover movement, moreover, was most certainly not unique, and was probably more truly representative of the women's movement at the grass-roots level than the feminist movements that emerged in liberal bastions such as Bremen. The decline of radical feminist influence within the BDF after 1906—and the national movement's steady drift to the right thereafter—certainly lends support to this assumption. It was, after all, the votes cast at the BDF's national congresses, by representatives from provincial towns across the empire, that produced this shift to the right; the Hanover movement therefore must have had counterparts in other cities. Once the bulk of bourgeois women was permitted to enter politics after 1908, and larger nonfeminist groups joined the BDF (such as the DEF and Housewives' League), this shift to the right was almost inevitable.

Whether the BDF was still "feminist" or not after 1908 (or 1914) is open to discussion, depending on the definition of feminism that is used. Certainly, even the women within the right wing of the movement were still working to broaden women's opportunities and rights and hoped to strengthen women's influence in German society. What seems clear, however, is that the majority of the movement's members (in Hanover and in the moderate wing of the BDF) combined their vision of spiritual motherhood and women's role with a larger social analysis that was politically conservative. An agenda grounded in gender difference is not inherently linked to nationalism, but the Hanover movement shows that, in practice, it often was. After 1919, this mixture would develop and intensify into a potent brew, one that ultimately proved poisonous for many Germans.

Methods Used to Determine

Social Background, Marital Status,

Confession, and Political Affiliation

of Clubwomen

The information about the women discussed in this study was collected from a variety of sources. Full or partial lists of members were located for sixteen associations; the sources for these lists are given at the end of this appendix. The names of individual clubwomen were also collected from other sources, including correspondence between associations or between the city government and individual associations, newspaper accounts of club meetings, and lists of officers of associations given in the city directory, the *Adressbuch der königlichen Haupt- und Residenzstadt Hannover*. The 1885 edition of the *Adressbuch* was used in collecting the names of the clubwomen discussed in Chapter 2, and the 1906 edition was used to prepare the tables in Chapter 6.

A total of 1,090 names of clubwomen were collected from these sources. In most cases, the source that listed a clubwoman's name either gave her address or included her husband's job title as a part of her honorific, as for example in the case of *Frau Stadtdirektor* Tramm. Using this information, I looked up each woman in the *Adressbuch*, which gave the address and job title for the head of each household in the city. Thus, if I knew a woman's address, I could usually determine her husband's or father's occupation, and if I knew her husband's job title, then I could almost always locate her address. In some cases, however, women who lived alone (widows or spinsters) were listed without reference to their husbands' or fathers' occupation; in other instances, the job title of a woman's husband was known, but the name was too common to permit the determination of the address, as in the case of a *Frau Lehrer* Hoffmann.

Using this method, I was able to determine the occupation of the husband or father for 719 of the 1,090 clubwomen. Of the remaining 371 women, the overwhelming majority (288) were single women whose addresses were unknown; most of them probably lived at home with their parents and were thus not listed individually in the *Adressbuch*. The remaining women were widows or married women who did not include a job title in their honorifics, and who could not be located in the *Adressbuch*.

Once the job title of the husband or father had been determined, the social background category for a particular clubwoman (that is, academic professional, military officer, or artisan) was usually obvious. In cases where I was unsure about the educational level associated with a particular job title—for example, if it was unclear if a civil servant had attended a university and therefore should be classified as a high-level civil servant or not—I referred to the job descriptions given in the 1902 edition of *Meyers Grosses Konversations-Lexikon*, which included the educational qualifications required in each instance.

Determining the marital status of each clubwoman was easier; I was able to identify the marital status of all but 63 of the 1,090 clubwomen. Single women were clearly identified by the honorific *Fräulein*. Women with the honorific *Frau* who could be located in the *Adressbuch* were assumed to be widowed if they were shown in the directory as living alone; it is possible that a few were divorced or separated, but there was no way to determine this. In other cases, widows lived at the same address as one of their sons, but were identified in the *Adressbuch* as the mother, not the wife, of the head of household. I was unable to locate the addresses for 63 women who were listed with the honorific of *Frau*, and thus could not positively determine if they were married or widowed; I included these cases in the category of married women.

The political affiliations of the husbands and fathers of clubwomen were determined by using several sources. Members of the National Liberal Party were identified by comparing the names I had located with a list of hundreds of local National Liberals published in the *Hannoverscher Anzeiger* on January 18, 1907. Guelph sympathizers were more difficult to identify, since no lists of German Hanoverian Party members were available. Fortunately, the provincial government kept dossiers on local Guelph sympathizers (located in the Niedersächsisches Hauptstaatsarchiv, file number Hann 122a XI 65a), which proved useful. In addition, clubwomen were identified as Guelph sympathizers if their husbands or fathers were on the executive committees of voluntary associations that were known to consist largely of Guelph partisans.

The confessional affiliation of individual clubwomen was determined largely by their membership in confessional associations; if a woman belonged to the DEF, for example, she was assumed to be Protestant. In addition, some Jewish clubwomen were located in a special card catalog of Jewish Hanoverians, maintained by and located in the Hanover Municipal Archive. Using these sources and methods, the confessional affiliations of all but 148 clubwomen were determined.

The information gathered about each clubwoman—her name, marital status, social background, political affiliation, and confession—was entered into a database and processed using the "Perfect Filer" software system marketed by Perfect Software, Incorporated. The database was compiled using the following membership lists:

Association	*Source of List*
Women's Association for the People's Welfare	1905–6 annual report STAH, XV Gb 171
Patrons of the Hanover Girls' Gymnasium and Association for the Reform of Female Education and Society for the Foundation of a Hanover Girls' Gymnasium	Report of the 12th General Assembly of the Association for the Reform of Female Education, STAH, Schulamt 845; also STAH, Kettler Nachlass

Boedeker Creche Society	1907 annual report, STAH, Schulamt 2357
Female Auxiliary of the Society for the Improvement of Public Morals	1905–6 annual report, LKAH, S 3d 531
DEF, Hanover chapter	DEF, *Frauenkalender für 1906*, 168–76
"Frauenwohl" Association	"Frauenwohl" Association, *Satzungen des Vereins "Frauenwohl,"* NH Hann 122a XX 142
Orphans' Officers	Städtische Armenverwaltung der königlichen Haupt- und Residenzstadt Hannover, *Einteilung der Waisenrats-Bezirke* (Hanover, 1908)
Municipal Almoners	Städtische Armenverwaltung der königlichen Haupt- und Residenzstadt Hannover, *Einteilung der königlichen Haupt- und Residenzstadt Hannover in Armendistrikte und Armenquartiere* (Hanover, 1909)
Parish Almoners	Verein für freiwillige Armenpflege, *Übersicht über die Organisation der freiwilligen Armenpflege* . . . (Hanover, 1906)
Women's Club	Satzungen des Vereins "Frauenklub Hannover 1900" in LKAH, E 2 395
Childbed Association	NH, Kleine Erwerbungen A 28
Frederica Association	1906 annual report in LKAH, S 3d 226
Association for the Advancement of Female Education	1908 catalog

Notes

ABBREVIATIONS

ADEF   Archiv des Deutschen Evangelischen Frauenbundes
ADF   Allgemeiner Deutscher Frauenverein
ADLV   Allgemeiner Deutscher Lehrerinnenverein
AKDFB   Archiv des Katholischen Deutschen Frauenbundes
BDF   Bund Deutscher Frauenvereine
BfM   Bund für Mutterschutz
DDP   Deutsche Demokratische Partei
DEF   Deutsch-Evangelischer Frauenbund
DNVP   Deutschnationale Volkspartei
DVP   Deutsche Volkspartei
LB   Landesarchiv Berlin
LKAH   Landeskirchliches Archiv der Evangelisch-lutherischen Landeskirche Hannover
NH   Niedersächsisches Hauptstaatsarchiv
SPD   Sozialdemokratische Partei Deutschlands
STAH   Stadtarchiv Hannover
STBH   Stadtbibliothek Hannover
VEFD   Vereinigung Evangelischer Frauenverbände Deutschlands

INTRODUCTION

1. Karen Offen, in a thoughtful analysis of the repercussions of essentialism within nineteenth-century feminist theory, refers to equal rights feminism as "individualist feminism." She distinguishes individualist feminism from a second school of thought that emerged during the same period, which tended to acknowledge and incorporate essentialism into its agenda to a greater degree: she calls this second school "relational feminism." "Relational feminism," she writes, "emphasized women's rights as women (defined principally by their childbearing and/or nurturing capacities) in relation to men," Offen, "Defining Feminism," 134–36. It is important to note that "relational feminists," as defined by Offen, did not reject equal political rights for women, including the right to vote, and envisioned roles for women that were different *but equal* to men's roles. Most of the Hanoverian women who are the subjects of this study rejected political equality for all women, which is why I do not refer to them as feminists.

2. Although some of them can be seen as relational feminists, the German moderates did not focus primarily on women's roles within the family, but instead sought a maternal role for women in the public sphere, as will be discussed. Bärbel Clemens, in her elegant study of both wings, notes that the difference between "radicals" and "moderates" was primarily analytical, and was not always reflected in strict organizational divisions. See Clemens, *Menschenrechte*, 4–5; Scott, "Deconstructing

Equality-Versus-Difference," 33–50, points out the limitations of an analysis that categorizes feminist thought according to its stress on "difference" versus equality.

3. See Clemens, *Menschenrechte*, 77–82; Stoehr, "'Organisierte Mütterlichkeit,'" 221–49; Bussemer, *Frauenemanzipation und Bildungsbürgertum*, 245–49; see also Wobbe, "Die Frau als zoon politicon," 326–37.

4. One of the earliest studies that criticized the movement was Evans, *Feminist Movement*. For another analysis of the BDF, see Greven-Aschoff, *Die bürgerliche Frauenbewegung*; see also Hackett, "Politics of Feminism," and "The German Women's Movement and Suffrage, 1890–1914," 354–86. For the movement's shift to the right following its rejection of equal rights for women, see Gerhard, *Unerhört*, 125, 177. See also Bussemer, "Bürgerliche Frauenbewegung und männliches Bildungsbürgertum," 199–201.

5. For more nuanced critiques of specific Weimar women's organizations that combined essentialism with political conservatism, see Bridenthal, Grossmann, and Kaplan, *When Biology Became Destiny*, 22; Bridenthal, "'Professional Housewives,'" 153–62. See also Koonz, *Mothers in the Fatherland*, 144–45.

6. Allen, *Feminism and Motherhood*, 7–8. In this theoretically sophisticated study, Allen points out that most of the women active in the kindergarten movement of the mid-nineteenth century supported the Revolution of 1848, and that the kindergarten movement itself was suppressed in the subsequent crackdown. Her analysis of the socially critical aspects of the early German women's movement is both persuasive and enlightening. Her argument is less convincing, however, as she traces the development of this maternalist ideology after the foundation of the BDF in 1894. In order to continue to depict maternalism as potentially radical and socially critical, Allen tends to focus on women who were really on the fringes of the bourgeois women's movement (members of the radical Bund für Mutterschutz or even SPD members), or does not examine the political conservatism of some of the mainstream leaders she includes. For example, Allen mentions in passing that one of the three women showcased in her analysis of the movement's work in child welfare, Anna v. Gierke, was later elected to the Reichstag as a representative of the right-wing Deutschnationale Volkspartei, a fact that ought to have raised questions about the political context of v. Gierke's ideas. Another "maternalist" studied by Allen, Hedwig Heyl, became the national head of the Women's Division of the German Colonial Society in 1910.

7. Meyer-Renschhausen, *Weibliche Kultur*, 6–7, 14–16, 209–13, 364–68. See also Meyer-Renschhausen, "Die weibliche Ehre," 80–101. Stoehr, "Fraueneinfluss oder Geschlechterversöhnung," 159–90, also questions how the "radicals" have been characterized and categorized in the literature on the women's movement.

8. Meyer-Renschhausen herself concludes that the Bremen movement was among the most radical in the empire; see Meyer-Renschhausen, *Weibliche Kultur*, 157, 335. This radicalism was reflected in its concentration on temperance and especially on the regulation of prostitution; Bremen women developed a more modest network of social welfare programs, which were the backbone of the "moderate" German women's movement, as for example in Hanover. Although its treatment of the temperance and morality movements is sensitive, imaginative, and extremely persuasive, this study is incomplete in some aspects. Meyer-Renschhausen does not

examine indications that members of the Bremen movement might have pursued interests based on their class or *Stand* identity. She does not analyze, for example, why the Bremen women's suffrage organization split irrevocably over the question of whether women should demand the right to vote based on the same property restrictions as men, or work for equal, secret, and direct voting rights for all women and men. This issue divided the suffrage movement both in Bremen and across Germany, and separated progressive liberal suffrage supporters from those who had more conservative affiliations. Ibid., 331–35. For the divisions at the national level, see Clemens, *Menschenrechte*, 59–61.

9. The comment on American female reformers is taken from Hewitt, "Beyond the Search for Sisterhood," 9. This essay summarizes the large body of literature in American women's history that testifies to the rarity of cross-class alliances among American women and to the frequency of class divisions between groups of women as well as divisions caused by racial or ethnic conflict.

10. There seems to be a consensus that the movement as a whole did shift to the right, although different writers see this as happening at different dates, including around 1908 or 1910. See Evans, *Feminist Movement*, 148–58, and Greven-Aschoff, *Die bürgerliche Frauenbewegung*, 105–6.

11. Allen, *Feminism and Motherhood*, 235.

12. That the Catholic and Protestant women's leagues should be included in a study of the women's movement will, I think, arouse little disagreement; the Jewish Women's League was always a stalwart pillar of the BDF. Some readers may be surprised at the inclusion of the Vaterländischer Frauenverein, but it did have its activist aspects, and has been studied before as a part of the movement. See Riemann, "Er mit der Waffe, sie mit Herz und Hand," 347–53.

13. In fact, during the 1920s, conservative women's associations in Hanover explicitly adopted this position, arguing that they need not belong to the BDF in order to belong the local women's movement, even claiming that the bulk of the local movement had distanced itself from the BDF. See Chapter 11.

14. See Clemens, *Menschenrechte*, 103; see also Hackett, "Politics of Feminism," 277–91.

15. See Chapter 11 for a discussion of Drechsler-Hohlt. For Gertrud Bäumer's political affiliations, see Gerhard, *Unerhört*, 294–95. That the linkage between essentialism and political conservatism was by no means automatic is also, of course, clearly demonstrated by Allen.

16. For a discussion of the mounting partisan tensions within the BDF, see Clemens, *Menschenrechte*, 59–61, 74–75; see also Gerhard, *Unerhört*, 286–92. For a discussion of the constraints imposed on the BDF by *Überparteilichkeit* during the Weimar period, see Stoehr, *Emanzipation*, 114–35; see also Schmidt-Waldherr, *Emanzipation durch Professionalisierung?*, ix–xi.

17. This was the motto of the politician who served as Hanover's mayor for most of the Wilhelmine period; see Röhrbein and Zankl, *Hannover im 20. Jahrhundert*, 28–30. For a discussion of the drive for professionalism and the political "neutrality" of liberal municipal officials in some German cities, see Sheehan, "Liberalism and the City in Nineteenth-Century Germany," 123–26; Heffter, *Die deutsche Selbstverwaltung im 19. Jahrhundert*, 609–11. For descriptions of several "nonpartisan" local

political elites, see Gall, *Stadt und Bürgertum*. In other cities, however, where the local franchise was not so severely restricted, municipal officials were elected in hotly partisan elections.

18. See Chapter 1 for a discussion of Hanover's antidemocratic political environment.

19. Clemens, *Menschenrechte*, 28; Gerhard, *Unerhört*, 124–25; Allen, *Feminism and Motherhood*, 100–103.

CHAPTER 1

1. Reulecke, *Geschichte der Urbanisierung*, 43–44, 220–25.

2. Röhrbein and Zankl, *Hannover im 20. Jahrhundert*, 7, 61–62.

3. Statistisches Amt, *Statistisches Jahrbuch*, 1st ed., 8.

4. Standard works on the Bürgertum in the nineteenth century include Henning, *Bürgertum*, and Vondung, *Das wilhelminische Bildungsbürgertum*. For more recent discussions of the emergence and composition of the Bürgertum, see Conze and Kocka, *Bildungsbürgertum im 19. Jahrhundert*; Kocka, "Family and Class Formation," 417–30; Koshar, *Social Life*, 13–16; and Jarausch, *Students, Society, and Politics*, 122–34.

5. Kaplan, *The Making of the Jewish Middle Class*, 13–15; Holborn, *Modern Germany*, 277–83; Craig, *Germany*, 67–78. The different strata of the Bürgertum were also in the process of consolidation and integration during this period, however. See Henning, *Bürgertum*, 125–26, 483–85; Jarausch, *Students, Society, and Politics*, 127–28.

6. Henning, *Bürgertum*, 33–34, 486–88; Koshar, *Social Life*, 12–13.

7. Meyer-Renschhausen, *Weibliche Kultur*, 14–19; Kaufmann, *Frauen zwischen Aufbruch und Reaktion*, 12, 32–34; Kaplan, *The Making of the Jewish Middle Class*, 69–78.

8. See Hausen, "Family and Role-Division," 51–83.

9. I am indebted here to the first-rate analysis of bourgeois housewifery and domesticity in Kaplan, *The Making of the Jewish Middle Class*, 25–41. Kaplan's study treats bourgeois Jewish Germans, but most of her observations apply to gentile Germans as well, since German Jews largely resembled gentile bourgeois culture in their domestic values and norms. See also Henning, *Bürgertum*, 274–75, 487–90; Meyer, *Das Theater mit der Hausarbeit*; Rosenbaum, *Formen der Familie*, 326–30.

10. Sidgwick, *Home Life*, 129, 136.

11. Ibid., 125.

12. Kaplan, *The Making of the Jewish Middle Class*, 29–30.

13. Ibid., 53–63.

14. Sidgwick, *Home Life*, 9–10. See also Kaplan, *The Making of the Jewish Middle Class*, 33.

15. Nipperdey, "Verein als soziale Struktur," 2–5. See also Koshar, *Social Life*, 4–8; Weber, "Rede auf dem ersten Deutschen Soziologentag," 442–45; Blackbourn, "The Discreet Charm of the Bourgeoisie," 196–98.

16. Nipperdey, "Verein als soziale Struktur," 26–27, 31–33.

17. Evans, *Feminist Movement*, 11.

18. See Sheehan, "Liberalism and the City," 119–20; Koshar, *Social Life*, 6–7. Sheehan and Koshar label this approach to politics "unpolitical" and "apolitical," respectively; I avoid using these terms, preferring the terms *partei-politisch neutral* or nonpartisan politics.

19. Sheehan, "Liberalism and the City," 131–32.

20. Röhrbein and Zankl, *Hannover im 20. Jahrhundert*, 34.

21. Hamann, "Politische Kräfte um 1880," 12–13; Aschoff, "Die welfische Bewegung," 42–44; Röhrbein and Zankl, *Hannover im 20. Jahrhundert*, 24.

22. See Hamann, "Politische Kräfte um 1880," 28–30; Röhrbein and Zankl, *Hannover im 20. Jahrhundert*, 9.

23. Röhrbein and Zankl, *Hannover im 20. Jahrhundert*, 9–10, 28–34. The National Liberals retained all of Hanover's seats in the Prussian Haus der Abgeordneten through 1907 because the Guelphs refused to campaign for seats in that body. For a discussion of the political "neutrality" of liberal municipal officials in Germany as a whole, see Sheehan, "Liberalism and the City," 125–26. See also the local case studies in Gall, *Stadt und Bürgertum*.

24. Sheehan, "Liberalism and the City," 123–25; Heffter, *Die deutsche Selbstverwaltung*, 609–11.

25. Sheehan, "Liberalism and the City," 134–35.

26. Röhrbein and Zankl, *Hannover im 20. Jahrhundert*, 24; Hamann, "Politische Kräfte am Vorabend des Ersten Weltkrieges," 439.

CHAPTER 2

1. Rothert, *Die innere Mission*, 281–82.

2. Bussemer, *Frauenemanzipation*, 12–13.

3. For an extended discussion of the "surplus women" issue, see Chapter 5.

4. Bussemer, *Frauenemanzipation*, 63–75.

5. Ibid., 107–12, 130–39. See also Stoehr, *Emanzipation*, 2–5.

6. Stoehr, *Emanzipation*, 2–5.

7. Bussemer, *Frauenemanzipation*, 186–88. See also Gerhard, *Unerhört*, 124.

8. Bussemer, *Frauenemanzipation*, 187–88; see also Sachsse, *Mütterlichkeit*, 110–16; Stoehr, "'Organisierte Mütterlichkeit,'" 222–24; Allen, *Feminism and Motherhood*, 36–38, 41, 66–71.

9. Bussemer, *Frauenemanzipation*, 151.

10. Hamann, "Politische Kräfte um 1880," 8–10.

11. Doerr, *Gemeinde-Handbuch*, 303–4.

12. Weisbrod, "Wohltätigkeit und 'symbolische Gewalt' in der Frühindustrialisierung," 356–57. On the Elberfeld system in general, see Sachsse and Tennstedt, *Geschichte der Armenfürsorge*, 214–22; see also Böhmert, *Das Armenwesen in 77 deutschen Städten*.

13. See Sachsse and Tennstedt, *Geschichte der Armenfürsorge*, 222–26; Reulecke, *Geschichte der Urbanisierung*, 33. For further discussion of bourgeois attempts to police the domestic lives of the poor or to inculcate them with bourgeois values, see Donzelot, *The Policing of Families*.

14. Rothert, *Die innere Mission*, 303–6.

15. From a letter from the Magistrat of Hanover to the Protestant Association, dated Nov. 8, 1884, in LKAH, E 2 114.

16. From an 1887 flyer of the association in LKAH, E 2 114.

17. From the associations's report, "Übersicht der Organisation der freiwilligen Armenpflege," in LKAH, E 2 114.

18. Rothert, *Die innere Mission* offers an incomplete list of these early associations in his Anhang I. The dates he gives for two of these organizations' foundations differ from the dates given in Table 2.1, since the sources used to compile this table gave slightly different dates. For a list of sources used to compile the tables in this chapter, see the appendix.

19. See minutes of the association's meetings in NH, Kleine Erwerbungen A 28; and the annual reports of the association, located in LKAH, Stadtkirchliches Archiv A362. For the "Prussian Colony," see Hamann, "Politische Kräfte um 1880," 17–20.

20. From reports of the society's activities that appeared in the parish's newsletter, *Der einzige Trost*, copies located in the archive of the Evangelisch-reformierte Kirche Hannovers.

21. See Rothert, *Die innere Mission*, 572. Information on the society's membership list is taken from the annual lists of private charities compiled by the Voluntary Poor Relief Association, located in LKAH, E 2 114.

22. The Jewish Women's League became an active participant in the local women's movement, but sources that mention it are, unfortunately, limited; in the late 1930s, its records in the municipal archives were purged. I had to reconstruct its history from published sources and surviving records in other associations' archives.

23. Report by Frau Eichhorn, *Der einzige Trost* 1 (1911–12): 95.

24. LKAH, S 3d 114, annual reports of the Magdalene Society.

25. Friederiken-Verein, *Die ersten fünfzig Jahre*, 7–8.

26. Ibid.

27. See Prelinger, *Charity, Challenge, and Change*, 29–38.

28. See the annual reports of each association, located in LKAH, S 3d 114 and S 3d 226.

29. Sociologists and anthropologists refer to such groups as "legal-rational associations," because they adopt "written statutes clearly defining the membership, participant obligations, leadership roles and conditions of convocation." See Anderson, "Voluntary Associations in History," 215.

30. See the annual reports of the Patriotic Association for this period in LKAH, S 3d 251.

31. From the *Adressbuch der königlichen Haupt- und Residenzstadt Hannover*, 1880 ed., part II, 54, and the 1890 ed., section II, 100.

32. This figure was derived by comparing the day-care centers' reported attendance, given in the *Adressbuch der königlichen Haupt- und Residenzstadt Hannover*, 1890 edition, section II, 100, with the city's census figures, reproduced in Statistisches Amt, *Statistisches Jahrbuch*, 1st ed., 6.

33. See STAH, Schulamt 2357, the 1907–8 annual report of the Boedeker Creche Society.

34. See STAH, Schulamt 1542, "Bericht über die Arbeit der Warteschule und des Kinderheims Limmer in den Jahren 1906–1917," 7.

35. Hanover's *Warteschulen* do not appear to have been run along the progressive

lines envisioned by leaders of the kindergarten movement studied by Ann Taylor Allen. Instead, these centers resembled the more restricted, regimented conservative infant schools, which were the new kindergartens' rivals. See Allen, *Feminism and Motherhood*, 60–61.

36. These figures are derived from an analysis of the society's steering committee lists, which appeared annually in the city's *Stadtadressbücher*; see also STAH, Schulamt 2357, which contains some of the society's annual reports.

37. From an interview with Friederike Feesche's granddaughter, Annamarie Feesche, held in Hanover on Oct. 3, 1986.

38. See STAH, XVI E VII 1–4, which contains the association's annual reports, as well as correspondence between the association's officers and municipal officials.

39. The information on the Educational Association's membership was derived from the membership lists in STAH, XVI E VII 1, and from information on the association presented annually in section II of the city's *Stadtadressbücher*. As far as could be determined, none of the twenty-three women was Catholic.

40. Report by Pastor Eichhorn, *Der einzige Trost* 2 (1913): 95.

CHAPTER 3

1. The morality movement (*Sittlichkeitsbewegung*) was a national network of Protestant men's morality associations. See Lewek, *Kirche und soziale Frage*; see also Fout, "The Moral Purity Movement," 5–31. In Hanover, the local branch was the Association for the Improvement of Public Morality (Verein zur Hebung der öffentlichen Sittlichkeit).

2. Weber's announcement is reprinted in Mueller, *Handbuch zur Frauenfrage*, 16.

3. Interview with Annamarie Feesche in Hanover, Oct. 3, 1986.

4. Taken from Pagenstecher's memoirs on the origins of the DEF, in ADEF, B 1.

5. Ibid.

6. These details were taken from ADEF, B 1, which contains biographical sketches of Mueller, written by her associates. See also Schroeder, *Sophie*, 250.

7. See especially Mueller's correspondence with other DEF officers and with other leaders of the women's movement in ADEF, B 1, O 12, O 9b.

8. Hilpert, "Die Geschichte des Deutsch-Evangelischen Frauenbundes," 100.

9. From the annual reports in ADEF, Akten der Ortsgruppe Hannover.

10. Countess Selma von der Groeben, Adelheid von Bennigsen, and Elisabeth von der Beck are examples of women who followed this "career path" within the DEF. See the lists of DEF national officers and Hanover branch officers, published in the 1906, 1908, and 1913 editions of the DEF *Frauenkalender*.

11. This information was derived from an analysis of the membership lists printed in the DEF *Frauenkalender für 1906*. For the methods used to ascertain the occupation of husbands and fathers of DEF members, see the appendix.

12. Kaufmann, "Die Ehre des Vaterlandes und die Ehre der Frauen," 283; Hilpert, "Geschichte des Deutsch-Evangelischen Frauenbundes," 17.

13. See the appendix for the methods used to determine the political affiliation of husbands and fathers of DEF members.

14. Hilpert, "Geschichte des Deutsch-Evangelischen Frauenbundes," 20; Schroeder, *Sophie*, 227, 237.

15. See Adelheid von Bennigsen's correspondence with Eyl, Wehrhahn, and Wespy in STAH, XV Gb 150.

16. See Erna von der Groeben's letter to Pastor Meyer, dated Oct. 26, 1904, in LKAH, E 2 379.

17. See Peukert, *Grenzen der Sozialdisziplinierung*, 54–55.

18. See Tenfelde, "Grossstadtjugend in Deutschland," 183–84, 187–88.

19. Peukert, *Grenzen der Sozialdisziplinierung*, 54–65.

20. Ibid.

21. See Nipperdey, "Jugend und Politik um 1900," 357–58; Saul, "Der Kampf um die Jugend," 97–143.

22. See LKAH, S 3d 270, "Festschrift zur Feier des 75. Jahresfestes des Christlichen Männer- und Jünglingsvereins Hannover," 22–23, 27.

23. See the list of youth groups in "Wo halte ich mich während meiner freien Zeit auf?" in STAH, Sportamt Sp 110, 8.

24. Berger, *Die Prostitution in Hannover*, 25.

25. Mueller, *Welche Aufgaben*, 3.

26. Ibid., 1.

27. For a discussion of the debate within the medical profession over the "social question," see Frevert, "Fürsorgliche Belagerung," 422–26; Peukert, *Grenzen der Sozialdisziplinierung*, 42–48 and 120–22, analyzes the role of philanthropists and jurists in the discussion of "social degeneration." See also Sachsse, *Mütterlichkeit*, 19–22. For an analysis of how women factory workers were depicted within this discursive domain, see Canning, "Feminist History," 380–84.

28. *Verwahrlosung* is often translated as "degeneration," and indeed "degeneration" is the best English term for the concept to which Hanover clubwomen were referring. *Verwahrlosung* does not mean the same thing as the word *Entartung*, however, which is also translated as "degeneration." *Entartung* is often associated with the National Socialists, who labeled cultural developments that they disliked, especially modern art, *entartet*; their term for modern art, *entartete Kunst*, is therefore translated as "degenerate art." *Entartung*, as the National Socialists used the term, has different connotations than *Verwahrlosung*. *Entartung* also means "contamination," "perversion," or "debasement," whereas *Verwahrlosung* can also mean "decay," or "neglect." *Verwahrlosung*, as it was used by social observers during the late nineteenth century, denoted a reversion to more primitive social conditions, which undermined civilized societies.

29. See Evans, "Prostitution, State, and Society," 106–15.

30. See Statistisches Amt, *Statistisches Jahrbuch*, 1st ed., 12.

31. Groeben, *Frauenarbeit und Frauenwert*, 5.

32. Mueller, *Welche Aufgaben*, 14.

33. Groeben, *Soziale Gegensätze und Frauenbewegung*, 14–15.

34. See her article on servants' associations in Mueller, *Handbuch zur Frauenfrage*, 145, 148.

35. Monthly reports on the association's activities appeared in *Der einzige Trost*.

36. From a flyer distributed by the Friends (n.d.), in LKAH, E 2 391.

37. Taken from a history of the Friends' Hanover branch and the society's annual reports, in LKAH, E 2 391 and E 2 393.

38. *Mitteilungen des Deutsch-Evangelischen Frauenbundes* 1 (1900–1901): 7–8.

39. *Evangelische Frauenzeitung* 5 (1904–5): 5, and 6 (1905–6): 62.

40. See STAH, XV Gb 150 vol. 1, and *Evangelische Frauenzeitung* 12 (1911–12): 75.

41. This estimate was compiled from membership figures for girls' associations given in the annual reports and memos of the Committee for *Jugendpflege* in STAH, Sportamt Sp110; see also the statistics given for local youth groups in a Mar. 1913 report, in STAH, Sportamt SP104; figures on girls' associations reprinted in the *Vierteljährliche Nachrichten des Landesvereins hannoverscher Jungfrauenvereine* 1, no. 2 (1913): 1–3. The total figure for all Hanover women between the ages of fourteen and twenty-one is given in the Statistisches Amt, *Statistisches Jahrbuch*, 1st ed., 6. See also the reports on local girls' groups in LKAH, S 3d 282.

42. See the minutes of the Hanover Committee for Youth Welfare meetings in STAH, Sportamt Sp109, particularly those of Jan. 16, 1912.

43. A copy of this pamphlet is in LKAH, E 2 247.

44. Interview with Frida Glindemann in Hanover, Oct. 10, 1986.

45. See a report on the city's youth organizations from Mar. 1913 in STAH, Sportamt, Sp104. For the failure of "patriotic" youth groups to attract boys nationally, see Lidtke, *The Alternative Culture*, 15.

46. I could find no detailed sources for socialist youth organizations in Hanover before 1914; municipal and provincial administrators were silent about such youth groups, and socialist youth leaders were excluded from the numerous conferences and committees on youth organizations. Socialist boys' groups did undoubtedly exist in Hanover before World War I, however, since municipal directories of youth groups issued after 1918 (when the SPD was able to force the city to recognize socialist youth organizations) include a number of socialist boys' associations, many of which were clearly of long standing. No socialist girls' groups were named in these first lists, however. See the lists of all youth organizations, dated Feb. 1919 and Apr. 1924 in STAH, Sportamt Sp110; see also Lidtke, *The Alternative Culture*, 51.

47. For the SPD's acceptance, by and large, of contemporary bourgeois sexual mores and socialists' own espousal of the values that made up "respectability," see Hurd, "The Illusive Alliance," 384, 390–91.

48. Ibid., 390–91.

49. Ibid., 433; see also Lidtke, *The Alternative Culture*, 159–65, 192–201.

50. LKAH, S 3d 282, "Leitsätze des Fünften Kursus zur Förderung der Arbeit an der weiblichen Jugend," 18.

51. Wallmann's salary for leading this group (work that was decidedly part-time) was about half the starting salary of (trained and state-certified) female teachers. See the correspondence between DEF officers and the city concerning the city's subsidies for this association in STAH, XV Gb 150. See also Verband Evangelische Arbeiterinnen-Vereine Deutschlands, *Verband Evangelischer Arbeiterinnen-Vereine Deutschlands*, 7–9. See also ADEF, Akten der Ortsgruppe Hannover, III Protokollbuch der Vorstandssitzungen der Ortsgruppe Hannover, meetings of Feb. 18, 1908, and Apr. 8, 1913.

52. *Mitteilungen des Deutsch-Evangelischen Frauenbundes* 1 (1900–1901): 43.

53. LKAH, E 2 379, "Ordnungen für die Mitglieder des Vereins," and Erna von der Groeben's correspondence. Groeben's group was not the only shopgirls' organization, however; local saleswomen and clerical workers had created their own

branch of the Commercial Union of Female Salaried Employees (Kaufmännischer Hilfsverein für weibliche Angestellte) in 1903. The union had its own set of club-rooms and maintained an unemployment insurance fund for members; it resented the association created by clubwomen, and argued that female white-collar workers ought to organize themselves independently. Ultimately, the union proved more attractive; by 1912, the Christian Association for Young Girls had been transformed into a servants' group, having lost its white-collar members. See the correspondence between the union and the Christian Association in LKAH, E 2 379.

54. From a DEF petition to the city, requesting funds for a girls' group, dated Feb. 4, 1911, in STAH, Gb 150 vol. 1.

55. Taken from ADEF, I 1a, "Entwurf eines Arbeitvertrages vom Zentralverband der Hausangestellten Deutschlands" (n.d.).

56. ADEF, I 1a, from a letter to Frau Dr. Klutner, dated Mar. 15, 1907.

57. See her article on servants' associations in Mueller, *Handbuch zur Frauenfrage*, 145–46.

58. ADEF, I 1a, contains a report on this conference.

59. Mueller, *Handbuch zur Frauenfrage*, 145, 148.

60. See the minutes of the first meeting of the commission, dated Jan. 11, 1908, in ADEF, I 1b.

61. Ibid. Although the Jewish Women's League was part of this coalition, it did not create a parallel servants' group; a small group for Jewish servants had existed in Hanover since 1868, but it was created not to fill members' leisure hours (and forestall unionization), but rather to award cash premiums to servants who worked for the same employer for many years. It also ran a pension fund for Jewish servants.

62. From the minutes of a 1913 follow-up conference on the "servant question," held in Munich, in ADEF, I 1a. A copy of the "model contract" is in ADEF, I 1b.

63. ADEF, I 1a, from a directive sent by Mueller to all DEF branch groups, directing DEF branches to participate in the foundation of housewives' associations (n.d., probably early 1908).

64. Ibid.

65. In five years, the court of arbitration heard only two cases. Both servants and employers evidently distrusted the court. Servants doubtless perceived it (correctly) as an agency of the Commission on Servants, which itself was a creation of house-wives. Housewives rejected the court perhaps because it might intervene in their relationship with their maids, and undermine housewives' authority. See ADEF, I 1a, minutes of the 1913 conference held in Munich on servants' associations.

66. Ibid.; see also minutes of the DEF Commission on Servants, Oct. 24, 1913, in the same file.

67. Schulte, "Dienstmädchen im Herrschaftlichen Haushalt," 884–85, 905–6.

68. ADEF, I 1a, minutes of the 1913 conference held in Munich on servants' groups.

69. ADEF, I 1a, "Satzungen des Evangelischen Hausgehilfinnenvereins Hannover."

70. STAH, XV Gb 150 vol. 1, correspondence between DEF officers and the city regarding the finances of the Servants' Association, and a 1918 report on the association's activities by Marie Gaster.

71. See ADEF, Akten der Ortsgruppe Hannover, III Protokollbuch der Vor-

standssitzungen der Ortsgruppe Hannover, meetings of Apr. 11, 1908, and May 21, 1910.

72. Except for the servants' association mentioned in n. 61, I could not locate any organizations that might have been created specifically for Jewish girls. The Jewish Women's League in Hanover did run a home to train girls for domestic service, however; see Chapter 4.

73. See *Die christliche Frau* 4 (1905–6): 402; 5 (1906–7): 439.

74. Catholic League members apparently had more success at organizing working-class Catholic girls than young women of their own class. The president of the Catholic youth group created for middle-class girls confessed sadly in 1912 that, although the auxiliary had forty-three members, only twelve came regularly to meetings, and only nine volunteered to do charitable work. "The rest cannot be persuaded by any means to join in our work," she wrote the league's leaders, "they all say either that they have no time, or that they are not suited to such work. . . . I myself am not suited [to lead the auxiliary], but no one else would accept the position." See AKDFB, "Generalversammlung 1912, Strassburg," letter from Toni Endler to the steering committee, dated June 29, 1912.

75. See Margarethe Haccius's memoir on her work with the Protestant Youths (she was the association's vice-president) in LKAH, N 30.

76. The Berlin association's name was the Mädchen- und Frauengruppen für soziale Hilfstätigkeit. See Gerhard, *Unerhört*, 237; Sachsse, *Mütterlichkeit*, 124–25.

77. From Haccius's memoir, in LKAH, N 30.

78. From a report on this work with schoolchildren in the *Vierteljährliche Nachrichten des Landesvereins hannoverscher Jungfrauenvereine* 2, no. 2 (1914): 2–3.

79. Ibid.

CHAPTER 4

1. The term "social poisons" (*Gifte*) did not originate with the Hanover movement, but was used widely by participants in the discussions about "social degeneration." See Peukert, *Grenzen der Sozialdisziplinierung*, 184.

2. The breadth and depth of the Hanover social services network reflected the fact that the Hanover movement resembled the "moderate" majority of the women's movement, compared with the more radical local movement in Bremen studied by Meyer-Renschhausen. The Bremen movement's radicalism was reflected in its concentration on temperance and especially on the regulation of prostitution, a cause that was fervently supported by the radical wing of the national movement. The Bremen women's movement appears to have spent less energy developing social welfare programs, which were the backbone of the German women's movement. As a result, the social welfare infrastructure in Bremen was insufficient to support a local National Women's Service (*Nationaler Frauendienst*) during World War I; the Women's Service created cartels of women's charitable and social welfare organizations in most German cities to handle the overwhelming load of social work that emerged during World War I. See Chapter 9 for a description of Hanover's Women's Service. The Bremen movement did create some private charitable organizations, but could not match the breadth of the social welfare network created in

Hanover. Instead, as Meyer-Renschhausen remarks, the temperance movement appears to have made up the heart of the Bremen movement. Meyer-Renschhausen, *Weibliche Kultur*, 245.

3. The origins of this discourse on social degeneration were discussed in Chapter 3. For the position advanced by the German Association for Poor Relief and Charity, see Peukert, *Grenzen der Sozialdisziplinierung*, 120–21.

4. See Canning, "Feminist History," 380–81.

5. Frevert, "Fürsorgliche Belagerung," 425.

6. Taken from a letter written by attorney von Issendorf, dated Oct. 13, 1910, in ADEF, V 24.

7. See Grundmann, *Gebhardts Handbuch*, 3:528.

8. NH, Hann 122a XX 142 vol. 2, 65.

9. See Meyer, *Das Theater mit der Hausarbeit*; Bock and Duden, "Arbeit aus Liebe," 118–99; Kaplan, *The Making of the Jewish Middle Class*, 30–35, 39–40; for France, see Smith, *Ladies of the Leisure Class*, 72–74.

10. Rosenbaum, *Formen der Familie*, 402–9.

11. Hagemann, *Frauenalltag und Männerpolitik*, 33–50, 90–98.

12. Interview with Ruth Grundmann, held in Hanover on Oct. 12, 1986.

13. Lewis, "The Working Class Wife and Mother and State Intervention, 1870–1918," 109–15, discusses the varying reactions of British working-class mothers to similar programs, some of which were viewed positively by clients, but most of which were seen as a "gross intrusion."

14. Hurd, "Morality and Working-Class Politics."

15. Women leaders successfully pushed for the introduction of obligatory domestic science courses within public schools before 1914 in Hamburg, Baden, and Saxony. The National Socialists mandated such courses nationwide in 1939. See Hagemann, *Frauenalltag und Männerpolitik*, 117–18.

16. Frevert, "Fürsorgliche Belagerung," 429–30.

17. This was the argument explicitly made in Hamburg by supporters of domestic science courses. See Hagemann, *Frauenalltag und Männerpolitik*, 120–21. Elisabeth Meyer-Renschhausen discusses similar domestic science courses offered by the women's movement in Bremen, but presents an analysis that differs sharply from the depiction given in this chapter or by Hagemann. She apparently agrees with club-women's descriptions about the deplorable state of working-class households and the potential value of these courses (or takes them at face value), and thus comes to much more positive and flattering conclusions about the bourgeois women who organized these classes. See Meyer-Renschhausen, *Weibliche Kultur*, 125–30.

18. See the correspondence and petitions concerning the creation of the Continuation School in STAH, Schulamt 1519.

19. STAH, Schulamt 1519, from a letter from Bertha Harder to the city, dated Jan. 17, 1902; also from the school's "Report on the Winter Courses, 1901/1902"; and from a 1902 report, "Zur Orientierung über die Fortbildungsschule"; see also the report on the school in *Evangelische Frauenzeitung* 6 (1905–6): 10.

20. STAH Schulamt 1519, from a petition dated Dec. 11, 1904.

21. Hagemann, *Frauenalltag und Männerpolitik*, 96–97.

22. Hurd, "The Illusive Alliance," 390–91.

23. Hagemann, *Frauenalltag und Männerpolitik*, 123.

24. See Duensing's work history in STAH, Lehrer: Personalakten von Volks-schullehrern: Bertha Duensing. Duensing was related to a more prominent leader of the German women's movement, Frieda Duensing, who pioneered professional social work, and was among the first to draw public attention to the problem of child abuse.

25. See the association's annual reports in STAH, XV Gb 171.

26. Ibid., from the annual reports for 1905, 1911, and 1914.

27. For an excellent discussion of Wilhelmine "pub culture," see Meyer-Rensch-hausen, *Weibliche Kultur*, 182–224, 252–57. Meyer-Renschhausen persuasively ar-gues that temperance was taken up by Bremen feminists, as well, because they felt that alcoholism led to domestic violence and marital rape. She does not, however, also analyze temperance as part of a conservative analysis that stressed social "de-generation." In fact, temperance, like "spiritual motherhood," could be politically malleable.

28. Doerr, *Gemeinde-Handbuch*, 310–19.

29. Rothert, *Die innere Mission*, 264–65.

30. ADEF, H 1a, 1906 annual report and *Beilage* of the DEF's Commission for the Protection of Children and Youths; see also the report in *Evangelische Frauenzeitung* 7 (1906–7): 20. Wallmann started at a salary of 1,200 Marks per year, approximately the same amount that beginning female elementary school teachers earned.

31. Doerr, *Gemeinde-Handbuch*, 294; *Evangelische Frauenzeitung* 11 (1910–11): 61.

32. See Sachsse and Tennstedt, *Geschichte der Armenfürsorge*, 233–35.

33. Rothert, *Die innere Mission*, 264–65.

34. See ibid., 101; Peukert, *Grenzen der Sozialdisziplinierung*, 144–45; ADEF, Akten der Ortsgruppe Hannover, 1903 annual report.

35. "Professional guardianship" (or *Berufsvormundschaft*) was adopted in other German cities as well. See Allen, *Feminism and Motherhood*, 146. See also ADEF, Akten der Ortsgruppe Hannover, III Protokollbuch der Vorstandssitzungen der Ortsgruppe Hannover, meetings of May 30, 1908, Oct. 28, 1908.

36. See the committee's correspondence and memorandums in LKAH, E 2 367, especially the correspondence between the members of the Protestant Association dated July 12, 1909, and July 15, 1909.

37. ADEF, Akten der Ortsgruppe Hannover, 1908 annual report.

38. See Selma von der Groeben's report on the police assistant in *Evangelische Frauenzeitung* 10 (1909–10): 131–33; Berger, *Die Prostitution*, 19.

39. See ADEF, Akten der Ortsgruppe Hannover, III Protokollbuch der Vor-standssitzungen der Ortsgruppe Hannover, meetings of May 21, 1910; June 12, 1911; Aug. 14, 1911; Aug. 20, 1912.

40. See the annual reports of the Magdalene Home in LKAH, S 3d 114, especially the 1906–7 report, 4–5, and the DEF's "Bericht des Versorgungshauses der Orts-gruppe Hannover, 1903–1905" in STAH, XV Gb 150 vol. 1.

41. See Selma von der Groeben's memo on the home in LKAH, E 2 219.

42. See the report on the home in *Evangelische Frauenzeitung* 6 (1905–6): 71–72.

43. ADEF, Akten der Ortsgruppe Hannover, III Protokollbuch der Vorstands-sitzungen der Ortsgruppe Hannover, meetings of Feb. 18, 1908; Jan. 4, 1909; May 12, 1909; Jan. 4, 1910; Feb. 1, 1910; Feb. 18, 1911; Apr. 4, 1911, Jan. 13, 1912.

44. ADEF, Akten der Ortsgruppe Hannover, file titled "Bau des Versorgungs-

hauses"; also III Protokollbuch der Vorstandssitzungen der Ortsgruppe Hannover, meeting of May 3, 1911; STAH, XV Gb 150 vol. 1, minutes of a city senate meeting, held on Dec. 5, 1912; *Mitteilungen des Statistischen Amts der Stadt Hannover* 1913, no. 2, 9.

45. ADEF, Akten der Ortsgruppe Hannover, III Protokollbuch der Vorstands-sitzungen der Ortsgruppe Hannover, meetings of Oct. 25, 1912, and Apr. 5, 1913. Mueller's father had been the *Landesdirektor* von der Wense's predecessor.

46. See the "Bericht über die Tätigkeit des hannoverschen Frauenbildungsverein für die Zeit vom 1. Januar 1896 bis 1. Januar 1901," 7–8, in STAH, XVI E VII 1; ADEF, CC 1, 1907 report of the legal advice bureau; reports on women's legal advice bureaus in *Evangelische Frauenzeitung* 4 (1903–4): 45, and 6 (1905–6): 56.

47. See the Hanover chapter's annual report in *Evangelische Frauenzeitung* 6 (1905–6): 62; DEF, *Frauenkalender für 1913*, 68; see also the correspondence between DEF officers and the city regarding the municipal subsidies in STAH, XV Gb 150 vol. 1, especially the letters dated Mar. 11, 1909; June 6, 1905; and Nov. 17, 1912.

48. ADEF, Akten der Ortsgruppe Hannover, III Protokollbuch der Vorstands-sitzungen der Ortsgruppe Hannover, meetings of Nov. 24, 1908; May 12, 1909; Feb. 1, 1910; Apr. 4, 1911; and May 3, 1911.

49. See STAH, XXX Sozialamt 134, which contains a collection of clippings from local newspapers, which were critical of the city's policies regarding the homeless; STAH, XV Gb 150a, memorandum by DEF officer Countess Wilhelmine von Finckenstein, dated Dec. 1, 1913.

50. STAH, XV Gb 150a, memorandum by Countess von Finckenstein, dated Dec. 1, 1913.

51. Ibid.; see also the minutes of the city senate meeting of Dec. 18, 1913, in STAH, XV Gb 150a; the 1912 report on the number of women referred to the shelter in STAH, XV Gb 150b. See also ADEF, Akten der Ortsgruppe Hannover, III Protokollbuch der Vorstandssitzungen der Ortsgruppe Hannover, meetings of Nov. 22, 1912; Mar. 15, 1913; Dec. 16, 1913; and Jan. 17, 1914.

52. See the minutes of a city senate debate, dated Dec. 18, 1913, in STAH, XV Gb 150a.

53. Mueller, *10 Jahre Deutsch-Evangelischer Frauenbund*, 12.

54. ADEF, B 1c, internal discussion on Verbandsthemen, *Leitsätze zur Stellung des DEFS in der neuen Zeit*, Dec. 1919.

55. See LKAH, S 3d 251, "Verwaltungsbericht des Vaterländischen Frauen-vereins für die königliche Residenzstadt Hannover und Umgebung für das Jahr 1885"; Rothert, *Die innere Mission*, 418–26; Tennstedt, *Sozialgeschichte der Sozial-politik*, 209–11.

56. Frevert, "Fürsorgliche Belagerung," 435–41.

57. Komitee zur Ermittlung der Säuglingsernährung, *Säuglingsernährung*, 115; Statistisches Amt, *Statistisches Jahrbuch*, 1st ed., 9–10.

58. A copy of this flyer is in NH, Hann 320 I no. 23. This particular copy dates from the 1920s, but it appears to be a reprint of flyers distributed before the war; it was written by Lina Ramsauer, the sister of Anna Ramsauer, a Hanover teacher and prominent association leader.

1. This estimate is taken from the 1899 program of the DEF, in LKAH, E 2 390; see also in particular the thorough discussion of the woman "surplus" question in Hackett, "Politics of Feminism," 40–66; Stodolsky, "Missionaries of the Feminine Mystique," 201–3; *Evangelische Frauenzeitung* 1 (1900–1901): 39, and 3 (1902–3): 42–43.

2. Riemann, "Zur Diskrepanz zwischen der Realität sozialer Arbeit," 71.

3. These are titles of pamphlets available in STAH, Kettler Nachlass.

4. From the 1899 DEF program in LKAH, E 2 390.

5. The only statistical survey with which I am familiar that offers any support for the claim that nuptuality rates varied drastically among different classes in Wilhelmine Germany is that given by Hackett in "Politics of Feminism," 64–66. Hackett herself writes, however, that this survey is inconclusive. She offers a study of the number of single women living in various neighborhoods in Frankfurt in 1895, which shows that wealthier neighborhoods had a higher percentage of single female inhabitants than working-class neighborhoods. Hackett defines "single women" as unmarried adult women over the age of eighteen, however, which is problematical. We must assume that many of the women in their late teens and twenties, whom she defines as single, would eventually marry; if Hackett's data had allowed her to break down these unmarried women into age groups, and given figures for unmarried women over age forty, then we would have a better idea of how many confirmed spinsters lived in wealthy neighborhoods, relative to poorer neighborhoods. In addition, the lower percentage of unmarried women over age eighteen in working-class neighborhoods does not conclusively prove that poorer women married more frequently. It is likely that, although unmarried daughters in better off families lived at home (and were included in Hackett's survey), working-class daughters must have often left home to seek work (as domestic servants, for example, they lived with their employers). The relatively low number of unmarried women in working-class neighborhoods therefore does not prove that working-class women had a higher nuptuality rate. It seems likely that there were class differences in nuptuality rates, but we have no evidence at the moment to tell us how great these differences were. Historians should therefore be cautious in evaluating Wilhelmine commentators' claims about the enormous "woman surplus."

6. Vicinus, *Independent Women*, 27.

7. See Bussemer, *Frauenemanzipation*, 29–39. This "woman surplus," and the problem of how to support unmarried daughters, was probably also a factor among German Jews, who suffered from a more severe demographic imbalance between marriageable men and women, which led to the steady inflation of dowries during the late nineteenth century. See Kaplan, *The Making of the Jewish Middle Class*, 93–98.

8. Mueller, "Bericht über die Jahresversammlung des Allgemeinen Deutschen Frauenvereins," *Evangelische Frauenzeitung* 4 (1903–4): 12. Mueller was apparently paraphrasing a speech given by ADF leader Ika Freudenberg.

9. The statements about the Society for the Advancement of Female Education given here, as well as the information that follows in the next paragraph, were taken

from the society's annual programs, and from the report on the society's activities in NH, Hann 122a XX 52, 3–10. Hanover women had begun working on this project as early as 1888, but the first official *Vorstand* was not elected until 1892.

10. See Dasey, "Women's Work and the Family: Women Garment Workers in Berlin before the First World War," 241–43.

11. See the *Vorstand* lists in NH, Hann 122a XX 52, 3–10, and in STBH, Signatur ZsH467.

12. Taken from STAH, Lehrer: Personalakten von Lehrkräften an höheren, mittleren, Berufs- und Fachschulen: Mathilde Drees, which contains Drees's autobiographical statement (*Lebenslauf*) and work history.

13. See Drechsler-Hohlt, "Mathilde Drees zum Gedächtnis," 632–38. Her personal politics were reflected in the fact that Drees became active in the DDP after 1918.

14. This dissertation offers only a brief discussion of the German secondary girls' school (*höhere Mädchenschule*) and its subsequent reform. For more detailed discussions, see Albisetti, *Schooling German Girls and Women*; Zinnecker, *Sozialgeschichte der Mädchenbildung*; Beckmann, *Die Entwicklung der höheren Mädchenbildung*; Lexis, *The History and Organization*.

15. See STAH, XVI A III b6, for the 1893 pay scale, as well as subsequent petitions relating to female teachers' salaries and the ensuing revised pay scales, especially the petition dated Aug. 20, 1902.

16. The "yellow brochure" is reprinted in Lange, *Kampfzeiten*, 1:7–58.

17. Ibid.

18. See Bogerts, *Bildung und berufliches Selbstverständnis lehrender Frauen*, 117.

19. See the *Centralblatt für das gesammte Unterrichtswesen in Preussen* 1894, 483.

20. See Albisetti, "Could Separate Be Equal?," 308–9.

21. From the minutes of a city council meeting, dated Jan. 19, 1898, in STAH, XVI A III b6.

22. Jarausch, *Students, Society, and Politics*, 52–64.

23. See the appendix attached to a teachers' petition, dated Dec. 16, 1904, in STAH, XVI A III b5.

24. See ADEF, Akten der Ortsgruppe Hannover, III Protokollbuch der Vorstandssitzungen der Ortsgruppe Hannover, meetings of June 29, 1907; Mar. 28, 1908.

25. See the appendix attached to a teachers' petition, dated Dec. 16, 1904, in STAH, XVI A III b5, which contains biographical information about these women.

26. Taken from Drees's and Ramsauer's personnel records in STAH, Lehrer: Personalakten von Lehrkräften an höheren, mittleren, Berufs- und Fachschulen.

27. See Albisetti, "Female Physicians," 120.

28. Ibid., 108–9.

29. Ibid.

30. Mary Poovey discusses husbands' investment in not having male doctors examine their wives, within the context of the debate over administering chloroform, in *Uneven Developments*, chap. 2.

31. Schroeder, *Sophie*, 123–27.

32. See the correspondence between the "Reform" officers and Kettler in STAH, Kettler Nachlass, especially the *Rundschreiben* dated Aug. 21 and Sept. 12, 1897. Richard Evans, in *Feminist Movement*, 38, states that Kettler was ousted from "Re-

form" in 1895, but the Hanover archival papers indicate that this did not occur until 1897.

33. See STAH, Schulamt 845, which contains the prospectus of the school, including the list of patrons and the "Committee to Assist" members, and also a short history of the school, published in 1909. See also STAH, Kettler Nachlass, for material on the Association for the Reform of Women's Education, including membership lists.

34. See the list of patrons in STAH, Schulamt 845, and the list of members of Kettler's association in the Kettler Nachlass. For the methods used to determine each individual's occupation, confession, or religious affiliation, see the appendix.

35. All of the information in the preceding paragraph is drawn from a 1909 history of the *Gymnasial* courses contained in STAH, Schulamt 845, 1–2, 10–12. Kettler, impatient with her Hanover associates' unwillingness to put pressure on the city and province to grant full *Gymnasium* status to the *Gymnasial* courses, resigned from the association in 1901. In fact, the city had tried to obtain permission from the Prussian government around 1900, and had failed. See Albisetti, "Could Separate Be Equal?," 310. Kettler proceeded to found a Committee for a Complete *Mädchengymnasium*, but it did not garner much local support. See the minutes of the Second Generalversammlung of the Association for the Reform of Women's Education in the Kettler Nachlass.

36. From an interview with Hedwig von Bülow, held in Hanover on Nov. 4, 1986.

37. Taken from a list of pupils, which included their family backgrounds and subsequent university majors, in the school's 1909 history in STAH, Schulamt 845, 13–14.

38. Ibid.

39. Taken from estimated local rents given in *Mitteilungen des Statistischen Amts der Stadt Hannover* 1912, no. 2, 11.

40. See Bennigsen, *Der soziale Frauenberuf*, 10–11; the report of a factory social worker in *Evangelische Frauenzeitung* 10 (1909–10): 83; and an article by Paula Mueller on the court system in *Evangelische Frauenzeitung* 13 (1912–13): 81–82.

41. Vicinus, *Independent Women*, 16.

42. See Bennigsen's announcement of the inauguration of a school for social work in *Evangelische Frauenzeitung* 5 (1904–5): 54.

43. See STAH, XV Gb 150 vol. 1, letter from Paula Mueller to city officials, dated Sept. 5, 1900.

44. Alice Salomon offered courses in social work within the Berlin Mädchen- und Frauengruppen as early as 1899, but these weren't consolidated into a school until 1906; see Sachsse, *Mütterlichkeit*, 141, 145.

45. See STAH, XV Gb 150 vol. 1, which contains the seminar's first prospectus and a directory of the school's first pupils. For the average rents paid by different social groups in Hanover, see the study in *Mitteilungen des Statistischen Amts der Stadt Hannover*, 1912, no. 2, 11.

46. See Bennigsen's correspondence with Eyl and Tramm in STAH, XV Gb 150 vol. 1, especially her letters of Nov. 14, 1909, Dec. 30, 1910, Apr. 17 and 25, 1911.

47. See STAH, XV Gb 150b, a letter from the seminar to the city, dated Mar. 9, 1934, and subsequent correspondence; see also STAH, Personalamt Abgabe 1 II 120/164, for the background of the city's first *Fürsorgerinnen*.

48. See Sachsse, *Mütterlichkeit*, 142–45.

49. See the collection of revised seminar curricula in STAH, XV Gb 150 vol. 1.

50. Bennigsen, *Der soziale Frauenberuf*, 1, 10, 14.

51. Interview with Jutta Rexhausen, held in Hanover on Nov. 18, 1986.

52. Dr. Pohlmann, "Erster Bericht über die private Handelsschule für Mädchen," in STAH, Schulamt 1479, 12–14.

53. See STAH, Schulamt 1519, for the Continuation School's annual reports, and a petition submitted to the city by the school, dated Apr. 1911.

54. See the discussion of this association in Chapter 3; for a discussion of the union's national organization, and its on-again-off-again relationship with the BDF, see Kerchner, *Beruf und Geschlecht*, 139–60.

55. From an interview with Jutta Rexhausen, held in Hanover on Nov. 18, 1986; see also the newspaper report on the sixth *Stiftungsfest* in the *Hannoverscher Anzeiger* 17 (1909), no. 32 (Feb. 7, 1909), 3–4; see also the association's letter to the Christian Association for Young Girls, dated Oct. 1904, in LKAH, E 2 379.

56. STAH, Lehrer: Personalakten von Volksschullehrern: Anna Dörries; this file includes correspondence which shows that Dörries was on very cordial terms with Senator Grote, and also with Albert Wehrhahn, who played a leading role in running the municipal school system.

57. See STAH, XVI A III g14, the 1908–9 annual report of the Association of German Music Teachers; STAH, XVI Schulamt A III g18, correspondence about the ADLV dated May 8, 1913, and subsequent correspondence; and NH, Hann 320 I no. 4, which contains a directory of Hanover women's associations.

58. Schroeder, *Sophie*, 139–55.

59. The Tonika Do method, which taught children to sing the scale of notes as "do-re-mi," was used by Julie Andrews in *The Sound of Music*.

60. Schroeder, *Sophie*, 149–54.

61. See STAH, XVI A III g18, correspondence between the ADLV and city in 1913; STAH, A III g14, correspondence between the music teachers' association and the city, especially the letters dated July 19, 1907, Aug. 21, 1908, and Mar. 31, 1914. See also STAH, XVI A III g7, for correspondence between the city and the elementary school teachers' association, especially the letters dated Aug. 26, 1899; Sept. 15, 1901; Dec. 8, 1903; and June 23, 1916.

62. From the minutes of a city council meeting, dated Feb. 19, 1906, in STAH, XVI A III b6; see this file also for the female teachers' petitions submitted between 1892 and 1920.

63. Paula Mueller's answer to the League against Women's Emancipation in *Evangelische Frauenzeitung* 10 (1909–10): 3; italics in original.

CHAPTER 6

1. Chickering, *We Men Who Feel Most German*, 155.

2. From the report on the meeting of regional chapter heads in *Evangelische Frauenzeitung* 6 (1905–6): 1–2.

3. Freudenthal, *Vereine in Hamburg*, 180.

4. From "Advice for New Chapters," *Evangelische Frauenzeitung* 12 (1911–12): 25–26.

5. Interview with Ruth Grundmann, held in Hanover on Oct. 12, 1986. See also ADEF, Akten der Ortsgruppe Hannover, 1906 annual report; *Die christliche Frau* 4 (1905–6): 402.

6. Ramstetter, "Eugen de Haen," 186–88.

7. See the membership lists of the following associations: that for the Association for the Reform of Women's Education in STAH, Schulamt 845; for the Women's Association for the People's Welfare, STAH, XV Gb 171, "Geschäftsbericht für die Jahre 1905/06 und 1906/07," 14–15; for the Women's Educational Association, STAH, XVI E VII 1, "Bericht über die Tätigkeit des hannoverschen Frauenbildungsvereins für die Zeit vom 1. Januar 1896 bis 1. Januar 1901"; and for the Frauenabteilung des Vereins zur Hebung der öffentlichen Sittlichkeit (which ran a daycare center), LKAH, S 3d 531.

8. For information on the Oppler family, see Ellitz, "Edwin Oppler," 132–36. For Ella Oppler's role in women's organizations, see LKAH, E 2 395, "Satzungen des Frauenklubs"; STAH, XVI E VII 1, "Bericht über die Tätigkeit des hannoverschen Frauenbildungsvereins für die Zeit vom 1. Januar 1896 bis 1. Januar 1901"; STAH, Nachlass Kettler, membership list of the Association to Found a Hanover Girl's Gymnasium; *Addressbuch der königlichen Haupt- und Residenzstadt Hannover*, 1910 ed., part V, 164, which contains lists of officers of Jewish charitable organizations.

9. STAH, Lehrer: Personalakten von Lehrkräften an höheren, mittleren, Berufs- und Fachschulen: Maria Mühry, letter by Wespy, dated Aug. 23, 1904.

10. Ibid., report by Mühry on 1912 Frauenkongress.

11. See STAH, Lehrer: Personalakten von Volksschullehrern: Toni Eicke.

12. See Hugo and Hugo, *Die Geschichte der Familie von Hugo*, 91–92.

13. Ibid.

14. See the appendix for a discussion of how the residences of individual clubwomen were located.

15. Hackett, "Politics of Feminism," 227, 271–74. For cohabitation among single women in all Western nations during the late nineteenth century, see Fadermann, *Surpassing the Love of Men*, 190–203.

16. From Elsbeth Kruckenberg, "Frauenfreundschaften," *Evangelische Frauenzeitung* 7 (1906–7): 43–44.

17. See the account of the club's creation in the *Hannoverscher Courier* 47 (1900), no. 22786 (Jan. 10, 1900), 5; see also the report on the club's twenty-fifth anniversary in the *Hannoverscher Anzeiger* 23 (1925), no. 269 (Nov. 15, 1925), Beilage. See also the club's constitution, with a list of officers, in LKAH, E 2 395.

18. See the *Hannoverscher Courier* 47 (1900), no. 22786 (Jan. 10, 1900), 5.

19. For examples of reports on the club's activities, see the *Hannoverscher Anzeiger* 14 (1906), no. 274 (Nov. 25, 1906), Beilage; 18 (1910), no. 232 (Oct. 4, 1910), third Beilage; 19 (1911), no. 239 (Oct. 11, 1911), second Beilage; 19 (1911), no. 275 (Nov. 22, 1911), 3.

20. The DEF, for example, did so in 1902. See the correspondence regarding this convention in LB, Helene Lange Archiv, Karton 12, Abt. 3 (film # 12-39, 1-5).

21. See the announcements about the *Fasching* celebration in the *Hannoverscher Anzeiger* 17 (1909), no. 29 (Feb. 4, 1909), Beilage; 17 (1909), no. 43 (Feb. 20, 1909), 3.

22. Bussemer, *Frauenemanzipation*, 223.

23. The shortage of Catholic activists was perhaps partly explained by the social profile of Hanover's Catholic population, which was heavily working class, and which therefore afforded a smaller number (in absolute and relative terms) of bourgeois women available for such work. See *Die christliche Frau* 4 (1905–6): 402.

24. From a letter from Mueller to Frau Steinhausen (n.d., probably 1903) in ADEF, B 1.

25. See *Frieda Duensing. Ein Buch der Erinnerung*, 63–64. For a biography of Duensing, see the introduction to this work.

26. Allen, *Feminism and Motherhood*, 219–27.

27. See STAH, XVI A III g14, "Bericht über das Geschäftsjahr 1.2.1908 bis 31.1.1909."

28. The years 1906–8 were chosen because the of availability of membership lists for these years for many of the city's women's organizations. In addition, 1906 was a crucial turning point in the history of the local women's movement, as is discussed in Chapter 7.

29. For a complete list of sources, as well as a discussion of the methods used, see the appendix.

30. For the social background of DEF officers, see Chapter 3.

31. Statistisches Amt, *Statistisches Jahrbuch*, 1st ed., 8.

32. See Lidtke, *The Alternative Culture*, 25–27; Blackbourn, "The Discreet Charm of the Bourgeoisie," 196–98.

33. From an editorial in the *Hannoverscher Anzeiger* 17 (1909), no. 39 (Feb. 16, 1909), 2.

34. For the ways in which bourgeois women's work and leisure time overlapped and blurred, see Kaplan, *The Making of the Jewish Middle Class*, 117–19.

CHAPTER 7

1. Evans, *Feminist Movement*, 37–38; Hackett, "Politics of Feminism," 83–100, 454–56.

2. See Chapter 2 for a discussion of the early German women's movement on the national level.

3. Hackett, "Politics of Feminism," 143–51; Evans, *Feminist Movement*, 38–41.

4. Evans, *Feminist Movement*, 48–52; Hackett, "Politics of Feminism," 155–65.

5. Evans, *Feminist Movement*, 146–47; Hackett, "Politics of Feminism," 168–71.

6. Evans, *Feminist Movement*, 93.

7. See Meyer-Renschhausen, *Weibliche Kultur*, 345–49.

8. See Schulte, *Sperrbezirke*, 249; Pappritz, *Einführung*, 30.

9. For an example of this schema of victimization in abolitionist rhetoric, see Pappritz, *Herrenmoral*, 17. For a discussion of how victimization was used in abolitionist rhetoric, see Meyer-Renschhausen, "Die weibliche Ehre," 84–92; see also Walkowitz, "Male Vice," 80–82.

10. This very real threat was present in internal discussions held within the bourgeois women's movement, and also in the culture as a whole, as evidenced by Henrik Ibsen's play, *Ghosts*.

11. For the rejection of this libertarian approach by the churches and conservatives, see Gibson, *Prostitution and the State*, 72–73.

12. Walkowitz, "Male Vice," 80–82. For more on the Victorian abolitionist movement by the same author, see *Prostitution and Victorian Society*. Throughout this chapter, I compare the British abolitionists studied by Walkowitz (along with abolitionist campaigns launched in other European nations) with the Hanover abolitionist campaign. Although I am aware of the problems inherent in using Britain as a standard for measuring German "progress," I think that it is justifiable to use the British case for comparison in this instance. The German abolitionists were part of an international antiregulation organization that had been founded by and was led by Josephine Butler and other British women. German abolitionists, including Hanover abolitionists, were familiar with British abolitionist rhetoric, tactics, and campaigns, as well as the tactics used by abolitionists in France and Italy. Thus, if Hanover abolitionists did not advance the same objections and arguments used by British abolitionists, it seems fair to conclude that these omissions were a deliberate choice on the part of Hanover abolitionists, a choice that is worth noting and analyzing.

13. For Butler's role in inspiring the creation of abolitionist movements in France and Italy, see Corbin, *Women for Hire*, 214–17; Gibson, *Prostitution and the State*, 41–45.

14. Gibson, *Prostitution and the State*, 50; Corbin, *Women for Hire*, 227–28.

15. Pappritz, *Herrenmoral*, 16–17 (italics in original).

16. Meyer-Renschhausen, *Weibliche Kultur*, 335–37.

17. Evans, *Feminist Movement*, 56–63.

18. Schulte, *Sperrbezirke*, 18–24. For a social profile of Hanover prostitutes, see Berger, *Die Prostitutionsfrage in Hannover*, 21–25. Berger's research also demonstrated the transient nature of prostitution in Hanover. Of the 261 women included in his study, 52 had been registered with the police as prostitutes for less than three months, 112 for less than a year, and 201 for less than five years. Most worked as prostitutes for a year or two, and then escaped police registration by moving to another city, or were struck from the registration lists after finding other gainful employment, or marrying. See Berger, *Die Prostitution in Hannover*, 20, 30. For a discussion of the social profile of Wilhelmine prostitutes as a whole, as well as an examination of those factors which drove women to prostitution, see Walser, "Prostitutionsverdacht und Geschlechterforschung," 101–3.

19. The text of this law is reprinted in Schulte, *Sperrbezirke*, 249.

20. Pappritz, *Einführung*, 30.

21. ADEF, V 23, "Sittenpolizeiliche Vorschriften."

22. Berger, *Die Prostitution in Hannover*, 40.

23. Ibid., 17–19.

24. ADEF, V 23, minutes of a meeting between DEF officers and police officials, dated Nov. 14, 1906. Unfortunately, it is not possible to determine how police arrived at their estimate of the number of unregistered prostitutes.

25. Berger, *Die Prostitution in Hannover*, 7, 25–26. See also Ulrich, *Bordelle, Strassendirnen, und bürgerliche Sittlichkeit*, 32; ADEF, V 23, "Bericht des Kriminal-Kommissars Haake über verschiedene Punkte der Broschöre des Kreisarztes Dr. med. Berger," 4. The same opportunities for escaping registration existed in Berlin; see Schulte, *Sperrbezirke*, 20.

26. This would have meant that approximately one out of every twenty young women in Hanover resorted to prostitution at least temporarily. This figure is based on the assumption that unregistered prostitutes, like registered prostitutes, were primarily drawn from women between the ages of eighteen and twenty-five (as were 68 percent of registered prostitutes), and that almost all were single, divorced, or separated. There were 16,592 single, divorced, or separated women in this age group in Hanover in 1905. If one assumes that approximately 1,250 women worked as prostitutes at any given time (1,000 unregistered and 250 registered), of whom 68 percent were between eighteen and twenty-five years old, then 1 out of every 20 single young women in this age group resorted to prostitution at least temporarily. This figure is not excessive when compared with contemporaries' estimates of the extent of prostitution in other large German cities; see Schulte, *Sperrbezirke*, 19–22.

27. ADEF, V 23, "Besondere Aktensammlung: Abänderung der sittenpolizei-lichen Vorschriften," "Kurze Notizen aus den Akten," 1, and "Bericht des Kriminal-Kommissars Haake über verschiedene Punkte der Broschöre des Kreisarztes Dr. med. Berger," 9. The existence of ADEF, V 23, "Besondere Aktensammlung," is itself important, and says a great deal about the relationship between municipal officials and the DEF leadership. The history of this file is as follows. In Feb. 1907, the head of police ordered that police files relating to the issue of prostitution in Hanover be loaned to the DEF, so that its officers could study the background of this question, as it was documented in the police archives (see the letter from the police to Mueller, dated Feb. 20, 1907, in ADEF, V 23). The DEF officers apparently studied these files, made extensive notes on their contents, and then returned the originals; thus, V 23 contains DEF notes and excerpts from the police files (this is fortunate, since the originals could not be located). The files included memorandums on internal police meetings about how best to regulate prostitution, copies of citizens' complaints about prostitutes' behavior, copies of the regulations applied to pros-titutes, reports by police officers on the activities of prostitutes in various neighbor-hoods, and a report by police commissioner Haake about Dr. Berger's book on prostitution in Hanover. The fact that the police would lend Mueller their own files speaks volumes about the congenial, collegial relationship that DEF officers had with the police and city officials, a relationship that is also documented in the DEF minutes made of meetings with police officials, also in ADEF, V 23.

28. See Vicinus, "Sexuality and Power: A Review of Current Work in the History of Sexuality," 136–37.

29. The police also began to experiment with allowing prostitutes to live together, and introduced a special class of registered prostitutes (*sozial feiner*, or "more re-fined" prostitutes, that is, call girls). *Sozial feiner* prostitutes had more freedom of movement and were required to report for medical examinations only once a month. See ADEF, V 23, "Besondere Aktensammlung: Abänderung der sittenpolizeilichen Vorschriften" and "Kurze Notizen aus den Akten."

30. ADEF, V 23, "Kurze Notizen aus den Akten," 1–5.

31. ADEF, V 23, memorandum from *Polizeirat* Titze to the *Regierungspräsident* (n.d.). The content of the document indicates that this memo was written in early Oct. 1906.

32. For a list of all Hanover women's associations that joined the anti-*Kaser-nierung* alliance, see the signatories to a petition reprinted in *Evangelische Frauen-*

zeitung 7 (1906–7): 28–29. The local branch of the Jewish Women's League did not sign this petition, which was somewhat surprising, considering its presence in other women's coalitions. The Hanover branch of the league may have joined later; one of its officers was active in the local chapter of the Abolitionist Federation.

33. The Hanover Federation chapter and the Women's Welfare (*"Frauenwohl"*) Association were the first local chapters to be founded by any "progressive" feminist women's organization, that is, the first local chapter of any of the organizations that belonged to the Verband Fortschrittlicher Frauenvereine, which is generally considered to define the "left" or feminist wing of the BDF.

34. For a list of officers of these two feminist groups, and a discussion of their size and memberships, see NH, Hann 122a XX 142 vol. 2, 122–24, 130–31.

35. Mueller, *Einsame Frauen*, 9 (this pamphlet is a reprint of a speech given by Mueller at several meetings during the last half of 1906).

36. From a petition submitted on Dec. 23, 1906, by twenty-two women's organizations to local authorities. A copy is in ADEF, V 23. See the reprint of the first petition submitted by the federation in the *Hannoverscher Anzeiger* 14 (1906), no. 245 (Oct. 19, 1906), 2–3.

37. See the petition reprinted in the *Hannoverscher Anzeiger* 14 (1906), no. 245 (Oct. 19, 1906), 2–3.

38. See the copy of the Dec. 26, 1906, petition submitted by the women's alliance in ADEF, V 23.

39. See Meyer-Renschhausen, "Die weibliche Ehre," 84–92.

40. See Walkowitz, "Male Vice," 80–84; see also Kent, *Sex and Suffrage*, 142–43.

41. Quoted in Meyer-Renschhausen, "Die weibliche Ehre," 91.

42. See Meyer-Renschhausen, *Weibliche Kultur*, 364–69; see also Kent, *Sex and Suffrage* 157–83.

43. In Bremen, where bourgeois women leaders did make alliances with working-class leaders, the alliance was with the local SPD; see Meyer-Renschhausen, *Weibliche Kultur*, 260, 365.

44. See Mueller, *Einsame Frauen*, 14; see also Mueller, *Welche Aufgaben*, 14–15.

45. See ADEF, V 23, memorandum from Mueller and von der Groeben to police, dated Nov. 26, 1906.

46. Ibid. (italics in original). This position echoed demands put forth by both the national abolitionist leadership and by local Hanover abolitionists. See "Verschiedenes," *Der Abolitionist* 5 (1906): 8; report on abolitionist meeting in *Hannoverscher Anzeiger* 14 (1906), no. 245 (Oct. 19, 1906), 2. Mueller was still espousing the same position ten years later when she proposed amending the penal code to read "it shall be a punishable offense to disturb public order or public decency through the commission of immoral acts, or through furthering or soliciting immoral acts." See the exchange of letters between Mueller and Herr Lic. Mumm dated Nov. 9 and 11, 1916, in ADEF, V 22b.

47. Minutes of these meetings, which were held on Oct. 14, Nov. 14, and Dec. 1, 1906, are in ADEF, V 23.

48. The police fell back upon "localization" in private meetings with the DEF as early as Nov. 14, 1906, but did not announce their change in plans publicly until Dec. 2, 1906. See the minutes of the Nov. 14 meeting with DEF leaders in ADEF, V 23; "Verschiedenes," *Der Abolitionist* 6 (1907): 16.

49. See ADEF, V 23, for the letter from the police that accompanied the copies of records sent to the DEF. See also Evans, *Feminist Movement*, 56–61, for Heymann's legal battles with the Hamburg police.

50. From the *Hannoversche Grundbesitzer Zeitung*, Oct. 28, 1906. It is not possible to give the volume number or page for this article, since the originals are no longer available. A copy of this article is preserved in ADEF, V 23. In addition, see ADEF, V 23, "Kurze Notizen aus den Akten," 5–7.

51. ADEF, V 23, copy of an article from the *Hannoversche Grundbesitzer Zeitung*, Oct. 28, 1906. Italics are in the original. In the same file, see the article from the *Hannoversche Grundbesitzer Zeitung*, Jan. 29, 1907. The same dualistic view of women was prevalent in Britain, a schema wherein women were assigned to one of two sexual categories, and the latter category (women "born hot") supposedly existed in order to provide a safety valve for men's sexuality; see Kent, *Sex and Suffrage*, 62–63.

52. ADEF, V 23, "Bericht des Kriminal-Kommissars Haake über verschiedene Punkte der Broschöre des Kreisarztes Dr. med. Berger," 4.

53. See the newspaper accounts in the *Hannoverscher Anzeiger* 15 (1907), no. 12 (Jan. 15, 1907), 6, and in the *Hannoversches Tageblatt* 56 (1907), no. 15 (Jan. 15, 1907), first Beilage, 5.

54. Regina Schulte notes that the need to distinguish between "decent women" and prostitutes was used to justify *Kasernierung* in several cities; Schulte, *Sperr-bezirke*, 27.

55. From the *Hannoverscher Anzeiger* 14 (1906), no. 294 (Dec. 16, 1906), 2.

56. The petition was dated Dec. 17, 1906; a copy is in ADEF, V 23.

57. See, for example, Lida Gustava Heymann's comment that to disrupt public meetings at the local level was unheard of in Wilhelmine bourgeois associational culture. In Gustava Heymann and Augspurg, *Erlebtes-Erschautes. Deutsche Frauen kämpfen für Freiheit, Recht und Frieden, 1850–1940*, 106.

58. From an editorial that appeared in the *Freie Meinung* on Jan. 19, 1907. Unfortunately, the volume and page numbers cannot be given, since the original is no longer available. A copy of the editorial is in ADEF, V 23.

59. See the *Hannoverscher Courier* 53 (1906), no. 26577 (Dec. 15, 1906), 5, and the *Hannoversches Tageblatt* 15 (1907), no. 78 (Mar. 29, 1907), third Beilage.

60. From the minutes of a meeting between DEF officers and Bertha Duensing, dated Feb. 13, 1907, in ADEF, V 23.

61. See the minutes of the Oct. 14 meeting with police in ADEF, V 23.

62. See the letters in the *Hannoverscher Courier* 54 (1907), no. 26756 (Apr. 5, 1907), 5, and the *Hannoversches Tageblatt* 56 (1907), no. 97 (Apr. 6, 1907), 5.

63. For the fears expressed by the chief of police, see the minutes of the Oct. 14 meeting with DEF leaders in ADEF, V 23. For the protests of the neighborhood associations and the divisions within the ranks of the pro-*Kasernierung* coalition, see the announcement of the *Bürgerverein Fernroder Stadtteile* in the *Hannoverscher Anzeiger* 14 (1906), no. 251 (Nov. 6, 1906), 5, and the *Hannoversches Tageblatt* 56 (1907), no. 103 (Apr. 12, 1907), 6.

64. See the report on a joint meeting of six neighborhood associations in the *Hannoverscher Anzeiger* 15 (1907), no. 27 (Feb. 10, 1907), 5–6, where property owners expressed their complaints about women leaders' influence within local government, particularly with the *Regierungspräsident*.

65. This claim is made in Pappritz, *Einführung*, 232; see also Meyer-Renschhausen, "Die weibliche Ehre," 85.

66. See the material on the cartel in ADEF, V 24, especially the minutes of the cartel meetings dated Dec. 4, 1908; Apr. 16, 1909; Sept. 20, 1909; and June 12, 1912. See also the letters from local newspaper publishers to the cartel, dated Nov. 2 and 3, 1910. For a survey of the national movement to combat *Schundliteratur*, see Schenda, "Schundliteratur."

67. See the descriptions of other, similar abolitionist campaigns in ADEF, V 22a vols. 1, 2 ("Prostitutionsfrage").

CHAPTER 8

1. See the report submitted by the Hanover chapter in *Die Frauenbewegung* 13 (1907): 31; see also the report in *Die Frauenbewegung* 15 (1909): 39.

2. See, for example, the report on a Suffrage Union meeting in the *Hannoverscher Anzeiger* 19 (1911), no. 66 (Mar. 18, 1911), 6.

3. See Hackett, "Helene Stöcker," 113–19; Allen, "Feminism, Venereal Diseases, and the State," 34–38; Evans, *Feminist Movement*, 119–25.

4. Evans, *Feminist Movement*, 126–28; Nowacki, *Der Bund für Mutterschutz*, 71.

5. Evans, *Feminist Movement*, 164–65.

6. Clemens, *Menschenrechte*, 59–62.

7. See NH, Hann 122a XX 142 vol. 2, 122–24; see also the account of a league meeting in the *Hannoverscher Anzeiger* 18 (1910), no. 40 (Feb. 17, 1910), 3. The Hanover group was not the only provincial chapter to reject the league. After the Hanover Women's Welfare Association dissolved a few years later, the Hanover group changed its name to the Association for the Protection of Motherhood. It functioned through the 1920s as an independent, local charity, which tried (unsuccessfully) to establish a home for unwed mothers, and gave advice (in a weekly *Sprechstunde*) to single pregnant women.

8. The Hanover Suffrage Union branch joined the Deutscher Reichsverband für Frauenstimmrecht, which did not demand universal suffrage for all adults; Clemens, *Menschenrechte*, 61, 156.

9. ADEF, V 24, minutes of the Cartel meeting of Sept. 20, 1909, and subsequent meetings; Akten der Ortsgruppe Hannover, III Protokollbuch der Vorstandssitzungen der Ortsgruppe Hannover, meeting of May 12, 1909. See also Mueller, *Die neue Ethik und ihre Gefahr*.

10. For a first-rate discussion of alcohol consumption by German men during this period, and the reaction of women temperance activists, see Meyer-Renschhausen, *Weibliche Kultur*, 182–224.

11. See NH, Hann 122a XX 142 vol. 2, 122–24.

12. Greven-Aschoff, *Die bürgerliche Frauenbewegung*, 106; Evans, *Feminist Movement*, 150–58.

13. Chickering, *We Men Who Feel Most German*, 197. The masculine German-national public realm is also analyzed in Eley, *Reshaping the German Right*, and in Coetzee, *German Army League*. See also Chickering, " 'Casting Their Gaze,' " 156–85.

14. Chickering, "'Casting Their Gaze,'" 166–67. See also Chickering, *We Men Who Feel Most German*, 170–71.

15. At least one chapter of the society tried to create an expanded role for women in this area, however. See Chickering, "'Casting Their Gaze,'" 167–71.

16. See the appendix for a discussion of the sources and methodology used to ascertain the social background and marital status of these activists.

17. See the accounts of the Women's Division's work in the *Hannoverscher Anzeiger* 18 (1910), no. 41 (Feb. 18, 1910), 2, and 19 (1911), no. 23 (Jan. 27, 1911), 11; Frauenbund der Deutschen Kolonialgesellschaft, *10 Jahre Frauenbund der Deutschen Kolonialgesellschaft*, 14. See also Chickering, "'Casting Their Gaze,'" 174–82. Chickering notes that although there was agreement between men and women in the Colonial Society about the goal of recruiting women for the colonies, there were also tensions about the division's finances generated by the subordination of the Women's Division to its masculine counterpart.

18. See the retrospective collection of division propaganda in Frobenius, *30 Jahre Koloniale Frauenarbeit*, 37.

19. See the account of the league's creation in the *Hannoverscher Anzeiger* 15 (1907), no. 18 (Jan. 22, 1907), 5; see also Chickering, "'Casting Their Gaze,'" 172–74.

20. See accounts of the women's league meetings in the *Hannoverscher Anzeiger* 15 (1907), no. 58 (Mar. 9, 1907), 2; *Deutsche Volkszeitung* 1907 volume, no. 10330 (Mar. 12, 1907), 3. At the national level, the men's Navy League also opposed the warship project, but urged the women to devote their funds to creating a convalescent home for sailors; this pressure was ultimately successful. See Chickering, "'Casting Their Gaze,'" 173–74.

21. From the *Deutsche Volkszeitung* 1907 volume, no. 10330 (Mar. 12, 1907), 3.

22. See the review in the *Hannoverscher Anzeiger* 17 (1909), no. 66 (Mar. 19, 1909), 5.

23. See the report on the tea in the *Hannoverscher Anzeiger* 18 (1910), no. 17 (Jan. 21, 1910), 2.

24. Roger Chickering also makes this argument in "'Casting Their Gaze,'" 172–74; the Hanover example confirms his observations.

25. For an account of the reform of the Law of Association, see Hackett, "Politics of Feminism," 675–79; for the affiliation of local feminists with the Progressive People's Party, see the party's announcement in the *Hannoverscher Anzeiger* 19 (1911), no. 29 (Feb. 3, 1911), 3.

CHAPTER 9

1. For the creation of the Conservative Women's Union, see the flyer announcing the union's creation in ADEF, H 1b; for the entrance of bourgeois women into almost all masculine political parties during this period, see Hackett, "Politics of Feminism," 781–808, 827–31.

2. Clemens, *Menschenrechte*, 96.

3. See Chapter 8 for a discussion of the divisions in the suffrage movement.

4. Evans, *Feminist Movement*, 153–54, 210–12; Greven-Aschoff, *Die bürgerliche Frauenbewegung*, 110–13, 148–49.

5. Evans, *Feminist Movement*, 195–99; Greven-Aschoff, *Die bürgerliche Frauen-bewegung*, 111–12.

6. See ADEF, FF 1, an exchange of letters between the DEF and the Red Cross in this file, beginning in 1912, as well as DEF secretary E. von der Beck's memo to all DEF Verbands-Vorsitzende, dated Feb. 7, 1913.

7. See the report on this meeting in *Evangelische Frauenzeitung* 13 (1913–14): 113–14. Italics are in the original.

8. Ibid.; see also the report in the *Vierteljährliche Nachrichten des Landesvereins hannoverscher Jungfrauenvereine* 1 (1913–14), no. 3, 2–3.

9. Quoted in Prokop, "Die Sehnsucht nach Volkseinheit," 179–80.

10. *Evangelische Frauenzeitung* 13 (1913–14): 172–73.

11. Boyd, " 'Nationaler Frauendienst,' " 59–62; Hackett, "Politics of Feminism," 906.

12. See the Women's Service organizational chart contained in ADEF, FF 1, Nationaler Frauendienst Hannover, *Tätigkeitsbericht vom 5. August bis 15. Oktober 1914*.

13. Feldman, *Army, Industry, and Labor*, 6–7.

14. Sachsse, *Mütterlichkeit*, 151; Seidel, *Frauenarbeit im Ersten Weltkrieg*, 36–39.

15. ADEF, FF 1, *Tätigkeitsbericht vom 5. August bis 15. Oktober 1914*, 7.

16. Sachsse, *Mütterlichkeit*, 157.

17. ADEF, FF 1, *Tätigkeitsbericht vom 5. August bis 15. Oktober 1914*, 6.

18. Ibid., 6–9.

19. Ibid.; see also ADEF, FF 1, *Zweiter Tätigkeitsbericht vom 15. Oktober 1914 bis 10. August 1915* and *Dritter Tätigkeitsbericht vom 10. August 1915 bis 10. August 1916*. See also Sachsse, *Mütterlichkeit*, 167–68; Wurms, " 'Krieg dem Kriege,' " 93.

20. Lüders, *Das unbekannte Heer*, 180.

21. Frevert, *Frauen-Geschichte*, 156–58.

22. Lüders, *Das unbekannte Heer*, 186.

23. See the report on the Housewives' Association (n.d., late 1915) in NH, Hann 320 I no. 2.

24. See the reports on the Housewives' Association cooperative stores in NH, Hann 320 I no. 4.

25. For Lüders's recollections of her work within the War Ministry, see Lüders, *Das unbekannte Heer*; Gersdorff, *Frauen im Kriegsdienst*, 22; Sachsse, *Mütterlichkeit*, 169.

26. Daniel, "Fiktionen," 295–97; Boyd, " 'Nationaler Frauendienst,' " 130–34, 146–51.

27. For a discussion of factors that affected women's wartime employment, see Daniel, "Fiktionen," 282–86, 299–304, 312–16; see also Seidel, *Frauenarbeit*, 238.

28. Seidel, *Frauenarbeit*, 222. See also Wurms, " 'Krieg dem Kriege,' " 103; Frevert, *Frauengeschichte*, 162–63. For an excellent analysis of the role that women played in popular protests in Berlin during this period, and of the debates that emerged during the war around women's wartime work, political mobilization, and nutritional needs, see Davis, "Food Scarcity," and "Home Fires Burning."

29. Röhrbein and Zankl, *Hannover im 20. Jahrhundert*, 16, 70.

30. ADEF, FF 1, Women's Service memos dated Oct. 25, 1917; May 29, 1918; and August 5, 1918.

31. ADEF, FF 1, *Dritter Tätigkeitsbericht vom 10. August 1915 bis 10. August 1916*, 3–5.

32. Magdalene v. Tilling, quoted in Kaufmann, "Die Ehre des Vaterlandes und die Ehre der Frauen," 287.

33. ADEF, FF 1, "Verantwortung," a flyer circulated by the Women's Service.

34. Ibid.

35. ADEF, FF 1, "An alle deutschen Frauen und Mädchen," a Women's Service flyer.

36. ADEF, FF 1, "Anruf an die deutschen Frauen," a Women's Service flyer.

37. ADEF, V 24, "Das Kartell Hannoverscher und Lindener Vereine zur Bekämpfung öffentlicher sittlicher Schäden," minutes of a meeting of the cartel, dated Oct. 24, 1914.

38. ADEF, FF 1, *Tätigkeitsbericht vom 5. August bis 15. Oktober 1914*, 8; *Zweiter Tätigkeitsbericht vom 15. Oktober 1914 bis 10. August 1915*, 9; report in *Evangelische Frauenzeitung* 13 (1913–14): 190; ADEF, V 23, letter from Mueller to Frau v. Schmeling, dated Dec. 16, 1916.

39. ADEF, FF 1, undated flyer distributed by Women's Service.

40. See the minutes of an assembly of leaders of youth organizations, dated Apr. 21, 1917, in STAH, Sportamt Sp110.

41. ADEF, FF 1, Mueller's memo to all Women's Service associations, dated May 22, 1916.

42. ADEF, FF 1, flyer "an alle deutschen Frauen und Mädchen"; see also the petition submitted by the cartel in 1916 to the local military authorities, which demanded a crackdown on adulterous wives and unsupervised youths in ADEF, V 24. The petition expressed anger, shock, and despair over the behavior of many Hanoverian women and youths. For the denunciation of German women who displayed an inappropriate interest in prisoners of war, see *Evangelische Frauenzeitung* 13 (1913–14): 177.

43. ADEF, FF 1, from a Women's Service memo dated Oct. 25, 1917, and from the program the lecture cited, dated July 1, 1917.

44. ADEF, FF 1, Mueller's memo to other service members, dated Oct. 16, 1918.

45. See Frevert, *Frauen-Geschichte*, 157–58.

46. ADEF, O 1, Mueller's correspondence from this period, especially her letter to Countess v. Schwerin-Löwitz, dated Oct. 14, 1917. See also Frevert, *Frauen-Geschichte*, 168. For the reaction of Hanover DEF officials to the break, see ADEF, Akten der Ortsgruppe Hannover, IV Protokollbuch der Vorstandssitzungen, meeting of Feb. 23, 1918.

47. Quoted in Evans, *Feminist Movement*, 226–27.

48. Kaufmann, *Frauen zwischen Aufbruch und Reaktion*, 45.

CHAPTER 10

1. For a first-rate analysis of this rhetoric, see Kaufmann, "Die Ehre des Vaterlandes," 290; see also Kaufmann, *Frauen zwischen Aufbruch und Reaktion*, 37–39.

2. ADEF, O 9b, Mueller's correspondence from Oct. to Dec. 1918. Mueller appar-

ently changed her last name in order to attract support by capitalizing on the fact that Otfried (a name from her mother's side of the family) was well known in Hanover because of an illustrious relative, and also to make her stand out from numerous other Muellers.

3. ADEF, O 9b, Countess Keyserlingk's letter to Mueller-Otfried, dated Nov. 22, 1918.

4. Quoted in Boyd, " 'Nationaler Frauendienst,' " 218–19.

5. Kaufmann, *Frauen zwischen Aufbruch und Reaktion*, 48–53.

6. See the report on the league in the *Hannoverscher Kurier*, Nov. 9, 1924, no. 528, "Die Frau" Beilage; see also the letter from Mathilde Drees to Bertha Hindenberg-Delbrück, dated July 11, 1928, in NH, Hann 320 I no. 10 vol. 1. The league's first national president, Marie von Alten, was also on the executive committee of the German Army League; Coetzee, *German Army League*, 57.

7. Geschichtswerkstatt Hannover, *Alltag zwischen Hindenburg und Haarmann*, 7.

8. See ADEF, Akten der Ortsgruppe Hannover, IV Protokollbuch der Vorstandssitzungen der Ortsgruppe Hannover, meeting of Nov. 9, 1917.

9. See ibid., meetings of Nov. 16, 1918; Nov. 22, 1918; Mar. 10, 1919; Oct. 15, 1919; Jan. 20, 1920; Apr. 30, 1920.

10. Ibid., meetings of Dec. 6, 1918, and May 3, 1919; see also ADEF, Akten der Ortsgruppe Hannover, III Protokollbuch der Mitgliederversammlungen der Ortsgruppe Hannover, meetings of Nov. 29, 1918, and Jan. 2, 1919.

11. Paula Mueller-Otfried, "Wir Wollen," *Evangelische Frauenzeitung* 25 (1924): 2.

12. See ADEF, Akten der Ortsgruppe Hannover, III Protokollbuch der Mitgliederversammlungen der Ortsgruppe Hannover, meetings of Jan. 11 and Feb. 23, 1925.

13. Frevert, *Frauen-Geschichte*, 166; Evans, *Feminist Movement*, 246.

14. Evans, *Feminist Movement*, 246–47.

15. STAH, Kartei: Mitglieder der städtischen Kollegien, 1919–33; STAH, Lehrer: Personalakten von Lehrkräften an höheren, mittleren, Berufs- und Fachschulen: Anna Ramsauer.

16. Röhrbein and Zankl, *Hannover im 20. Jahrhundert*, 72–73. "SPD" here refers to the majority socialists; the Independent Socialists and later the Communists found only limited support among Hanover's working-class voters.

17. Ibid., 77–81.

18. Ibid., 80, 119.

19. Ibid., 118–21.

20. STAH, Kartei: Mitglieder der städtischen Kollegien, 1919–33.

21. The new system is discussed in Schickenberg, *Neuordnung der Fürsorge*.

22. Marquardt, *Sozialpolitik und Sozialfürsorge*, 6–14; Sachsse, *Mütterlichkeit als Beruf*, 193–249.

23. Marquardt, *Sozialpolitik und Sozialfürsorge*, 47–51.

24. Ibid., 73–83; Sachsse, *Mütterlichkeit als Beruf*, 181–86.

25. See STAH, Wohlfahrtsausschuss, 1922–27, minutes of the meeting of Jan. 15, 1923. In practice, the district welfare committees were heavily influenced by the local SPD; as a result, they were abolished after the National Socialists took control of the Hanover city council.

26. Marquardt, *Sozialpolitik und Sozialfürsorge*, 84.

27. Schickenberg, *Neuordnung der Fürsorge*, 18.

28. Schmidt-Waldherr, *Emanzipation durch Professionalisierung?*, 206–7.

29. Sachsse, *Mütterlichkeit als Beruf*, 227–32; for an example in Hanover, see the minutes of the municipal finance committee meeting of Sept. 27, 1920, in STAH, XVI E VII 3.

30. STAH, XVI E VII 3, minutes for committee meeting of Sept. 27, 1920; XV Gb 150a, minutes of the city senate meeting of Aug. 27, 1920; Schulamt 1519, letter from Mathilde Drees to the city, dated Jan. 17, 1920; see also ADEF, Akten der Ortsgruppe Hannover, IV Protokollbuch der Vorstandssitzungen der Ortsgruppe Hannover, meeting of Nov. 12, 1921; see also III Protokollbuch der Mitgliederversammlungen der Ortsgruppe Hannover, meeting of Feb. 23, 1923.

31. See STAH, XV Gb 150 vol. 2, letter from Schickenberg to the mayor's office, dated Mar. 28, 1925.

32. Quoted in Clemens, *Menschenrechte*, 115.

33. ADEF, Akten der Ortsgruppe Hannover, IV Protokollbuch der Vorstandssitzungen der Ortsgruppe Hannover, meeting of May 3, 1919.

34. The quotation and the information on the Brunswick chapter are taken from Stoehr, *Emanzipation*, 95–96.

35. Ibid., 105.

36. Stoehr, "Neue Frau und alte Bewegung," 390.

37. Ibid., 390–94; see also Evans, *Feminist Movement*, 249–50.

38. *Hannoverscher Anzeiger*, 23 (1925), no. 269 (Nov. 15, 1925).

39. See Guckel, "Eine Welt aus Zuckerguss und Schmiedeeisen," and "Weltspiele Georgstrasse," 19–38.

40. Röhrbein and Zankl, *Hannover im 20. Jahrhundert*, 121–23.

41. See STAH, Personalamt Abgabe 1 II 120/164, petition of the City Women's Federation, dated Mar. 1, 1927; see also Marquardt, *Sozialpolitik und Sozialfürsorge*, 65–70.

42. See the correspondence during this period concerning a rental dispute between the club and the Housewives' Association in NH, Hann 320 I no. 3.

43. See ADEF, Akten der Ortsgruppe Hannover, III Protokollbuch der Mitgliederversammlungen der Ortsgruppe Hannover, meetings of Jan. 17, 1922; May 22, 1922; May 11, 1923.

44. See ADEF, Akten der Ortsgruppe Hannover, IV Protokollbuch der Vorstandssitzungen der Ortsgruppe Hannover, meetings of Mar. 20, 1920; Apr. 20, 1920; Mar. 14, 1921; Sept. 10, 1921; May 11, 1921. See also Protokollbuch der Vorstandssitzungen der Ortsgruppe Hannover (1925–28), meetings of Jan. 7, 1926; June 3, 1926; Apr. 13, 1928.

45. See Deutsch-Evangelischer Frauenbund, *25 Jahre Säuglingsheim und Versorgungshaus*, 7.

46. See Richter's petition, dated Feb. 18, 1925, in STAH, XXX Wohlfahrts- und Armenwesen 90, Martha Richter.

47. ADEF, III Protokollbuch der Mitgliederversammlungen der Ortsgruppe Hannover, meetings of Oct. 26, 1923, and Nov. 28, 1924. See also IV Protokollbuch der Vorstandssitzungen der Ortsgruppe Hannover, meeting of Apr. 21, 1921.

1. See Table 6.1; see also Bund Deutscher Frauenvereine, *Zusammenstellung der angeschlossenen Verbände*, 16; Statistisches Amt, *Statistisches Jahrbuch*, 2d ed., 137. In the case of the teachers' associations, both figures reflect the fact the teachers' groups had overlapping memberships: thus, the real number of teachers in Hanover was lower. For a discussion of the Commercial Union of Female Employees nationally, see Nienhaus, *Berufsstand weiblich*.

2. See, for example, STAH, XVI A 111 b6, letter from the Association of Hanover and Linden Female Teachers to the city, dated Sept. 1, 1920.

3. Kaufmann, *Frauen zwischen Aufbruch*, 37–39, 66–68. More broadly translated, *Deutschtum* refers to German customs and values, the German "way of life."

4. From a letter to Frau Falke, dated July 13, 1921, in ADEF, V 22b. For the *Schmachfrieden* protests organized by Hanover women, see ADEF, Akten der Orts-gruppe Hannover, III Protokollbuch der Mitgliederversammlungen der Orts-gruppe, meeting of Dec. 1, 1922. See also Kaufmann, *Frauen zwischen Aufbruch*, 39. Mueller-Otfried's letter reveals interesting differences in the way that nationalist men and women thought about this issue. The discussion within the women's movement acknowledged that German women in the occupied areas were volun-tarily consorting with foreign troops, while the masculine nationalist imagination conceptualized these relationships almost exclusively in terms of rape; nationalist men apparently could not admit that "their" women would fraternize with French (African) soldiers. This second approach, which saw these relationships as rape, was reflected in the popular Weimar film, *Die schwarze Schmach*. See Guckel, "Welt-spiele Georgstrasse," 34.

5. For an analogous debate in contemporary Britain, see Kent, *Making Peace*.

6. See Usborne, *Politics of the Body*, 69–84. See also Grossmann, *Reforming Sex*.

7. Quoted in Kaufmann, *Frauen zwischen Aufbruch*, 82–83.

8. See Usborne, *Politics of the Body*, 69–84, 203.

9. From ADEF, Akten der Ortsgruppe Hannover, III Protokollbuch der Mit-gliederversammlungen der Ortsgruppe, meeting of May 3, 1919; see also meeting of Jan. 11, 1925. See also ADEF B 1c, Leisätze zu der Stellung des DEFs in der neuen Zeit (Dec. 1919).

10. As noted in Chapter 10, by the mid-1920s even the DVP was beyond the pale, since it became part of governing coalitions.

11. As noted in Chapter 9, the housewives' organization formed before the war to deal with the "servant question" was long since moribund, and the organization was refounded in 1915 to work on war-related issues.

12. I am indebted here to the first-rate analysis of the Hanover chapter's parent organization, the National Federation of German Housewives' Associations, which includes an interesting section on Hindenberg-Delbrück herself, in Bridenthal, "'Professional Housewives,'" 153–73; see also Bridenthal, "Class Struggle around the Hearth," 243–64. Bridenthal also examines the work and politics of the urban housewives' sister organization, the National Federation of Agricultural House-wives' Associations, in "Organized Rural Women," 375–405.

13. For her views on the City League, see NH, Hann 320 I no. 20, her letter to the

Vorstand of the Housewives' Association, dated Mar. 31, 1925, as well as her letter to the Arbeitsausschuss für hausmütterliche Erziehung, Mar. 23, 1925.

14. NH, Hann 320 I no. 72 vol. 2, letter from Hindenberg-Delbrück to Frau Wiemann, Feb. 25, 1933.

15. See NH, Hann 320 I no. 21, letter to Freifrau von Bülow, Nov. 20, 1925.

16. See the announcement in *Mitteilungen des Hausfrauenvereins Hannover* 4 (June 1929): 1, and 4 (Nov. 1929): 1. For the National League's protectionism, see Bridenthal, " 'Professional Housewives,' " 161–62.

17. See NH, Hann 320 I no. 10 vol. 3, letter from Frau Wiemann to Frau Jecker (n.d., probably 1928).

18. For examples of Hindenberg-Delbrück's use of the Cinderella motif, see her letter to Franziska Wiemann, dated Nov. 22, 1926, in NH, Hann 320 I no. 45; see also her article, entitled "Die Hausfrau," in the Sonder-Beilage of the *Hannoverscher Kurier*, May 5, 1929.

19. Report on a speech given by Hindenberg-Delbrück in Goslar, Sept. 15, 1926, in NH, Hann 320 I no. 22.

20. *Doppelverdiener* referred to dual-income couples; the campaign targeted the wives in these couples, who opponents argued had no need to work (since their husbands could presumably support them) and who allegedly thus took positions that should have gone to unemployed men. See NH, Hann 320 I no. 24 vol. 1, draft of an article by the head of the Bund der Kinderreichen (n.d., probably 1927); see also *Mitteilungen der Hausfrauenvereins Hannover* 7 (May 1932): 48–49.

21. See the article in *Mitteilungen der Hausfrauenvereins Hannover* 7 (Jan. 1932): 7.

22. See NH, Hann 320 I no. 35, letter from the Reichsfrauenausschuss of the DNVP to Hindenberg-Delbrück, Dec. 20, 1929.

23. For a discussion of the new *Wohnkultur* of the 1920s, which included new styles of domestic architecture, new technology, and new styles of household management, see Saldern, *Neues Wohnen. Wohnungspolitik und Wohnkultur im Hannover der Zwanziger Jahren.*

24. See the article on the Leipzig testing office in the *Hannoverscher Kurier*, Mar. 29, 1928, "Die Frau" Beilage.

25. NH, Hann 320 I no. 9, 1926–29 annual reports.

26. The national movement to "reform" or "rationalize" the household and housework is discussed in Hagemann, *Frauenalltag und Männerpolitik*, 99–114; see also Nolan, *Visions of Modernity*, chap. 10.

27. See the letter from Menge to Hindenberg-Delbrück, dated Dec. 23, 1925, in NH, Hann 320 I no. 9; see also the 1925 Jahresbericht of the Hausfrauenverein in NH, Hann 320 I no. 6.

28. NH, Hann 320 I no. 6, 1925 annual report; see also the report issued by the Preisgericht in NH, Hann 320 I no. 44.

29. See, for example, the correspondence between Hindenberg-Delbrück and *Bürgervorsteher* von Wolff, dated Jan. 25, 1927, in NH, Hann 320 I no. 45.

30. See the report on this meeting in the 1927 annual report of the Housewives' Association in NH, Hann 320 I no. 9; a copy of this pamphlet is in NH, Hann 320 I no. 45.

31. For the reform movement's conception of the *Arbeitsküche*, see Hagemann,

Frauenalltag und Männerpolitik, 100–101. See also Reagin, "Die Werkstatt der Hausfrau."

32. For specific suggestions regarding the design of kitchens, see the pamphlet issued by the Housewives' Association in NH, Hann 320 I no. 45. For the association's claims that it was successful in influencing Hanover's building policies, see the chapter's report to the Reichsverband, dated Mar. 15, 1927, in NH, Hann 320 I no. 45; see also an article by Hindenberg-Delbrück, entitled "Hausfrauen und Wohnungsbau in Hannover," in NH, Hann 320 I no. 45; see also the association's annual reports in NH, Hann 320 I no. 9.

33. See the guide to this exhibition in *Mitteilungen des Hausfrauenvereins Hannover* 3 (Mar. 15, 1928).

34. Ibid.; see also Ilse Gropius's letter to Hindenberg-Delbrück, dated Jan. 10, 1927, in NH, Hann 320 I no. 45.

35. Hindenberg-Delbrück's speech was quoted in the *Hannoverscher Kurier*, Mar. 15, 1928, "Die Frau" Beilage; see also the report in the *Niederdeutsche Zeitung*, Mar. 15, 1928, p. 5. See also Hindenberg-Delbrück's article in the *Hannoverscher Kurier*, May 5, 1929, "Die Frau" Beilage.

36. From the guide to the exhibition in NH, Hann 320 I no. 47, p. 50.

37. NH, Hann 320 I no. 34, copy of a speech by Hindenberg-Delbrück, (n.d., probably 1928). The law was never passed. For the parallel lobbying done by rural housewives' associations against this proposed reform, see Bridenthal, "Organized Rural Women," 397.

38. NH, Hann 320 I no. 35, Bertha Hindenberg-Delbrück, "Hausfrauen und Hausgehilfen. Das kommende Hausgehilfinnengesetz."

39. Ibid.

40. See NH, Hann 320 I no. 23, Petition by the Arbeitsgemeinschaft für hauswirtschaftliche-hausmütterliche Erziehung to the city, Nov. 24, 1925. The form the *Pflichtjahr* would take varied, depending on the advocate. The first year of courses, followed by one year in private households, was favored by the Housewives' Association, while some other women leaders thought one year of domestic science courses alone would suffice. Later, Hindenberg-Delbrück would argue for two years' training in households. The rural housewives associations were in fact able to create voluntary apprenticeship programs in agricultural housewifery, albeit on a small scale. See Bridenthal, "Organized Rural Women," 395–96.

41. See NH, Hann 320 I no. 31, Bericht über die Arbeit der Arbeitsgemeinschaft für hauswirtschaftliche-hausmütterliche Erziehung in Hannover vom Sept. 1925–Sept. 1926, and correspondence between Hindenberg-Delbrück and the head of the municipal *Ordnungsblock*, Mar. 8, 1926, and following. Also in no. 31, see the clipping from the Oct. 13, 1927, edition of *Volkswille*, which reported on the mandatory courses for unemployed women. The idea of the *hauswirtschaftliches Pflichtjahr* was not unique to Hanover. A *Pflichtjahr* was actually introduced during the 1920s in Halle and Bremen. See the newspaper reports on both city's programs in NH, Hann 320 I no. 22.

42. See ADEF, Akten der Ortsgruppe Hannover, Protokollbuch der Vorstandssitzungen der Ortsgruppe Hannover (1925–28), meetings of Mar. 5, Mar. 17, and June 22, 1926. See also the report on the courses in the *Hannoverscher Kurier*, Apr. 12, 1928, "Die Frau" Beilage.

43. See Hagemann, *Frauenalltag und Männerpolitik*, 111–17.

44. Kaufmann, *Frauen zwischen Aufbruch und Reaktion*, 66–68.

45. Ibid., 57; for Hanover, see ADEF, Akten der Ortsgruppe Hannover, III Protokollbuch der Mitgliederversammlungen der Ortsgruppe Hannover, meeting of Jan. 2, 1919.

46. Frauenbund der Deutschen Kolonialgesellschaft, *Jahresbericht 1929–1930*, 10, 23.

47. Ibid., 3–7; see also Frauenbund der Deutschen Kolonialgesellschaft, *10 Jahre Frauenbund*, 14–18. *Heimatart* is difficult to translate, but broadly speaking, refers to native (German) manners or life-style.

48. See the report on the league's work in the *Hannoverscher Kurier*, Nov. 9, 1924, "Die Frau" Beilage.

49. See reports on the league's work in the *Hannoverscher Kurier*, "Die Frau" Beilage of Feb. 24, 1925; Apr. 29, 1926; Jan. 12, 1928; Apr. 12, 1928. I was unable to locate exact membership figures for the league, but it was repeatedly referred to by other organizations as one of the largest women's associations in Hanover, which meant that its membership must have been at least several hundred; see, for example, the references to the league in the correspondence surrounding the Housewives' Association's withdrawal from the Women's City League in NH, Hann 320 I no. 10 vols. 1–3.

50. See the report in the *Hannoverscher Kurier*, Mar. 13, 1927, "Die Frau" Beilage.

51. See the report on the league's meeting in the *Hannoverscher Kurier*, Feb. 2, 1928, "Die Frau" Beilage.

52. See the report on the *Pflichtjahr* proposal in ADEF, Protokollbuch der Vorstandssitzungen der Ortsgruppe Hannover (1925–28), meeting of Mar. 5, 1926.

53. See ADEF, Akten der Ortsgruppe Hannover, Protokollbuch der Vorstandssitzungen der Ortsgruppe Hannover (1925–28), meeting of Feb. 10, 1928.

54. For the list maintained by the Housewives' Association, see NH, Hann 320 I no. 22; for the report on the German Women's League assembly, see the *Hannoverscher Kurier*, Apr. 29, 1926, "Die Frau" Beilage. See also the annual report of the Women's City League in *Der Frauenstadtbund* 2 (Feb. 1931): 2.

55. See Drechsler-Hohlt's 1925 essay, "Politische Frauenarbeit," in LB, Bestand des Allgemeinen Deutschen Lehrerinnenvereins, 13/22, Film L000035. See also Drees's statement in *Der Frauenstadtbund* 1 (Mar. 1929): 3.

56. Stoehr, *Emanzipation*, 113–14.

57. Ibid.; Drechsler-Hohlt, "Politische Frauenarbeit."

58. See Mathilde Drechsler-Hohlt, "Der nationale Gedanke und die Frauen," *Hannoverscher Kurier*, Aug. 1, 1925, "Die Frau" Beilage.

59. On the national level, these tensions between housewives' and professional women's organizations had their origins in the prewar period; see Kerchner, *Beruf und Geschlecht*, 219–20.

60. See NH, Hann 320 I no. 10 vol. 3, letter from Drechsler-Hohlt to Reichsverband Deutscher Hausfrauen, June 26, 1928, comments by Hindenberg-Delbrück attached to this letter. *Frauenrechtlerinnen* literally refers to those who support women's rights. In this context, however, the connotations were closer to those associated with the modern pejorative, "women's libber."

61. NH, Hann 320 I no. 9, minutes of *Vorstand* meeting of the Housewives' Association, Jan. 23, 1928.

62. This was at most a minor faux pas in the culture of the local women's movement, where associations frequently invited each other's members to meetings, but the Housewives' Association claimed to be offended that the privacy of its members had been violated by the exploitation of the membership list. A considerable amount of correspondence was generated by this dispute, including claims and counterclaims, and petitions. See NH, Hann 320 I no. 10 vols. 1–3, for this material. In her responses to the City League, Hindenberg-Delbrück made it clear that the Housewives' Association could leave the City League (and the BDF), yet still belong to the local women's movement; her definition of the "women's movement" was flexible, and included the other conservative women's associations discussed previously. She, and her nationalist allies, obviously did not believe that the women's movement was coterminous with the BDF.

63. See NH, Hann 320 I no. 10 vol. 3, letter from Drechsler-Hohlt to Reichsverband Deutscher Hausfrauen, June 26, 1928; see also no. 10 vol. 1, letter from Hindenberg-Delbrück to Reichsverband Deutscher Hausfrauen, Oct. 9, 1928.

64. NH, Hann 320 I no. 72 vol. 1, letter to Frau Dralle, Mar. 30, 1933. In 1935, Hindenberg-Delbrück boasted that she had been so successful at driving out left-wing and Jewish members that "we did not need to cull our membership politically or racially after 1933 [in accordance with National Socialist *Gleichschaltung* guidelines]." See also a pamphlet by Hindenberg-Delbrück, *20 Jahre Hausfrauenvereinsarbeit in Hannover*, 12.

65. See also *Mitteilungen des Hausfrauenvereins Hannover* 4 (June 1929): 1. For the nationwide protests mounted by conservative women against the Berlin Congress, see Stoehr, *Emanzipation*, 129–31.

66. As mentioned in Chapter 1, the SPD had held the local Reichstag seat since 1884, although its influence in local politics was repressed before 1918 due to the restrictions on the local franchise. After 1918, the SPD was largely dominant in local elections, since the Communist Party attracted relatively little support in Hanover. See Historisches Museum, *Hannover 1933*, 17, 21–24, 29. Sources to account for the actions of bourgeois women's associations in Hanover during this period, between 1930 and 1933, were difficult to locate. In many cases, such as in the DEF archives, files appear to have been selectively purged; for example, the ADEF file on the DEF's correspondence with the National Socialists consists of one innocuous letter. For the last few years of the Weimar period, I was forced to rely primarily on newspaper accounts and on the archives of the Housewives' Association, which fortunately contained a substantial amount of material from and correspondence with other associations. I also used the reports contained in the *Frauenstadtbund*, a newsletter issued by the local Women's City League, which contained reports from BDF-affiliated associations.

67. See Stoehr, *Emanzipation*, 132–35; Schmidt-Waldherr, *Emanzipation durch Professionalisierung?*, xi, 89–144; Bridenthal, "'Professional Housewives,'" 161–65. Schmidt-Waldherr argues plausibly that much of the BDF's propaganda during this period was really "disguised texts of struggle" against the Nazis, but there is no getting away from the fact that the BDF's campaign against the National Socialists

was "disguised," and therefore weakened, and less aggressive. The BDF could not do otherwise, especially before the conservative housewives' associations left it in late 1932, since it was bound by the ideal of "neutrality."

68. Holborn, *History of Modern Germany*, 683–707.

69. See the Women's Citizens' announcements in *Der Frauenstadtbund* 2 (Aug. 1930): 1, and 2 (Oct. 1930): 1.

70. See the BDF announcement in *Der Frauenstadtbund* 4 (July–Aug. 1932): 1.

71. See the BDF announcement in *Der Frauenstadtbund* 5 (Mar. 1933): 1.

72. Available sources do not indicate whether Drechsler-Hohlt was ousted or resigned of her own accord. For Hering-Hessel's election to head the ADF, see *Der Frauenstadtbund* 4 (Dec. 1932): 3. For her subsequent career in the Nazi Frauenschaft, see Manns, "Zur NS-Frauenschaft in Niedersachsen." I am grateful to Christiane Schröder for drawing this point to my attention. For the meetings organized by Hering-Hessel in 1932, see *Der Frauenstadtbund* 4 (Apr. 1932): 1. The National Socialist speaker was scheduled, but apparently never actually came. Perhaps other members opposed Hering-Hessel in this matter.

73. Holborn, *History of Modern Germany*, 686–87; for the Harzburg women's coalition, see Schmidt-Waldherr, *Emanzipation durch Professionalisierung?*, 122–24.

74. See the DEF's call for a boycott of all foreign products in *Evangelische Frauenzeitung* 32 (1931–32): 182; see also Hindenberg-Delbrück, *20 Jahre Hausfrauenvereinsarbeit in Hannover*, 12.

75. Schmidt-Waldherr, *Emanzipation durch Professionalisierung?*, 122–28. At the local level, nationalist women attacked the Women's City League for supporting this resolution. See the City League announcement in *Der Frauenstadtbund* 4 (Jan. 1932): 1.

76. Schmidt-Waldherr, *Emanzipation durch Professionalisierung?*, 137–44.

77. Bertha Hindenberg-Delbrück, "Geistige Ziele der Hausfrauenbewegung," *Mitteilungen des Hausfrauenvereins Hannover* 7 (Aug. 1932): 74–76 (italics in original).

78. See ADEF, B 1c, Paula Mueller-Otfried, "1931 Verbandsthemenschrift."

79. Evans, *Feminist Movement*, 257–59; Bridenthal, " 'Professional Housewives,' " 165–68. The DEF and other confessional organizations were permitted to continue to operate during the Third Reich, but only if they confined themselves to religious activities. For a discussion of the activities of Jewish women's organizations after 1933, see Kaplan, "Jewish Women in Nazi Germany." For the dissolution of the Hanover Women's City League, along with most of its member organizations, see *Der Frauenstadtbund* 5 (May 1933): 1–3.

CONCLUSION

1. Bridenthal, Grossmann, and Kaplan, *When Biology Became Destiny*, 21.

2. Koonz, *Mothers in the Fatherland*, 144; Richard Evans, in a less nuanced study, gives a sweeping conclusion, writing that the BDF's ideas were "*völkisch* and protofascist," and that the BDF's response to the National Socialists was "ambivalent," in part because the similarity between some of the BDF's ideas "and much of what the NSDAP had to say about women [which] was too striking to overlook." Evans, *Feminist Movement*, 273, 258–59.

3. Stoehr, "Machtergriffen," 26, 32. Stoehr's implicit endorsement of "indifference" as a strategy of resistance assumes that, for women, there were no meaningful differences between the National Socialists and the other male-dominated parties; meaningful, significant differences would have required engagement on behalf of those parties which offered more to women. This is surely an untenable position; the SPD's policies, disappointing though they may have been to feminists in some regards, still cannot be equated with those of the National Socialists. I am indebted to the imaginative, pioneering body of work that Stoehr has produced on the women's movement, but in my opinion Schmidt-Waldherr, in *Emanzipation durch Professionalisierung?*, is nevertheless more persuasive when she argues that it was the BDF's policy of *Überparteilichkeit*, not indifference, that hobbled the movement's resistance to the Nazis.

4. Meyer-Renschhausen argues that Bremen feminists were politically "neutral" and cannot be classified using "male" political categories because their agenda was based on women's values, which led them to be critical of men's political parties and norms. Her argument is useful, illuminating, and persuasive in her analysis of Bremen's temperance and abolitionist organizations. Her study only covers the movement up to 1927, however, and does not address the question of how this "neutrality" affected the movement's response to the rise of National Socialism. Her decision to end her study in 1927, and her failure to discuss the movement's shift to the right after 1918, or any possible relationship between the women's movement and the Nazis implies that there was no such relationship, a conclusion that this book has argued against. The only section of *Weibliche Kultur* that discusses the reaction of the movement to the Nazi seizure of power at length is a passage that describes how one of the largest Bremen women's organizations tried to "get through the winter" of the Third Reich by acquiescing in *Gleichschaltung* and incorporation into a Nazi women's organization. Although Meyer-Renschhausen does not acknowledge this, this strategy presumably also involved the expulsion of Jewish members, which was a prerequisite for *Gleichschaltung*; see *Weibliche Kultur*, 6–7, 14–16, 166.

5. Allen, *Feminism and Motherhood*, 236.

6. Stoehr, *Emanzipation*, 132–33. For an account of a scathing analysis of the Nazis offered by Velsen, see Schmidt-Waldherr, *Emanzipation durch Professionalisierung?*, 97–103.

7. Schmidt-Waldherr, *Emanzipation durch Professionalisierung?*, 89–91, 104–5, 137–42; see also Evans, *Feminist Movement*, 242, 255.

Select Bibliography

UNPUBLISHED PRIMARY SOURCES

Archiv des Deutschen Evangelischen Frauenbundes, Hanover
  Akten der Ortsgruppe Hannover
  Annual Reports for the Ortsgruppe, 1903–8
  Bau des Versorgungshauses

III	Protokollbuch der Vorstandssitzungen der Ortsgruppe Hannover (1907–13)
IV	Protokollbuch der Vorstandssitzungen der Ortsgruppe Hannover (1913–21)Protokollbuch der Vorstandssitzungen der Ortsgruppe Hannover (no number, 1925–28)
II	Protokollbuch der Mitgliederversammlungen der Ortsgruppe Hannover (1904–15)
III	Protokollbuch der Mitgliederversammlungen der Ortsgruppe Hannover (1915–27)
B 1	Material über die Gründung des Deutsch-Evangelischen Frauenbundes und seine Entwicklung bis 1934
B 1c	Verbandsthemen
CC 1	Rechtskommission
CC 2	Rechtsschutzstelle
FF 1	Nationaler Frauendienst Hannover
H 1a	Kommission für Kinderschutz und Jugendfürsorge
H 1b	Kommission für Kinderschutz und Jugendfürsorge
I 1a	Die Dienstbotenfrage
I 1b	Hausdienstausschuss
O 1	Correspondence
O 9b	Correspondence
O 12	Briefwechsel mit rechtsstehenden Frauenvereinen
V 22a	Die Prostitutionsfrage (vols. 1 and 2)
V 22b	Die Prostitutionsfrage
V 23	Die Prostitutionsfrage, Hannover
V 24	Das Kartell Hannoverscher und Lindener Vereine zur Bekämpfung öffentlicher sittlicher Schäden

Archiv des Katholischen Deutschen Frauenbundes, Cologne
  Zweigvereine   Material und Schreiben betr. Gründungen der Zweigvereine
  Generalversammlungen   Generalversammlung 1912, Strassburg
Landesarchiv Berlin
  Helene Lange Archiv Bestand
  Karton 12/Abt.3   Correspondence of Bund Deutscher Frauenvereine Vorstand, esp. with DEF

Karton 13/Abt. 4   Suffrage movement materials

Karton 46/Abt. 8   Materials related to prostitution, venereal disease, white slavery

Bestand des Allgemeinen Deutschen Lehrerinnenvereins

13/22   Correspondence

102/1–19   Correspondence, Vorstand, 1902

105/1–91   Correspondence, Vorstand, 1904

84/46–50   Correspondence, Vorstand, 1919

157/1–14   Correspondence, Vorstand, 1919–20

113/1–50   Records of 12th congress, 1911

107/1–31   Records of 15th congress, 1919

29/1–41   Frauen in der kommunalen Schulverwaltung, Preussen

76/1–190   Correspondence, Vorstand, 1919

17/3–145   Correspondence, Vorstand, 1921–22

68/1–139   Correspondence, Vorstand, 1919

86/1–119   Correspondence, Vorstand, 1919–20

Landeskirchliches Archiv der Evangelisch-lutherischen Landeskirche Hannover

E 2 114   Verein für freiwillige Armenpflege

E 2 196   Verwahrloste Jugend

E 2 219   Versorgungshaus für Gefährdete

E 2 224   Polizeiassistentin

E 2 247   Verein zur Hebung der öffentlichen Sittlichkeit

E 2 367   Fürsorgeausschuss

E 2 373   Verein zur Fürsorge für die schulentlassene Jugend

E 2 379   Jungmädchenvereine

E 2 390   Deutsch-Evangelischer Frauenbund

E 2 391   Verein Freundinnen junger Mädchen

E 2 393   Verein Freundinnen junger Mädchen

E 2 395   Weibliche Berufsverbände

N 30   Margarethe Haccius Nachlass

S 3d 114   Magdalenen-Asyl

S 3d 185   Kinderpflegeanstalten, Horte, Krippen, Kinderheime

S 3d 226   Friederikenstift

S 3d 251   Vaterländischer Frauenverein

S 3d 270   Christlicher Männer- und Jünglingsverein

S 3d 282   Jungfrauenvereine

S 3d 330   Hauptverein für Volkswohlfahrt

S 3d 384   Haushaltungsschulen

S 3d 531   Verein zur Hebung der öffentlichen Sittlichkeit

Niedersächsisches Hauptstaatsarchiv, Hanover

Kleine Erwerbungen A 28 "Frauen-Verein"

Hann 122a XX 5   Wohlfahrtspflege (Allgemeines)

Hann 122a XX 52   Verein zur Förderung weiblicher Bildung

Hann 122a XX 58a   Verschiedene Frauenvereine

Hann 122a XX 65a   Politische Personalien, 1894–1904

Hann 122a XX 104   Magdalenen-Verein
Hann 122a XX 112   Nationaler Frauendienst
Hann 122a XX 142   Gemeinnützige Anstalten und Vereine, vol. 2 Ver-
                     schiedenes, 1905–12
Hann 320 I nos. 2–72 Hannoverscher Hausfrauenverein
Stadtarchiv Hannover
  Hedwig Kettler Nachlass
  Wohlfahrtsausschuss 1922–27
  XV Gb 88   Christlicher Verein junger Männer
  XV Gb 150   Deutsch-Evangelischer Frauenbund (vols. 1 and 2)
  XV Gb 150a   Frauenherberge zur Heimat
  XV Gb 150b   Deutsch-Evangelischer Frauenbund
  XV Gb 171   Frauenverein "Volkswohl"
  XV Gb 174   Hannoverscher Hausfrauenverein
  XV Gb 290   Evangelischer Hausgehilfinnenverein
  XVI A III b5   Oberlehrerinnen Gründsätze
  XVI A III b6   Lehrerinnen Gründsätze
  XVI A III g7   Landesverein preussischer Volksschullehrerinnen
  XVI A III g8   Verein preussischer technischer Lehrerinnen
  XVI A III g14   Verband deutscher Musiklehrerinnen
  XVI A III g18   Allgemeiner Deutscher Lehrerinnenverein, Ortsgruppe
  XVI E VII 1   Frauenbildungsverein
  XVI E VII 2   Frauenbildungsverein
  XVI E VII 3   Frauenbildungsverein
  XVI E VII 4   Frauenbildungsverein
  XXX Sozialamt 134 Obdachlosigkeit
  XXX Sozialamt 145 Jugendamt
  XXX Wohlfahrts- und Armenwesen 90. Martha Richter
  Kartei: Mitglieder der städtischen Kollegien, 1919–33
  Lehrer: Personalakten von Lehrkräften an höheren, mittleren, Berufs- und
     Fachschulen: Mathilde Drees, Anna Ramsauer, Anna Wuillemin, Marie
     Mühry
  Lehrer: Personalakten von Volksschullehrern: Bertha Duensing, Anna Keller-
     mann, Anna Dörries, Toni Eicke, Emmi Langer, Anna Ziegler
  Personalamt Abgabe 1 II 120/164 Fürsorgerinnen
  Schulamt 845   Das Hannoversche Mädchengymnasium
  Schulamt 1479   Gewerbliche Fortbildungsschule
  Schulamt 1519   Fortbildungsschule für Mädchen der Hannoverschen und
                     Lindener Frauenvereine, 1901–23
  Schulamt 1542   Warteschulverein
  Schulamt 2357   Boedeker Krippe und Warteheim
  Sportamt Sp104   Jugendpflege
  Sportamt Sp109   Jugendpflege
  Sportamt Sp110   Organisation und Entwicklung der Jugendpflege in Han-
                     nover
  Sportamt Sp113   Jugendvereine

Periodicals
Der Abolitionist, 1906–8
Adressbuch der königlichen Haupt- und Residenzstadt Hannover, 1860–1918
Centralblatt für das gesammte Unterrichtswesen in Preussen, 1894
Die christliche Frau, 1905–13
Deutsche Volkszeitung, 1906–8
Der einzige Trost, 1911–13
Evangelische Frauenzeitung, 1901–26
Die Frau. Monatsschrift für das gesamte Frauenleben unserer Zeit, 1894–1918
Die Frauenbewegung, 1900–1919
Der Frauenstadtbund. Nachrichtenblatt des Frauenstadtbundes Hannover, e.V., 1929–33
Hannoverscher Anzeiger, 1900–1925
Hannoverscher Courier, later *Kurier*, 1899–1933
Hannoversches Tageblatt, 1900–1914, 1930–33
Mitteilungen des Deutsch-Evangelischen Frauenbundes, 1899–1901
Mitteilungen des Hausfrauenvereins Hannover, 1926–32
Mitteilungen des statistischen Amts der Stadt Hannover, 1912–13
Niederdeutsche Zeitung, 1928
Vierteljährliche Nachrichten des Landesvereins hannoverscher Jungfrauenvereine, 1913–14
Volkswille. Organ für die Interessen der arbeitenden Bevölkerung der Provinz Hannovers, 1914

Books, Articles, and Pamphlets
Altmann-Gottheimer, Elisabeth. *Jahrbuch der Frauenbewegung*. Berlin, 1913.
Bennigsen, Adelheid von. *Der soziale Frauenberuf*. Berlin, 1914.
Berger, Heinrich. *Die Prostitution in Hannover*. Berlin, 1902.
Böhmert, Victor. *Das Armenwesen in 77 deutschen Städten und einigen Landarmenverbänden*. Dresden, 1888.
Bund Deutscher Frauenvereine. *Zusammenstellung der angeschlossenen Verbände und ihrer Mitgliedsvereine, der Mitglieder des engeren und des Gesamtvorstandes, der Mitglieder des Frauenberufamtes, sowie der Stadtverbände*. Mannheim, 1922.
Deutsch-Evangelischer Frauenbundes. *Festschrift zum 25 jährigen Bestehen des Christlich-Sozialen Frauenseminars des Deutsch-Evangelischen Frauenbundes in Hannover*. Hanover, 1930.
——. *Frauenkalender für 1908. Jahrbuch des Deutsch-Evangelischen Frauenbundes*. Berlin, 1908.
——. *Frauenkalender für 1913. Jahrbuch des Deutsch-Evangelischen Frauenbundes*. Berlin, 1913.
——. *Frauenkalender für 1906. Jahrbuch des Deutsch-Evangelischen Frauenbundes*. Berlin, 1906.
——. *25 Jahre Säuglingsheim und Versorgungshaus*. Hanover, 1928.
Doerr, Wilhelm. *Gemeinde-Handbuch der Stadt Hannover*. Hanover, 1914.

Drechsler-Hohlt, Mathilde. "Wirkende Frauenkraft. Mathilde Drees zum Gedächtnis." *Die Frau* 45 (1937–38): 632–38.

Frauenbund der Deutschen Kolonialgesellschaft. *10 Jahre Frauenbund der Deutschen Kolonialgesellschaft*. Berlin, 1918.

——. *Jahresbericht 1928–1929*. Berlin, 1929.

——. *Jahresbericht 1929–1930*. Berlin, 1930.

Frieda Duensing. Ein Buch der Erinnerung. Herausgegeben von ihren Freunden. . . . Berlin, 1926.

Friederiken-Verein. *Die ersten fünfzig Jahre des Frederikenstiftes, 1840–1890*. Hanover, 1890.

Frobenius, Else. *30 Jahre Koloniale Frauenarbeit*. Berlin, 1936.

Groeben, Countess Selma von der. *Frauenarbeit und Frauenwert*. Berlin, 1908.

——. *Soziale Gegensätze und Frauenbewegung*. Berlin, 1912.

Heymann, Lida Gustava, and Anita Augspurg. *Erlebtes, Erschautes. Deutsche Frauen kämpfen für Freiheit, Recht und Frieden, 1850–1940*. Meisenheim am Glan, 1972.

Hindenberg-Delbrück, Bertha. *20 Jahre Hausfrauenvereinsarbeit in Hannover*. Hanover, 1935.

Hugo, Karl von, and Kurt von Hugo. *Die Geschichte der Familie von Hugo*. Hanover, 1919.

Kaiserliches Statististisches Amt, Abteilung für Arbeiterstatistik. *Statistik der Frauenorganisationen im Deutschen Reich (1. Sonderheft zum Reichsarbeitsblatte)*. Berlin, 1909.

Katholischer Frauenbund. *Jahrbuch des Katholischen Frauenbundes*. Cologne, 1907.

——. *Katholischer Frauenkalender*. Cologne, 1914.

——. *Katholischer Frauenkalender*. Cologne, 1915.

——. *Katholischer Frauenkalender*. Cologne, 1916.

——. *Katholischer Frauenkalender*. Cologne, 1918.

Komitee zur Ermittlung der Säuglingsernährung. *Säuglingsernährung, Säuglingssterblichkeit, und Säuglingsschutz in den Städten Hannover und Linden*. Berlin, 1913.

Lange, Helene. *Kampfzeiten. Aufsätze und Reden aus vier Jahrzehnten*. 2 vols. Berlin, 1928.

Lange, Helene, and Gertrud Bäumer, eds. *Handbuch der Frauenbewegung*. 5 vols. Berlin, 1901–6.

Lüders, Marie-Elisabeth. *Das unbekannte Heer. Frauen kämpfen für Deutschland, 1914–1918*. Berlin, 1936.

Meyers Grosses Konversations-Lexikon. Leipzig, 1902.

Mueller, Paula. *Einsame Frauen*. Berlin, 1906.

——. *Die Frauen im kirchlichen Gemeindeleben*. Hanover, 1904.

——. *Die neue Ethik und ihre Gefahr*. Berlin, 1908.

——. "Die soziale Ursache der Prostitution." In *Die Bedeutung der Sittlichkeitsfrage für die deutsche Zukunft. Vorträge gehalten auf der Fruaenkonferenz zum Studium der Sittlichkeitsfrage*, 54–70. Berlin, 1917.

——. *Die Verantwortung der Frau für die religiössittliche Erneuerung des Volkslebens*. Berlin, 1918.

——. *Welche Aufgaben erwachsen der Frau aus der sittlichen Not unserer Zeit?*. Hanover, 1906.

——. *Weltanschauung und Frauenbewegung*. Berlin, 1910.

——, ed. *Handbuch zur Frauenfrage. Der Deutsch-Evangelische Frauenbund in seiner geschichtlichen Entwicklung, seinen Zielen und seiner Arbeit*. Berlin, 1908.

——. *10 Jahre Deutsch-Evangelischer Frauenbund*. Berlin, 1910.

——. *25 Jahre Deutsch-Evangelischer Frauenbund*. Berlin, 1924.

Pappritz, Anna. *Herrenmoral*. 8th ed. Leipzig, n.d.

——, ed. *Einführung in die Prostitutionsfrage*. Leipzig, 1919.

Rothert, Wilhelm. *Die innere Mission in Hannover in Verbindung mit der sozialen und provinzialen Volkswohlfahrtspflege*. 3d ed. Gütersloh, 1909.

Schickenberg, Wilhelm. *Die Neuordnung der Fürsorge in der Stadt Hannover*. Hanover, 1919.

Schmidt, Direktor Dr. "Die Verteilung der Unterrichtsfächer in den deutschen Gymnasial-, Realgymnasial-, und Real-Bildungsanstalten für Mädchen." *Frauenbildung* 4 (1905): 481–95.

Sidgwick, Mrs. Alfred. *Home Life in Germany*. New York, 1908.

Silbergleit, Heinrich. *Finanzstatistik der Armenverwaltung von 108 deutschen Städten*. Leipzig, 1902.

Städtische Armenverwaltung der königlichen Haupt- und Residenzstadt Hannover. *Einteilung der königlichen Haupt- und Residenzstadt Hannover in Armendistrikte und Armenquartiere*. Hanover, 1909.

——. *Einteilung der Waisenrats-Bezirke*. Hanover, 1908.

Statistisches Amt der Stadt Hannover. *Statistisches Jahrbuch der Stadt Hannover*. 1st ed. Hanover, 1914.

——. *Statistisches Jahrbuch der Stadt Hannover*. 2d ed. Hanover, 1930.

Venzmer, Dr. B. *Wider die sozialdemokratische Jugendbewegung*. [1913?].

Verband Evangelischer Arbeiterinnen-Vereine Deutschlands. *Verband Evangelischer Arbeiterinnen-Vereine Deutschlands*. Hanover, n.d.

Verein für freiwillige Armenpflege. *Übersicht über die Organisation der freiwilligen Armenpflege in der königlichen Haupt- und Residenzstadt Hannover*. Hanover, 1906.

Wegner, Marie. *Die Armen- und Waisenpflege*. Leipzig, 1908.

——, ed. *Merkbuch der Frauenbewegung*. Leipzig, 1908.

Wespy, Schulrat Dr. Leon. "Über den Stand der höheren Mädchenschulen in Preussen." *Frauenbildung* 4 (1905): 267–84.

INTERVIEWS

Bülow, Hedwig von. Interview by author, November 4, 1986, Hanover.

Feesche, Annamarie. Interview by author, October 3, 1986, Hanover.

Glindemann, Frida. Interview by author, October 10, 1986, Hanover.

Grundmann, Ruth. Interview by author, October 12, 1986, Hanover.

Kahrno, Anna. Interview by author, October 12, 1986, Hanover.

Rexhausen, Jutta. Interview by author, November 18, 1986, Hanover.

Albisetti, James. "Could Separate Be Equal? Helene Lange and Women's Education in Imperial Germany." *History of Education Quarterly* 22 (1982): 301–17.

———. "The Fight for Female Physicians in Imperial Germany." *Central European History* 15 (1982): 99–123.

———. *Schooling German Girls and Women*. Princeton, 1988.

Allen, Ann Taylor. *Feminism and Motherhood in Germany, 1800–1914*. New Brunswick, N.J., 1991.

———. "Feminism, Venereal Diseases, and the State in Germany, 1890–1918." *Journal of the History of Sexuality* 4 (1993): 27–50.

———. "Mothers of the New Generation: Adele Schreiber, Helene Stoecker, and the Evolution of a German Idea of Motherhood, 1900–1914." *Signs* 10 (1985): 418–38.

———. "Spiritual Motherhood: German Feminists and the Kindergarten Movement, 1848–1911." *History of Education Quarterly* 22 (1982): 319–39.

Anderson, Robert. "Voluntary Associations in History." *American Anthropologist* 73 (1971): 209–22.

Aschoff, Hans-Georg. "Die welfische Bewegung und die Deutsch-hannoversche Partei zwischen 1866 und 1914." *Niedersächsisches Jahrbuch für Landesgeschichte* 53 (1981): 41–64.

Beckmann, Emily. *Die Entwicklung der höheren Mädchenbildung in Deutschland von 1870 bis 1914. Dargestellt in Dokumenten*. Berlin, 1936.

Blackbourn, David. "The Discreet Charm of the Bourgeoisie: Reappraising German History in the Nineteenth Century." In *The Peculiarities of German History*, by David Blackbourn and Geoff Eley. Oxford, 1984.

Bock, Gisela, and Barbara Duden. "Arbeit aus Liebe—Liebe als Arbeit: Zur Entstehung der Hausarbeit im Kapitalismus." In *Frauen und Wissenschaft. Beiträge zur Berliner Sommeruniversität für Frauen*, ed. Gruppe Berliner Dozentinnen, 118–99. Berlin, 1977.

Bogerts, Hildegard. *Bildung und berufliches Selbstverständnis lehrenden Frauen in der Zeit von 1885 bis 1920*. Frankfurt, 1977.

Boyd, Catherine E. " 'Nationaler Frauendienst': German Middle Class Women in Service to the Fatherland, 1914–1918." Ph.D. diss., University of Georgia, 1979.

Bridenthal, Renate. "Class Struggle around the Hearth: Women and Domestic Service in the Weimar Republic." In *Towards the Holocaust: Anti-Semitism and Fascism in Weimar Germany*, ed. Michael Dobkowski and Isidor Walliman, 243–64. Westport, Conn, 1983.

———. "Organized Rural Women in the Conservative Mobilization of the German Countryside in the Weimar Republic." In *Between Reform, Reaction, and Resistance: Studies in the History of German Conservatism from 1789 to 1945*, ed. Larry Eugene Jones and James N. Retallack, 375–405. New York, 1993.

———. " 'Professional Housewives': Stepsisters of the Women's Movement." In *When Biology Became Destiny: Women in Weimar and Nazi Germany*, ed. Renate Bridenthal, Atina Grossmann, and Marion Kaplan, 153–73. New York, 1984.

Bridenthal, Renate, Atina Grossmann, and Marion Kaplan. *When Biology Became Destiny: Women in Weimar and Nazi Germany*. New York, 1984.

Bussemer, Herrad-Ulrike. "Bürgerliche Frauenbewegung und männliches Bildungsbürgertum 1860–1880." In *Bürger und Bürgerinnen*, ed. Ute Frevert, 190–205. Göttingen, 1988.

———. *Frauenemanzipation und Bildungsbürgertum. Sozialgeschichte der Frauenbewegung in der Reichsgründungszeit*. Weinheim, 1985.

Canning, Kathleen. "Feminist History after the Linguistic Turn: Historicizing Discourse and Experience." *Signs* 19 (1994): 368–404.

Chickering, Roger. " 'Casting Their Gaze More Broadly': Women's Patriotic Activism in Imperial Germany." *Past and Present* 118 (1988): 156–85.

———. *We Men Who Feel Most German: A Cultural Study of the Pan-German League, 1866–1914*. Boston, 1984.

Clemens, Bärbel. *Menschenrechte haben kein Geschlecht. Zum Politikverständnis der bürgerlichen Frauenbewegung*. Pfaffenweiler, 1988.

Coetzee, Marilyn Shevin. *The German Army League: Popular Nationalism in Wilhelmine Germany*. New York, 1990.

Conze, Werner, and Jürgen Kocka, eds. *Bildungsbürgertum im 19. Jahrhundert*. Stuttgart, 1985.

Corbin, Alain. *Women for Hire: Prostitution and Sexuality in France after 1850*. London, 1990.

Craig, Gordon. *Germany, 1866–1945*. New York, 1978.

Daniel, Ute. "Fiktionen, Friktionen, und Fakten—Frauenarbeit im Ersten Weltkrieg." In *Arbeiterschaft in Deutschland, 1914–1918*, ed. Gunther Mai, 277–323. Düsseldorf, 1985.

Dasey, Robyn. "Women's Work and the Family: Women Garment Workers in Berlin before the First World War." In *The German Family*, ed. Richard J. Evans and W. R. Lee, 221–53. London, 1981.

Davis, Belinda. "Food Scarcity and the Empowerment of the Female Consumer in World War I Germany." In *The Sex of Things: Gender and Consumption in Historical Perspective*, ed. Victoria de Grazia. Berkeley, forthcoming.

———. "Home Fires Burning: Politics, Identity, and Food in World War I Berlin." Ph.D. diss., University of Michigan, 1992.

Diessenbacher, Hartmut. "Der Armenbesucher: Missionar im eigenen Land. Armenfürsorge und Familie in Deutschland um die Mitte des 19. Jahrhunderts." In *Soziale Sicherheit und soziale Disziplinierung. Beiträge zu einer historischen Theorie der Sozialpolitik*, ed. Christoph Sachsse and Florian Tennstedt, 209–45. Frankfurt, 1986.

Donzelot, Jacques. *The Policing of Families*. New York, 1979.

Eley, Geoff. *Reshaping the German Right: Radical Nationalism and Political Change after Bismarck*. London, 1980.

Ellitz, Peter. "Leben und Werke des königlichen hannoverschen Baurats Edwin Oppler." *Hannoversche Geschichtsblätter*, n.s., 25 (1971): 132–48.

Evans, Richard J. *The Feminist Movement in Germany, 1894–1933*. London, 1976.

———. "Prostitution, State, and Society in Imperial Germany." *Past and Present* 70 (1976): 106–29.

Fadermann, Lillian. *Surpassing the Love of Men: Romantic Friendship and Love between Women from the Renaissance to the Present*. New York, 1981.

Feldman, Gerald. *Army, Industry, and Labor in Germany, 1914–1918*. Princeton, 1966.

Fout, John C. "The Moral Purity Movement in Wilhelmine Germany and the Attempt to Regulate Male Behavior." *Journal of Men's Studies* 1 (1992): 5–31.

———, ed. *German Women in the Nineteenth Century*. New York, 1984.

Freudenthal, Herbert. *Vereine in Hamburg. Ein Beitrag zur Geschichte und Volkskunde der Geselligkeit*. Hamburg, 1968.

Frevert, Ute. *Frauen-Geschichte zwischen Bürgerlicher Verbesserung und Neuer Weiblichkeit*. Frankfurt, 1986.

———. "Fürsorgliche Belagerung. Hygienebewegung und Arbeiterfrauen im 19. und frühen 20. Jahrhundert." *Geschichte und Gesellschaft* 11 (1985): 420–46.

Gall, Lothar, ed. *Stadt und Bürgertum im 19. Jahrhundert*. Munich, 1990.

Gerhard, Ute. *Unerhört. Die Geschichte der deutschen Frauenbewegung*. Reinbeck bei Hamburg, 1990.

———. *Verhältnisse und Verhinderungen. Frauenarbeit, Familie und Rechte der Frauen im 19. Jahrhundert. Mit Dokumentation*. Frankfurt, 1978.

Gersdorff, Ursula von. *Frauen im Kriegsdienst, 1914–1945*. Stuttgart, 1969.

Geschichtswerkstatt Hannover. *Alltag zwischen Hindenburg und Haarmann. Ein anderer Stadtführer durch das Hannover der 20er Jahre*. Hamburg, 1987.

Gibson, Mary. *Prostitution and the State in Italy*. London, 1986.

Gordon, C. Wayne, and Nicholas Babchuk. "A Typology of Voluntary Associations." *American Sociological Review* 24 (1959): 22–29.

Greven-Aschoff, Barbara. *Die bürgerliche Frauenbewegung in Deutschland, 1894–1933*. Göttingen, 1981.

Grossmann, Atina. *Reforming Sex: German Sex Reform, 1920 to 1950*. Oxford, forthcoming.

Grundmann, Herbert, ed. *Gebhardts Handbuch der deutschen Geschichte*. 9th ed. Stuttgart, 1973.

Guckel, Sabine. "Eine Welt aus Zuckerguss und Schmiedeeisen. Tivoli Varieté in der Tivolistrasse." In *Alltag zwischen Hindenburg und Haarmann*, ed. Geschichtswerkstatt Hannover, 19–26. Hamburg, 1987.

———. "Weltspiele Georgstrasse. Kinos in Hannover." In *Alltag zwischen Hindenburg und Haarmann*, ed. Geschichtswerkstatt Hannover, 27–38. Hamburg, 1987.

Gusfield, Joseph. "The Problem of Generations in an Organizational Structure." *Social Forces* 35 (1957): 323–30.

Hackett, Amy. "The German Women's Movement and Suffrage 1890–1914—A Study of National Feminism." In *Modern European Social History*, ed. Robert J. Bezucha, 354–86. New York, 1978.

———. "Helene Stöcker: Left Wing Intellectual and Sex Reformer." In *When Biology Became Destiny: Women in Weimar and Nazi Germany*, ed. Renate Bridenthal, Atina Grossmann, and Marion Kaplan, 109–30. New York, 1984.

———. "The Politics of Feminism in Wilhelmine Germany, 1890–1918." Ph.D. diss., Columbia University, 1976.

Hagemann, Karen. *Frauenalltag und Männerpolitik. Alltagsleben und gesellschaftliches Handeln von Arbeiterfrauen in der Weimarer Republik*. Bonn, 1990.

Hamann, Manfred. "Politische Kräfte in der Provinz Hannover am Vorabend des Ersten Weltkrieges." In *Beiträge zur niedersächsischen Landesgeschichte*, ed. Dieter Brosius and Martin Last, 421–53. Hildesheim, 1984.

——. "Politische Kräfte und Spannungen in der Provinz Hannover um 1880." *Niedersächsisches Jahrbuch für Landesgeschichte* 53 (1981): 1–40.

Hasenclever, Christa. *Jugendhilfe und Jugendgesetzgebung seit 1900*. Göttingen, 1978.

Hausen, Karin. "Family and Role Division: The Polarization of Sexual Stereotypes in the Nineteenth Century—An Aspect of the Disassociation of Work and Family Life." In *The German Family*, ed. Richard J. Evans and W. R. Lee, 51–83. London, 1981.

——, ed. *Frauen suchen ihre Geschichte*. Munich, 1983.

Heffter, Heinrich. *Die deutsche Selbstverwaltung im 19. Jahrhundert. Geschichte der Ideen und Institutionen*. Stuttgart, 1950.

Henning, Hansjoachim. *Das westdeutsche Bürgertum in der Epoche der Hochindustrialisierung 1860–1914. Teil 1: Das Bildungsbürgertum in den preussischen Westprovinzen*. Wiesbaden, 1972.

Hewitt, Nancy. "Beyond the Search for Sisterhood: American Women's History in the 1980s." In *Unequal Sisters: A Multicultural Reader in U.S. Women's History*, ed. Vicki Ruiz and Ellen Carol DuBois, 1-19. New York, 1994.

Hilpert, Christiana. "Die Geschichte des Deutsch-Evangelischen Frauenbundes, 1899–1914." M.A. thesis, Ruhr University at Bochum, 1982.

Historisches Museum am Hohen Ufer, Hanover. *Hannover 1933. Eine Grossstadt wird national-sozialistisch*. Hanover, 1981.

Holborn, Hajo. *A History of Modern Germany, 1840–1945*. Princeton, 1969.

Hurd, Madeleine. "The Illusive Alliance: Liberals, Socialists, and Democracy in Hamburg and Stockholm, 1870–1914." Ph.D. diss., Harvard University, 1993.

——. "Morality and Working-Class Politics in Turn-of-the-Century Hamburg." Paper presented at the German Studies Association conference, Washington, D.C., October 8, 1993.

Jarausch, Konrad. *Students, Society, and Politics in Imperial Germany: The Rise of Academic Illiberalism*. Princeton, 1982.

John, Michael. "Liberalism and Society in Germany, 1850–1880: The Case of Hanover." *English Historical Review* 102 (1987): 579–98.

Kaiser, Jochen-Christoph. "Kirchliche Frauenarbeit in Westfalen. Ein Beitrag zur Geschichte des Provinzialverbandes der westfälischen Frauenhilfe 1906–1945." *Jahrbuch für westfälische Kirchengeschichte* 74 (1981): 159–90.

Kaplan, Marion. *The Jewish Feminist Movement in Germany: The Campaigns of the Jüdischer Frauenbund, 1904–1938*. Westport, Conn., 1979.

——. "Jewish Women in Nazi Germany: Daily Life, Daily Struggles, 1933–1939." *Feminist Studies* 16 (1990): 579–606.

——. *The Making of the Jewish Middle Class: Women, Family, and Identity in Imperial Germany*. New York, 1991.

——. "Prostitution, Morality Crusades, and Feminism: German-Jewish Feminists and the Campaign against White Slavery." *Women's Studies International Forum* 5 (1982): 619–27.

Kater, Michael. *The Nazi Party: A Profile of Members and Leaders*. Cambridge, Mass., 1983.

Kaufmann, Doris. "Die Ehre des Vaterlandes und die Ehre der Frauen oder der Kampf an der äusseren und inneren Front. Der Deutsch-Evangelische Frauenbund im Übergang vom Kaiserreich zur Weimarer Republik." *Evangelische Theologie* 46 (1986): 277–92.

———. *Frauen zwischen Aufbruch und Reaktion. Protestantische Frauenbewegung in der ersten Hälfte des 20. Jahrhunderts.* Munich 1988.

Kent, Susan Kingsley. *Making Peace: The Reconstruction of Gender in Interwar Britain.* Princeton, 1993.

———. *Sex and Suffrage in Britain, 1860–1914.* Princeton, 1987.

Kerchner, Brigitte. *Beruf und Geschlecht. Frauenberufsverbände in Deutschland, 1848–1908.* Göttingen, 1992.

Kocka, Jürgen. "Family and Class Formation." *Journal of Social History* 17 (1984): 417–30.

Koonz, Claudia. *Mothers in the Fatherland: Women, the Family, and Nazi Politics.* New York, 1987.

Koshar, Rudy. *Social Life, Local Politics, and Nazism: Marburg, 1880–1935.* Chapel Hill, 1986.

Kuhn, Annette, and Jörn Rüsen, eds. *Frauen in der Geschichte.* 5 vols. Düsseldorf, 1982–84.

Laqueur, Walter. *Young Germany: A History of the German Youth Movement.* New Brunswick, N.J., 1984.

Lasch, Christopher. *Haven in a Heartless World: The Family Besieged.* New York, 1977.

Lewek, Gert. *Kirche und soziale Frage um die Jahrhundertwende. Dargestellt am Wirken Ludwig Webers.* Neukirchen-Vluyn, 1963.

Lewis, Jane. "The Working Class Wife and Mother and State Intervention, 1870–1918." In *Labour and Love: Women's Experiences of Home and Family, 1850–1940,* ed. Jane Lewis, 99–122. Oxford, 1986.

Lexis, Wilhelm. *The History and Organization of Public Education in the German Empire.* Berlin, 1904.

Lidtke, Vernon. *The Alternative Culture: Socialist Labor in Imperial Germany.* New York, 1985.

Manns, Haide. "Zur NS-Frauenschaft in Niedersachsen am Beispiel der Zeitschrift 'Niedersachsen.'" In *Ausser Haus—Frauengeschichte in Hannover,* ed. Christiane Schröder and Monika Sonneck. Hanover, 1994.

Marquardt, Doris. *Sozialpolitik und Sozialfürsorge der Stadt Hannover in der Weimarer Republik.* Hanover, 1994.

Meyer, Sibylle. *Das Theater mit der Hausarbeit. Bürgerliche Repräsentation in der Familie der wilhelminischen Zeit.* Frankfurt, 1982.

Meyer-Renschhausen, Elisabeth. "Die weibliche Ehre. Ein Kapitel aus dem Kampf von Frauen gegen Polizei und Ärzte." In *Frauenkörper, Medizin, Sexualität,* ed. Johanna Geyer-Kordesch and Annette Kuhn, 80–101. Düsseldorf, 1986.

———. *Weibliche Kultur und soziale Arbeit. Eine Geschichte der Frauenbewegung am Beispiel Bremens, 1810–1927.* Cologne, 1989.

Mlynek, Klaus, and Waldemar R. Röhrbein. *Hannover Chronik. Von den Anfängen bis zur Gegenwart.* Hanover, 1991.

Nienhaus, Ursula. *Berufsstand weiblich. Die ersten weiblichen Angestellten.* Berlin, 1982.

Nipperdey, Thomas. "Jugend und Politik um 1900." In *Gesellschaft, Kultur, Theorie,* 338–59. Göttingen, 1976.

——. "Verein als soziale Struktur in Deutschland im späten 18. und frühen 19. Jahrhundert." In *Geschichtswissenschaft und Vereinswesen im 19. Jahrhundert,* ed. Hartmut Brockmann, 2–43. Göttingen, 1972.

Nolan, Mary. *Visions of Modernity: American Business and the Modernization of Germany.* Oxford, 1994.

Nowacki, Bernd. *Der Bund für Mütterschutz 1905–1933.* Husum, 1983.

Offen, Karen. "Defining Feminism: A Comparative Historical Approach." *Signs* 14 (1988): 119–57.

Ottmüller, Uta. *Die Dienstbotenfrage.* Munster, 1978.

——. " 'Mütterpflichten'—Die Wandlungen ihrer inhaltlichen Ausformung durch die akademische Medizin." *Beiträge zur marxistischen Theorie* 14 (1981): 97–138.

Peukert, Detlev. *Grenzen der Sozialdisziplinierung: Aufstieg und Krise der deutschen Jugenfürsorge von 1878 bis 1932.* Cologne, 1986.

Poovey, Mary. *Uneven Developments: The Ideological Work of Gender in Mid-Victorian England.* Chicago, 1988.

Prelinger, Catherine. *Charity, Challenge, and Change: Religious Dimensions of the Mid-Nineteenth Century Women's Movement in Germany.* New York, 1987.

Prokop, Ulrike. "Die Sehnsucht nach Volkseinheit. Zum Konservatismus der bürgerlichen Frauenbewegung vor 1933." In *Die Überwindung der Sprachlosigkeit. Texte aus der neuen Frauenbewegung,* ed. Gabriele Dietze, 176–202. Darmstadt, 1979.

Ramstetter, M. Heiner. "Eugen de Haen." *Hannoversche Geschichtsblätter,* n.s., 20 (1966): 107–91.

Reagin, Nancy. " 'A True Woman Can Take Care of Herself': The Debate over Prostitution in Hanover, 1906." *Central European History* 24, no. 4 (Winter 1991): 347–80.

——. "Die Werkstatt der Hausfrau: Bürgerliche Frauenbewegung und Wohnungspolitik im Hannover der Zwanziger Jahre." In *Altes und neues Wohnen: Linden und Hannover im frühen 20. Jahrhundert,* ed. Adelheid von Saldern and Sid Auffarth. Seelze-Velber, 1992.

Reulecke, Jürgen. "Bürgerliche Sozialreformer und Arbeiterjugend im Kaiserreich." *Archiv für Sozialgeschichte* 22 (1982): 299–329.

——. *Geschichte der Urbanisierung in Deutschland.* Frankfurt, 1985.

Riemann, Ilka. "Er mit der Waffe, sie mit Herz und Hand. Die Rolle der Frauenvereine in der Sozialpolitik, insbesondere die der Vaterländischen Frauenvereine." In *Frauenmacht in der Geschichte. Beiträge des Historikerinnentreffs 1985 zur Frauengeschichtsforschung,* ed. Jutta Dalhoff, Uschi Frey, and Ingrid Scholl, 347–53. Düsseldorf, 1986.

——. "Zur Diskrepanz zwischen der Realität Sozialer Arbeit als Frauenberuf und dem Mythos dieser Arbeit als Karriereberuf von Mittelschichtsfrauen." *Beiträge zur feministischen Theorie und Praxis* 5 (1981): 69–76.

Röhrbein, Waldemar R., and Franz R. Zankl, eds. *Hannover im 20. Jahrhundert. Aspekte der neueren Stadtgeschichte.* Hanover, 1978.

Rosenbaum, Heidi. *Formen der Familie. Untersuchung zum Zusammenhang von Familienverhältnissen, Sozialstruktur und sozialem Wandel in der deutschen Gesellschaft des 19. Jahrhunderts.* Frankfurt, 1982.

Rüschemeyer, D. "Professionalisierung. Theoretische Probleme für die vergleichende Geschichtsforschung." *Geschichte und Gesellschaft* 6 (1980): 311–25.

Sachsse, Christoph. *Mütterlichkeit als Beruf. Sozialarbeit, Sozialreform und Frauenbewegung, 1871–1929.* Frankfurt, 1986.

Sachsse, Christoph, and Florian Tennstedt. *Geschichte der Armenfürsorge in Deutschland.* Stuttgart, 1980.

Saldern, Adelheid von. *Neues Wohnen. Wohnungspolitik und Wohnkultur im Hannover der Zwanziger Jahre.* Hanover, 1992.

Saul, Klaus. "Der Kampf um die Jugend zwischen Volksschule und Kaserne. Ein Beitrag zur 'Jugendpflege' im wilhelminischen Reich, 1890–1914." *Militärgeschichtliche Mitteilungen* 9 (1971): 97–143.

Schenda, Rudolf. "Schundliteratur und Kriegsliteratur." In *Die Lesestoff der kleinen Leute,* 78–95. Munich, 1976.

Schmidt-Waldherr, Hiltraud. *Emanzipation durch Professionalisierung? Politische Strategien und Konflikte innerhalb der bürgerlichen Frauenbewegung während der Weimarer Republik und die Reaktion des bürgerlichen Antifeminismus und des Nationalsozialismus.* Frankfurt, 1987.

Schroeder, Hiltrud, ed. *Sophie und Co. Bedeutende Frauen Hannovers.* Hanover, 1991.

Schulte, Regina. "Dienstmädchen im herrschaftlichen Haushalt. Zur Genese ihrer Sozialpsychologie." *Zeitschrift für bayerische Landesgeschichte* 41 (1978): 879–920.

———. *Sperrbezirke. Tugendhaftigkeit und Prostitution in der bürgerlichen Welt.* Frankfurt, 1984.

Scott, Joan. "Deconstructing Equality-Versus-Difference: Or, The Uses of Poststructuralist Theory for Feminism." *Feminist Studies* 14 (1988): 33–50.

———. "Gender: A Useful Category of Historical Analysis." *American Historical Review* 91 (1986): 1053–75.

Seidel, Anneliese. *Frauenarbeit im Ersten Weltkrieg als Problem der staatlichen Sozialpolitik. Dargestellt am Beispiel Bayerns.* Frankfurt, 1979.

Sheehan, James. "Liberalism and the City in Nineteenth Century Germany." *Past and Present* 51 (1971): 116–37.

Smith, Bonnie. *Ladies of the Leisure Class: The Bourgeoises of Northern France in the Nineteenth Century.* Princeton, 1984.

Smith, Constance, and Anne Freedman. *Voluntary Associations: Perspectives on the Literature.* Cambridge, Mass., 1972.

Stehlin, Stewart. *Bismarck and the Guelph Problem.* The Hague, 1973.

Stodolsky, Catherine. "Missionaries of the Feminine Mystique: Female Teachers in Prussia and Bavaria: 1880–1920." Ph.D. diss., State University of New York at Stony Brook, 1988.

Stoehr, Irene. *Emanzipation zum Staat? Der Allgemeine Deutsche Frauenverein— Deutscher Staatsbürgerinnenverband (1893–1933).* Pfaffenweiler, 1990.

———. "Fraueneinfluss oder Geschlechterversöhnung? Zur Sexualitätsdebatte in der deutschen Frauenbewegung um 1900." In *Frauenkörper, Medizin, Sexualität,* ed. Johanna Geyer-Kordesch and Annette Kuhn, 159–90. Düsseldorf, 1986.

——. "Machtergriffen? Die deutsche Frauenbewegung 1933." *Courage* (1983): 24–32.

——. "Neue Frau und alte Bewegung? Zum Generationskonflikt in der Frauenbewegung der Weimarer Republik." In *Frauenmacht in der Geschichte. Beiträge des Historikerinnentreffs 1985 zur Frauengeschichtsforschung*, ed. Jutta Dalhoff, Uschi Frey, and Ingrid Scholl, 390–402. Düsseldorf, 1986.

——. "'Organisierte Mütterlichkeit.' Zur Politik der deutschen Frauenbewegung um 1900." In *Frauen suchen ihre Geschichte*, ed. Karin Hausen, 221–49. Munich, 1983.

Tenfelde, Klaus. "Grossstadtjugend in Deutschland vor 1914." *Vierteljahrschrift für Sozial- und Wirtschaftsgeschichte* 69 (1982): 182–218.

Tennstedt, Florian. *Sozialgeschichte der Sozialpolitik in Deutschland*. Göttingen, 1981.

Ulrich, Anita. *Bordelle, Strassendirnen, und bürgerliche Sittlichkeit in der Belle Epoche*. Zurich, 1985.

Usborne, Cornelie. *The Politics of the Body in Weimar Germany*. Ann Arbor, Mich., 1992.

Vicinus, Martha. *Independent Women: Work and Community for Single Women, 1850–1920*. Chicago, 1985.

——. "Sexuality and Power: A Review of Current Work in the History of Sexuality." *Feminist Studies* 8 (1982): 133–56.

Vondung, Klaus, ed. *Das wilhelminische Bildungsbürgertum*. Göttingen, 1976.

Walkowitz, Judith. "Male Vice and Feminist Virtue: Feminism and the Politics of Prostitution in 19th Century Britain." *History Workshop* 13 (1982): 79–93.

——. *Prostitution and Victorian Society: Women, Class, and the State*. Cambridge, 1980.

Walser, Karin. "Prostitutionsverdacht und Geschlechterforschung. Das Beispiel der Dienstmädchen um 1900." *Geschichte und Gesellschaft* 11 (1985): 99–111.

Warriner, Charles K., and Jane Emily Prather. "Four Types of Voluntary Associations." *Sociological Inquiry* 35 (1965): 138–48.

Weber, Max. "Rede auf dem ersten Deutschen Soziologentag in Frankfurt, 1910." Chap. in *Gesammelte Aufsätze zur Soziologie und Sozialpolitik*. Tübingen, 1924.

Weisbrod, Bernd. "Wohltätigkeit und 'symbolische Gewalt' in der Frühindustrialisierung. Städtische Armut und Armenpolitik in Wuppertal." In *Vom Elend der Handarbeit*, ed. Hans Mommsen and Werner Schulze, 334–57. Stuttgart, 1981.

Wells, Roger H. *German Cities: A Study of Contemporary Municipal Politics and Administration*. Princeton, 1932.

Wittrock, Christine. *Weiblichkeitsmythen. Das Frauenbild im Faschismus und seine Vorläufer in der Frauenbewegung der 20er Jahre*. Frankfurt, 1983.

Wobbe, Theresa. "Die Frau als zoon politicon. Überlegungen zur historischen Rekonstruktion der Politik der bürgerlichen Frauenbewegung um 1900." In *Frauenmacht in der Geschichte. Beiträge des Historikerinnentreffs 1985 zur Frauengeschichtsforschung*, ed. Jutta Dalhoff, Uschi Frey, and Ingrid Scholl, 326–37. Düsseldorf, 1986.

——. "'Die Frauenbewegung ist keine Parteisache.' Politische Positionen der Gemässigten und Fortschrittlichen der bürgerlichen Frauenbewegung im Kaiserreich." *Feministische Studien* 5 (1986): 50–65.

Wurms, Renate. " 'Krieg dem Kriege'—'Dienst am Vaterlande': Frauenbewegung im Ersten Weltkrieg." In *Geschichte der deutschen Frauenbewegung*, ed. Florence Hervé, 84–118. Cologne, 1982.

Zinnecker, Jürgen. *Sozialgeschichte der Mädchenbildung*. Weinheim, 1973.

Zwerschke, Manfred. *Jugendverbände und Sozialpolitik. Zur Geschichte der deutschen Jugendverbände*. Munich, 1963.

Index

graphic profile of membership, 47–48, 135–40; relationship with local authorities, 48–49, 85–87, 89–90, 107–8, 114, 163–64, 167, 169, 172, 214, 218, 251, 284 (n. 27); and the Social Democratic Party, 53–54, 57–58, 61; functioning as a surrogate for local government programs, 81–84, 87–88; and social work, 113–16; and Abolitionism, 157–59, 169, 170; and the Hanover Women's City League, 206–8, 240–41, 252; partisan tensions within, 207, 252; after 1933, 246–47

Deutsche Volkspartei (DVP), 206, 207, 209, 225, 237

Deutschnationale Volkspartei (DNVP), 204, 205, 207, 209, 225, 226, 228, 234, 244, 255

Deutschtum, 10, 223, 224, 234, 236. *See also* Nationalist women's associations

Domestic science courses, 58, 63, 65, 74–80, 95, 97, 104, 224, 232–33, 236, 250, 274 (n. 17), 295 (n. 40)

Doppelverdiener, 227

Dorcas Society, 30–32, 37, 134

Drechsler-Hohlt, Mathilde, 6, 206–8, 237–43, 250

Drees, Mathilde, 104–6, 108, 115, 123, 128, 130, 206–9, 217, 233, 238–42, 252

Duensing, Bertha, 80, 81, 123, 126–28, 132, 157, 158, 167, 172, 178, 242

Eichhorn, Maria, 38, 41, 54, 80

Eicke, Toni, 127, 128

Elberfeld system, 27–28

Embourgeoisement, 71, 97, 250

Essentialism, 1–3, 6, 250, 263 (n. 1)

Feesche, Friederike, 36–38

Feesche, Marie, 36, 45

Female education, 48, 103–12, 114–15, 213–14, 232–33. *See also* Gymnasium for Girls; Oberlehrerinnen; Social Work: seminar for training in; Soci-ety for the Advancement of Female Education; Women's Educational Association

Female physicians, 108–9, 112–13

Female teachers, 79, 103–8, 111, 118-121, 126, 215, 222–23, 237. *See also* Oberlehrerinnen

Feminism, 1–3, 5, 6, 24–25, 102, 180, 253–54, 256–57, 263 (nn. 1, 2). *See also* Essentialism; Spiritual motherhood

Feminists, 147, 152, 159, 160, 185, 191, 208, 251–53, 256–57, 264 (n. 6); within national women's movement, 4, 6, 24–25, 148–49, 174–76, 214–15, 254; goals and strategies at local level, 71, 157–58, 168–70; demographic profile of, 143, 177; within Hanover women's movement, 157–58, 172–79; and abolitionism, 157–68; DEF's attacks upon, 174–80; and temper-ance, 178; and male political parties, 184, 187, 252. *See also* Abolitionism; Bund Deutscher Frauenvereine: pro-gressive wing of; German Union for Women's Suffrage; League for the Protection of Motherhood; Women's Movement: in Bremen, in Hamburg; Women's Welfare Association

Foster Care Committee, 83, 84

Frederica Association, 30, 33, 34, 39, 67, 134

Froebel, Friedrich, 1, 25

German General Association of Female Teachers, 104, 119

German Revolution, 8, 201, 203, 204, 206, 236

German Union for Women's Suffrage, 149, 174–76, 184

German Women's League, 205, 207, 223, 235, 236, 237, 239, 241, 244, 246, 255. *See also* Nationalist women's associations

German Women's Navy League, 133, 180–83, 255

Girls' groups, 44, 49, 53–57, 65, 67–70,

191, 211, 212; bourgeois fear of, 7, 8, 20–22, 28, 50, 53–54, 68, 206, 226, 227, 231, 246, 250, 255; and local elections, 18–19, 205, 242; and respectability, 57–58, 77; and servants, 60–63, 232–33; within Hanover's municipal government, 209–10, 214, 216–17, 218, 251. *See also* Nationalist women's associations; Social degeneration

Social welfare programs, 8, 9, 11, 17, 23, 42, 43, 52, 58, 67, 71, 81, 84, 88–90, 97, 99, 122, 128, 132, 135, 137, 140, 143, 147, 162, 175, 176, 184, 192–93, 195–96, 210–14, 216, 219, 221, 250

Social work, 8, 23, 42, 70, 71, 77, 132, 146; and spiritual motherhood, 2, 7, 26; professional social work, 97, 98, 102, 113–16, 143; 195–96, 210–13, 208, 217, 222; as a solution for "surplus" women, 97, 99; seminar for training in, 113–15; local employment of social workers, 115; in World War I, 187, 190–93, 195–96

Society for the Advancement of Female Education, 78, 103, 104, 108, 113, 119, 157, 213, 237

Society for the Sale of Female Needlework, 30, 31

Society to Combat Venereal Diseases, 164, 165

Spiegelberg, Elsbeth, 181, 255

Spiritual motherhood, 1–3, 6, 25, 26, 42, 49, 59, 69, 70, 96, 116, 147, 249, 250, 252–54, 256, 257

"Surplus" women, 24–25, 99–102, 121–22

Teachers' associations, 119–21, 125, 133–34, 222–23, 251; providing leadership within the local women's movement, 44, 56, 78, 81, 84, 118, 157, 170, 191

Temperance movement, 73, 126–27, 128, 157, 237, 251; in Bremen, 2, 178, 264 (n. 8), 275 (n. 27); demographic profile of, 135–40; and feminism, 178

Temperance restaurants, 80–81, 96, 123

Trade school for female clerical workers, 117–18, 214

Tramm, Heinrich (mayor), 20, 21, 88, 107, 114, 121, 209, 216

Tramm, Olga, 21, 86, 130, 206

Treaty of Versailles, 10, 203, 223, 226, 241, 246, 255

Venereal diseases, 149, 150, 152, 155, 156, 159, 165; and married women, 160–61. *See also* Prostitution; Society to Combat Venereal Diseases

Vereinigung Evangelischer Frauenverbände Deutschlands (VEFD), 200, 205, 224, 234, 237, 255. *See also* Deutsch-Evangelischer Frauenbund

Voluntary Poor Relief Association, 29, 38

War Welfare Office, 192, 195, 210, 211

Women's Club, 129–32, 216. *See also* Recreational associations for women

Women's Division of the Colonial Society, 181, 206, 234, 236–37, 246–47. *See also* Nationalist women's associations

Women's Educational Association, 30, 37, 39–42, 62, 86, 119, 126–28, 157, 191, 218, 222, 251; demographic profile of membership, 40–44, 103, 134, 136, 139–40; and girls' groups, 56, 69; courses offered by, 78–80, 117–18, 233; collapse of, 213, 215, 237, 252. *See also* Commission on Servants; Girls' groups; Legal advice bureau for women

Women's movement, 16, 23, 24, 25, 39, 40, 43, 44, 45, 57, 70, 104, 106, 108, 109, 115, 116, 118, 164; and equal rights feminism, 1–2, 5–6; and essentialism, 1–3, 5–6, 58, 96, 102–3, 106, 112–13, 121, 196–97, 233, 249, 255; in Bremen, 2–4, 147, 152, 157, 159–62, 172, 178, 253, 257, 264 (n. 8), 273 (n. 2), 299 (n. 4); and class interests, 3, 8, 53, 60–62, 71, 76–77, 97, 130,

9841